THE DAILY STUDY BIBLE

THE GOSPEL
of
MATTHEW

Volume 1

THE GOSPEL

of

MATTHEW

Volume 1

(*Chapters 1 to 10*)

Translated
with an Introduction and Interpretation
by

WILLIAM BARCLAY

THE WESTMINSTER PRESS
PHILADELPHIA

First published by The Saint Andrew Press
Edinburgh, Scotland
First Edition, September, 1956
Second Edition, May, 1958

Library of Congress Catalog Card No. 59-8233

Typeset in Great Britain
Printed in the United States of America

To
A. McC.
ALWAYS MY FRIEND
AND SOMETIMES MY TASK-MASTER
WITHOUT WHOSE HELP AND ENCOURAGEMENT
THIS BOOK WOULD NEVER HAVE BEEN WRITTEN

GENERAL INTRODUCTION

It may truly be said that this series of Daily Bible Studies began almost accidently. A series which the Church of Scotland was using came to an end, and another series was immediately required. I was asked to write a volume on *Acts*, and, at the moment, had no intention beyond that. But one volume followed another, until the demand for one volume became a plan to write on the whole New Testament.

The translation which is given in each volume claims no special merit. It was included in order that the reader might be able to carry both the text of the New Testament and the comments on it wherever he went, and that he might be able to read it anywhere. While I was making the translation, the translations of Moffatt, Weymouth, and Knox were ever beside me. *The American Revised Standard Version*, *The Twentieth Century New Testament*, and *The New Testament in Plain English*, by Charles Kingsley Williams, have been in constant use. Since its publication, I have consistently consulted *The Authentic New Testament*, translated by Hugh J. Schonfield.

I cannot see another edition of these books going out to the public without expressing my very deep and sincere gratitude to the Church of Scotland Publications Committee for allowing me the privilege of first beginning, and then continuing, this series. And in particular I wish to express my very great gratitude to the convener, Rev. R. G. Macdonald, O.B.E., M.A., D.D., and to the committee's secretary and manager, Rev. Andrew McCosh, M.A., S.T.M., for constant encouragement and never-failing sympathy and help.

As these volumes went on, the idea of the whole series developed. The aim is to make the results of modern scholarship available to the non-technical reader in a form that it does not require a theological education to understand; and then to seek to make the teaching of the New Testament books relevant to life and work to-day. The whole aim of these books is summed up in Richard of Chichester's famous prayer; they are meant to enable men and women to know Jesus Christ more clearly, to love Him more dearly, and to follow Him more nearly. It is my prayer that they may do something to make that possible.

FOREWORD

ONCE again I must begin this foreword by expressing my most grateful thanks to the Publications Committee of the Church of Scotland for allowing me to add yet another volume to this series of Daily Bible Studies. Once again I would like very specially to thank the Rev. R. G. Macdonald, O.B.E., M.A., D.D., the Convener of that Committee, and the Rev. Andrew McCosh, M.A., S.T.M., the Committee's Secretary and Manager, for unfailing kindness and constant encouragement. I am quite sure that without their help and encouragement I could not have gone on producing these volumes as I have done.

I should like to say certain things by way of explanation about this volume on *Matthew*. If I could have assumed that everyone who reads it had already read the volumes on *Mark* and on *Luke*, there are certain things which could have been omitted; but each volume in this series has to stand on its own feet, and that has meant that this volume has been bound to say again certain things which have already been said in the other two volumes on the Synoptic Gospels. Further, this volume may seem to have taken a great deal of space to cover a short section of the gospel. But it must be remembered that in this volume we study the Sermon on the Mount, and the Sermon on the Mount is so central to the Christian faith and the Christian life that it has often to be taken sentence by sentence, and even word by word. I am convinced that in this section o *Matthew* detailed study will amply repay those who are prepared to make it.

Strangely enough, *Matthew* has not been very fortunate in its commentators. The commentary by A. B. Bruce in the *Expositor's Greek Testament* is still full of illumination. That by W. C. Allen in the *International Critical Commentary* is more for the expert than for the general reader. Of all the commentaries on the Greek text that by A. H. McNeile in the Macmillan series is by far the best. Alfred Plummer's *Exegetical Commentary on the Gospel according to Saint Matthew* is solidly helpful. T. H. Robinson's commentary in the *Moffatt Commentary* is suggestive, but rather slight. The most helpful, if sometimes the most disturbing of all the commentaries, is that by C. G. Montefiore in his *Synoptic Gospels*. C. G. Montefiore was himself a liberal Jew, and therefore his commentary is bound to be of special interest.

There are two great characteristics of Matthew's gospel. It is pre-eminently the gospel of the teacher, for in no other gospel is the teaching of Jesus so systematically assembled and gathered together. And it is pre-eminently the gospel which is concerned to show us Jesus as the man born to be King. It is my prayer that this book will do something to help us better to understand the teaching of Jesus, and to move us to enthrone Him more fully as King in our own lives.

WILLIAM BARCLAY.

TRINITY COLLEGE,
   GLASGOW.
     September, 1956.

CONTENTS

	Page
Introduction to Matthew	xvii
The Lineage of the King (1: 1-17)	1
The Three Stages (1: 1-17) (contd.)	3
The Realization of Men's Dreams (1: 1-17) (contd.) ..	5
Not the Righteous, but Sinners (1: 1-17) (contd.) ..	7
The Saviour's Entry into the World (1: 18-25) ..	8
Born of the Holy Spirit (1: 18-25) (contd.)	10
Creation and Re-creation (1: 18-25) (contd.)	12
The Birth Place of the King (2: 1, 2)	14
The Homage of the East (2: 1, 2) (contd.)	16
The Crafty King (2: 3-9)	19
Gifts for Christ (2: 9-12)	22
Escape to Egypt (2: 13-15)	24
The Slaughter of the Children (2: 16-18)	27
Return to Nazareth (2: 19-23)	29
The Years Between	32
The Emergence of John the Baptizer (3: 1-6) ..	34
The Message of John—The Threat (3: 7-12) ..	38
The Message of John—The Promise (3: 7-12) (contd.)	40
The Message of John—The Promise and The Threat (3: 7-12) (contd.)	42
The Message of John—The Demand (3: 7-12) (contd.)	43
The Message of John—The Demand (3: 7-12) (contd.)	47
Jesus and His Baptism (3: 13-17)	51
The Testing Time	54
The Temptations of Christ (4: 1-11)	54
The Sacred Story (4: 1-11) (contd.)	57
The Attack of the Tempter (4: 1-11) (contd.) ..	60
The Son of God goes forth (4: 12-17)	64
The Herald of God (4: 12-17) (contd.)	68
Christ calls the Fishermen (4: 18-22)	70
The Methods of the Master (4: 23-25)	74
The Activities of Jesus (4: 23-25) (contd.)	77
The Sermon on the Mount	78

THE GOSPEL OF MATTHEW

CONTENTS

	Page
The Supreme Blessedness (5: 3)	82
The Bliss of the Destitute (5: 3) (contd.)	85
The Bliss of the Broken Heart (5: 4)	88
The Bliss of the God-controlled Life (5: 5)	91
The Bliss of the Starving Spirit (5: 6)	94
The Bliss of Perfect Sympathy (5: 7)	97
The Bliss of the Clean Heart (5: 8)	101
The Bliss of Bringing Men together (5: 9)	103
The Bliss of the Sufferer for Christ (5: 10-12)	106
The Bliss of the Blood-stained Way (5: 10-12) (contd.)	110
The Salt of the Earth (5: 13)	114
The Light of the World (5: 14, 15)	118
Shining for God (5: 16)	121
The Eternal Law (5: 17-20)	122
The Essence of the Law (5: 17-20) (contd.)	126
The Law and the Gospel (5: 17-20) (contd.)	128
The New Authority (5: 21-48)	130
The New Standard (5: 21-48) (contd.)	132
The Forbidden Anger (5: 21, 22)	134
Words of Insult (5: 21, 22) (contd.)	136
The Insurmountable Barrier (5: 23, 24)	139
Make Peace in Time (5: 25, 26)	141
The Forbidden Desire (5: 27, 28)	144
The Surgical Cure (5: 29, 30)	145
The Bond which Must not be Broken (5: 31, 32)	148
The Bond that Cannot be Broken (5: 31, 32) (contd.)	150
The Bond that Cannot be Broken (5: 31, 32) (contd.)	153
A Word is a Pledge (5: 33-37)	155
The End of Oaths (5: 33-37) (contd.)	158
The Ancient Law (5: 38-42)	160
The End of Resentment and of Retaliation (5: 38-42) (contd.)	163
Gracious Giving (5: 38-42) (contd.)	167
Christian Love (5: 43-48)	170
Christian Love (5: 43-48) (contd.)	174

THE GOSPEL OF MATTHEW

CONTENTS

	Page
The Reward Motive in the Christian Life	177
Right Things from the Wrong Motive (6: 1)	184
How not to Give (6: 2-4)	186
The Motive of Giving (6: 2-4) (contd.)	187
How not to Pray (6: 5-8)	190
How not to Pray (6: 5-8) (contd.)	193
How not to Pray (6: 5-8) (contd.)	195
The Disciple's Prayer (6: 9-15)	197
The Father in Heaven (6: 9)	200
The Father in Heaven (6: 9) (contd.)	202
The Father in Heaven (6: 9) (contd.)	203
The Hallowing of the Name (6: 9) (contd.)	205
The Prayer for Reverence (6: 9) (contd.)	206
God's Kingdom and God's Will (6: 10, 11)	210
God's Kingdom and God's Will (6: 10, 11) (contd.)	213
Our Daily Bread (6: 12)	215
Our Daily Bread (6: 12) (contd.)	218
Forgiveness Human and Divine (6: 12, 14, 15)	220
Forgiveness Human and Divine (6: 12, 14, 15) (contd.)	223
The Ordeal of Temptation (6: 13)	225
The Attack of Temptation (6: 13) (contd.)	228
The Attack of Temptation (6: 13) (contd.)	230
The Defence against Temptation (6: 13) (contd.)	232
How not to Fast (6: 16-18)	234
How not to Fast (6: 16-18) (contd.)	237
The True Fasting (6: 16-18) (contd.)	239
The True Treasure (6: 19-21)	240
Treasure in Heaven (6: 19-21) (contd.)	243
The Distorted Vision (6: 22, 23)	245
The Necessity of the Generous Eye (6: 22, 23) (contd.)	247
The Exclusive Service (6: 24)	250
The Place of Material Possessions (6: 24) (contd.)	253
The Two Great Questions about Possessions (6: 24) (contd.)	256
The Forbidden Worry (6: 25-34)	257

THE GOSPEL OF MATTHEW

CONTENTS

	Page
Worry and Its Cure (6: 25-34) (contd.)	259
The Folly of Worry (6: 25-34) (contd.)	262
The Error of Judgment (7: 1-5)	264
No Man can Judge (7: 1-5)	266
The Truth and the Hearer (7: 6)	269
Reaching those who are unfit to Hear (7: 6) (contd.) ..	271
The Charter of Prayer (7: 7-11)	273
The Everest of Ethics (7: 12)	276
The Golden Rule of Jesus (7: 12) (contd.)	279
Life at the Cross-Roads (7: 13, 14)	281
The False Prophets (7: 15-20)	285
Known by their Fruits (7: 15-20) (contd.)	288
The Fruits of Falseness (7: 15-20) (contd.)	290
On False Pretences (7: 21-23)	293
The Only True Foundation (7: 24-27)	295
Love in Action	298
The Living Death (8: 1-4)	300
Compassion Beyond the Law (8: 1-4) (contd.) ..	302
True Prudence (8: 1-4) (contd.)	303
A Good Man's Plea (8: 5-13)	305
The Passport of Faith (8: 5-13) (contd.)	308
The Power which Annihilates Distance (8: 5-13) (contd.)	310
A Miracle in a Cottage (8: 14, 15)	313
Miracles in a Crowd (8: 16, 17)	315
The Summons to Count the Cost (8: 18-22)	317
The Tragedy of the Unseized Moment (8: 18-22) (contd.)	319
The Peace of the Presence (8: 23-27)	322
Calm Amidst the Storm (8: 23-27) (contd.)	324
The Demon-Haunted Universe (8: 28-34)	325
The Defeat of the Demons (8: 28-34) (contd.)	328
The Growth of Opposition	330
Get Right with God (9: 1-8)	332
The Man whom all Men Hated (9: 9)	336
A Challenge Issued and Received (9: 9) (contd.) ..	338
Where the Need is Greatest (9: 10-13)	339

THE GOSPEL OF MATTHEW

CONTENTS

	Page
Present Joy and Future Sorrow (9: 14, 15)	342
The Problem of the New Idea (9: 16, 17)	344
The Imperfect Faith and the Perfect Power (9: 18-31)	348
The Awakening Touch (9: 18, 19, 23-26)	350
All Heaven's Power for One (9: 20-22)	354
Faith's Test and Faith's Reward (9: 27-31)	357
The Two Reactions (9: 32-34)	359
The Threefold Work (9: 35)	361
The Divine Compassion (9: 36)	363
The Waiting Harvest (9: 37, 38)	365
The Messengers of the King (10: 1-4)	367
The Making of the Messengers (10: 1-4) (contd.) ..	369
The Commission of the King's Messenger (10: 5-8a)	371
The Words and Works of the King's Messenger (10: 5-8a) (contd.)	374
The Equipment of the King's Messenger (10: 8b-10) ..	376
The Conduct of the King's Messenger (10: 11-15) ..	379
The Challenge of the King to His Messengers (10: 16-22)	382
The King's Honesty to His Messengers (10: 16-22) (contd.)	385
The Reasons for the Persecution of the King's Messengers (10: 16-22) (contd.)	387
The Prudence of the King's Messenger (10: 23) ..	389
The Coming of the King (10: 23) (contd.)	391
The King's Messenger and the King's Sufferings (10: 24, 25)	394
The King's Messenger's Freedom from Fear (10: 26-31)	396
The Courage of the Right (10: 26-31) (contd.)	398
God Cares! (10: 26-31) (contd.)	400
The Loyalty of the King's Messenger and its Reward (10: 32, 33)	402
The Warfare of the King's Messenger (10: 34-39) ..	405
The Cost of being a Messenger of the King (10: 34-39) (contd.)	407
The Reward of those who Welcome the King's Messenger (10: 40-42)	409

INTRODUCTION TO THE GOSPEL ACCORDING TO SAINT MATTHEW

The Synoptic Gospels

THE first three gospels, *Matthew*, *Mark* and *Luke*, are usually known as the *Synoptic Gospels*. The word *synoptic* comes from two Greek words which mean *to see together*. *Synoptic* literally means *able to be seen together*. The reason for that name is this. These three gospels each give an account of the same events in Jesus' life. There are in each of them additions and omissions; but broadly speaking their material is the same and their arrangement is the same. It is therefore possible to set them down in three parallel columns, and so to read them together, and to compare the one with the other. When that is done, it is quite clear that there is the closest possible relationship between these three gospels. If we, for instance, compare the story of the feeding of the five thousand in the three gospels (*Matthew* 14: 12-21; *Mark* 6: 30-44; *Luke* 9 10-17) we find exactly the same story told in almost exactly the same words. A very clear instance of this is the story of the healing of the man who was sick with the palsy (*Matthew* 9: 1-8; *Mark* 2: 1-12; *Luke* 5: 17-26). These three accounts are so similar that even a little parenthesis— " then saith he to the sick of the palsy "—occurs in all three as a parenthesis in exactly the same place. The correspondence between the three gospels is so close that we are bound to come to the conclusion either that all three are drawing their material from a common source, or that two of them must be based on the third.

The Earliest Gospel

When we begin to examine the matter more closely we begin to see that there is every reason for believing that *Mark* must have been the first of the gospels to be written, and that the other two, *Matthew* and *Luke*, are using *Mark* as a basis. *Mark* can be divided into 105 sections. Of these sections 93 occur in *Matthew* and 81 in *Luke*. Of *Mark's* 105 sections there are only 4 which do not occur either in *Matthew* or in *Luke*. *Mark* has 661 verses: *Matthew* has 1068 verses: *Luke* has 1149 verses. *Matthew* reproduces no fewer than 606 of *Mark's* verses; and *Luke* reproduces 320. Of the 55 verses of *Mark* which *Matthew* does not reproduce *Luke* reproduces 31; so there are only 24 verses in the whole of *Mark* which are not reproduced somewhere in *Matthew* or *Luke*. It is not only the substance of the verses which is reproduced; the very words are reproduced. *Matthew* uses 51 per cent of *Mark's* words; and *Luke* uses 53 per cent.

Still further, both *Matthew* and *Luke* as a general rule follow *Mark's* order of events. Occasionally either *Matthew* or *Luke* differs from *Mark* as to the order of events; but they never in any case *both* differ against him; always at least one of them follows *Mark's* order of events.

Improvements on Mark

Since *Matthew* and *Luke* are both much longer than *Mark*, it might just possibly be suggested that *Mark* is a summary of *Matthew* and *Luke;* but there is one other set of facts which show that *Mark* is earlier. It is the custom of *Matthew* and *Luke* to improve and to polish *Mark*, if we may put it so. Let us take some instances of that. Sometimes *Mark* seems to limit the power of Jesus; at least an ill-disposed critic might try to prove that he was doing so. Let us take three passages which are all accounts of the same incident:

> *Mark* 1: 34: And He healed *many* that were sick with divers diseases, and cast out *many* devils;

> *Matthew* 8: 16: And He cast out the spirits with a word, and healed *all* that were sick;

> *Luke* 4: 40: And He laid hands on *everyone* of them, and healed them.

Let us take other three similar examples:

Mark 3: 8: For He had healed *many*;

Matthew 12: 15: And He healed them *all*;

Luke 6: 19: He healed them *all*.

Matthew and *Luke* both change *Mark's many* into *all* so that there may be no suggestion of any limitation of the power of Jesus Christ.

There is a very similar change in the account of the events of Jesus' visit to Nazareth. Let us compare the account of *Mark* and of *Matthew*.

Mark 6: 5, 6: And *He could there do* no mighty work . . . and He marvelled because of their unbelief;

Matthew 13: 57: And *He did not* many mighty works there, because of their unbelief.

Matthew shrinks from saying that Jesus *could not do* any mighty works; and changes the form of the expression so that there may be no possibility of any limitation of the power of Jesus.

Sometimes *Matthew* and *Luke* leave out little touches in *Mark* in case they could be taken to belittle Jesus. *Matthew* and *Luke* omit three statements in *Mark*:

Mark 3: 5: When He had looked round on them *with anger, being grieved* at the hardness of their hearts;

Mark 3: 21: And when His friends heard it, they went out to lay hold on Him: for they said, *He is beside Himself;*

Mark 10: 14: He was *moved with indignation.*

Matthew and *Luke* hesitate to attribute human emotions of anger and grief to Jesus, and shudder to think that anyone should even have suggested that Jesus was mad.

Sometimes *Matthew* and *Luke* slightly alter things in *Mark* in order to get rid of statements which might seem to show the apostles in a bad light. We may take but one instance, from the occasion on which James and John sought to ensure themselves of the highest places in the coming Kingdom. Let us compare the introduction to that story in *Mark* and in *Matthew:*

> *Mark* 10: 35: And there came near unto him *James and John,* the sons of Zebedee, saying unto him . . . ;
> *Matthew* 20: 20: There came to Him *the mother of the sons of Zebedee* with her two sons, worshipping Him, and asking a certain thing of Him.

Matthew hesitates to ascribe motives of ambition directly to the two apostles, and so he ascribes them to their mother.

All this makes it clear that *Mark* is the earliest of the gospels. *Mark* gives a simple, vivid, direct narrative; but *Matthew* and *Luke* have already begun to be affected by doctrinal and theological considerations which make them much more careful of what they say.

The Teaching of Jesus

We have seen that *Matthew* has 1068 verses; and that *Luke* has 1149 verses; and that between them they reproduce 582 of *Mark's* verses. That means that in *Matthew* and *Luke* there is much more material than *Mark* contains and supplies. When we examine that material we find that more than 200 verses of it are almost identical. For instance such passages as *Luke* 6: 41, 42 and *Matthew* 7: 3, 5; *Luke* 10: 21, 22 and *Matthew* 11: 25-27; *Luke* 3: 7-9 and *Matthew* 3: 7-10 are almost identically the same. But here we notice a difference. The material which *Matthew* and *Luke* drew from *Mark* was almost entirely material dealing with the events of Jesus' life; but the 200 common verses which *Matthew* and *Luke* have over and above that is entirely composed of *the teaching of Jesus;* these verses tell us, not so much what Jesus *did,* as what Jesus *said.* Clearly in these 200 verses *Matthew* and *Luke* are drawing from *a common source-book of the teaching of Jesus.* That book does not now exist; but to it scholars have given the letter Q which stands for *Quelle,* which is the German word for *source*. In its day it must have been an extraordinarily important book, for it was the first handbook of the teaching of Jesus.

Matthew's Place in the Gospel Tradition

It is here that we come to Matthew the apostle. Scholars are agreed that the first gospel as it stands does not come directly from the hand of Matthew. One who had himself been an eye-witness of the life of Christ would not have needed to use *Mark* as a source-book for the life of Jesus as *Matthew* does. But one of the earliest Church historians, a man called Papias, gives us this intensely important piece of information: " Matthew collected the sayings of Jesus in the Hebrew tongue." So, then, we can believe that it was none other than Matthew who collected the first handbook of the teaching of Jesus, that book which was the source from which all men must draw, if they wished to know what Jesus taught. And it was because so much of that source-book is incorporated in the first gospel that Matthew's name was attached to it. We must be for ever grateful to Matthew, when we remember that it is to him that we owe the Sermon on the Mount and nearly all we know about the teaching of Jesus. Broadly speaking, to Mark we owe our knowledge of the *events* of Jesus' life; to Matthew we owe our knowledge of the substance of Jesus' *teaching*.

Matthew the Taxgatherer

About Matthew himself we know very little. We read of his call in *Matthew* 9: 9. We know that he was a taxgatherer and that he must therefore have been a bitterly hated man, for the Jews hated the members of their own race who had entered the civil service of their conquerors. Matthew would be regarded as nothing better than a quisling. But there was one gift which Matthew would possess. Most of the disciples were fishermen. They would have little skill and little practice in putting words together on paper; but Matthew would be an expert in that. When Jesus called Matthew, as he sat at the receipt of custom, Matthew rose up and followed him and left everything behind him except one thing—his pen. And Matthew nobly used his literary skill to become the first man ever to compile an account of the teaching of Jesus.

The Gospel of the Jews

Let us now look at the chief characteristics of Matthew's gospel so that we may watch for them as we read it. First and foremost, *Matthew is the gospel which was written for the Jews.* It was written by a Jew in order to convince Jews. One of the great objects of *Matthew* is to demonstrate that all the prophecies of the Old Testament are fulfilled in Jesus, and that, therefore, He must be the Messiah. It has one phrase which runs through it like an ever-recurring theme—" All this was done that it might be fulfilled which was spoken by the prophet, saying." That phrase occurs in the gospel as often as 16 times. Jesus' birth and Jesus' name are the fulfilment of prophecy (1: 21-23); so are the flight to Egypt (2: 14, 15); the slaughter of the children (2: 16-18); Joseph's settlement in Nazareth and Jesus' upbringing there (2: 23); Jesus' use of parables (13: 34, 35); the triumphal entry (21: 3-5); the betrayal for thirty pieces of silver (27: 9); the casting of lots for Jesus garments as He hung on the Cross (27: 35). It is *Matthew's* primary and deliberate purpose to show how the Old Testament prophecies received their fulfilment in Jesus; how every detail of Jesus' life was foreshadowed in the prophets; and thus to compel the Jews to admit that Jesus was the Messiah.

(i) The main interest of *Matthew* is in the Jews. Their conversion is especially near and dear to the heart of its writer. When the Syro-Phoenician woman sought His help, Jesus' first answer is: " I am not sent but unto the lost sheep of the house of Israel " (15: 24). When Jesus sends out the Twelve on the task of evangelization, His instruction is: " Go not into the way of the Gentiles, and into any city of the Samaritans enter ye not: but go rather to the lost sheep of the house of Israel " (10: 5, 6). Yet it is not to be thought that this gospel by any means excludes the Gentiles. Many are to come from the east and the west to sit down in the kingdom of God (8: 11). "The gospel is to be preached to the whole world (24: 14). And it is *Matthew* which gives us the marching orders of the Church: " Go ye therefore and teach all nations " (28: 19). It is clear that *Matthew's* first interest is in the Jews, but that it foresees the day when all nations will be gathered in.

The Jewishness of *Matthew* is also seen in its attitude to the Law. Jesus did not come to destroy, but to fulfil the Law. The least part of the Law will not pass away. Men must not be taught to break the Law. The righteousness of the Christian must exceed the righteousness of the Scribes and Pharisees (5: 17-20). *Matthew* was written by one who knew and loved the Law, and who saw that even the Law has its place in the Christian economy.

Once again there is an apparent paradox in the attitude of *Matthew* to the Scribes and Pharisees. They are given a very special authority: " The Scribes and the Pharisees sit on Moses' seat; all things therefore whatsoever they bid you, these do and observe " (23: 2). But at the same time there is no gospel which so sternly and consistently condemns the Scribes and the Pharisees. Right at the beginning there is John the Baptist's savage denunciation of them as a brood of vipers (3: 7-12). They complain that Jesus eats with publicans and sinners (9: 11). They ascribe the power of Jesus, not to God, but to the prince of devils (12: 24). They plot to destroy Him (12: 14). The disciples are warned against the leaven, the evil teaching, of the Scribes and Pharisees (16: 12). They are like evil plants doomed to be rooted up (15: 13). They are quite unable to read the signs of the times (16: 3). They are

the murderers of the prophets (21: 31). There is no chapter
of condemnation in the whole New Testament like *Matthew*
23 which is the condemnation of the Scribes and the
Pharisees. *Matthew's* condemnation of the Scribes and
Pharisees is not a condemnation of what they teach, but
of what they are. He condemns them for falling so far
short of their own teaching, and of falling so far below the
ideal of what they ought to be.

(ii) There are certain other special interests in *Matthew*.
Matthew is especially interested in the Church. *Matthew* is in
fact the only one of the Synoptic Gospels which uses the
word Church at all. It is only *Matthew* which introduces
the passage about the Church after Peter's confession at
Caesarea Philippi (*Matthew* 16: 13-23; cp. *Mark* 8: 27-33;
Luke 9: 18-22). It is only *Matthew* which says that disputes are to be settled by the Church (18: 17). By the
time *Matthew* came to be written the Church had become
a great organisation and institution; the Church had
indeed become the dominant factor in the life of the
Christian.

(iii) *Matthew has a specially strong apocalyptic interest*.
That is to say, *Matthew* has a specially strong interest in all
that Jesus said about His own Second Coming, about the
end of the world, and about the judgment. *Matthew* 24
gives us a fuller account of Jesus' apocalyptic discourse
than any of the other gospels. *Matthew* alone has the
parables of the talents (25: 14-30); the wise and the
foolish virgins (25: 1-13); and the sheep and the goats
(25: 31-46). *Matthew* has a special interest in the last
things and in judgment.

(iv) But we have not yet come to the greatest of all the
characteristics of *Matthew*. *Matthew is supremely the
teaching gospel*. We have already seen that the apostle
Matthew was responsible for the first collection and the

THE GOSPEL OF MATTHEW

first handbook of the teaching of Jesus. Matthew was the great systematizer. It was his habit and his custom to gather together in one place all that he knew and could find about the teaching of Jesus on any given subject. The result is that in *Matthew* we find five great blocks of Jesus' teaching, five great sections in which the teaching of Jesus is collected and systematized: all these sections have to do with the Kingdom of God. They are as follows:

(a) The Sermon on the Mount, or The Law of the Kingdom (5-7).

(b) The Duties of the Leaders of the Kingdom (10).

(c) The Parables of the Kingdom (13).

(d) Greatness and Forgiveness in the Kingdom (18).

(e) The Coming of the King (24, 25).

Matthew does more than collect and systematize. It must be remembered that Matthew was writing in an age when printing had not been invented, when books were few and far between because they had to be hand-written. In an age like that comparatively few people could possess a book; and, therefore, if they wished to know and to use the teaching and the story of Jesus, they had to carry it in their memories. Matthew therefore always arranges things in a way that it is easy for the reader to memorise. He arranges things in threes and sevens. There are three messages to Joseph; there are three denials of Peter; there are three questions of Pilate. There are seven parables of the Kingdom in chapter 13; there are seven woes to the Scribes and Pharisees in chapter 23. The genealogy of Jesus with which the gospel begins is a good example of this. The genealogy is to prove that Jesus is the Son of David. In Hebrew there are no figures; when figures are necessary the letters of the alphabet stand for the figures. In Hebrew there are no written vowels. The Hebrew letters for David are DWD; if these letters be taken as figures and not as letters, they add up to 14; and the genealogy consists of three groups of names, and in each group there are 14 names. Matthew does everything possible to systematize and to arrange the teaching of Jesus in such a way that people will be able to assimilate and to remember it.

Every teacher owes a debt of gratitude to Matthew, for Matthew wrote what is above all the teacher's gospel.

(v) *Matthew* has one final characteristic *Matthew's dominating idea is the idea of Jesus as King.* He writes to demonstrate the royalty of Jesus. Right at the beginning the genealogy is to prove that Jesus is the Son of David (I: I-17). The title, Son of David, is used oftener in *Matthew* than in any other gospel (15: 22; 21: 9; 21: 15). The wise men come looking for Him who is King of the Jews (2: 2). The triumphal entry is a deliberately dramatized claim to be King (21: I-II). Before Pilate, Jesus deliberately accepts the name of King (27: II). Even on the Cross the title of King is affixed, even if it be in mockery, over his head (27: 37). In the Sermon on the Mount *Matthew* shows us Jesus quoting the Law and five times abrogating it with a regal: " But I say unto you . . . " (5: 21, 27, 34, 38, 43). The final claim of Jesus is: " All power is given unto me " (28: 18). *Matthew's* picture of Jesus is the picture of the man born to be King. Jesus walks through *Matthew's* pages as if in the purple and gold of royalty. *Matthew* is concerned to show to men the lordship of Jesus Christ, to show us that indeed His is the Kingdom and the Power and the Glory.

MATTHEW

THE LINEAGE OF THE KING

This is the record of the lineage of Jesus Christ, the son of David, the son of Abraham.

Abraham begat Isaac, and Isaac begat Jacob. Jacob begat Judah and his brothers. Judah begat Phares and Zara, whose mother was Thamar. Phares begat Esrom. Esrom begat Aram. Aram begat Aminadab. Aminadab begat Naasson. Naasson begat Salmon. Salmon begat Booz, whose mother was Rachab. Booz begat Obed, whose mother was Ruth. Obed begat Jesse. Jesse begat David, the king.

David begat Solomon, whose mother was Uriah's wife. Solomon begat Roboam. Roboam begat Abia. Abia begat Asaph. Asaph begat Josaphat. Josaphat begat Joram. Joram begat Ozias. Ozias begat Joatham. Joatham begat Achaz. Achaz begat Ezekias. Ezekias begat Manasses. Manasses begat Amos. Amos begat Josias. Josias begat Jechonias, and his brothers, in the days when the exile to Babylon took place.

After the exile to Babylon Jechonias begat Salathiel. Salathiel begat Zorobabel. Zorobabel begat Abioud. Abioud begat Eliakim. Eliakim begat Azor. Azor begat Zadok. Zadok begat Acheim. Acheim begat Elioud. Elioud begat Eleazar. Eleazar begat Matthan. Matthan begat Jacob. Jacob begat Joseph, the husband of Mary, who was the mother of Jesus, who is called Christ.

From Abraham to David there were in all fourteen generations. From David to the exile to Babylon there were also fourteen generations. From the exile to Babylon to the coming of Christ there were also fourteen generations.

IT might seem to a modern reader that Matthew chose an extraordinary way in which to begin his gospel. It might seem a daunting proceeding to present the reader right at the very beginning of his book with a long list of names to wade through. But to a Jew this was the most natural, and the most interesting, and indeed the most essential way to begin the story of any man's life.

I

The Jews were exceedingly interested in genealogies. Matthew calls this *the book of the generation* (*biblos geneseōs*) of Jesus Christ. That to the Jews was a common phrase; and it means the record of a man's lineage, with a few explanatory sentences, where such comment was necessary. In the Old Testament we frequently find lists of the *generations* of famous men (*Genesis* 5: 1; 10: 1; 11: 10; 11: 27). When Josephus, the great Jewish historian, wrote his own autobiography, he began it with his own pedigree, which, he tells us, he found in the public records. The reason for this interest in pedigrees was that the Jews set the greatest possible store on purity of lineage. If in any man there was the slightest admixture of foreign blood, he lost his right to be called a Jew, and a member of the people of God. A priest, for instance, was bound to produce an unbroken record of his pedigree stretching back to Aaron; and, if he married, the woman he married must produce her pedigree for at least five generations back. When Ezra was reorganizing the worship of God, when the people returned from exile, and when he was setting the priesthood to function again, the children of Habaiah, the children of Koz, and the children of Barzillai were debarred from office, and were labelled as polluted because " they sought their register among those who were reckoned by genealogy, but they were not found " (*Ezra* 2: 61, 62). These genealogical records were actually kept by the Sanhedrin. Herod the Great was always despised by the pure-blooded Jews because he was half an Edomite; and we can see the importance that even Herod attached to these genealogies from the fact that he had the official registers destroyed, so that no one could prove a purer pedigree than his own. This may seem to us an uninteresting passage, but to the Jew it would be a most impressive matter that the pedigree of Jesus could be traced back to Abraham.

It is further to be noted that this pedigree is most carefully arranged. It is arranged in three groups of fourteen people each. It is in fact what is technically known as a mnemonic, that is to say a thing so arranged that it is easy to memorize. It is always to be remembered that the gospels were composed and written hundreds of years before there was any such thing as a printed book. Very few people would be able to possess actual copies of them; and, if they wished to possess them, they would be compelled to memorize them. So this pedigree is arranged in such a way that it is easy to memorize. The Hebrews did not possess any separate signs for figures; the letters of the alphabet served for figures as well, as if we used A to mean 1, and B to mean 2 and so on. Now the consonants of the name *David* in Hebrew are D W D. In Hebrew D stands for 4 and W stands for 6; therefore D W D stands for $4 + 6 + 4$, which adds up to 14. This genealogy is meant to prove that Jesus was the son of David, and it is so arranged as to make it easy for people to memorize it, and to carry it in their memories.

THE THREE STAGES

Matthew 1: 1-17 (*continued*)

THERE is something symbolic of the whole of human life in the way in which this pedigree is arranged. It is arranged in three sections, and the three sections are based on three great stages in Jewish history. The first section takes the story of history up to David. David was the man who welded Israel into a nation, and who made the Jews a power in the world. The first section takes the story up to the rise of Israel's greatest king. The second section takes the story down to the exile to Babylon. It is the section which tells of the nation's shame, and tragedy, and disaster. The third section takes the story down to Jesus Christ. Jesus Christ was the person who liberated men from their slavery, who rescued them from their disaster, and in whom the tragedy was turned into triumph.

These three sections stand for three stages in the spiritual history of mankind.

(i) *Man was born for greatness.* " God created man in His own image, in the image of God created He him " (*Genesis* I: 27). God said: " Let us make man in our own image, after our likeness " (*Genesis* I: 26). Man was created in the image of God. God's dream for man was a dream of greatness. Man was designed for fellowship with God. He was created that he might be nothing less than kin to God. As Cicero, the Roman thinker, saw it, " The only difference between man and God is in point of time." Man was essentially man born to be king.

(ii) *Man lost his greatness.* Instead of being the servant of God man became the slave of sin. As G. K. Chesterton said of man, " whatever else is true of man, man is not what he was meant to be." He used his free-will to defy and to disobey God, rather than to enter into friendship and fellowship with God. He became the rebel against God rather than the friend of God. Left to himself man had frustrated the design and plan of God in His creation.

(iii) *Man can regain his greatness.* Even then God did not abandon man to himself and to his own devices. God did not allow man to be destroyed by his own folly. Even then the end of the story was not left to be tragedy. Into this world God sent His Son, Jesus Christ, that Jesus Christ might rescue man from the morass of sin in which he had lost himself, and liberate him from the chains of sin with which he had bound himself, and that through Him man might regain the fellowship with God which he had lost.

In his genealogy Matthew shows us the royalty of king-ship gained; the tragedy of freedom lost; the glory of liberty restored. And that, in the mercy of God, is the story of mankind, and of each individual man.

4

THE REALIZATION OF MEN'S DREAMS

Matthew 1: 1-17 (continued)

THIS passage stresses two special things about Jesus.

(i) It stresses the fact that He was the son of David. It was, in fact, mainly to prove that that this genealogy was composed. That is a fact which the New Testament stresses again and again. Peter states it in the first recorded sermon of the Christian Church (*Acts* 2: 29-36). Paul speaks of Jesus Christ made of the seed of David according to the flesh (*Romans* 1: 3). The writer of the Pastoral Epistles urges men to remember that Jesus Christ, of the seed of David, was raised from the dead (2 *Timothy* 2: 8). The writer of the *Revelation* hears the Risen Christ say: " I am the root and the offspring of David " (*Revelation* 22: 16).

Repeatedly Jesus is so addressed in the gospel story. After the healing of the blind and dumb man, the people exclaim, " Is not this the son of David? " (*Matthew* 12: 23). The woman of Tyre and Sidon, who wished for Jesus' help for her daughter, calls him: " Thou son of David " (*Matthew* 15: 22). The blind men cry out to Jesus as son of David (*Matthew* 20: 30, 31). It is as son of David that the crowds greeted Jesus when He entered Jerusalem for the last time (*Matthew* 21: 9, 15).

There is something of great significance here. It is clear that it was the crowd, the common people, the ordinary folk, who addressed Jesus as son of David. The Jews were a waiting people. They never forgot, and never could forget, that they were the chosen people of God. Although their history was one long series of disasters, although at this very time they were a subject people, they never forgot their destiny. And it was the dream of the common people that into this world there would come a descendant of David who would lead them to the glory which they believed to be theirs by right. That is to say, Jesus is the answer to the dreams of men. It is true that so often men do not see it so. They see the answer to their dreams in power, in wealth, in material plenty, and in the realisation of the ambitions which they cherish. But if ever men's dreams of peace and loveliness, and greatness and satisfaction, are to be realized, they can only find their realization in Jesus Christ. Jesus Christ and the life He offers is the answer to the dreams of men. In the old Joseph story there is a text which goes far beyond the story itself. When Joseph was in prison, Pharaoh's chief butler and chief baker were prisoners along with him. They had their dreams, and their dreams troubled them, and their bewildered cry is, " We have dreamed a dream, and there is no interpreter of it " (*Genesis* 40: 8). Because man is man, because he is a child of eternity, man is always haunted by his dream; and the only way to the realization of it lies in Jesus Christ.

(ii) This passage also stresses that Jesus was the fulfilment of prophecy. In Him the message of the prophets came true. We tend nowadays to make very little of prophecy. We are not really interested for the most part in searching for sayings in the Old Testament which are fulfilled in the New Testament. But prophecy does contain this great and eternal truth, the truth that this is a planned universe, that in this universe there is purpose and design, that God is meaning and willing certain things to happen. J. H. Withers quotes a saying from Gerald Healy's play *The Black Stranger*. The scene is in Ireland, in the terrible days of famine in the mid-nineteenth century. For want of something better to do, and for lack of some other solution, the government had set men to digging roads to no purpose and to no destination. Michael finds out about this and comes home one day, and says in poignant wonder to his father, " They're makin' roads that lead to nowhere ". If we believe in prophecy that is what we can never say. History can never be a road that leads to nowhere. We may not use prophecy in the same way as our fathers did, but at the back of the fact of prophecy there lies the eternal fact that life and the world are not on the way to nowhere, but on the way to the goal of God.

NOT THE RIGHTEOUS, BUT SINNERS

Matthew I: I-17 (*continued*)

BY far the most amazing thing about this pedigree is the names of the women who appear in it.

It is not normal to find the names of women in Jewish pedigrees at all. The woman had no legal rights; she was regarded, not as a person, but as a thing. She was merely the possession of her father or of her husband, and in his disposal to do with as he liked. In the regular form of morning prayer the Jew thanked God that God had not made him a Gentile, a slave, or a woman. The very existence of these names in any pedigree at all is a most surprising and extraordinary phenomenon.

But it is when we look at who these women were, and at what they did, that the matter becomes even more amazing. Rachab, or as the Old Testament calls her, Rahab, was a harlot of Jericho (*Joshua* 2: I-7). Ruth was not even a Jewess; she was a Moabitess (*Ruth* I: 4), and does not the law itself lay it down, " An Ammonite or a Moabite shall not enter into the congregation of the Lord; even to their tenth generation shall they not enter into the congregation of the Lord for ever " (*Deuteronomy* 23: 3)? Ruth belonged to an alien and a hated people. Thamar was a deliberate seducer and an adulteress (*Genesis* 38). Bathsheba, the mother of Solomon, was the woman whom David seduced from Uriah, her husband, with an unforgivable cruelty (2 *Samuel* II and I2). If Matthew had ransacked the pages of the Old Testament for improbable candidates he could not have discovered four more incredible ancestors for Jesus Christ. But, surely, there is something very lovely here. Here, at the very beginning of his gospel, Matthew shows us in symbol the very essence of the gospel of God in Jesus Christ, for here he shows us the barriers going down.

(i) *The barrier between Jew and Gentile is down.* Rahab, the woman of Jericho, and Ruth, the woman of Moab, find their place within the pedigree of Jesus Christ. Already the great truth is there that in Christ there is neither Jew or Greek. Here, at the very beginning, there is the universalism of the gospel and of the love of God.

(ii) *The barriers between male and female are down.* In no ordinary pedigree would the name of any woman be found; but such names are found in Jesus' pedigree. The old contempt is gone; and men and women stand equally dear to God, and equally important to His purposes.

(iii) *The barrier between saint and sinner is down.* Somehow God can use for His purposes, and fit into His scheme of things, those who have sinned greatly. " I am not come," said Jesus, " to call the righteous, but sinners to repentance " (*Matthew* 9: 13).

Here at the very beginning of the gospel we are given a hint of the all-embracing width of the love of God. God can find His servants amongst those from whom the respectable orthodox would shudder away in horror.

THE SAVIOUR'S ENTRY INTO THE WORLD

Matthew 1: 18-25

The birth of Jesus Christ happened in this way. Mary, His mother, was betrothed to Joseph, and, before they became man and wife, it was discovered that she was carrying a child in her womb through the action of the Holy Spirit. Although Joseph, her husband, was a man who kept the law, he did not wish publicly to humiliate her, so he wished to divorce her secretly. When he was planning this, behold, an angel of the Lord came to him in a dream. " Joseph, son of David," said the angel, " do not hesitate to take Mary as your wife; for that which has been begotten within her has come from the Holy Spirit. She will bear a son, and you must call His name Jesus, for it is He who will save His people from their sins. All this has happened that there might be fulfilled that which was spoken by the Lord through the prophet, ' Behold, the maiden will conceive and bear a son, and you must call His name Emmanuel, which is

8

translated: God with us '." So Joseph woke from his
sleep, and did as the angel of the Lord had commanded
him; and he accepted his wife: and he did not know
her until she had borne a son; and he called His
name Jesus.

To our western ways of thinking the relationships in
this passage are very bewildering. First, Joseph is said
to be *betrothed* to Mary; then he is said to be planning
quietly to *divorce* her; and then she is called his *wife*.
The relationships represent normal Jewish marriage
procedure. In Jewish marriage there were three steps.

(i) There was the *engagement*. The engagement was
often made when the couple were only children. It was
usually made through the parents, or through a professional
match-maker. And it was often made without the couple
involved ever having seen each other. Marriage was held
to be far too serious a step to be left to the dictates of
human passion and the human heart.

(ii) There was the *betrothal*. The betrothal was what
we might call the ratification of the engagement into
which the couple had previously entered. At this point
the engagement, entered into by the parents or the match-
maker, could be broken if the girl was unwilling to go
on with it. But once the betrothal was entered into it was
absolutely binding. It lasted for one year. During that
year the couple were known as man and wife, although
they had not the rights of man and wife. It could not be
terminated in any other way than by divorce. In the Jewish
law we frequently find what is to us a curious phrase.
A girl whose fiancé had died during the year of betrothal is
called " a virgin who is a widow ". It was at this stage
that Joseph and Mary were. They were betrothed, and
if Joseph wished to end the betrothal, he could do so in
no other way than by divorce; and in that year of betrothal
Mary was legally known as his wife.

(iii) The third stage was *the marriage proper* which
took place at the end of the year of betrothal.

If we remember the normal Jewish wedding customs, then the relationships in this passage are perfectly usual and perfectly clear.

So at this stage it was told to Joseph that Mary was to bear a child, that that child had been begotten by the Holy Spirit, and that he must call the child by the name Jesus. *Jesus* is the Greek form of the Jewish name *Joshua*, and *Joshua* means *Jehovah is salvation*. Long ago the Psalmist had heard God say, " He shall redeem Israel from all his iniquities " (*Psalm* 130: 8). And Joseph was told that the child who was to be born would grow into the Saviour who would save God's people from their sins. Jesus was not so much The Man born to be King, as He was The Man born to be Saviour. He came to this world, not for His own sake, but for us men and for our salvation.

BORN OF THE HOLY SPIRIT

Matthew 1: 18-25 (*continued*)

THIS passage tells us how Jesus was born by the action of the Holy Spirit. It tells us of what we call the Virgin Birth. The Virgin Birth is a doctrine which presents us with many difficulties; and it is a doctrine which our Church does not compel us to accept in the literal and the physical sense. This is one of the doctrines on which the Church says that we have full liberty to come to our own belief and our own conclusion. At the moment we are concerned only to find out what this means for us.

If we come to this passage with fresh eyes, and if we read it as if we were reading it for the first time, we will find that the fact which it stresses is not so much that Jesus was born of a woman who was a virgin, as that the birth of Jesus is the work of the Holy Spirit. " It was discovered that Mary was carrying a child in her womb through the action of the Holy Spirit." " That which has been begotten within her has come from the Holy

Spirit." It is as if these sentences were underlined, and printed large. That is what Matthew wishes to say to us in this passage. What then does it mean to say that in the birth of Jesus the Holy Spirit of God was specially operative? Let us leave aside all the doubtful and debatable things, and let us here concentrate on that great truth, as Matthew would wish us to do.

In Jewish thought the Holy Spirit had certain very definite functions. We cannot bring to this passage the *Christian* idea of the Holy Spirit in all its fulness, because Joseph would know nothing about that. We must interpret it in the light of the *Jewish* idea of the Holy Spirit, for it is that idea that Joseph would inevitably bring to this message, for that was all he knew.

(i) According to the Jewish idea, *the Holy Spirit was the person who brought God's truth to men.* It was the Holy Spirit who taught the prophets what to say; it was the Holy Spirit who taught men of God what to do; it was the Holy Spirit who, throughout the ages and the generations, brought God's truth to men. So then, Jesus is the one person who brings God's truth to men. Let us put it in another way. Jesus is the one person who can tell us what God is like, and what God means us to be. In Jesus alone we see what God is like, and we see what man ought to be like. Before Jesus came men had only vague and shadowy, and often quite wrong, ideas about God; they could only at best guess and grope; but Jesus could say, " He that hath seen Me hath seen the Father " (*John* 14: 9). In Jesus we see the love, the compassion, the mercy, the seeking heart, the purity of God as nowhere else in all this world. With the coming of Jesus the time of guessing is gone, and the time of certainty is come. Before Jesus came men did not really know what goodness was. In Jesus alone we see true manhood, true goodness true obedience to the will of God. Jesus came to tell us the truth about God and the truth about ourselves.

(ii) The Jews believed that the Holy Spirit not only brought God's truth to men, but also *enabled men to recognize that truth when they saw it.* So then Jesus opens men's eyes to the truth. Men are blinded by their own ignorance; they are led astray by their own prejudices; their minds and eyes are darkened by their own sins and their own passions. Jesus can open our eyes until we are able to see the truth. In one of William J. Locke's novels there is a picture of a woman who has any amount of money, and who has spent half a lifetime on a tour of the sights and picture galleries of the world. She was weary and bored. Then she met a Frenchman who had little of this world's goods, but who had a wide knowledge and a great love of beauty. He came with her, and in his company things were completely different. " I never knew what things were like," she said to him, " until you taught me how to look at them." Life is quite different when Jesus teaches us how to look at things. When Jesus comes into our hearts, our eyes see things quite differently, for He opens our eyes that we may see them truly.

CREATION AND RE-CREATION

Matthew I: 18-25 *(continued)*

(iii) The Jews specially *connected the Spirit of God with the work of creation.* It was through His Spirit that God performed His creating work. In the beginning the Spirit of God moved upon the face of the waters and chaos became a world (*Genesis* I: 2). " By the word of the Lord were the heavens made," said the Psalmist, " and all the host of them by the breath of His mouth " (*Psalm* 33: 6). (Both in Hebrew, *ruach,* and in Greek, *pneuma,* the word for *breath* and *spirit* is the same word). " Thou sendest forth Thy Spirit, they are created " (*Psalm* 104: 30). " The Spirit of God hath made me," said Job, " and the breath of the Almighty hath given me life " (*Job* 33: 4).

The Spirit is the Creator of the World and the Giver of Life. So, then, in Jesus there came into the world God's life-giving and creating power. In Jesus there entered the world the very life and power of God Himself. That power, which reduced the primal chaos to order, is come to bring order to our disordered life. That power, which breathed life into that in which there was no life, is come to breathe life into our weaknesses and frustrations. We could put it this way—we are not really alive until Jesus enters into our lives.

(iv) The Jews specially connected the Spirit, not only with the work of creation, but *with the work of re-creation.* Ezekiel draws his grim picture of the valley of dry bones. He goes on to tell how the dry bones came alive; and then he hears God say, " I shall put my Spirit in you and you shall live " (*Ezekiel* 37: 1-14). The Rabbis had a saying, " God said to Israel: ' In this world my Spirit has put wisdom in you, but in the future my Spirit will make you to live again ' ". When men are dead in sin and in lethargy, and in the death of the mind and soul and heart, it is the Spirit of God which can waken them to life anew. So then, in Jesus there came to this world the power which can re-make and re-create life. He can bring to life again the soul which is dead in sin; He can revive again the ideals which have died; He can make strong again the will to goodness which has perished. He can renew and re-create life, when men have lost all that life means.

There is much more in this chapter than the crude fact that Jesus Christ was born of a virgin mother. The essence of Matthew's story is that in the birth of Jesus the Spirit of God was operative as never before in this world. It is the Spirit who brings God's truth to men; it is the Spirit who enables men to recognize that truth when they see it; it was the Spirit who was God's agent in the creation of the world; it is the Spirit who alone can re-create the human soul when it has lost the life it ought to have. Jesus enables us to see what God is and what man ought

13

to be; Jesus opens the eyes of our minds so that we can see the truth of God for us; Jesus is the creating power come amongst men; Jesus is the re-creating power which can release the souls of men from the death of sin.

THE BIRTH PLACE OF THE KING

Matthew 2: 1, 2

> When Jesus was born in Bethlehem in Judaea, in the days of Herod the King, behold there came to Jerusalem wise men from the East. " Where," they said, " is the newly born King of the Jews? For we have seen His star in its rising and we have come to worship Him."

IT was in Bethlehem that Jesus was born. Bethlehem was quite a little town six miles to the south of Jerusalem. In the olden days it had been called Ephrath or Ephratah. The name *Bethlehem* means *The House of Bread,* and Bethlehem stood in a fertile countryside, which made its name a fitting name. It stood high up on a grey limestone ridge more than two thousand five hundred feet in height. The ridge had a summit at each end, and a hollow like a saddle between them. So, from its position, Bethlehem looked like a town set in an amphitheatre of hills.

Bethlehem had a long history. It was there that Jacob had buried Rachel, and had set up a pillar of memory beside her grave (*Genesis* 48: 7; 35: 20). It was there that Ruth had lived when she married Boaz (*Ruth* 2: 1), and from Bethlehem Ruth could see the land of Moab, her native land, across the Jordan valley. But above all Bethlehem was the home and the city of David (I *Samuel* 16: 1; 17: 12; 20: 6); and it was for the water of the well of Bethlehem that David longed when he was a hunted fugitive upon the hills (2 *Samuel* 23: 14, 15). In later days we read that Rehoboam fortified the town of Bethlehem (2 *Chronicles* 11: 6). But in the history of

Israel, and to the minds of the people, Bethlehem was uniquely the city of David. It was from the line of David that God was to send the great deliverer of His people. As the prophet Micah had it: " Thou Bethlehem Ephratah, though thou be little among the thousands of Judah, yet out of thee shall He come forth unto me that is to be the ruler of Israel; whose goings forth have been from of old, from everlasting " (*Micah* 5: 2).

It was in Bethlehem, David's city, that the Jews expected great David's greater Son to be born; it was there that they expected God's Anointed One to come into the world, and it was so.

The picture of the stable and the manger as being the birthplace of Jesus is a picture which is indelibly etched in our minds; but it may well be that that picture is not altogether correct. Justin Martyr, one of the greatest of the early fathers, who lived about A.D. 150, and who came from the district near Bethlehem, tells us that Jesus was born in a cave near the village of Bethlehem (Justin Martyr, *Dialogue with Trypho*, 78, 304); and it may well be that Justin's information is correct. The houses in Bethlehem are built on the slope of the limestone ridge; and it is very common for them to have a cave-like stable hollowed out in the limestone rock below the house itself; and it is very likely that it was in such a cave-stable that Jesus was born.

To this day such a cave is shown in Bethlehem as the birthplace of Jesus and above it the great Roman Church of the Nativity has been built. For very long that cave has been shown as the birthplace of Jesus. It was so in the days of the Roman Emperor, Hadrian, for Hadrian, in a deliberate attempt to desecrate the place, erected a shrine to the heathen god Adonis above it. When the Roman Empire became Christian, early in the fourth century, the first Christian Emperor, Constantine, built a great church there, and that church still stands. H. V. Morton tells how he visited that Church of the Nativity in Bethlehem. He came to a great wall, and in the wall there was a door so low that even a dwarf would have to stoop to enter it; and through the door, and on the other side of the wall, there was the church. Beneath the high altar of the church, there is the cave, and when the pilgrim descends into it he finds a little dark cavern about fourteen yards long and four yards wide, lit by fifty-three silver lamps; and in the floor there is a star, and round it a Latin inscription: " Here Jesus Christ was born of the Virgin Mary."

When the Lord of Glory came to this earth, He was born in a cave where men sheltered the beasts. The cave, which is now in the Church of the Nativity in Bethlehem, may be that same cave, or it may not be. That, we will never know for certain. But there is something beautiful in the symbolism that the church where the cave is has a door so low that all who enter it must stoop to enter. It is supremely fitting that every man should approach the infant Jesus upon his knees.

THE HOMAGE OF THE EAST

Matthew 2: 1, 2 (continued)

WHEN Jesus was born in Bethlehem there came to do Him homage wise men from the East. The name of these men is the *Magi*, and that is a word which is difficult to translate. Herodotus (1: 101, 132) has certain information about these men called the Magi. He says that the Magi were originally a Median tribe. The Medes were part of the Empire of the Persians; they tried to overthrow the Persians and to substitute the power of the Medes. The attempt failed. From that time the Magi ceased to have any ambitions for power or prestige, and became a tribe of priests. They became in Persia almost exactly what the Levites were in Israel. They became the teachers and instructors of the Persian kings. In Persia no sacrifice could be offered unless one of the Magi was present. They became men of holiness and wisdom.

These Magi were men who were skilled in philosophy, medicine and natural science. They were soothsayers and interpreters of dreams. In later times the word Magus developed a much lower meaning, and came to mean little more than a fortune-teller, a sorcerer, a magician, and a charlatan. Such was Elymas, the sorcerer (*Acts* 13: 6, 8), and Simon who is commonly called Simon Magus (*Acts* 8: 9, 11). But at their best the Magi were not like that; at their best they were good and holy men, who sought for truth.

In those ancient days all men believed in astrology. They believed that they could foretell the future from the stars, and they believed that a man's destiny was settled by the star under which he was born. It is not difficult to see how that belief arose. The stars pursue their unvarying courses; they represent the order of the universe. If then there suddenly appeared some brilliant star, if the unvarying order of the heavens was broken by some special phenomenon, it did look as if God was breaking into His own order, and announcing some special thing.

We do not know what brilliant star these ancient Magi saw. Many suggestions have been made. About 11 B.C. Halley's comet was visible shooting brilliantly across the skies. About 7 B.C. there was a brilliant conjunction of Saturn and Jupiter. In the years 5 to 2 B.C. there was an unusual astronomical phenomenon. In these years, on the first day of the Egyptian month, Mesori, Sirius, the dog star, rose heliacally, that is at sunrise, and shone with extraordinary brilliance. Now the name *Mesori* means *the birth of a prince*, and to those ancient astrologers such a star would undoubtedly mean the birth of some great king. We cannot tell what star the Magi saw; but it was their profession to watch the heavens, and some heavenly brilliance spoke to them of the entry of a king into the world.

It may seem to us extraordinary that these men should set out from the East to find a king, but the strange thing is that, just about the time when Jesus was born, there was in the world a strange feeling of expectation, a waiting for the coming of a king. Even the Roman historians knew about this. Not so very much later than this, on the days of Vespasian, Suetonius could write, " There had spread over all the Orient an old and established belief, that it was fated at that time for men coming from Judaea to rule the world " (Suetonius, *Life of Vespasian*, 4: 5). Tacitus tells of the same belief that " there was a firm persuasion . . . that at this very time the East was to grow powerful, and rulers coming from Judaea were to acquire universal empire " (Tacitus, *Histories*, 5: 13). The Jews had the belief that " about that time one from their country should become governor of the habitable earth " (Josephus, *Wars of the Jews*, 6: 5, 4). At a slightly later time we find Tiridates, King of Armenia, visiting Nero at Rome with his Magi along with him (Suetonius, *Life of Nero*, 13: 1). We find the Magi in Athens sacrificing to the memory of Plato (Seneca, *Epistles*, 58: 31). Almost at the same time as Jesus was born we find Augustus, the Roman Emperor, being hailed as the Saviour of the World, and Virgil, the Roman poet, writing his Fourth Eclogue, which is known as the Messianic Eclogue, about the golden days to come.

There is not the slightest need to think that the story of the coming of the Magi to the cradle of Christ is only a lovely legend. It is exactly the kind of thing that could easily have happened in that ancient world. When Jesus Christ came into this world the world was in an eagerness of expectation. Men were waiting for God. The desire for God was in the hearts of men. They had discovered that they could not build the golden age without God. It was to a waiting world that Jesus came; and, when He came, the ends of the earth were gathered at His cradle. It was the first sign and symbol of the world conquest of Christ.

THE CRAFTY KING

Matthew 2: 3-9

> When Herod the king heard of this he was disturbed, and so was all Jerusalem with him. So he collected all the chief priests and scribes of the people, and asked them where the Anointed One of God was to be born. They said to him, " In Bethlehem in Judaea. For so it stands written through the prophets, ' And you Bethlehem, land of Judah, are by no means the least among the leaders of Judah. For there shall come forth from you the leader, who will be a shepherd to my people Israel.' " Then Herod secretly summoned the wise men, and carefully questioned them about the time when the star appeared. He sent them to Bethlehem. " Go," he said, " and make every effort to find out about the little child. And, when you have found Him, send news to me, that I, too, may come and worship Him." When they had listened to the king they went on their way.

IT came to the ears of Herod that the wise men had come from the East, and that they were searching for the little child who had been born to be King of the Jews. Any king would have been worried at the report that a child had been born who was to occupy his throne. But Herod was doubly disturbed. Herod was half Jew and half Idumæan. There was Edomite blood in his veins. He had made himself useful to the Romans in the wars and civil wars of Palestine, and they trusted him. He had been appointed governor in 47 B.C.; in 40 B.C. he had received the title of king; and he was to reign until 4 B.C. He had wielded power for long. He was called Herod the Great, and in many ways he deserved the title. He was the only ruler of Palestine who ever succeeded in keeping the peace and in bringing order into disorder. He was a great builder; he was indeed the builder of the Temple in Jerusalem. He could be generous. In times of difficulty he remitted the taxes to make things easier for the people; and in the famine of 25 B.C. he had actually melted down his own gold plate to buy corn for the starving people. But Herod had one terrible flaw in his character. He was almost insanely suspicious. He had always been suspicious, and the older he became the more suspicious he grew, until, in his old age, he was, as someone said, " a murderous old man." If he suspected anyone as a rival to his power, that person was promptly eliminated. He murdered his wife Mariamne and her mother Alexandra. His eldest son, Antipater, and two other sons, Alexander and Aristobulus, were all assassinated by him. Augustus, the Roman Emperor, had said, bitterly, that it was safer to be Herod's pig than Herod's son. (The saying is even more epigrammatic in Greek, for in Greek *hus* is the word for a *pig*, and *huios* is the word for a *son*). Something of Herod's savage, bitter, warped nature can be seen from the provisions he made when death came near. When he was seventy he knew that he must die. He retired to Jericho, the loveliest of all his cities. He gave orders that a collection of the most distinguished citizens of Jerusalem should be arrested on trumped up charges and imprisoned. And he ordered that the moment he died, they should all be killed. He said grimly that he was well aware that no one would mourn for his death, and that he was determined that some tears should be shed when he died.

It is clear how such a man would feel when news reached him that a child was born who was destined to be king. Herod was troubled, and Jerusalem was troubled too, for Jerusalem well knew the steps that Herod would take to pin down this story and to eliminate this child. Jerusalem knew Herod, and Jerusalem shivered as it waited for Herod's inevitable reaction.

Herod summoned the chief priests and the scribes. The scribes were the experts in scripture and in the law. The chief priests consisted of two kinds of people. They consisted of ex-high priests. The high priesthood was confined to a very few families. They were the priestly aristocracy, and the members of these select families were called the chief priests. So Herod summoned the religious aristocracy and the theological scholars of his day, and asked them where, according to the scriptures, the Anointed One of God should be born. They quoted the text in *Micah* 5: 2 to him. Herod sent for the wise men, and despatched them to make diligent search for the little child who had been born. He said that he, too, wished to come and worship the child, but his one desire was to murder the child born to be king.

No sooner was Jesus born into this world than we see men grouping themselves into these three groups in which men are always to be found in regard to Jesus Christ. Let us look at the three reactions.

(i) There was the reaction of Herod, *the reaction of hatred and hostility*. Herod was afraid that this little child was going to interfere with his life, his place, his power, his influence, and therefore his first instinct was to destroy Him. There are still those who would gladly destroy Jesus Christ, because they see in Him the one who inter- feres with their lives. They wish to do what they like, and Christ will not let them do what they like; and so they would kill Him. The man whose one desire is to do what he likes has never any use for Jesus Christ. The Christian is the man who has ceased to do what he likes, and who has dedicated his life to do as Christ likes.

(ii) There was the reaction of the chief priests and scribes. *Their reaction was complete indifference*. It did not make the slightest difference to them. They were so engrossed in their Temple ritual and their legal discussions that they simply completely disregarded Jesus. He meant nothing to them. There are still those who are so interested in their own affairs that Jesus Christ means nothing to them. The prophet's poignant question can still be asked: " Is it nothing to you, all ye that pass by? " (*Lamentations* I: 12).

(iii) There was the reaction of the wise men, *the reaction of adoring worship*, the desire to lay at the feet of Jesus Christ the noblest gifts which they could bring. Surely, when any man realizes the love of God in Jesus Christ, he too should be lost in wonder, love and praise.

GIFTS FOR CHRIST

Matthew 2: 9-12

> And, behold, the star, which they had seen in its rising, led them on until it came and stood over the place where the little child was. When they saw the star, they rejoiced with exceeding great joy. When they came into the house, they saw the little child with Mary, His mother, and they fell down and worshipped Him; and they opened their treasures, and offered to Him gifts, gold, frankincense and myrrh. And because a message from God came to them in a dream, telling them not to go back to Herod, they returned to their own country by another way.

So the wise men found their way to Bethlehem. We need not think that the star literally moved like a guide across the sky. There is poetry here, and we must not turn lovely poetry into crude and lifeless prose. But over Bethlehem the star was shining. There is a lovely legend which tells how the star, its work of guidance completed, fell into the well at Bethlehem, and that it is still there and can still be seen sometimes by those whose hearts are pure.

Later legends have been busy with the wise men. In the early days eastern tradition said that there were twelve of them. But now the tradition that there were three of them is almost universal. The New Testament does not say that there were three, but the idea that there were three of them no doubt arose from the threefold gift which they brought. Later legend made them kings. And still later legend gave them names, Caspar, Melchior and Balthasar. Still later legend assigned to each a personal description, and distinguished the gift which each of them gave to Jesus. Melchior was an old man, grey haired, and with a long beard, and it was he who brought the gift of gold. Caspar was young and beardless, and ruddy in countenance, and it was he who brought the gift of frankincense. Balthasar was swarthy, with the beard newly grown upon him, and it was he who brought the gift of myrrh.

From very early times men have seen a peculiar fitness

in the gifts the wise men brought. They have seen in each gift something which specially matched some characteristic of Jesus and His work.

(i) *Gold is the gift for a king.* Seneca tells us that in Parthia it was the custom that no one could ever approach the king without a gift. And gold, the king of metals, is the fit gift for a king of men. So then Jesus was " the Man born to be King." But He was to reign, not by force, but by love; and He was to rule over men's hearts, not from a throne, but from a Cross. We do well to remember that Jesus Christ is King. We can never meet Jesus on an equality. We must always meet Him on terms of complete submission and complete surrender. Nelson, the great admiral, always treated his vanquished opponents with the greatest kindness and courtesy. After one of his naval victories, the defeated admiral was brought aboard Nelson's flagship and on to Nelson's quarter-deck. Knowing Nelson's reputation for courtesy, and thinking to trade upon it, he advanced across the quarter-deck with hand outstretched as if he was advancing to shake hands with an equal. Nelson's hand remained by his side. " Your sword first," he said, " and then your hand." Before we must be friends with Christ, we must submit to Christ.

(ii) *Frankincense is the gift for a priest.* It was in the Temple worship and at the Temple sacrifices that the sweet perfume of frankincense was used. The function of a priest is to open the way to God for men. The Latin word for *priest* is *pontifex*, which means a *bridge-builder*. The priest is the man who builds a bridge between men and God. That is what Jesus did. He opened the way to the presence of God; He made it possible for men to enter into the very presence of God.

(iii) *Myrrh is the gift for one who is to die.* Myrrh was used to embalm the bodies of the dead. Jesus came into the world to die. Holman Hunt has a famous picture of Jesus. It shows Jesus at the door of the carpenter's shop in Nazareth. He is still only a boy. The setting sun is shining in at the door, and the lad, Jesus, has come to the door to stretch His limbs which had grown cramped over the bench. He stands there in the doorway withs arm outstretched, and behind Him, on the wall, the setting sun throws His shadow, and it is the shadow of a cross. And in the background there stands Mary, and as she sees that shadow there is the fear of coming tragedy in her eyes. Jesus came into the world to live for men, and, in the end, to die for men. He came to give for men His life and His death.

Gold for a king, frankincense for a priest, myrrh for one who was to die—these were the gifts of the wise men, and, even at the cradle of Christ, they foretold that He was to be the true King, the perfect High Priest, and in the end the supreme Saviour of men.

ESCAPE TO EGYPT

Matthew 2: 13-15

> When they had gone away, behold, an angel of the Lord appeared in a dream to Joseph. " Rise," he said, " and take the little child and His mother, and flee into Egypt, and stay there until I tell you; for Herod is about to search for the little child, in order to kill Him." So he arose and took the little child and His mother by night and went away into Egypt, and he remained there until the death of Herod. This happened that the word spoken by the Lord through the prophet might be fulfilled: " Out of Egypt have I called My Son."

THE ancient world had no doubt that God sent His messages to men in dreams. So Joseph was warned in a dream to flee into Egypt to escape Herod's murderous intentions. The flight into Egypt was entirely natural. Often, throughout the troubled centuries before Jesus came, when some peril and some tyranny and some persecution made life intolerable for the Jews, they sought refuge in Egypt. The result was that every city in Egypt had its colony of Jews; and in the city of Alexandria there were actually more than a million Jews, and certain districts of the city were entirely handed over to them. Joseph in his hour of peril was doing what many a Jew had done before; and when Joseph and Mary reached Egypt they would not find themselves altogether amidst strangers, for in every town and city they would find Jews who had sought refuge there.

It is an interesting fact that in the after days the foes of Christianity and the enemies of Jesus used the stay in Egypt as a peg to attach their slanders to Him. Egypt was proverbially the land of sorcery, of witchcraft and of magic. The *Talmud* says, " Ten measures of sorcery descended into the world; Egypt received nine, the rest of the world one ". So the enemies of Jesus declared that it was in Egypt that Jesus had learned a magic and a sorcery which made Him able to work miracles, and to deceive men. When the pagan philosopher, Celsus, directed his attack against Christianity in the third century, that attack which Origen met and defeated, he said that Jesus was brought up as an illegitimate child, that He served for hire in Egypt, that He came to the knowledge of certain miraculous powers, and returned to His own country and used these powers to proclaim Himself God (Origen, *Contra Celsum* I: 38). A certain Rabbi, Eliezer ben Hyrcanus, said that Jesus had the necessary magical formulae tattooed upon His body so that He would not forget them. Such were the slanders that twisted minds connected with the flight to Egypt; but they are obviously false, for it was as a little baby that Jesus was taken to Egypt, and it was as a little child that He was brought back.

Two of the loveliest New Testament legends are connected with the flight into Egypt. The first is a legend about the penitent thief. Legend calls the penitent thief Dismas, and tells that he did not meet Jesus for the first time when they both hung on their crosses on Calvary. The story runs like this. When Joseph and Mary were on their way to Egypt, they were waylaid by robbers.

One of the robber chiefs wished to murder them at once and to steal their little store of goods. But something about the baby Jesus went straight to Dismas' heart, for Dismas was one of these robbers. He refused to allow any harm to come to Jesus or His parents. He looked at Jesus and said, " O most blessed of children, if ever there come a time for having mercy on me, then remember me, and forget not this hour ". So, the legend says, Jesus and Dismas met again at Calvary, and Dismas on the cross found forgiveness and mercy for his soul.

The other legend is a child's story, but it is very lovely. When Joseph and Mary and Jesus were on their way to Egypt, the story runs, as the evening came they were weary, and they sought refuge in a cave. It was very cold, so cold that the ground was white with hoar frost. A little spider saw the little baby Jesus, and he wished so much that he could do something for Him to keep Him warm in the cold night. He decided to do the only thing he could do, to spin his web across the entrance of the cave, to make, as it were, a curtain there. Along the path there came a detachment of Herod's soldiers, seeking for children to kill to carry out Herod's bloodthirsty order. When they came to the cave they were about to burst in to search it, to see if anyone was hiding there, but their captain noticed the spider's web. It was covered with the white hoar frost and stretched right across the entrance to the cave. " Look," he said, " at the spider's web there. It is quite unbroken and there cannot possibly be anyone in the cave, for anyone entering the cave would certainly have torn the web." So the soldiers passed on, and left the holy family in peace, because a little spider had spun his web across the entrance to the cave. And that, so they say, is why to this day we put tinsel on our Christmas trees, for the glittering tinsel streamers stand for the spider's web, white with the hoar frost, stretched across the entrance of the cave on the way to Egypt. It is a lovely story, and this much, at least, is true, that no gift which Jesus receives is ever forgotten.

The last words of this passage introduce us to a custom which is characteristic of Matthew. He sees in the flight to Egypt a fulfilment of the word spoken by Hosea. He quotes it in the form: Out of Egypt have I called my son. That is a quotation from *Hosea* 11: 1, which reads: " When Israel was a child, then I loved him, and called my son out of Egypt." It can be seen at once that in its original form this saying of Hosea had nothing to do with Jesus, and nothing to do with the flight to Egypt. It was nothing more than a simple statement of how God had delivered the nation of Israel from slavery and from bondage in the land of Egypt. We shall see, again and again, that this is typical of Matthew's use of the Old Testament. He is prepared to use as a prophecy about Jesus any text at all which can be made verbally to fit, even although originally it had nothing to do with the question in hand, and was never meant to have anything to do with it. Matthew knew that almost the only way to convince the Jews that Jesus was the promised Anointed One of God was to prove that He was the fulfilment of Old Testament prophecy. And in his eagerness to do that he finds prophecies in the Old Testament where no prophecies were ever meant. When we read a passage like this we must remember that, though it seems strange and unconvincing to us, it would appeal to those Jews for whom Matthew was writing.

THE SLAUGHTER OF THE CHILDREN
Matthew 2: 16-18

> Then Herod saw that he had been tricked by the wise men, and he sent and slew all the children in Bethlehem, and in all the districts near by. He slew every child of two years and under, reckoning from the time when he had made his inquiries from the wise men. Then the word which was spoken through Jeremiah the prophet was fulfilled: " A voice was heard in Rama, weeping and much lamenting, Rachel weeping for her children, and she refused to be comforted, for they were no more."

WE have already seen that Herod was a past master in the art of assassination. He had no sooner come to the throne than he began by annihilating the Sanhedrin, the supreme court of the Jews. Later he had slaughtered three hundred court officers out of hand. Later he had murdered his wife Mariamne, and her mother Alexandra, his eldest son Antipater, and two other sons, Alexander and Aristobulus. And in the hour of his death he had arranged for the slaughter of the notable men of Jerusalem It was not to be expected that Herod would calmly accept the news that a child had been born who was going to be king. We have read how he had carefully enquired of the wise men when they had seen the star. Even then he was craftily working out the age of the child so that he might take steps towards murder, and now he put his plans into swift and savage action. He gave orders that every child under two years of age in Bethlehem and the surrounding district should be slaughtered.

There are two things which we must note. Bethlehem was not a large town, and the number of the children would not exceed from twenty to thirty babies. We must not think in terms of hundreds. It is true that this does not make Herod's crime any the less terrible, but we must get the picture right.

Secondly, there are certain critics who hold that this slaughter cannot have taken place because there is no mention of it in any writer outside this one passage of the New Testament. The Jewish historian Josephus, for instance, does not mention it. There are two things to be said. First, as we have just seen, Bethlehem was a comparatively small place, and in a land where murder was so widespread the slaughter of twenty or thirty babies would cause little stir, and would mean very little except to the broken-hearted mothers of Bethlehem. Second, Carr notes that Macaulay, in his history, points out that Evelyn, the famous diarist, who was a most assiduous and voluminous recorder of contemporary events, never mentions the massacre of Glencoe. The fact that a thing is not mentioned, even in the places where one might expect it to be mentioned, is no proof at all that it did not happen. The whole incident is so typical of Herod that we need not doubt that Matthew is passing the truth down to us.

Here is a terrible illustration of what men will do to get rid of Jesus Christ. If a man is set on his own way, if he sees in Christ someone who is liable to interfere with his ambitions and rebuke his ways, then his one desire is to eliminate Christ; and then he is driven to the most terrible things, for then, if he does not break men's bodies, he will break their hearts.

Here again, at the end of this passage, we see Matthew's characteristic way of using the Old Testament. He quotes *Jeremiah* 31: 15, " Thus saith the Lord: a voice was heard in Ramah, lamentation and bitter weeping; Rachel weeping for her children refused to be comforted for her children, because they were not." Very certainly the verse in Jeremiah has no connection with Herod's slaughter of the children. The picture in Jeremiah was this. Jeremiah was picturing the people of Jerusalem being led away in exile. In their sad way to an alien land they pass Ramah, and Ramah was the place where Rachel lay buried (I *Samuel* 10: 2); and Jeremiah pictures Rachel weeping, even in the tomb, for the fate that had befallen the people. Here again Matthew is doing what he so often did. He is finding a prophecy in his eagerness where no prophecy is. But, again, we must remind ourselves that what seems strange to us seemed in no way strange to those for whom Matthew was writing in his day.

RETURN TO NAZARETH

Matthew 2: 19-23

When Herod died, behold, the angel of the Lord appeared in a dream to Joseph in Egypt. " Rise," he

said, " and take the little child and his mother, and
go into the land of Israel. For those who seek the
little child's life are dead." So he rose and took the
little child and his mother, and went into the land
of Israel. When he heard that Archelaus was king
in Judaea instead of Herod, his father, he was afraid
to go there. So, when he had received a message
from God in a dream, he withdrew to the districts
of Galilee, and he came and settled in a town called
Nazareth. This happened so that the word spoken
through the prophets might be fulfilled: " He shall
be called a Nazarene."

IN due time Herod died, and when Herod died the whole
kingdom over which he had ruled was split up. The Romans
had trusted Herod, and they had allowed him to reign
over a very considerable territory, but Herod well knew
that none of his sons would be allowed a like power. So
he had divided his kingdom into three, and in his will
he had left a part to each of three of his sons. He had
left Judaea to Archelaus; he had left Galilee to Herod
Antipas; and he had left the region away to the north-
east and beyond Jordan to Philip. But the death of Herod
did not solve the problem. Archelaus was a bad king, and
he was not to last long upon the throne. In point of fact
he had begun his reign with an attempt to out-Herod
Herod, for he had opened his rule with the deliberate
slaughter of three thousand of the most influential people
in the country. Clearly, even now that Herod was dead,
it was still unsafe to return to Judaea with the savage
and reckless Archelaus on the throne. So Joseph was
guided to go to Galilee where Herod Antipas, a much
better king, reigned.

It was in Nazareth that Joseph settled, and it was in
Nazareth that Jesus was brought up. It must not be
thought that Nazareth was a little quiet backwater, quite
out of touch with life and with events. Nazareth lay in a
hollow in the hills in the south of Galilee. But a lad had
only to climb the hills for half the world to be at his door.
He could look west and the waters of the Mediterranean,

blue in the distance, would meet his eyes; and he would see the ships going out to the ends of the earth. He had only to look at the plain which skirted the coast, and he would see, slipping round the foot of the very hill on which he stood, one of the greatest roads in the world. It was the road from Damascus to Egypt, the land bridge to Africa. It was one of the greatest caravan routes in the world. It was the road by which centuries before Joseph had been sold down into Egypt as a slave. It was the road that three hundred years before Alexander the Great and his legions had followed. It was the road by which centuries later Napoleon was to march. It was the road which in the twentieth century Allenby was to take. Sometimes it was called The Way of the South, and sometimes the Road of the Sea. On it Jesus would see all kinds of travellers from all kinds of nations on all kinds of errands, coming and going from the ends of the earth. But there was another road. There was the road which left the sea coast at Acre or Ptolemais and went out to the East. It was the Road of the East. It went out to the eastern bounds and frontiers of the Roman Empire. Once again the cavalcade of the caravans and their silks and spices would be continually on it; and on it also the Roman legions clanked out to the frontiers. Nazareth indeed was no backwater. Jesus was brought up in a town where the ends of the earth passed the foot of the hilltop. From His boyhood days He was confronted with scenes which must have spoken to him of a world for God.

We have seen how Matthew clinches each event in the early life of Jesus with a passage from the Old Testament which he regards as a prophecy. Here Matthew cites a prophecy: " He shall be called a Nazarene "; and here Matthew has set us an insoluble problem, for there is no such text in the Old Testament. In fact Nazareth is never mentioned in the Old Testament. No one has ever satisfactorily solved the problem of what part of the Old Testament Matthew is thinking. The ancient writers liked puns and plays on words. It has been suggested that Matthew is playing on the words of Isaiah in *Isaiah* 11: 1: " And there shall come forth a rod out of the stem of Jesse, and a branch shall grow out of his roots." The word for *branch* is *nezer*; and it is just possible that Matthew is playing on the word *Nazarene* and the word *Nezer*; and that he is saying at one and the same time that Jesus was from *Nazareth* and that Jesus was the *nezer*, the promised Branch from the stock of Jesse, the descendant of David, the promised Anointed King of God. No one can tell. What prophecy Matthew had in mind must remain a mystery.

So now the stage is set; Matthew has brought Jesus to Nazareth and in a very real sense Nazareth was the gateway to the world.

THE YEARS BETWEEN

BEFORE we move on to the third chapter of Matthew's gospel there is something at which we would do well to look. The second chapter of the gospel closes with Jesus as a little child; the third chapter of the gospel opens with Jesus as a man of thirty (cp. *Luke* 3: 23). That is to say, between the two chapters there are thirty silent years. Why should it have been so? What was happening in those silent years? Jesus came into the world to be the Saviour of the world, and for thirty years He never moved beyond the town of Palestine, except to the Passover at Jerusalem. He died when He was thirty-three, and of these thirty-three years thirty were spent without record in Nazareth. To put it in another way, ten-elevenths of Jesus' life were spent in Nazareth. What was happening then?

(i) Jesus was growing up to boyhood, and then to manhood, in a good home; and there can be no greater start to life than that. J. S. Blackie, the famous Edinburgh professor, once said in public, " I desire to thank God for the good stock-in-trade, so to speak, which I inherited from my parents for the business of life." George Herbert once said, " A good mother is worth a hundred school-masters." So for Jesus the years passed, silently but mouldingly, in the circle of a good home.

(ii) Jesus was fulfilling the duties of an eldest son. It seems most likely that Joseph died before the family had grown up. Maybe he was already much older than Mary when they married. In the story of the Wedding Feast at Cana of Galilee there is no mention of Joseph, although Mary is there, and it is natural to suppose that Joseph had died. So Jesus became the village craftsman of Nazareth to support His mother and His younger brothers and sisters. A world was calling Him, and yet He first fulfilled His duty to His mother and to His own folks and to His own home. When his mother died, Sir James Barrie could write, " I can look back, and I cannot see the smallest thing undone." There lies happiness. It is on those who faithfully and ungrudgingly accept the simple duties that the world is built. One of the great examples of that is the great doctor, Sir James Y. Simpson, the discoverer of chloroform. He came from a poor home. One day his mother took him on her knee and began to darn his stockings. When she had finished, she looked at her neat handi-work. " My, Jamie," she said, " mind when your mither's awa' that she was a grand darner." Jamie was the " wise wean, the little box of brains," and his family knew it. They had their dreams for him. His brother Sandy said, " I aye felt he would be great some day." And so, without jealousy and willingly, his brothers worked in the bake-shop and at their jobs that the lad might have his college education and his chance. There would have been no Sir James Simpson had there not been simple folk willing to do simple things and to do without things that the brilliant lad might have his chance. Jesus is the great example of one who accepted the simple duties of the home.

(iii) Jesus was learning what it was like to be a working man. He was learning what it was like to have to earn a living, to save to buy food and clothes, and maybe sometimes a little pleasure; to meet the dissatisfied and the critical customer, and the customer who would not pay his debts. If Jesus was to help men, He must first know what men's lives were like. He did not come into a protected cushioned life; He came into the life that any man must live. He had to do that, if He was ever to understand the life of ordinary people. There is a famous story of Marie Antoinette, the Queen of France, in the days when the storm of the French Revolution was brooding over the country before it broke. Men were starving; the mob was rioting. The Queen asked what all the uproar was about. She was told: " They have no bread." " If they have no bread," she said, " let them eat cake." The idea of a life without plenty was an idea which did not come within her horizon. She did not understand. Jesus worked in Nazareth for all the silent years in order that He might know what our life was like, and that, understanding, He might be able to help.

(iv) Jesus was faithfully performing the lesser task before the greater task could be given to Him to do. The great fact is that, if Jesus had failed in the smaller duties, the great task of being the Saviour of the world could never have been given to Him to do. He was faithful in little that He might become master of much. It is a thing never to be forgotten that in the everyday duties of life we make or mar a destiny, and we win or lose a crown.

THE EMERGENCE OF JOHN THE BAPTIZER

Matthew 3: 1-6

> In those days John the Baptizer arrived on the scene, preaching in the wildnerness of Judaea. " Repent," he said, " for the Kingdom of the Heavens has come near." It was this man who was spoken of by Isaiah

the prophet when he said, " The voice of one crying in the wilderness: ' Make ready the road by which the Lord is coming, and make straight the paths which He must travel! ' " John himself wore a garment made from camel's hair, and he had a leathern belt round his waist; and his food was locusts and wild honey. Then Jerusalem and all Judaea, and all the district around the Jordan, went out to him. They were baptized in the river Jordan, and, as they were baptized, they confessed their sins.

THE emergence of John was like the sudden sounding of the voice of God. At this time the Jews were sadly conscious that the voice of the prophets spoke no more. They said that for four hundred years there had been no prophet. Throughout the long centuries the voice of prophecy had been silent. As they put it themselves, " There was no voice, nor any that answered." But in John the prophetic voice spoke again. What then were the characteristics of John and his message?

(i) He fearlessly denounced evil wherever he might find it. If Herod the king sinned by contracting an evil and unlawful marriage, John rebuked him. If the Sadducees and Pharisees, the leaders of orthodox religion, the church-men of their day, were sunk in ritualistic formalism, John never hesitated to say so. If the ordinary people were living lives which were unaware of God, John would tell them so. Wherever John saw evil—in the state, in the Church, in the crowd—he fearlessly rebuked it. He was like a light which lit up the dark places; he was like wind which swept from God throughout the country. It was said of a famous journalist who was great, but who never quite fulfilled the work he might have done, " He was perhaps not easily enough disturbed." There is still a place in the Christian message for warning and denunciation. " The truth," said Diogenes, " is like the light to sore eyes." " He who never offended anyone," he said, " never did anyone any good." It may be that there have been times when the Church was too careful not to offend. There come occasions when the time for smooth politeness has gone, and the time for blunt rebuke has come.

(ii) He urgently summoned men to righteousness. John's message was not a mere negative denunciation; it was a positive erecting of the moral standards of God. He not only denounced men for what they had done; he summoned them to what they ought to do. He not only condemned men for what they were; he challenged them to be what they could be. He was like a voice calling men to higher things. He not only rebuked evil, he also set before men the good. It may well be that there have been times when the Church was too occupied in telling men what not to do; and too little occupied in setting before them the height of the Christian ideal.

(iii) John came from God. He came out of the desert. He came to men only after he had undergone years of lonely preparation by God. As Alexander Maclaren said, " John leapt, as it were, into the arena full-grown and full-armed." He came, not with some opinion of his own, but with a message from God. Before he spoke to men, he had companied long with God. The preacher, the teacher with the prophetic voice must always come into the presence of men out of the presence of God.

(iv) John pointed beyond himself. The man was not only a light to illumine evil, a voice to rebuke sin, he was also a signpost to God. It was not himself he wished men to see; he wished to prepare them for the one who was to come. It was the Jewish belief that Elijah would return before the Messiah came, and that he would be the herald of the coming King. " Behold I will send you Elijah the prophet before the coming of the great and dreadful day of the Lord " (*Malachi* 4: 5). John wore a garment of camel's hair, and a leathern belt around his waist. That is the very description of the raiment which Elijah had worn (2 *Kings* I: 8). Matthew connects him with a prophecy from Isaiah (*Isaiah* 40: 3). In ancient times in the East the roads were bad. There was an eastern proverb which said, " There are three states of misery—sickness, fasting and travel." Before a traveller set out upon a journey he was advised " to pay all debts, provide for dependants, give parting gifts, return all articles under trust, take money and good-temper for the journey; then bid farewell to all." The ordinary roads were no better than tracks. They were not surfaced at all because the soil of Palestine is hard and will bear the traffic of mules and asses and oxen and carts. A journey along such a road was an adventure, and indeed an undertaking to be avoided. There were some few surfaced and artificially made roads. Josephus, for instance, tells us that Solomon laid a causeway of black basalt stone along the roads that lead to Jerusalem to make them easier for the pilgrims, and " to manifest the grandeur of his riches and government." All such surfaced and artificially made roads were originally built by the king and for the use of the king. They were called " the king's highway." They were kept in repair only as the king needed them for any journey that he might make. Before the king was due to arrive in any area, a message was sent out to the people to get the king's roads in order for the king's journey. John was preparing the way for the king. The preacher and the teacher with the prophetic voice, points, not at himself, but at God. His aim is not to focus men's eyes on his own cleverness, but on the majesty of God. The true preacher is obliterated in his message.

Men recognized John as a prophet, even after years when no prophetic voice had spoken, because he was a *light* to light up evil things, a *voice* to summon men to righteousness, a *signpost* to point men to God, and because he had on him that unanswerable authority which clings to the man who comes into the presence of men out of the presence of God.

THE MESSAGE OF JOHN—THE THREAT

Matthew 3: 7-12

> When he saw many of the Pharisees and Sadducees coming to his baptism, he said to them, " Brood of vipers! Who put it into your minds to flee from the coming wrath? Produce fruit to fit repentance. Do not think that you can say to yourselves, ' We have Abraham as a father.' For I tell you that God can raise up children to Abraham from these stones. The axe is already applied to the root of the trees. Therefore every tree which does not produce good fruit is on the point of being cut down, and thrown into the fire. I baptize you with water that you may repent. He who is coming after me is stronger than I. I am not fit to carry His sandals. He will baptize you with the Holy Spirit and with fire. His fan is in His hand, and He will thoroughly cleanse His threshing-floor; and He will gather the corn into His storehouse, but He will burn the chaff with a fire that no man can quench."

IN John's message there is both a threat and a promise. This whole passage is full of vivid pictures.

John calls the Pharisees and the Sadducees a brood of vipers, and asks them who has suggested to them to flee from the coming wrath. There may be one of two pictures there. John knew the desert. The desert had in places thin, short, dried-up grass, and stunted thorn bushes, brittle for want of moisture. Sometimes a desert fire would break out. When that happened the fire swept like a river of flame across the grass and the bushes, for they were as dry as tinder. And in front of the fire there would come scurrying and hurrying the snakes and the scorpions, and the living creatures who found their shelter in the grass and in the bushes. They were driven from their lairs by this river of flame, and they ran for their lives before it. But it may be that there is another picture here. There are many little creatures in a standing field of corn—the field mice, the rats, the rabbits, the birds. But when the reaper comes they are driven from their nests and their shelters, and as the field is laid bare they have to flee for their lives. It is in terms of these pictures that John is thinking. If the Pharisees and Sadducees are really coming for baptism, they are like the animals scurrying for life before a desert fire or in front of the sickle of the harvester.

He warns them that it will avail them nothing to plead that Abraham is their father. To the orthodox Jew that was an incredible statement. To the Jew Abraham was unique. So unique was he in his goodness and in his favour with God, that his merits sufficed not only for himself but for all his descendants also. He had built up a treasury of merit which not all the claims and needs of his descendants could exhaust. So the Jews believed that a Jew simply because he was a Jew, and not for any merits of his own, was safe in the life to come. They said, " All Israelites have a portion in the world to come." They talked about " the delivering merits of the fathers." They said that Abraham sat at the gates of Gehenna to turn back any Israelite who might by chance have been consigned to its terrors. They said that it was the merits of Abraham which enabled the ships to sail safely on the seas; that it was because of the merits of Abraham that the rain descended on the earth; that it was the merits of Abraham which enabled Moses to enter into heaven and to receive the Law; that it was because of the merits of Abraham that David was heard. Even for the wicked these merits sufficed. " If thy children," they said of Abraham, " were mere dead bodies, without blood vessels or bones, thy merits would avail for them! " It is that spirit which John is rebuking. Maybe the Jews carried it to an unparalleled distance, but there is always need of a warning that we cannot live on the spiritual capital of the past. A degenerate age cannot hope to claim salvation for the sake of an heroic past; and an evil son cannot hope to plead the merits of a saintly father.

Then, once again, John returns to his harvest picture.

At the end of the season the keeper of the vineyards and the fig trees would look at his vines and his trees; and those which were fruitless and useless would be rooted out. They only cumbered the ground. Uselessness always invites disaster. The man who is useless to God and to his fellow-men is in grave and serious peril, and is under condemnation.

THE MESSAGE OF JOHN—THE PROMISE

Matthew 3: 7-12 (continued)

BUT after John's threat there came the promise—which had also a threat within it. As we have said John pointed beyond himself to the one who was to come. At the moment he was enjoying a vast reputation, and he was wielding a most powerful influence. Yet he said that he was not fit to carry the sandals of the one who was to come— and to carry sandals was the duty of a slave. John's whole attitude was self-obliteration, not self-importance. His only importance was, as he saw it, as a signpost pointing to the one who was to come.

He said that the one who was to come would baptize them with the Holy Spirit and with fire.

All through their history the Jews had looked for the time when the Spirit would come. Ezekiel heard God say, " A new heart will I give you, and a new spirit will I put into you. . . . And I will put my Spirit within you, and cause you to walk in my statutes, and ye shall keep my judgments and do them " (*Ezekiel* 36: 26, 27). " And I shall put my Spirit in you and ye shall live " (*Ezekiel* 37: 14). " Neither will I hide my face any more from them; for I have poured out my Spirit upon the house of Israel, saith the Lord " (*Ezekiel* 39: 29). " I will pour water upon him that is thirsty, and floods upon the dry ground; I will pour my Spirit upon thy seed, and my blessing upon thine offspring " (*Isaiah* 44: 3). " And it shall come to pass afterward, that I will pour out my Spirit upon all flesh "

THE GOSPEL OF MATTHEW

(*Joel* 2: 28). What then is the gift and work of this Spirit of God? When we try to answer that question, we must remember to answer it in Hebrew terms. John was a Jew, and it was to Jews that he was speaking. He is thinking and speaking, not in terms of the Christian doctrine of the Holy Spirit, but in terms of the Jewish doctrine of the Spirit.

(i) The word for *spirit* is *ruach*, and *ruach*, like *pneuma* in Greek, means not only *spirit*; it also means *breath*. *Breath is life*; and therefore the promise of the Spirit is *the promise of life*. The Spirit of God breathes God's life into a man. When the Spirit of God enters a man, the tired lack-lustre, weary defeatedness of life is gone, and a surge of new life enters our life.

(ii) This word *ruach* not only means *breath*; it also means *wind*. It is the word for the storm wind, the mighty rushing wind that once Elijah heard. *Wind means power.* The gale of wind sweeps the ship before it and uproots the tree. The wind has an irresistible power. *The Spirit of God is the Spirit of power.* When the Spirit of God enters into a man, his weakness is clad with the power of God. He is enabled to do the undoable, and to face the unfaceable, and to bear the unbearable. Frustration is banished; victory arrives.

(iii) The Spirit of God is connected with *the work of creation*. It was the Spirit of God who moved upon the face of the waters and made the chaos into a cosmos, turned disorder into order, and made a world out of the uncreated mists. The Spirit of God can recreate us. When the Spirit of God enters into a man the disorder of human nature becomes the order of God; our dishevelled, disorderly, uncontrolled lives are moulded by the Spirit into the harmony of God.

(iv) To the Spirit the Jews assigned special functions. *The Spirit brought God's truth to men.* It is the Spirit who reveals the truth of God to men. Every new discovery in every realm of thought is the gift of the Spirit. The Spirit

41

enters into a man's mind and turns his human guesses into divine certainty, and changes his human ignorance into divine knowledge.

(v) *The Spirit enables men to recognize God's truth when they see it.* When the Spirit enters our hearts, our eyes are opened. The prejudices which blinded us are taken away. The self-will which darkened us is removed. The Spirit enables a man to see.

Such are the gifts of the Spirit, and, as John saw it, such were the gifts the one who was to come would bring.

THE MESSAGE OF JOHN—THE PROMISE AND THE THREAT

Matthew 3: 7-12 (continued)

THERE is a word and a picture in John's message which combine both *promise* and *threat*.

John says that the baptism of the one who is to come will be with *fire*. In the thought of a baptism with fire there are three ideas.

(i) There is the idea of *illumination*. The blaze of a flame sends a light through the night and illuminates the darkest corners. The flame of the beacon guides the sailor to the harbour and the traveller to his goal. In fire there is not only destruction; there is light and guidance. Jesus is the beacon light to lead men into truth and to guide them home to God.

(ii) There is the idea of *warmth*. A great and a kindly man was described as one who lit fires in cold rooms. When Jesus comes into a man's life, He kindles his heart with the warmth of love towards God and towards his fellow men. Christianity is always the religion of the kindled heart.

(iii) There is the idea of *purification*. In this sense purification involves destruction; for the purifying flame burns away the false and leaves the true. The flame tempers and strengthens and purifies the metal. When Christ comes into a man's heart, the evil dross is purged away. Sometimes that has to happen through painful experiences, but, if a man throughout all the experiences of life believes that God is working together all things for good, he will emerge from them with a character which is cleansed and purified, until, being pure in heart, he can see God.

So, then, the word fire has in it the illumination, the warmth and the purification of the entry of Jesus Christ into the heart of a man.

But there is also a picture which has in it a promise and a threat—the picture of the threshing floor. The fan was the great wooden winnowing shovel. With it the grain was lifted from the threshing floor and tossed into the air. When that was done the heavy grain fell to the ground, but the light chaff was blown away by the wind. The grain was then collected and stored in the barns, while any chaff which remained was used as fuel for the fire.

The coming of Christ necessarily involves a separation. Either men accept Him or reject Him. When they are confronted with Him, they are confronted with a choice which cannot be avoided. They are either for or against. And it is precisely that choice which settles destiny. Men are separated by their reaction to Jesus Christ.

In Christianity there is no escape from the eternal choice. On the village green in Bedford, John Bunyan heard the voice which drew him up all of a sudden and left him looking at eternity: " Wilt thou leave thy sins and go to heaven, or wilt thou have thy sins and go to hell? " In the last analysis that is the choice which no man can evade.

THE MESSAGE OF JOHN—THE DEMAND
Matthew 3: 7-12 (*continued*)

In all John's preaching there was one basic demand— and that basic demand was: " Repent! " (*Matthew* 3: 2).

That was also the basic demand of Jesus Himself, for Jesus came saying, " Repent ye, and believe the gospel " (*Mark* 1: 15). Obviously we will do well to seek to understand what this repentance is, and what this basic demand of the King and His herald means.

It is to be noted that both Jesus and John use the word *repent* without any explanation of its meaning. They use it as a word which they were sure their hearers would know and understand.

Let us then look at the Jewish teaching about repentance.

To the Jew repentance was central to all religious faith and to all relationship with God. G. F. Moore writes, " Repentance is the sole, but inexorable, condition of God's forgiveness and the restoration of His favour, and the divine forgiveness and favour are never refused to genuine repentance." He writes, " That God fully and freely remits the sins of the penitent is a cardinal doctrine of Judaism." The Rabbis said, " Great is repentance for it brings healing upon the world. Great is repentance for it reaches to the throne of glory." C. G. Montefiore wrote, " Repentance is the great mediatorial bond between God and man." The Law was created two thousand years before creation, but, the Rabbis taught, repentance was one of the things created even before the Law; the six things are repentance, paradise, hell, the glorious throne of God, the celestial temple, and the name of the Messiah. " A man," they said, " can shoot an arrow for a few furlongs, but repentance reaches even to the throne of God." There is a famous rabbinic passage which sets repentance in the first of all places: " Who is like God a teacher of sinners that they may repent? " They asked Wisdom, " What shall be the punishment of the sinner? " Wisdom answered: "Evil pursues sinners" (*Proverbs* 13: 21). They asked Prophecy. It replied: " The soul that sinneth it shall die" (*Ezekiel* 18: 4). They asked the Law. It replied: " Let him bring a sacrifice" (*Leviticus* 1: 4). They asked God, and He

44

replied: " Let him repent and obtain his atonement. My children, what do I ask of you? *Seek me and live.*" So, then, to the Jew the one gateway back to God is the gateway of repentance.

The Jewish word which is commonly used for repentance is itself interesting. It is the word *teshubah* which is the noun for the verb *shub* which means *to turn*. Repentance is a turning away from evil and a turning towards God. G. F. Moore writes, " The transparent primary meaning of repentance in Judaism is always a change in man's attitude towards God, and in the conduct of life, a religious and moral reformation of the people or the individual." C. G. Montefiore writes, " To the Rabbis the essence of repentance lay in such a thorough change of mind that it issues in a change of life and a change of conduct." Maimonides, the great medieval Jewish scholar, defines repentance thus: " What is repentance? Repentance is that the sinner forsakes his sin and puts it away out of his thoughts and fully resolves in his mind that he will not do it again; as it is written, ' Let the wicked forsake his way, and the bad man his plans.' " G. F. Moore very interestingly and very truly points out that, with the single exception of the two words in brackets, the Westminster Confession definition of repentance would be entirely acceptable to a Jew: " Repentance unto life is a saving grace, whereby a sinner, out of a true sense of sin, and apprehension of the mercy of God (in Christ), doth, with grief and hatred of his sin, turn from it unto God, with full purpose of and endeavour after, new obedience." Again and again the Bible speaks of this *turning away* from sin, and this *turning towards* God. Ezekiel had it: " As I live, saith the Lord God, I have no pleasure in the death of the wicked; but that the wicked turn from his way and live; turn ye, turn ye from your evil ways; for why will ye die, O house of Israel " (*Ezekiel* 33: 11). Jeremiah had it: " Turn Thou me, and I shall be turned; for Thou art the Lord my God " (*Jeremiah* 33: 18). Hosea had it: " O Israel, return unto

45

the Lord thy God. . . . Take with you words and turn unto the Lord " (*Hosea* 14: 1, 2).

From all this it is quite clear that in Judaism repentance has in it an ethical demand. It is a turn from evil to God, with a corresponding change in action. John was fully within the tradition of his people when he demanded that his hearers should bring forth fruit meet for repentance. There is a beautiful synagogue prayer which runs, " Cause us to return, O Father, unto Thy law; draw us near, O King, unto Thy service; bring us back in perfect repentance unto Thy presence. Blessed art Thou, O Lord, who delightest in repentance." But that repentance had to be shown in a real change of life.

A Rabbi, commenting on *Jonah* 3: 10, wrote, " My brethren, it is not said of the Ninevites that God saw their sackcloth and their fasting, but that God saw their *works*, that they turned from their evil way." The Rabbis said, " Be not like fools, who, when they sin, bring a sacrifice but do not repent. If a man says, ' I will sin and repent, I will sin and repent,' he is not allowed to repent." Five unforgivable sinners are listed, and the list includes " Those who sin in order to repent, and those who repent much and always sin afresh." They said: " If a man has an unclean thing in his hands, he may wash them in all the seas of the world, and he will never be clean; but if he throws the unclean thing away, a little water will suffice." The Jewish teachers spoke of what they called " the nine norms of repentance," the nine necessities of real repentance. They found them in the series of commandments in *Isaiah* 1: 16: " Wash you, make you pure, remove the evil of your misdeeds from before my eyes, cease doing evil, learn to do well, seek after justice, relieve the oppressed, do justice to the orphan, take up the cause of the widow." The son of Sirach writes in *Ecclesiasticus*: " Say not, I sinned, and what happened to me? For the Lord is long-suffering. Do not become rashly confident about expiation, and go on adding sin to sins; and do not say, His compassion is great, He will forgive the multitude of my sins; for mercy and wrath are with Him, and upon sinners His anger will rest. Delay not to turn to the Lord, and do not put it off from day to day" (*Ecclesiasticus* 5: 4-7). He writes again, " A man who bathes to purify himself from contact with a dead body and touches it again, what profit was there in his bath? So a man who fasts for his sins and goes again and does the same things—who will listen to his prayer, and what profit was there is his afflicting himself?" (*Ecclesiasticus* 31: 30, 31).

The Jew held that true repentance issues, not merely in a sentimental sorrow, but in a real change in life—and so does the Christian. The Jew had a holy horror of seeking to trade on the mercy of God—and so has the Christian. The Jew held that true repentance brings forth fruits which demonstrate the reality of the repentance—and so does the Christian.

But the Jews had still more things to say about repentance and we must go on to look at them.

THE MESSAGE OF JOHN—THE DEMAND

Matthew 3: 7-12 (*continued*)

THERE is an almost terrifying note in the ethical demand of the Jewish idea of repentance, but there are other comforting things.

Repentance is always available. " Repentance," they said, " is like the sea—a man can bathe in it at any hour." There may be times when even the gates of prayer are shut; but the gates of repentance are never closed. The door of repentance is a door which no man can ever shut.

Repentance is completely essential. There is a story of a kind of argument that Abraham had with God. Abraham said to God, " Thou canst not lay hold of the cord at both ends at once. If Thou desirest strict justice the world cannot endure. If Thou desirest the preservation of the world, strict justice cannot endure." The world itself cannot continue to exist without the mercy of God, and the gateway of repentance. If there was nothing but the justice of God, it would be the end of all men and of all things. So essential is repentance that in order to make it possible God cancels His own demands: "Beloved is repentance before God, for He cancels His own words for its sake." The threat of the destruction of the sinner is cancelled by the acceptance of repentance for the sinner's sins.

Repentance lasts as long as life. So long as life remains, there remains the possibility of repentance. "God's hand is stretched out under the wings of the heavenly chariot to snatch the penitent from the grasp of justice." Rabbi Simeon ben Yohai said, "If a man has been completely righteous all his days, and rebels at the end, he destroys it all, for it is said, 'The righteousness of the righteous man will not save him, in the day when he transgresses' (*Ezekiel* 33: 12); if a man has been completely wicked all his days, and repents at the end, God receives him, for it is said, 'And as for the wickedness of the wicked, he shall not stumble by it in the day when he turns from his wickedness'" (*Ezekiel* 33: 12). "Many," they said, "can go into the world to come only after years and years; while another gains it in an hour." As the poet said of the man who gained the mercy of God in the instant of death:

> "Between the saddle and the ground,
> I mercy sought, and mercy found."

Such is the mercy of God that He will receive even secret repentance. Rabbi Eleazar said, "It is the way of the world, when a man has insulted his fellow in public, and after a time seeks to be reconciled to him, that the other says, 'You insult me publicly, and now you would be reconciled to me between us two alone! Go bring the men in whose presence you insulted me, and I will be reconciled to you.' But God is not so. A man may stand and rail and blaspheme in the market place, and the Holy One says, ' Repent between us two alone, and I will receive you.' " God's mercy is open to the man who is so ashamed that he can tell his shame to no one except God.

There is no forgetfulness in God, because He is God, but such is the mercy of God that He not only forgives, but, incredible as it may sound, He even forgets the sin of the penitent: " Who is a God like Thee that forgets iniquity and passes over the transgressions of the remnant of His inheritance? " (Micah 7: 18). " Thou hast forgotten the iniquity of Thy people, Thou hast covered all their sin " (Psalm 85: 3). To forgive may be a human achievement, but to forget is divine.

Loveliest of all, God comes halfway and more to meet the penitent: " Return so far as you can, and I will come to you the rest of the way." The Rabbis at their highest had a glimpse of the Father who in His love ran to meet the prodigal son.

Yet, even remembering all this mercy, it remains true that in true repentance reparation is necessary in so far as it can be made. The Rabbis said, " Injury must be repaired, and pardon sought and forgiven. The true penitent is he who has the opportunity to do the same sin again, in the same circumstances, and who does not do it." The Rabbis stressed again and again the importance of human relationships, and of setting them right. There is one curious rabbinic passage. (A zadik is a righteous man). " He who is good towards heaven and towards his fellow men is a good zadik. He who is good towards heaven and not towards his fellow men, is a bad zadik. He who is wicked against heaven and wicked against his fellow men, is a bad sinner. He who is wicked against heaven, but not wicked against his fellow men is not a bad sinner." It is because reparation is so necessary that he who teaches others to sin is the worst of sinners, for he cannot make reparation for he can never tell how far his sin has gone out and how many it has gone on to influence.

Not only is reparation necessary for true repentance; confession is equally necessary. Again and again we find that demand within the Bible itself. " When a man or a woman has committed any of all the sins of men . . . they shall confess their sins they have committed " (*Numbers* 5: 6, 7). " He who conceals his transgressions shall not succeed; but he who confesses and forsakes them shall obtain mercy " (*Proverbs* 28: 13). " I acquaint Thee with my sin, and do not conceal my guilt. I say, I will confess on my part my transgressions to the Lord, and Thou dost pardon the guilt of my sin " (*Psalm* 32: 5). It is the man who says that he is innocent and who refuses to admit that he has sinned who is condemned (*Jeremiah* 2: 35). Maimonides gives the formula which a man may use to confess his sin: " O God, I have sinned, I have done iniquity, I have transgressed before Thee, and have done thus and so. I am sorry and ashamed for my deed, and I will never do it again." True repentance necessitates the humility to admit and to confess our sin.

No case is hopeless for repentance, and no man is beyond repentance. The Rabbis said, " Let not a man say, ' Because I have sinned, no repair is possible for me,' but let him trust in God and repent, and God will receive him." The classical example of a seemingly impossible reformation was the case of Manasseh. He worshipped the Baals; he brought strange gods into Jerusalem; he even sacrificed children to Moloch in the valley of Hinnom. Then he was taken away captive to Assyria, and there in fetters he lay upon the thorns. Then he prayed to God in his distress, and God heard his supplication and brought him again to Jerusalem. " Then Manasseh knew that the Lord He is God " (2 *Chronicles* 33: 13). Sometimes it takes God's threat and God's discipline to bring a man home, but none is beyond the power of God to bring him home.

There is one last Jewish belief about repentance, and it is a belief which must have been in John's mind. Certain, at least, of the Jewish teachers taught that if Israel could repent perfectly for even one day the Messiah would come. It was only the hardness of the hearts of men which delayed the sending of God's Redeemer into the world.

Repentance was the very centre of the Jewish faith as it is the very centre of the Christian faith, for repentance is the turning away from sin and the turning towards God, and towards the life that God means us to live.

JESUS AND HIS BAPTISM

Matthew 3: 1-17

> Then Jesus came from Galilee to the Jordan to John to be baptized by him. But John tried to prevent Him. " It is I," he said, " who need to be baptized by you, and are you coming to me? " Jesus answered him, " Let it be just now, for so it befits us to fulfil all righteousness." Then he allowed Jesus to be baptized. After Jesus had been baptized He came up immediately from the water and, lo, the heavens were opened for Him, and He saw the Spirit of God descending, like a dove, and coming upon Him. And, lo, there came a voice from heaven, saying, " This is my Son, the Beloved One, in whom I am well pleased."

WHEN Jesus came to John to be baptized John was startled and unwilling to baptize Him. It was John's conviction that it was he who needed what Jesus could give, not Jesus who needed what he could give.

Ever since men began to think about the gospel story at all, they have found the baptism of Jesus difficult to understand. In John's baptism there was a summons to repentance, and the offer of a way to the forgiveness of sins. But, if Jesus is who we believe Him to be, Jesus did not stand in need of repentance, and did not need forgiveness from God. John's baptism was for sinners conscious of their sin, and therefore it does not seem applicable to Jesus at all.

A very early writer suggested that Jesus came to be baptized only to please His mother and His brothers, and that it was in answer to their entreaties that He was almost compelled to let this thing be done. *The Gospel according to the Hebrews*, which is one of the very early gospels which failed to be included in the New Testament, has a passage like this: " Behold the mother of the Lord and His brethren said to Him, ' John the Baptist baptizeth for the remission of sins; let us go and be baptized by him.' But He said to them, ' What sin have I committed, that I should go and be baptized by him? Except perchance this very thing that I have said is ignorance.' "

It can be seen that from the very earliest times thinkers were puzzled by the fact that Jesus submitted to be baptized. But there were reasons, and good reasons, why Jesus should go to John to be baptized.

(i) For thirty years Jesus had waited in Nazareth, faithfully performing the simple duties of the home and of the carpenter's shop. All the time He knew that a world was waiting for Him. All the time He was increasingly conscious of His waiting task. The success of any undertaking is determined by the wisdom with which the moment to embark upon it is chosen. Jesus must have waited for the hour to strike, for the moment to come, for the summons to sound. And when John emerged He knew that the time had arrived.

(ii) Why should that be so? There was one very simple and very vital reason. It is the simple fact that never in all history before this had any Jew submitted to being baptized. The Jews knew and used baptism, but only for proselytes who came into Judaism from some other faith. It was natural that the sin-stained, polluted proselyte should be baptized, but no Jew had ever conceived that he, a member of the chosen people, a son of Abraham, assured of God's salvation, could ever need baptism. Baptism was for sinners, and no Jew ever conceived of himself as a sinner shut out from God, for was he not a son of Abraham and therefore safe for eternity? For the first time in their national history the Jews realized their own sin and their own clamant need of God. Never in all history had there been such a unique national movement of penitence and of search for God.

This was the very moment for which Jesus had been waiting. Men were conscious of their sin and conscious of their need of God as never before. This was His opportunity, and in His baptism He identified Himself with the search of men for God. When Jesus went to be baptized He was identifying Himself with the men He came to save, in the hour of their new consciousness of their own sin, and of their search for God.

The voice which Jesus heard at the baptism is of supreme importance. " This is my beloved Son," it said, " in whom I am well pleased." That sentence is composed of two quotations. " This is my beloved Son," is a quotation from *Psalm* 2: 7. Every Jew accepted that Psalm as a description of the Messiah, the mighty King of God who was to come. " In whom I am well pleased " is a quotation from *Isaiah* 42: 1, which is a description of the Suffering Servant, a description which culminates in *Isaiah* 53. So in the baptism there came to Jesus two certainties— the certainty that He was indeed the chosen One of God, and the certainty that the way in front of Him was the way of the Cross. In that moment He knew that He was chosen to be King, but He also knew that His throne must be a Cross. In that moment He knew that He was destined to be a conqueror, but that His conquest must have as its only weapon the power of suffering love. In that moment there was set before Jesus both His task and the only way to the fulfilling of it.

THE TESTING TIME

STEP by step Matthew unfolds the story of Jesus. He began by showing us how Jesus was born into this world. He went on to show us, at least by implication, that Jesus had to perform faithfully His duties to His home before He began on His duty to the world, that He had to show Himself faithful in the smaller tasks before God gave to Him the greatest task in all the world.

He went on to show us how, with the emergence of John the Baptist, Jesus knew that the hour had struck, and that the time had come to enter upon His work. He shows us Jesus identifying Himself with a people's unprecedented search for God. In that moment he shows us Jesus' realization that He was indeed the chosen one of God, but that His way to victory lay through the Cross.

If any man has a vision, his immediate problem is how to turn that vision into fact; he has to find some way to turn the dream into reality. That is precisely the problem which faced Jesus. He had come to lead men home to God. How was He to do it? What method was He to adopt? Was He to adopt the method of a mighty conqueror, or was He to adopt the method of patient, sacrificial love? That was the problem which faced Jesus in His temptations. The task had been committed into His hands. What method was He to choose to work out the task which God had given Him to do?

THE TEMPTATIONS OF CHRIST

Matthew 4: I-II

Then Jesus was led by the Spirit into the wilderness to be tempted by the devil. After He had deliberately gone without food for forty days and forty nights He was hungry. So the tempter came and said to Him, " If you really are the Son of God, tell these stones to become bread." He answered: " It stands written, ' Man shall not live by bread alone, but by every word which proceeds through the mouth of God.'" Then the devil took Him to the holy city, and set Him on the pinnacle of the Temple. "If you really are the Son of God," he said to Him, "fling yourself down, for it stands written, 'He will give His angels orders to care for you, and they will lift you upon their hands, lest at any time you should strike your foot against a stone.'" Jesus said to him, "Again it stands written, 'You must not try to put the Lord your God to the test.'" Again the devil took Him to a very lofty mountain, and showed Him all the kingdoms of the world, and their glory, and said to Him, "I will give you all these things, if you will fall down and worship me." Then Jesus said to him, "Begone, Satan! For it stands written, 'You shall worship the Lord your God, and Him alone you will serve.'" Then the devil left Him alone, and behold, angels came and gave Him their service.

THERE is one thing which we must carefully note right at the beginning of our study of the temptations of Jesus, and that is the meaning of the word *to tempt*. The Greek word is *peirazein*. In English the word *tempt* has a uniformly and consistently bad meaning. It always means to entice a man to do wrong, to seek to seduce him into sin, to try to persuade him to take the wrong way. But *peirazein* has a quite different element in its meaning. It means *to test* far more than it means *to tempt* in our sense of the word. One of the great Old Testament stories is the story of how narrowly Abraham escaped sacrificing his only son Isaac. Now that story begins like this: "And it came to pass after these things that God did *tempt* Abraham" (*Genesis* 22: 1). Quite clearly the word *to tempt* cannot there mean *to seek to seduce into evil*. It is unthinkable that God should try to make any man a wrong-doer. It is inconceivable that God should be the agent in seeking to make any man a sinner. But the thing is quite clear when we understand that it means: "And it came to pass after these things that God *tested* Abraham." The time had come for a supreme test of the loyalty of Abraham. Just as metal has to be tested far beyond any stress and strain

55

that it will ever be called upon to bear, before it can be used for any useful purpose, so a man has to be tested before God can use him for His purposes. The Jews had a saying, " The Holy One, Blessed be His Name, does not elevate a man to dignity till He has first tried and searched him; and if he stands in temptation, then He raises him to dignity."

Now here is a great and uplifting truth. What we call temptation is not meant to make us sin; it is meant to enable us to conquer sin. It is not meant to make us bad, it is meant to make us good. It is not meant to weaken us, it is meant to make us emerge stronger and finer and purer from the ordeal. Temptation is not the penalty of being a man, temptation is the glory of being a man. It is the test which comes to a man whom God wishes to use. So, then, we must think of this whole incident and experience, not so much as the *tempting*, as the *testing* of Jesus.

We have to note further where this test took place. It took place in *the wilderness*. Between Jerusalem, which stands on the central plateau, which is the backbone of Palestine, and the Dead Sea there stretches the wilderness. The Old Testament calls it Jeshimmon, which means The Devastation, and it was a fitting name. It stretches over an area of thirty-five by fifteen miles. Sir George Adam Smith who travelled over it describes it. It is an area of yellow sand, of crumbling limestone, and of scattered shingle. It is an area of contorted strata, where the ridges run in all directions as if they were warped and twisted. The hills are like dust heaps; the limestone is blistered and peeling; rocks are bare and jagged; often the very ground sounds hollow when the footfall or the 'horse's hoof falls upon it. It glows and shimmers with heat like some vast furnace. It runs right out to the Dead Sea, and then there comes a drop of twelve hundred feet, a drop of limestone, flint, and marl, through crags and corries and precipices down to the Dead Sea. In that wilderness Jesus could be more alone than anywhere else

In Palestine. Jesus went into the wilderness to be alone. His task had come to Him; God had spoken to Him; He must think how He was to attempt the task which God had given Him to do; He had to get things straightened out before He started; and He had to be alone.

It may well be that we so often go wrong simply because we never try to be alone. There are certain things which a man has got to work out alone. There are times when no one else's advice is any good to him. There are certain times when a man has got to stop acting and start thinking. It may be that we make many a mistake because we do not give ourselves a chance to be alone with God.

THE SACRED STORY

Matthew 4: 1-11 (continued)

THERE are certain further things which we must note before we proceed to the detailed study of the story of the temptations.

(i) All the three gospel writers seem to stress the immediacy with which the temptations followed the baptism of Jesus. As Mark has it: "And *immediately* the Spirit driveth Him into the wilderness" (*Mark* 1: 12). It is one of the great truths of life that after every great moment there comes a moment of reaction—and again and again it is in the reaction that the danger lies. That is what happened to Elijah. With magnificent courage Elijah in all his loneliness faced and defeated the prophets of Baal on Mount Carmel (1 *Kings* 18: 17-40). That was Elijah's greatest moment of courage and of witness. But the slaughter of the prophets of Baal provoked the wicked Jezebel to wrath, and she threatened Elijah's life. "And when he saw that, he arose and went for his life and came to Beer-sheba" (1 *Kings* 19: 3). The man who had stood fearlessly against all comers is now fleeing for his life with terror at his heels. The moment of reaction had come.

Always after some great moment or some great experience there comes the moment of reaction. It seems to be the law of life that just after our resistance power has been highest it nose dives until it is at its lowest. The tempter carefully, subtly, and skilfully chose his time to attack Jesus—but Jesus conquered him. We will do well to be specially carefully on our guard after every time when life has brought us to the heights, for it is just then that we are n gravest danger of the depths.

(ii) We must not think of this experience of Jesus as an outward experience. It was a struggle that went on in His own heart and mind and soul. The proof of that is that there is no possible mountain from which all the kingdoms of the earth could be seen. This is an inner struggle. It is through our inmost thoughts and desires that the tempter comes to us. His attack is launched in our own minds. It is true that that attack can be so real that we almost see the devil. To this day you can see the ink-stain on the wall of Luther's room in the Castle of the Wartburg in Germany; Luther caused that ink-stain by throwing his ink-pot at the devil as he tempted him. But the very power of the devil lies in the fact that he breaches our defences and attacks us from within. He finds his allies and his weapons in our own inmost thoughts and desires.

(iii) We must not think that in one campaign Jesus for ever conquered the tempter and that the tempter never came to Him again. The tempter spoke again to Jesus at Caesarea Philippi when Peter tried to dissuade Him from taking the way to the Cross, and when He had to say to Peter the very same words as He said to the tempter in the wilderness, " Satan begone! " (*Matthew* 16: 23). At the end of the day Jesus could say to His disciples, " Ye are they which have continued with me in my temptations " (*Luke* 22: 28). And never in all history was there such a fight with temptation as Jesus waged in Gethsemane when the tempter sought to deflect Him from the Cross (*Luke* 22: 42-44). " Eternal vigilance is the price of freedom." In the Christian warfare there is no release. Sometimes people grow worried because they think that they should reach a stage when they are beyond temptation, a stage at which the power of the tempter is for ever broken. Jesus never reached that stage. From the beginning to the end of the day He had to fight His battle; that is why He can help us to fight ours.

(iv) One thing stands out about this story—the temptations are temptations which could only come to a person who had very special powers and who knew that he had them. Sanday described the temptations as " the problem of what to do with supernatural powers." The temptations which came to Jesus are temptations which could only have come to one who knew that there were amazing things which he could do. We must always remember that again and again we are tempted *through our gifts.* The person who is gifted with charm will be tempted to use that charm " to get away with anything." The person who is gifted with the power of words will be tempted to use his command of words to produce glib excuses to justify his own conduct. The person with a vivid and sensitive imagination will undergo agonies of temptation that a more stolid person will never experience. The person with great gifts of mind will be tempted to use these gifts for himself and not for others, to become the master and not the servant of men. It is the grim fact of temptation that it is just where we are strongest that we must be for ever on the watch.

(v) No one can ever read this story without remembering one thing about it—its only source must have been Jesus Himself. In the wilderness He was alone. No one was with Him when this struggle was being fought out. And we only know about it because Jesus Himself must have told His men about it. It is Jesus telling us His own spiritual autobiography. We must always approach this story with a unique and special reverence, for in it Jesus is laying bare His inmost heart and soul. He is telling men what He went through. It is the most sacred of all stories, for in it Jesus is saying to us that He can help others who are tempted, in that He Himself was tempted. He draws the veil from His own struggles to help us in our struggle.

THE ATTACK OF THE TEMPTER

Matthew 4: 1-11 (continued)

THE tempter launched his attack against Jesus along three lines, and in every one of them there was a certain inevitability.

(i) There was the temptation to turn the stones into bread. The desert was littered with little round pieces of limestone rock which were exactly like little loaves; even they would suggest this temptation to Jesus. This was a double temptation. It was a temptation to Jesus *to use His powers selfishly and for His own use*, and that is precisely what Jesus always refused to do. There is always the temptation to use selfishly whatever powers God has given to us. God has given every man a gift, and every man can ask one of two questions. He can ask, " What can I make for myself out of this gift? " or, " What can I do for others with this gift? " This kind of temptation can come out in the simplest thing. A person may possess, for instance, a voice which it is good to hear in music; he may thereupon " cash in on it ", and refuse to use it unless he is paid to do so. There is no reason why he should not use it for pay, but there is every reason why he should never use it for anything else but pay. There is no man who will not be tempted to use selfishly the gift which God has given to him.

But there was another side to this temptation. Jesus was God's Messiah, and He knew it. In the wilderness He was facing the choice of a method whereby He could win men to God. What method was He to use to embark upon the task which God had given Him to do? How was he to turn the vision into actuality, and the dream into fact? One sure way to persuade men to follow Him was to give them bread, to give them material things. Did not history justify that? Had not God given His people manna in the wilderness? Had God not said, " I will rain bread from heaven for you "? Did not the visions of the future golden age include that very dream? Had not Isaiah said, " They shall not hunger or thirst? " (*Isaiah* 49: 10). Was the Messianic Banquet not a settled feature in the dreams of the kingdom between the Testaments? If Jesus had wished to give men bread, He could have produced justification enough for it.

But to give men bread would have been a double mistake. First, it would have been to bribe men to follow Him. It would have been to persuade men to follow Him for the sake of what they could get out of it, and the reward that Jesus had to offer was a Cross. He called men to a life of giving, not of getting. To bribe men with material things would have been the denial of all He came to say; it would have been ultimately to defeat His own ends. Second, it would have been to remove the symptoms without dealing with the disease itself. Men are hungry. But the question is, *why are they hungry?* Is it because of their own foolishness, and their own shiftlessness, and their own carelessness? Is it because there are some who selfishly possess too much while others possess too little? The real way to cure hunger is to remove the causes which cause hunger—and these causes are in men's souls. And above all there is a hunger of the heart which it is not in material things to satisfy. So Jesus answered the tempter in the very words which express the whole lesson which God had sought to teach His people in the wilderness: " Man shall not live by bread alone, but by every word which proceeds through the mouth of God " (*Deuteronomy* 8: 3). The only real way to true satisfaction is the way which has learned its complete dependence on God.

(ii) So the tempter repeated his attack from another angle. In a vision he took Jesus to the *pinnacle of the Temple*. That may mean one of two things. The Temple was built on the top of Mount Sion. The top of the mountain was levelled out into a plateau, and on that plateau the whole area of the Temple buildings stood. There was one corner at which Solomon's porch and the Royal porch met, and at that corner there was a sheer drop of four hundred and fifty feet into the valley of the Kedron below. Why should not Jesus stand on that pinnacle, and leap down, and land unharmed in the valley beneath? That would startle men into following a man who could do a thing like that. On the top of the roof of the Temple itself there was a stance where every morning a priest stood; he stood there with a trumpet in his hands, waiting for the first flush of the dawn across the hills of Hebron, and at the first dawn light he sounded the trumpet to tell men that the hour of morning sacrifice had come. Why should not Jesus stand there, and leap down right into the Temple court, and amaze men into following Him? Had not Malachi said, " The Lord whom ye seek will suddenly come to His Temple "? (*Malachi* 3: 1). Was there not a promise that the angels would bear God's man upon their hands lest any harm should come to him? (*Psalm* 90: 11, 12).

This was the very method that the false Messiahs who were continually arising promised. Theudas had led the people out, and had promised with a word to split the waters of Jordan in two. The famous Egyptian pretender (*Acts* 21: 38) had promised that with a word he would lay flat the walls of Jerusalem. Simon Magus, so it is said, had promised to fly through the air, and had perished in the attempt. These pretenders had offered sensations which they could not perform. Jesus could perform anything He promised. Why should He not do it?

There were two good reasons why Jesus should not adopt that course of action. First, he who seeks to attract men to him by providing them with sensations has adopted a way in which there is most literally no future. The reason is simple. To retain his power he must produce ever greater and greater sensations. Wonders are apt to be nine day wonders. This year's sensation is next year's commonplace. A gospel founded on sensation-mongering is foredoomed to failure. Second, that is not the way to use the power of God. " You must not put the Lord your God to the test," said Jesus (*Deuteronomy* 6: 16). He meant this; there is no good seeing how far you can go with God; there is no good in putting yourself deliberately into a threatening situation, and doing it quite recklessly and quite needlessly, and then expecting God to rescue you from it. God expects a man to take risks in order to be true to Him, but He does not expect him to take risks to enhance his own prestige. The very faith which is dependent on signs and wonder is not faith. If faith cannot believe without sensations it is not really faith, it is doubt looking for proof and looking in the wrong place. God's rescuing power is not something to be played and experimented with, it is something to be quietly trusted in the life of every day.

Jesus refused the way of sensations because He knew that it was the way to failure—it still is—and because to long for sensations is not to trust, but to distrust, God.

(iii) So the tempter tried his third avenue of attack. It was the world that Jesus came to save, and into His mind there came the picture of the world. The tempting voice said: " Fall down and worship me, and I will give you all the kingdoms of this world." Had not God Himself said to His chosen one, " Ask of me and I will give thee the heathen for thine inheritance, and the uttermost parts of the earth for thy possession "? (*Psalm* 2: 8). What the tempter was saying was, " Compromise! Come to terms with me! Don't pitch your demands quite so high! Wink just a little at evil and questionable things—and then people will follow you in their hordes." This was the temptation to come to terms with the world, instead of uncompromisingly presenting God's demands to the world. It was the temptation to try to advance by retreating, to try to change the world by becoming like the world. Back came Jesus' answer: " You shall worship the Lord your God, and Him alone you will serve " (*Deuteronomy* 6: 13). Jesus was quite certain that we can never defeat evil by compromising with evil. He laid down the uncompromisingness of the Christian faith. Christianity cannot stoop to the level of the world; it must lift the world to its own level. Nothing less will do.

So Jesus made His decision. He decided that He must never bribe men into following Him; He decided that the way of sensations was not for Him; He decided that there could be no compromise in the message He preached and in the faith He demanded. That choice inevitably meant the Cross—but the Cross just as inevitably meant the final victory.

THE SON OF GOD GOES FORTH

Matthew 4: 12-17

> When Jesus heard that John had been delivered into the hands of the authorities, He withdrew into Galilee. He left Galilee and came and made His home in Capernaum, which is on the lake-side, in the districts of Zebulun and Naphtali. This was done that there might be fulfilled that which was spoken through Isaiah the prophet, when he said, " Land of Zebulun, land of Naphtali, by the way of the sea, beyond Jordan, Galilee of the Gentiles— the people who sat in darkness have seen a great light, and a light has risen for those who sat in the land and in the shadow of death." From that time Jesus began to proclaim His message and to say, " Repent, for the Kingdom of the Heavens has come near! "

BEFORE very long disaster came to John. He was arrested and imprisoned in the dungeons of the Castle of Machaerus by Herod the king. His crime was that he had publicly denounced Herod for seducing his brother's wife, and making her his own wife, after he had put away the wife he had. It is never safe to rebuke an eastern despot, and John's courage brought him first imprisonment and then death. We shall come later to the details of that story which Matthew does not tell until *Matthew* 14: 3-12.

For Jesus the time had come when He must go forth to His task.

Let us note what He did first of all. He left Nazareth and He took up residence in the town of Capernaum. There was a kind of symbolic finality in that move. In that moment Jesus left His home never again to return to live in it. It is as if He shut the door that lay behind Him before He opened the door that stood in front of Him. It was the clean cut between the old and the new. One chapter was ended and another had begun. Into life there come these moments of decision. It is always better to meet them with an even surgical cut than to vacillate undecided between two courses of action.

Let us note where Jesus went. He went into Galilee. When Jesus went into Galilee to begin His mission and His ministry, He knew what He was doing. Galilee was the most northerly district of Palestine. It stretched from the Litany River in the north to the Plain of Esdraelon in the south. On the west it did not reach the sea coast of the Mediterranean, because the coastal strip was in the possession of the Phoenicians. On the north-east it was bounded by Syria, and its eastern limit was the waters of the Sea of Galilee. Galilee was not large; it was only fifty miles from north to south, and twenty-five miles from east to west.

But, small as it was, Galilee was densely populated. It was by far the most fertile region of Palestine; its fertility was indeed phenomenal and proverbial. There was a saying that it was easier to raise a legion of olives in Galilee than it was to bring up one child in Judaea.

Josephus, who was at one time governor of the province, says, "It is throughout rich in soil and pasturage, producing every variety of tree, and inviting by its productiveness even those who have the least inclination for agriculture; it is everywhere tilled; no part is allowed to lie idle, and everywhere it is productive." The result of this was that for its size Galilee had an enormous population. Josephus tells us that in it there were two hundred and four villages, none with a population of fewer than fifteen thousand people. So, then, Jesus began His mission in that part of Palestine where there were most people to hear Him; He began His work in an area teeming with men to whom the gospel proclamation might be made.

But not only was Galilee a populous district; its people were people of a certain kind. Of all parts of Palestine Galilee was most open to new ideas. Josephus says of the Galileans, "They were ever fond of innovations, and by nature disposed to changes, and delighted in seditions." They were ever ready to follow a leader and to begin an insurrection. They were notoriously quick in temper and given to quarrelling. Yet withal they were the most chivalrous of men. "The Galileans," said Josephus, "have never been destitute of courage." "Cowardice was never a characteristic of the Galileans." "They were ever more anxious for honour than for gain." The inborn characteristics of the Galileans were such as to make them most fertile ground for a new gospel to be preached to them.

This openness to new ideas was due to certain facts.

(i) The name *Galilee* comes from the Hebrew word *galil* which means a *circle*. The full name of the area was *Galilee of the Gentiles*. Plummer wishes to take that to mean "heathenish Galilee." But the phrase came from the fact that Galilee was literally surrounded by Gentiles. On the west, the Phoenicians were its neighbours. To the north and the east, there were the Syrians. And even to the south, there lay the territory of the Samaritans.

Galilee was in fact the one part of Palestine that was inevitably in touch with non-Jewish influences and ideas. Galilee was bound to be open to new ideas in a way that no other part of Palestine was.

(ii) The great roads of the world passed through Galilee, as we saw when we were thinking of the town of Nazareth. The Way of the Sea led from Damascus through Galilee right down to Egypt and to Africa. The Road to the East led through Galilee away out to the frontiers. The traffic of the world passed through Galilee. Away in the south Judaea is tucked into a corner, isolated and secluded. As it has been well said, " Judaea is on the way to nowhere: Galilee is on the way to everywhere." Judaea could erect a fence and keep all foreign influence and all new ideas out; Galilee could never do that. Into Galilee the new things were bound to come.

(iii) Galilee's geographical position had affected its history. Again and again it had been invaded and conquered, and the tides of the foreigners had often flowed over it and had sometimes engulfed it. Originally it had been assigned to the tribes of Asher, Naphtali and Zebulun when the Israelites first came into the land (*Joshua* 9) but these tribes had never been completely successful in expelling the native Canaanite inhabitants, and from the beginning the population of Galilee was mixed. More than once foreign invasions from the north and east had swept down on it from Syria, and in the eighth century B.C. the Assyrians had engulfed it completely, the greater part of its population had been taken away into exile, and strangers had been settled in the land. Inevitably this brought a very large injection of foreign blood into Galilee. From the eighth until the second century B.C. it had been largely in Gentile hands. When the Jews returned from exile under Nehemiah and Ezra, many of the Galileans came south to live in Jerusalem. In 164 B.C. Simon Maccabaeus chased the Syrians north from Galilee back to their own territory; and on his way back he took with him to Jerusalem the remnants of the Galileans who were left. The most amazing thing of all is that in 104 B.C. Aristobulus reconquered Galilee for the Jewish nation, and proceeded forcibly to circumcise the inhabitants of Galilee, and thus to make them Jews whether they liked it or not. History had compelled Galilee to open its doors to new strains of blood and to new ideas and to new influences.

The natural characteristics of the Galileans, and the preparation of history had made Galilee the one place in all Palestine where a new teacher with a new message had any real chance of being heard, and it was there that Jesus began His mission and first announced His message.

THE HERALD OF GOD

Matthew 4: 12-17 (continued)

BEFORE we leave this passage there are certain other things which we must note.

It was to the town of Capernaum that Jesus went. The correct form of the name is *Capharnaum*; the form *Capernaum* does not occur at all until the fifth century A.D., but the name Capernaum is so fixed in our minds and memories that it would not be wise to try to change it, even though Capharnaum is more correct.

There has been much argument about the site of Capernaum. Two places have been suggested. The commonest, and the likeliest, identification is that Capernaum is Tell Hum, which is on the west side of the extreme north of the Sea of Galilee; the alternative, and the less likely, identification is that Capernaum is Khan Minyeh, which is about two and a half miles to the south-west of Tell Hum. In any event, there is now nothing but ruins left to show where Capernaum once stood.

It was Matthew's habit to find in the Old Testament something which he could use as a prophecy about every event in Jesus' life. He finds such a prophecy in *Isaiah* 9: 1, 2. In point of fact that is another of the prophecies which Matthew tears violently from its context and uses in his own extraordinary way. It is a prophecy which dates back to the reign of Pekah. In those days the northern parts of Palestine, including Galilee, had been despoiled by the invading armies of the Assyrians; and this was originally a prophecy of the deliverance which would some day come to these conquered territories. Matthew finds in it a prophecy which foretold of the light that Jesus was to bring.

Finally, Matthew gives us a brief one-sentence summary of the message which Jesus brought. The Authorised Version says that Jesus began to *preach*. The word *preach* has come down in the world; it is all too unfortunately true that it is connected in the minds of far too many people with boredom. The word in Greek is *kērussein*, which is the word of a herald's proclamation from a king. *Kērux* is the Greek word for herald, and the herald was the man who brought a message direct from the king.

This word tells us of certain characteristics of the preaching of Jesus, and these are characteristics which should be in all preaching.

(i) The herald had in his voice a note of *certainty*. There was no doubt about his message; he did not come with perhapses and maybes and probablys; he came with a definite and indisputable message. Goethe had it: " Tell me of your certainties: I have doubts enough of my own." Preaching is the proclamation of certainties, and a man cannot make others sure of that about which he himself is in doubt.

(ii) The herald had in his voice the note of *authority*. He was speaking for the king; he was laying down and announcing the king's law, the king's commands, and the king's decision. As was said of a great preacher, " He did not cloudily guess; he knew." Preaching, as it has been put, is the application of prophetic authority to the present situation.

(iii) The herald's message came from *a source beyond himself*; it came from the king. Preaching speaks from a source beyond the preacher. It is not the expression of one man's personal opinions; it is the voice of God transmitted through one man to the people. It was with the voice of God that Jesus spoke to men.

The message of Jesus consisted of a command which was the consequence of a new situation. " Repent! " He said. " Turn from your own ways, and turn to God. Lift your eyes from earth and look to heaven. Reverse your direction, and stop walking away from God and begin walking towards God." That command had become urgently necessary because the reign of God was about to begin. Eternity had invaded time; God had invaded earth in Jesus Christ, and therefore it was of paramount and tremendous importance that a man should choose the right side and the right direction.

CHRIST CALLS THE FISHERMEN

Matthew 4: 18-22

> While He was walking beside the Sea of Galilee, He saw two brothers, Simon, who is called Peter, and Andrew, his brother, casting their net into the sea, for they were fishermen. He said to them, " Follow me, and I will make you fishers of men." They immediately left their nets and followed Him. He went on from there and saw other two brothers, James, Zebedee's son, and John, his brother. They were in the boat with Zebedee their father getting ready their nets for use. So He called them. They immediately left their boat and their father, and followed Him.

ALL Galilee centred round the Sea of Galilee. It was thirteen miles long from north to south, and eight miles across from east to west. The Sea of Galilee is therefore

small, and it is interesting to note that Luke, the Gentile,
who had seen so much more of the world, never calls it
the *sea* (*thalassa*), but always the *lake* (*limnē*). It is the
shape of an oval, wider at the top than at the bottom.
It lies in that great rift in the earth's surface in which
the Jordan valley runs, and the surface of the Sea of Galilee
is six hundred and eighty feet below sea level. The fact
that it lies in this dip in the earth's surface gives it a very
warm climate, and makes the surrounding countryside
phenomenally fertile. It is one of the loveliest lakes in
the world. W. M. Thomson describes it: " Seen from
any point of the surrounding heights it is a fine sheet
of water—a burnished mirror set in a framework of rounded
hills and rugged mountains, which rise and roll backward
and upward to where Hermon hangs the picture against
the blue vault of heaven."

In the days of Josephus there were no fewer than nine
populous cities on its shore. In the 1930's, when H. V.
Morton saw it, only Tiberias was left and it was little
more than a village.

In the time of Jesus the Sea of Galilee was thick with
fishing boats. Josephus on a certain expedition had no
difficulty in assembling no fewer than two hundred and
forty fishing boats to set out from Tarichaea; but nowadays
the fishermen are few and far between.

There were three methods of fishing. There was fishing
by line. There was fishing with the casting net. The
casting net was circular, and might be as much as nine feet
across. It was skilfully cast into the water from the land,
or from the shallow water at the edge of the lake. It was
weighted with pellets of lead round the circumference.
It sank into the sea and surrounded the fishes; it was then
drawn through the water as if the top of a bell tent were
being drawn to land, and in it the fish were caught. That
was the kind of net that Peter and Andrew, and James
and John, were handling when Jesus saw them. Its name
was the *amphiblēstron*. The drag net was used from a boat,

or better from two boats. It was cast into the water with ropes at each of the four corners. It was weighted at the foot so that, as it were, it stood upright in the water. When the boats were rowed along with the net behind them, the effect was that the net became a great cone, and in the cone the fishes were caught and brought into the boat. This kind of net is the net in the parable of the dragnet; and is called the *sagēnē*.

So Jesus was walking by the lakeside; and as He walked He called Peter and Andrew, James and John. It is not to be thought that this was the first time that He had seen them, or they Him. As John tells the story, at least some of them were already disciples of John the Baptist (*John* I: 35). No doubt they had already talked with Jesus and had already listened to Him, but in this moment there came to them the challenge once and for all to throw in their lot with Him.

The Greeks used to tell how Xenophon first met Socrates. Socrates met him in a narrow lane and barred his path with his stick. First of all Socrates asked him if he knew where he could buy this and that, and if he knew where this and that were made. Xenophon gave the required information. Then Socrates asked him, "Do you know where men are made good and virtuous?" "No," said the young Xenophon. "Then," said Socrates, "follow me and learn!"

Jesus, too, called on these fishermen to follow Him. It is interesting to note what kind of men they were. They were not men of great scholarship, or influence, or wealth, or social background. They were not poor, they were simple working people with no great background, and certainly, anyone would have said, with no great future. It was these ordinary men whom Jesus chose. Once there came to Socrates a very ordinary man called Aeschines. "I am a poor man," said Aeschines. "I have nothing else, but I give you myself." "Do you not see," said Socrates, "that you are giving me the most precious thing of all?" What Jesus needs is ordinary folk who will give Him themselves. He can do anything with people like that.

Further these men were fishermen. It has been pointed out by many scholars that the good fisherman must possess these very qualities which will turn him into the good fisher of men.

(i) He must have *patience*. He must learn to wait patiently until the fish will take the bait. If he is restless and quick to move he will never make a fisherman. The good fisher of men will have need of patience. It is but rarely in preaching or in teaching that we will see quick results. We must learn to wait.

(ii) He must have *perseverance*. He must learn never to be discouraged, but always to try again. The good preacher and teacher must not be discouraged when nothing seems to happen. He must always be ready to try again.

(iii) He must have *courage*. As the old Greek said when he prayed for the protection of the gods: "My boat is so small and the sea is so large." He must be ready to risk and to face the fury of the sea and of the gale. The good preacher and teacher must be well aware that there is always a danger in telling men the truth. The man who tells the truth more often than not takes his reputation and his life in his hands.

(iv) He must have *an eye for the right moment*. The wise fisherman knows well that there are times when it is hopeless to fish. He knows when to cast and when not to cast. The good preacher and teacher chooses his moment. There are times when men will welcome the truth, and times when they will resent the truth. There are times when the truth will move them, and times when the truth will harden them in their opposition to the truth. The wise preacher and teacher knows that there is a time to speak and a time to be silent.

(v) He must *fit the bait to the fish*. One fish will rise

to one bait and another to another. Paul said that he became all things to all men if by any chance he might win some. The wise preacher and teacher knows that the same approach will not win all men. He may even have to know and recognize his own limitations. He may have to discover that there are certain spheres in which he himself can work, and others in which he cannot.

(vi) The wise fisherman must *keep himself out of sight*. If he obtrudes his own presence, even his own shadow, the fish will very certainly not bite. The wise preacher and teacher will always seek to present men, not with himself, but with Jesus Christ. His aim is to fix men's eyes, not on himself, but on that figure beyond.

THE METHODS OF THE MASTER

Matthew 4: 23-25

> Jesus made a circular tour of Galilee, teaching in the Synagogues, proclaiming the good news of the Kingdom, and healing all kinds of diseases and ailments among the people: and the report of His activities went out all over Syria. So they brought to Him all those who were ill, those who were in the grip of the most varied diseases and pains, those who were possessed by demons, those who were epileptics, and those who were paralysed; and He healed them. And great crowds followed Him from Galilee, and from the Decapolis, and from Jerusalem, and from Judaea, and from beyond Jordan.

JESUS had chosen to begin His mission in Galilee, and we have seen how well-prepared Galilee was to receive the seed. Within Galilee Jesus chose to launch His campaign in the Synagogues. The Synagogue was the most important institution in the life of any Jew. There was a difference between the Synagogues and the Temple. There was only one Temple, the Temple in Jerusalem, but wherever there was the smallest colony of Jews there was a Synagogue. The Temple existed solely for the offering of sacrifice;

in it there was no preaching or teaching. The Synagogue was essentially a teaching institution. The Synagogues have been defined as " the popular religious universities of their day." If a man had any religious teaching or religious ideas to disseminate, the Synagogue was unquestionably the place to start.

Further, the Synagogue service was such that it gave the new teacher his chance. In the Synagogue service there were three parts. The first part consisted of prayers. The second part consisted of readings from the Law and from the Prophets, readings in which members of the congregation took part. The third part was the address. The important fact is that there was no one person to give the address. There was no such thing as a professional ministry. The president of the Synagogue presided over the arrangements for the service. Any distinguished stranger could be asked to give the address, and anyone with a message to give might volunteer to give it; and, if the ruler or president of the Synagogue judged him to be a fit person to speak, he was allowed to speak. Thus at the beginning the door of the Synagogue and the pulpit of the Synagogue were open to Jesus. He began in the Synagogue because it was there He would find the most sincerely religious people of His day, and the way to speak to them was open to Him. After the address there came a time for talk, and questions, and discussion. The Synagogue was the ideal place in which to get a new teaching across to the people.

But not only did Jesus preach; He also healed the sick. It was little wonder that reports of what He was doing went out and people came crowding to hear Him, and to see Him, and to benefit from His pity.

They came from Syria. Syria was the great province of which Palestine was only a part. It stretched away to the north and the north-east with the great city of Damascus as its centre. It so happens that one of the loveliest legends passed down to us by Eusebius (*Ecclesiastical History* I: 13) goes back to this time. The story goes that there was a king called Abgar, in Edessa, and he was ill. So, it is said, he wrote to Jesus: " Abgar, ruler of Edessa, to Jesus, the most excellent Saviour, who has appeared in the country of Jerusalem—greeting. I have heard of you and of your cures, performed without medicine and without herb; for, it is said, you make the blind to see and the lame to walk, you cleanse the lepers, you cast out evil spirits and demons, you heal those afflicted with lingering diseases, and you raise the dead. Now, as I have heard all this about you, I have concluded that one of two things must be true; either, you are God, and having descended from heaven, you do these things, or else, you are a Son of God by what you do. I write to you, therefore, to ask you to come and cure the disease from which I am suffering. For I have heard that the Jews murmur against you, and devise evil things against you. Now, I have a very small but an excellent city which is large enough for both of us." Jesus was said to have written back: " Blessed are you for having believed in me without seeing me. For it is written concerning me that those who have seen me will not believe in me, while they who have not seen me will believe and be saved. But, as to your request that I should come to you, I must fulfil all things here for which I have been sent, and, after fulfilling them, be taken up again to Him who sent me. Yet, after I am taken up, I will send you one of my disciples to cure your disease, and to give life to you and to yours." So, the legend goes on, Thaddeus went to Edessa and cured Abgar. It is only a legend, but it does show how men believed that even in distant Syria men had heard of Jesus and longed with all their hearts for the help and the healing which He alone could give.

Very naturally they came from Galilee, and the word about Jesus had spread south to Jerusalem and Judaea also, and they came from there. They came from the land across the Jordan, which was known as Peraea, and which stretched from Pella in the north to Arabia Petra in the south. They came from the Decapolis. The Decapolis was a federation of ten independent Greek cities, all of which, except Scythopolis, were on the far side of the Jordan.

This list is symbolic for in it we see not only the Jews but the Gentiles also coming to Jesus Christ for what He alone could give them. Already the ends of the earth are gathering to Him.

THE ACTIVITIES OF JESUS

Matthew 4: 23-25 (*continued*)

THIS passage is of great importance because it gives us in brief summary the three great activities of Jesus' life.

(i) He came *proclaiming* the gospel, or, as the Authorised Version has it, He came *preaching*. Now, as we have already seen, preaching is the proclamation of certainties. Therefore, *Jesus came to defeat men's ignorance*. He came to tell them the truth about God, to tell them that which by themselves they could never have found out. He came to put an end to guessing and to groping, and to show men what God is like.

(ii) He came *teaching* in the synagogues. What is the difference between *teaching* and *preaching*? Preaching is the uncompromising proclamation of certainties; teaching is the explanation of the meaning and the significance of them. Therefore, *Jesus came to defeat man's misunderstandings*. There are times when man knows the truth and misinterprets it. He knows the truth and draws the wrong conclusions from it. Jesus came to tell men the meaning of true religion.

(iii) He came *healing* all those who had need of healing. That is to say, *Jesus came to defeat man's pain*. The important thing about Jesus is that He was not satisfied with simply telling men the truth in *words*; He came to turn

77

that truth into deeds. Florence Allshorn, the great missionary teacher, said, " An ideal is never yours until it comes out of your finger tips." The ideal is not yours until it is realized in action. Jesus realized His own teaching in deeds of help and healing.

Jesus came *preaching* that He might defeat all *ignorance*. He came *teaching* that He might defeat all *misunderstandings*. He came *healing* that He might defeat all *pain*. We, too, must proclaim our certainties; we, too, must be ready to explain our faith; we, too, must turn the ideal into action and into deeds.

THE SERMON ON THE MOUNT

As we have already seen, Matthew has a careful pattern in his gospel.

In his story of the Baptism of Jesus he shows us Jesus realising that the hour has struck, that the call to action has come, and that He must go forth on His crusade. In his story of the Temptations he shows us Jesus deliberately choosing the method He will use to carry out His task, and deliberately rejecting methods which He knew to be against the will of God. If a man sets his hand to a great task, he needs his helpers, his assistants, his staff. So Matthew goes on to show us Jesus selecting the men who will be His fellow-workers and His fellow-labourers. But if helpers and assistants are to do their work intelligently and effectively, they must first have instruction. And now, in the Sermon on the Mount, Matthew shows us Jesus instructing His disciples in the message which was His and which they were to take to men. In Luke's account of the Sermon on the Mount this becomes even clearer. In Luke the Sermon on the Mount follows immediately after what we might call the official choosing of the Twelve (*Luke* 6: 13 ff). For that reason one great scholar called the Sermon on the Mount " The Ordination Address to the Twelve." Just as a young minister has his task set out before him, when he is called to his first charge, so the Twelve received from Jesus their ordination address before they went out to their task. It is for that reason that other scholars have given other titles to the Sermon on the Mount. It has been called " The Compendium of Christ's Doctrine," " The Magna Charta of the Kingdom," " The Manifesto of the King." All are agreed that in the Sermon on the Mount we have the core and the essence and the distillation of the teaching of Jesus to the inner circle of His chosen men.

The Summary of the Faith.

In actual fact this is even truer than at first sight appears. We speak of the Sermon on the Mount as if it was one single sermon preached on one single occasion. But it is far more than that. There are good and compelling and convincing reasons for thinking that the Sermon on the Mount is far more than one sermon, that it is, in fact, a kind of epitome of all the sermons that Jesus ever preached.

(i) Anyone who heard it in its present form would be exhausted long before the end. There is far too much in it for one hearing. It is one thing to sit and *read* it, and to pause and linger as we read; it would be entirely another thing to *listen* to it for the first time in spoken words. We can read at our own pace and with a certain familiarity with the words; but to hear it in its present form for the first time would be to be dazzled with excess of light long before the end.

(ii) There are certain sections of the Sermon on the mount which emerge, as it were, without warning; they have no connection with what goes before and no connection with what comes after. For instance, *Matthew* 5: 31, 32 and *Matthew* 7: 7-11 are quite detached from their context. They neither emerge from what went before nor lead up to what comes after. There is a certain disconnection in the Sermon on the Mount.

(iii) The most important point is this. Both Matthew

and Luke give us a version of the Sermon on the Mount. In Matthew's version there are 107 verses. Of these 107 verses 29 are found all together in *Luke* 6: 20-49; 47 have no parallel in Luke's version and 34 are found scattered all over Luke's gospel in different contexts. For instance, the simile of the salt is in *Matthew* 5: 13 and in *Luke* 14: 34, 35; the simile of the lamp is in *Matthew* 5: 15 and in *Luke* 8: 16; the saying that not one jot or tittle of the law shall pass away is in *Matthew* 5: 18 and in *Luke* 16: 17. That is to say, passages which are consecutive in Matthew's gospel appear in widely separated chapters in Luke's gospel. To take another example, the saying about the mote in our brother's eye and the beam in our own is in *Matthew* 7: 1-5 and in *Luke* 6: 37-42; the passage in which Jesus bids men to ask and seek and find is in *Matthew* 7: 7-12 and in *Luke* 11: 9-13. If we tabulate these things, the matter will become clear:

> *Matthew* 5: 13 = *Luke* 14: 34, 35
> *Matthew* 5: 15 = *Luke* 8: 16
> *Matthew* 5: 18 = *Luke* 16: 17
> *Matthew* 7: 1-5 = *Luke* 6: 37-42
> *Matthew* 7: 7-12 = *Luke* 11: 9-13

Now, as we have seen *Matthew* is essentially the teaching gospel; it is Matthew's characteristic that he collects the teaching of Jesus under certain great headings; and it is surely far more likely that Matthew collected Jesus' teaching into one whole pattern, than that Luke took the pattern and broke it up and scattered the pieces all over his gospel. The Sermon on the Mount is not one single sermon which Jesus preached on one definite situation; it is the epitome, the distillation, the summary of His consistent teaching to His disciples. It has been suggested that, after Jesus definitely chose the Twelve, He may have taken them away into a quiet place for a week or even a longer period of time, and that, during that space, He taught them all the time, and the Sermon on the Mount is the summary of that teaching.

THE GOSPEL OF MATTHEW

Matthew's Introduction.

In point of fact Matthew's introductory sentence goes a long way to make that clear.

> " When Jesus saw the crowds, He went up into the mountain; and when He had sat down, His disciples came to Him; and when He had opened His mouth, this is what He used to teach them."

In that brief verse there are three clues to the real significance of the Sermon on the Mount.

(i) Jesus began to teach *when He had sat down.* When a Jewish Rabbi was teaching officially he sat to teach. We still speak of a professor's *chair;* the Pope still speaks *ex cathedra,* from his seat. Often a Rabbi gave instruction when he was standing or strolling about; but his really official teaching was done when he had taken his seat. So, then, the very intimation that Jesus sat down to teach His disciples is the indication that this teaching is central, that it is official, that it is the very essence of His teaching.

(ii) Matthew goes on to say that *when He had opened His mouth,* He taught them. This phrase *He opened His mouth* is not simply a decoratively roundabout way of saying *He said.* In Greek the phrase has a double significance. *(a)* In Greek it is used of a solemn, grave and dignified utterance. It is used, for instance, of the saying of an oracle. It is the natural preface for a most weighty saying. *(b)* It is used of a person's utterance when he is really opening his heart and fully pouring out his mind. It is used of intimate teaching with no barriers between. Again the very use of this phrase indicates that the material in the Sermon on the Mount is no chance piece of teaching. It is the grave and solemn utterance of the central things; it is the opening of Jesus' heart and mind to the men who were to be His right-hand men in His task.

(iii) The Authorised Version has it that when Jesus had sat down, He opened His mouth and *taught them saying.* In Greek there are two past tenses of the verb. There is the *aorist* tense, and the aorist tense expresses one particular action, done and completed in past time. In the sentence, " He shut the gate," *shut* would be an aorist in Greek because it describes one completed action in past time. There is the *imperfect* tense, and the imperfect tense describes repeated, continuous, or habitual action in past time. In the sentence, " It was his custom to go to Church every Sunday," in Greek *it was his custom to go* would be expressed by a single verb in the imperfect tense, because it describes continuous and often-repeated action in the past. Now the point is that in the Greek of this sentence, which we are studying, the verb *taught* is not an *aorist*, but an *imperfect* and therefore it describes repeated and habitual action, and therefore the translation should be: " This is what He used to teach them." Matthew has said as plainly as Greek will say it that the Sermon on the Mount is not one sermon of Jesus, given at one particular time and on one particular occasion; it is the summary, and the essence, and the core of all that Jesus continuously and habitually taught His disciples.

The Sermon on the Mount is greater even than we think. Matthew in his introduction wishes us to see that it is the official teaching of Jesus; that it is the opening of Jesus' whole mind to His disciples; that it is the summary of the teaching which Jesus habitually gave to his inner circle. The Sermon on the Mount is nothing less than the concentrated memory of many hours of heart to heart communion between the disciples and their Master.

As we study the Sermon on the Mount, we are going to set at the head of each of the beatitudes the translation of the authorised version; and then at the end of our study of each beatitude we shall see what the words mean in modern English.

THE SUPREME BLESSEDNESS
Matthew 5: 3

Blessed are the poor in spirit, for theirs is the Kingdom of Heaven.

BEFORE we study each of the beautitudes in detail there are two general facts which we must note.

(i) It can be seen that every one of the beatitudes has precisely the same form. As we read them as they are commonly printed in our Bibles we note that in each one of them in the English version the word *are* is printed in italic, or sloping, type. When a word appears in italic type in the Authorised Version it means that in the Greek, or in the Hebrew, there is no equivalent word, and that that word has had to be added to bring out the meaning of the sentence. This is to say that in the beatitudes there is no verb, there is no *are*. Why should that be? Jesus did not speak the beatitudes in Greek; He spoke them in Aramaic, which was the kind of Hebrew which people spoke in His day. Aramaic and Hebrew have a very common kind of expression, which is in fact an exclamation and which means, " O the blessedness of . . ." That expression (*asherē* in the Hebrew) is very common in the Old Testament. For instance, the first Psalm begins in the Hebrew: " O the blessedness of the man that walketh not in the counsel of the ungodly " (*Psalm* I: I). That is the form in which Jesus first spoke the beatitudes. The beatitudes are not simple statements; they are exclamations: " O the blessedness of the poor in spirit! "

That is most important, for it means that the beatitudes are not pious hopes of what shall be; they are not glowing, but nebulous prophecies of some future bliss; they are congratulations on what is. The blessedness which belongs to the Christian is not a blessedness which is postponed to some future world of glory; it is a blessedness which exists here and now. It is not something into which the Christian *will enter;* it is something into which he *has entered.* True, it will find its fulness and its consummation in the presence of God; but for all that it is a present reality to be enjoyed here and now. The beatitudes in effect say, " O the bliss of being a Christian! O the joy of following Christ! O the sheer happiness of knowing Jesus Christ as Master, Saviour

THE GOSPEL OF MATTHEW

and Lord! " The very form of the beatitudes is the statement of the joyous thrill and the radiant gladness of the
Christian life. In face of the beatitudes a gloom-encompassed Christianity is unthinkable.

(ii) The word *blessed* which is used in each of the beatitudes is a very special word. It is the Greek word *makarios*.
Makarios is the word which specially describes the gods.
In Christianity there is a divine and godlike joy. The
meaning of *makarios* can best be seen from one particular
usage of it. The Greeks always called Cyprus *hē makaria*
(the feminine form of the adjective), which means *The
Happy Isle*, and they did so because they believed that
Cyprus was so lovely, so rich, and so fertile an island
that a man would never need to go beyond its coastline to
find the perfectly happy life. It had such a climate, such
flowers and fruits and trees, such minerals, such natural
resources that it contained within itself all the materials
for perfect happiness. *Makarios* then describes that
joy which has its secret within itself, that joy which is
serene and untouchable, and self-contained, that joy which
is completely independent of all the chances and the changes
of life. The English word *happiness* gives its own case away.
It contains the root *hap* which means *chance*. Human
happiness is something which is dependent on the chances
and the changes of life, something which life may give and
which life may also destroy. The Christian blessedness is
completely untouchable and unassailable. " Your joy,"
said Jesus, " no man taketh from you " (*John* 16: 22).
The beatitudes speak of that joy which seeks us through
our pain, that joy which sorrow and loss, and pain and
grief, are powerless to touch, that joy which shines through
tears, and which nothing in life or death can take away.

The world can win its joys, and the world can equally
well lose its joys. A change in fortune, a collapse in health,
the failure of a plan, the disappointment of an ambition,
even a change in the weather, can take away the fickle joy
the world can give. But the Christian has the serene and

untouchable joy which comes from walking for ever in the company and in the presence of Jesus Christ.

The greatness of the beatitudes is that they are not wistful glimpses of some future beauty; they are not even golden promises of some distant glory; they are triumphant shouts of bliss for a permanent joy that nothing in the world can ever take away.

THE BLISS OF THE DESTITUTE

Matthew 5: 3 (*continued*)

IT seems a surprising way to begin talking about happiness by saying, " Blessed are the poor in spirit." There are two ways in which we can come at the meaning of this word *poor*.

As we have them the beatitudes are in Greek, and the word that is used for *poor* is the word *ptōchos*. In Greek there are two words for poor. There is the word *penēs*. *Penēs* describes a man who has to work for his living; it is defined by the Greeks as describing the man who is *auto-diakonos*, that is, *the man who serves his own needs with his own hands*. *Penēs* describes the working man, the man who has nothing superfluous, the man who is not rich, but who is not destitute either. But, as we have seen, it is not *penēs* that is used in this beatitude, it is *ptōchos*, which describes *absolute and abject poverty*. It is connected with the root *ptōssein*, which means *to crouch* or *to cower*; and it describes the poverty which is beaten to its knees. As it has been said, *penēs* describes the man who has nothing superfluous; *ptōchos* describes the man who has nothing at all. So this beatitude becomes even more surprising. Blessed is the man who is abjectly and completely poverty-stricken. Blessed is the man who is absolutely destitute.

As we have also seen the beatitudes were not originally spoken in Greek, but in Aramaic. Now the Jews had a special way of using the word *poor*. In Hebrew the word is 'ani or ebiōn. These words in Hebrew underwent a four-stage development of meaning. (i) They began by meaning simply *poor*. (ii) They went on to mean, *because poor, therefore having no influence or power, or help, or prestige.* (iii) They went on to mean, *because having no influence, therefore down-trodden and oppressed by men.* (iv) Finally, they came to describe *the man who, because he has no earthly resources whatever, puts his whole trust in God.* So in Hebrew the word *poor* was used to describe the humble and the helpless man who put his whole trust in God. It is thus that the Psalmist used the word, when he writes, " This *poor man* cried, and the Lord heard him, and saved him out of all his troubles " (*Psalm* 34: 6). It is in fact true that in the Psalms the poor man, in this sense of the term, is the good man who is dear to God. " The expectation of the poor shall not perish for ever " (*Psalm* 9: 18). God delivers the poor (*Psalm* 35: 10). " Thou, O God, hast prepared of Thy goodness for the poor " (*Psalm* 68: 10). " He shall give justice to the poor of the people " (*Psalm* 72: 4). " Yet setteth He the poor on high from affliction, and maketh him families like a flock " (*Psalm* 107: 41). " I will satisfy the poor with bread " (*Psalm* 132: 15). In all these cases the *poor* man is the humble, helpless man who has put his trust in God.

Let us now take the two sides, the Greek and the Aramaic, and put them together. *Ptōchos* describes the man who is absolutely destitute, the man who has nothing at all; *'ani* and *ebiōn* describe the poor, and humble, and helpless man who has put his whole trust in God. Therefore, " Blessed are the poor in spirit " means:

> Blessed is the man who has realised his own utter helplessness, and who has put his whole trust in God.

If a man has realised his own utter helplessness, and has put his whole trust in God, there will enter into his life two things which are opposite sides of the same thing. He will become completely *detached from things*, for he will know that things have not got it in them to bring happiness or security; and he will become completely *attached to God*, for he will know that God alone can bring him help, and hope, and strength. The man who is poor in spirit is the man who has realised that things mean nothing, and that God means everything.

We must be careful not to think that this beatitude calls actual material poverty a good thing. Poverty is not a good thing. Jesus would never have called blessed a state where people live in slums and have not enough to eat, and where health rots because conditions are all against it. That kind of poverty it is the aim of the Christian gospel to remove. The poverty which is blessed is the poverty *of spirit*, the spirit which realises its own utter lack of resources to meet life, and which finds its help and strength in God.

Jesus says that to such a poverty belongs the Kingdom of Heaven. Why should that be so? If we take the two petitions of the Lord's Prayer and set them together:

Thy Kingdom come.
Thy will be done in earth as it is in heaven,

we get the definition: The Kingdom of God is a society where God's will is as perfectly done in earth as it is in heaven. That means that only he who does God's will is a citizen of the Kingdom; and we can only do God's will when we realize our own utter helplessness, our own utter ignorance, our own utter inability to cope with life, and when we put our whole trust in God. Obedience is always founded on trust. The Kingdom of God is the possession of the poor in spirit, because the poor in spirit have realised their own utter helplessness without God, and have learned to trust and obey.

So then, the first beatitude means:

O THE BLISS OF THE MAN WHO HAS REALISED HIS OWN UTTER HELPLESSNESS, AND WHO HAS PUT HIS WHOLE TRUST IN GOD, FOR THUS ALONE HE CAN RENDER TO GOD THAT PERFECT OBEDIENCE WHICH WILL MAKE HIM A CITIZEN OF THE KINGDOM OF HEAVEN!

THE BLISS OF THE BROKEN HEART

Matthew 5: 4

> Blessed are they that mourn, for they shall be comforted.

It is first of all to be noted about this beatitude that the Greek word for *to mourn*, used here, is the strongest word for mourning in the Greek language. It is the word which is used for mourning for the dead, for the passionate lament for one who was loved. In the Septuagint, the Greek version of the Old Testament, it is the word which is used of Jacob's grief when he believed that Joseph, his son, was dead (*Genesis* 37: 34). It is defined as the kind of grief which takes such a hold on a man that it cannot be hid. It is not only the sorrow which brings an ache to the heart; it is the sorrow which brings the unrestrainable tears to the eyes. Here then indeed is an amazing kind of bliss:

> Blessed is the man who mourns like one mourning for the dead.

There are three ways in which this beatitude has been taken, and can be taken.

(i) It can be taken quite literally: Blessed is the man who has endured the bitterest sorrow that life can bring. The Arabs have a proverb: "All sunshine makes a desert." The land on which the sun always shines will soon become an arid place in which no fruit will grow. There are certain things which only the rains will produce; and certain experiences which only sorrow can beget. Sorrow can do two things for us. It can show us, as nothing else can, the essential kindness of our fellow-men; and it can show us as nothing else can the comfort and the compassion of God. Many and many a man in the hour of his sorrow has discovered his fellow-men and his God as he never did before. When things go well it is possible to live for years on the surface of things; but when sorrow comes a man is driven to the deep things of life, and, if he accepts it aright, a new strength and beauty enter into his soul.

" I walked a mile with Pleasure,
  She chattered all the way,
But left me none the wiser
  For all she had to say.

I walked a mile with Sorrow,
  And ne'er a word said she,
But, oh, the things I learned from her
  When Sorrow walked with me! "

(ii) Some people have taken this beatitude to mean:

Blessed are those who are desperately sorry for the sorrow and the suffering of this world.

When we were thinking of the first beatitude we saw that it is always right to be detached from *things*, but it is never right to be detached from *people*. This world would have been a very much poorer place, if there had not been those who cared intensely about the sorrows and the sufferings of others. Lord Shaftesbury probably did more for ordinary working men and women and for little children than any social reformer ever did. It all began very simply. When he was a boy at Harrow, he was going along the street one day, and he met a pauper's funeral. The coffin was a shoddy, ill-made box. It was on a hand-barrow. The barrow was being pushed by a quartette of men who were drunk; and as they pushed the barrow along, they were singing ribald songs, and joking and jesting among themselves. As they pushed the barrow up the hill the box, which was the coffin, fell off the barrow and burst open. Some people would have thought the whole business a good joke; some would have turned away in fastidious disgust; some would have shrugged their shoulders and would have felt that it had nothing to do with them, although it might be a pity that such things should happen. The young Shaftesbury saw it and said to himself, " When I grow up, I'm going to give my life to see that things like that don't happen." So he dedicated his life to caring for others. Christianity *is* caring. This beatitude does mean: Blessed is the man who cares intensely for the sufferings, and for the sorrows, and for the needs of others.

(iii) No doubt both these thoughts are in this beatitude, but the main thought of this beatitude undoubtedly is: Blessed is the man who is desperately sorry for his own sin and his own unworthiness. As we have seen, the very first word of the message of Jesus was, " Repent! " No man can repent unless he is sorry for his sins. The thing which really changes men is when they suddenly come up against something which opens their eyes to what sin is and to what sin does. A boy or a girl may go his or her own way, and may never think of effects and consequences; and then some day something may happen, and that boy or girl may see the stricken look in a father's or a mother's eyes; and suddenly sin is seen for what it is. That is what the Cross does for us. As we look at the Cross, we are bound to say, " That is what sin can do. Sin can take the loveliest life in all the world and smash it on a Cross." One of the great functions of the Cross is to open the eyes of men and women to the horror of sin. And when a man sees sin in all its horror he cannot do anything else but experience this intense sorrow for his sin.

Christianity begins with a sense of sin. Blessed is the man who is intensely sorry for his sin, the man who is heart-broken for what his sin has done to God and to Jesus Christ, the man who sees the Cross and who is appalled by the havoc wrought by sin.

It is the man who has that experience who will indeed be comforted; for that experience is what we call penitence, and the broken and the contrite heart God will never despise (*Psalm* 51: 17). The way to the joy of forgiveness is through the desperate sorrow of the broken heart.

The real meaning of the second beatitude is:

O THE BLISS OF THE MAN WHOSE HEART IS BROKEN FOR THE WORLD'S SUFFERING AND FOR HIS OWN SIN, FOR OUT OF HIS SORROW HE WILL FIND THE JOY OF GOD!

THE BLISS OF THE GOD-CONTROLLED LIFE

Matthew 5: 5

Blessed are the meek, for they shall inherit the earth.

IN our modern English idiom the word *meek* is hardly one of the honourable words of life. Nowadays it carries with it an idea of spinelessness, and subservience, and mean-spiritedness. It paints the picture of a submissive and ineffective creature. But it so happens that the word *meek*—in Greek *praus*—was one of the great Greek ethical words.

Aristotle has a great deal to say about the quality of *meekness* (*praotēs*). It was Aristotle's fixed method to define every virtue as the mean between two extremes. On the one hand there was the extreme of excess; on the other hand there was the extreme of defect; and in between there was the virtue itself, the happy medium. To take an example, on the one extreme there is the spendthrift; on the other extreme there is the miser; and in between there is the generous man. Aristotle defines *meekness*, *praotēs*, as the mean between *orgilotēs*, which means *excessive anger*, and *aorgēsia*, which means *excessive angerlessness*. *Praotēs*, *meekness*, as Aristotle saw it, is the happy medium between too much and too little anger. And so the first possible translation of this beatitude is:

> Blessed is the man who is always angry at the right time, and never angry at the wrong time.

If we ask what the right time and the wrong time are, we may say as a general rule for life that it is never right to be angry for any insult or injury done to ourselves; that is something that no Christian must ever resent; but that it is often right to be angry at injuries done to other people. Selfish anger is always a sin; selfless anger can be one of the great moral dynamics of the world.

But the word *praus* had a second standard Greek usage. It is the regular word for an animal which has been domesticated, which has been trained to obey the word of command, which has learned to answer to the reins. It is the word for an animal which has learned to accept control. So the second possible translation of this beatitude is:

> Blessed is the man who has every instinct, every impulse, every passion under control. Blessed is the man who is entirely self-controlled.

The moment we have stated that, we see that it needs a change. It is not so much the blessing of the man who is *self*-controlled, for such complete self-control is beyond human capacity; rather, it is the blessing of the man who is completely *God*-controlled, for only in His service do we find our perfect freedom, and in doing His will our peace.

But there is still a third possible side from which we may approach this beatitude. The Greeks always contrasted the quality which they called *praotēs*, and which the Authorised Version translates *meekness*, with the quality which they called *hupsēlokardia*, which means *lofty-heartedness*. In *praotēs* there is the true humility which banishes all pride.

Without humility a man cannot learn, for the first step to learning is the realisation of our own ignorance. Quintilian, the great Roman teacher of oratory, said of certain of his scholars, " They would no doubt be excellent students, if they were not already convinced of their own knowledge." No one can teach the man who knows it all already. Without humility there can be no such thing as love, for the very beginning of love is a sense of unworthiness. Without humility there can be no true religion, for all true religion begins with a sense and a realisation of our own weakness and of our need for God. Man only reaches true manhood when he is always conscious that he is the creature and that God is the Creator, and that without God he can do nothing.

Praotēs describes the humility, the acceptance of the necessity to learn and of the necessity to be forgiven. It describes man's only possible attitude to God. So then, the third possible translation of this beatitude is:

Blessed is the man who has the humility to know his own ignorance, his own weakness, and his own need.

It is this meekness, Jesus says, which will inherit the earth. It is the fact of history that it has always been the men with this gift of self-control, the men with their passions, and instincts, and impulses under discipline, who have been great. *Numbers* says of Moses, the greatest leader and the greatest law-giver the world has ever seen: " Now the man Moses was very meek, above all men which were upon the face of the earth " (*Numbers* 12: 3). Moses was no milk and water character; he was no spineless creature; he could be blazingly angry; but he was a man whose anger was on the leash, only to be released when the time was right. The writer of *Proverbs* has it: " He that ruleth his spirit is better than he that taketh a city " (*Proverbs* 16: 32). It was the lack of that very quality which ruined Alexander the Great, who, in a fit of uncontrolled temper in the middle of a drunken debauch, hurled a spear at his best friend and killed him. No man can lead others until he has mastered himself; no man can serve others until he has subjected himself; no man can be in control of others until he has learned to control himself. But the man who gives himself into the complete control of God will gain this meekness which will indeed enable him to inherit the earth.

It is clear that this word *praus* means far more than the English word *meek* now means; it is, in fact, clear that there is no one English word which will translate it, although perhaps the word *gentle* comes nearest to it. The full translation of this third beatitude must read:

O THE BLISS OF THE MAN WHO IS ALWAYS ANGRY AT THE RIGHT TIME AND NEVER ANGRY AT THE WRONG TIME, WHO HAS EVERY INSTINCT, AND IMPULSE, AND PASSION UNDER CONTROL BECAUSE HE HIMSELF IS GOD-CONTROLLED, WHO HAS THE HUMILITY TO REALISE HIS OWN IGNORANCE AND HIS OWN WEAKNESS, FOR SUCH A MAN IS A KING AMONG MEN!

THE BLISS OF THE STARVING SPIRIT

Matthew 5: 6

> Blessed are they which do hunger and thirst after righteousness, for they shall be filled.

WORDS do not exist in isolation; they exist against a background of experience and of thought; and the meaning of any word is conditioned by the background of the person who speaks it. That is particularly true of this beatitude. It would convey to those who heard it for the first time an impression which is quite different from the impression which it conveys to us.

The fact is that very few of us in modern conditions of life know what it is to be really hungry or really thirsty. In the ancient world it was very different. A working man's wage was the equivalent of eight pence a day, and, even making every allowance for the difference in the purchasing power of money, no man ever got fat on that wage. In the ancient world it was very different. A working man in Palestine ate meat only once a week, and in Palestine the working man and the day labourer were never far from the border-line of real hunger and actual starvation. It was still more so in the case of thirst. In the ancient world it was not possible for the vast majority of people to turn a tap and find the clear, cold water pouring into their house. A man might be on a journey, and in the midst of it the hot wind which brought the sand-storm might begin to blow. There was nothing for him to do but to wrap his head in his burnous and turn his back to the wind, and wait, while the swirling sand filled his nostrils and his throat until he was like to suffocate for breath, and until he was parched with an imperious thirst. In the conditions of modern western life there is no parallel at all to that.

So, then, the hunger which this beatitude describes is no genteel hunger which could be satisfied with a mid-morning snack; the thirst of which it speaks is no thirst which could be slaked with a cup of coffee or an iced-drink.

94

It is the hunger of the man who is starving for food, and of the man who will die unless he drinks.

Since that is so this beatitude is in reality a question and a challenge. In effect it demands, " How much do you want goodness? Do you want it as much as a starving man wants food, and as much as a man dying of thirst wants water? " How intense is our desire for goodness?

Most people have an instinctive desire for goodness, but that desire is wistful and nebulous rather than sharp and intense; and when the moment of decision comes they are not prepared to make the effort, the sacrifice which real goodness demands. Most people suffer from what Robert Louis Stevenson called " the malady of not wanting." It would obviously make the biggest difference in the world if we literally desired goodness more than anything else in the world.

When we approach this beatitude from that side it is the most demanding, and indeed the most frightening, of all the beatitudes. But not only is it the most demanding beatitude; in its own way it is also the most comforting beatitude. At the back of it there is the meaning that the man who is blessed is not necessarily the man who attains and achieves this goodness, but the man who longs for it with his whole heart. If blessedness came only to him who achieved, then none would be blessed. But blessedness comes to the man who, in spite of failures and failings, still clutches to him the passionate love of the highest. H. G. Wells somewhere said, "A man may be a bad musician and yet be passionately in love with music." Robert Louis Stevenson spoke of even those who have sunk to the lowest depths " clutching the remnants of virtue to them in the brothel and on the scaffold." Sir Norman Birkett, the famous lawyer and judge, was once speaking of the criminals with whom he had come in contact in his work. He spoke of the inextinguishable something in every man. Goodness, " the implacable hunter," is always at their heels. The worst of men is " condemned to some kind of nobility." The true wonder of man is not that he is a sinner, but that even in his sin he is haunted by goodness, that even in the mud he can never wholly forget the stars. David had always wished to build the Temple of God; he never achieved that ambition; it was denied and forbidden to him; but God said to him, " Thou didst well that it was in thine heart " (*I Kings* 8: 18). In His mercy God judges us, not only by our achievements, but also by our dreams. Even if a man never attains goodness, if to the end of the day he is still hungering and thirsting for it, he is not shut out from blessedness.

There is one further point in this beatitude, a point which only emerges in the Greek. It is a rule of Greek grammar that verbs of hungering and thirsting are followed by the genitive case. The genitive case is the case which, in English, is expressed by the word *of*; *of the man* is the genitive case. The genitive which follows verbs of hungering and thirsting in Greek is called the partitive genitive, that is the genitive of the part. The idea is this. The Greek said, " I hunger for of bread." It was some bread he desired, a part of the bread, not the whole loaf. The Greek said, " I thirst for of water." It was some water he desired, a drink of water, not all the water in the tank. But in this beatitude most unusually *righteousness* is in the direct accusative, and not in the normal genitive. Now, when verbs of hungering and thirsting in Greek take the accusative instead of the genitive, the meaning is that the hunger and the thirst is for *the whole thing*. To say I hunger for bread in the accusative means, I want the whole loaf. To say I thirst for water in the accusative means, I want the whole pitcher. Therefore the correct translation of this is:

> Blessed are those who hunger and thirst for the whole of righteousness, for total righteousness, for complete righteousness.

That is in fact what people so seldom do. They are content with a part of righteousness. A man, for instance, may be a good man in the sense that, however hard one tried, one could not pin a moral fault on to him. His honesty, his morality, his respectability may be beyond question; but no one could go to that man and weep out a sorry story of failure on his breast; he would freeze, if he tried to do so. There can be a goodness which is accompanied with a hardness, a censoriousness, a lack of sympathy. Such a goodness is a partial goodness. On the other hand a man may have all kinds of faults; he may drink, and swear, and gamble, and lose his temper; and yet, if any one is in trouble, he would give him the last penny out of his pocket and the very coat off his back. Again that is a partial goodness. This beatitude says, it is not enough to be satisfied with a partial goodness. Blessed is the man who hungers and thirsts for the goodness which is total and complete. Neither an icy faultlessness nor a faulty warm-heartedness is enough.

So, then, the translation of the fourth beatitude could run:

O THE BLISS OF THE MAN WHO LONGS FOR TOTAL RIGHTEOUSNESS AS A STARVING MAN LONGS FOR FOOD, AND A MAN PERISHING OF THIRST LONGS FOR WATER, FOR THAT MAN WILL WILL BE TRULY SATISFIED!

THE BLISS OF PERFECT SYMPATHY

Matthew 5: 7

Blessed are the merciful, for they shall obtain mercy.

EVEN as it stands this is surely a great enough saying; and it is the statement of a principle which runs all through the New Testament. The New Testament is insistent that to be forgiven we must be forgiving. As James had it: " He shall have judgment without mercy that hath showed no mercy " (*James* 2: 13). Jesus finishes the story of the unforgiving debtor with the warning: " So likewise shall my heavenly Father do also unto you, if ye from your heart forgive not every one his brother their trespasses " *Matthew* 18: 35). The Lord's Prayer is followed by the

two verses which explain and underline the petition,
" Forgive us our debts as we forgive our debtors ": " For
if ye forgive men their trespasses, your heavenly Father
will also forgive you. But if ye forgive not men their
trespasses, neither will your Father forgive your trespasses " (*Matthew* 6: 12, 14, 15). It is the consistent
teaching of the New Testament that indeed only the
merciful shall receive mercy.

But there is even more to this beatitude than that. The
Greek word for merciful is *eleēmōn*. But, as we have
repeatedly seen, the Greek of the New Testament as we
possess it goes back to an original Hebrew and Aramaic.
The Hebrew word for mercy is *chesedh*; and it is an
untranslatable word. It does not mean only to sympathise
with a person in the popular sense of the term; it does not
mean simply to feel sorry for someone in trouble. *Chesedh,
mercy*, means the ability to get right inside the other person's
skin until we can see things with his eyes, think things with
his mind, and feel things with his feelings. Clearly this is
much more than an emotional wave of pity; clearly this
demands a quite deliberate effort of the mind and of the
will. It denotes a sympathy which is not given, as it were,
from outside, but which comes from a deliberate identification with the other person, until we see things as he sees
them, and feel things as he feels them. This is *sympathy* in
the literal sense of the word. *Sympathy* is derived from two
Greek words, *sun* which means *together with*, and *paschein*
which means *to experience* or *to suffer*. *Sympathy* means
experiencing things together with the other person, literally
going through what he is going through.

This is precisely what so many people do not even try to
do. Most people are so concerned with their own feelings
that they are not much concerned with the feelings of
anyone else. When they are sorry for someone else, it is,
as it were, from the outside; they do not make this deliberate effort to get inside the other person's mind and heart,
until they see and feel things as he sees and feels them.

If we did make this deliberate attempt, and if we did achieve this identification with the other person, it would obviously make a very great difference to life.

(i) It would save us from being kind in the wrong way. There is one outstanding example of insensitive and mistaken kindness in the New Testament. It is in the story of Jesus' visit to the house of Martha and Mary at Bethany (*Luke* 10: 38-42). When Jesus paid that visit, the Cross was only a few days ahead. All that He wanted was an opportunity for so short a time to rest and to relax, and to lay down the terrible tension of living. Martha loved Jesus; He was her most honoured guest; and because she loved Him she would provide the best meal the house could supply. She bustled and scurried here and there with the clatter of dishes and the clash of pans; and every moment was torture to the tense nerves of Jesus. All he wanted was quiet. Martha meant to be kind, but she could hardly have been more cruel. But Mary understood that Jesus wished only for peace. So often when we wish to be kind the kindness has to be given in our way, and the other person has to put up with it whether he likes it or not. Our kindness would be doubly kind, and would be saved from much quite unintentional unkindness, if we would only make the effort to get inside the other person.

(ii) It would make forgiveness, and it would make tolerance ever so much easier. There is one principle in life which we so often forget—there is always a reason why a person thinks and acts as he does, and if we knew that reason, it would be so much easier to understand and to sympathise and to forgive. If a person thinks, as we see it, mistakenly, he may have come through experiences, he may have a heritage which has made him think as he does. If a person is irritable and discourteous, he may be worried or he may be in pain. If a person treats us in a certain way, he does it because there is some idea in his mind which may be quite mistaken. Truly, as the French proverb has it, " To know all is to forgive all," but we will never know all until we make the deliberate attempt to get inside the other person's mind and heart.

(iii) In the last analysis, is not that what God did in Jesus Christ? In Jesus Christ, in the most literal sense, God got inside the skin of men. He came as a man; He came seeing things with men's eyes, feeling things with men's feelings, thinking things with men's minds. God knows what life is like, because God came right inside life. Queen Victoria was a close friend of Principal and Mrs. Tulloch of St. Andrews. Prince Albert died and Victoria was left alone. Just at the same time Principal Tulloch died and Mrs. Tulloch was left alone. All unannounced Queen Victoria came to call on Mrs. Tulloch when she was resting on a couch in her room. When the Queen was announced Mrs. Tulloch struggled to rise quickly from the couch and to curtsey. The Queen stepped forward: " My dear," she said, " don't rise. I am not coming to you to-day as a queen to a subject, but as one woman who has lost her husband to another." It is just that that God did; He came to men, not as the remote, detached, isolated, majestic God; but as a man. The supreme instance of *mercy, chesedh,* is the coming of God in Jesus Christ.

It is only those who show this mercy who will receive this mercy. This is true on the human side, for it is the great truth of life that in other people we see the reflection of ourselves. If we are detached and disinterested in them, they will be detached and disinterested in us. If they see that we care, their hearts will respond in caring. It is supremely true on the divine side, for he who shows this mercy has become nothing less than like God.

So the translation of the fifth beatitude might read:

O THE BLISS OF THE MAN WHO GETS RIGHT INSIDE OTHER PEOPLE, UNTIL HE CAN SEE WITH THEIR EYES, THINK WITH THEIR THOUGHTS, FEEL WITH THEIR FEELINGS, FOR HE WHO DOES THAT WILL FIND OTHERS DO THE SAME FOR HIM, AND WILL KNOW THAT THAT IS WHAT GOD IN JESUS CHRIST HAS DONE!

THE BLISS OF THE CLEAN HEART

Matthew 5: 8

Blessed are the pure in heart, for they shall see God.

HERE is the beatitude which demands that every man who reads it should stop, and think, and examine himself.

The Greek word for *pure* is *katharos*, and it has a variety of usages, all of which have something to add to the meaning of this beatitude for the Christian life.

(i) Originally it simply meant *clean*, and could, for instance, be used of soiled clothes which have been washed clean. (ii) It is regularly used for corn which has been winnowed or sifted and cleansed of all chaff. In the same way it is used of an army which has been purged of all discontented, cowardly, unwilling and inefficient soldiers, and which is a force composed solely of first-class fighting men. (iii) It very commonly appears in company with another Greek adjective—*akēratos*. *Akēratos* can be used of milk or wine which is unadulterated with water, or of metal which has in it no tinge of alloy.

So, then, the basic meaning of *katharos* is *unmixed, unadulterated, unalloyed*. That is why this beatitude is so demanding a beatitude. It could be translated:

Blessed is the man whose motives are always entirely unmixed, for that man shall see God.

It is very seldom indeed that we do even our finest actions from absolutely unmixed motives. If we give generously and liberally to some good cause, it may well be that there lingers in the depths of our hearts some contentment in basking in the sunshine of our own self-approval, some pleasure in the praise and thanks and credit which we will receive. If we do some fine thing, which demands some sacrifice from us, it may well be that we are not altogether free from the feeling that men will see something heroic in us and that we may regard ourselves as a martyr. Even a preacher at his most sincere is not altogether free from the danger of self-satisfaction in having preached a good sermon. Was it not John Bunyan who was once told by someone that he had preached well that day, and who answered sadly, " The devil already told me that as I was coming down the pulpit steps"?

This beatitude demands from us the most exacting self-examination. Is our work done from motives of service or from motives of pay? Is our service given from selfless motives or from motives of self-display? Is the work we do in Church done for Christ or for our own prestige? Is even our Church-going an attempt to meet God or a fulfilling of an habitual and conventional respectability? Is even our prayer and our Bible reading engaged upon with the sincere desire to company with God or because it gives us a pleasant feeling of superiority to feel that we do these things? Is our religion a thing in which we are conscious of nothing so much as the need of God within our hearts, or a thing in which we have comfortable thoughts of our own piety? To examine one's own motives is a daunting and a shaming thing, for there are few things in this world that even the best of us do with completely unmixed motives.

Jesus went on to say that only the pure in heart will see God. It is one of the simple facts of life that we see only what we are able to see; and that is true not only in the physical sense; it is also true in every other possible sense. If the ordinary person goes out on a night of stars, he sees only a host of pinpoints of light in the sky; he sees what is fit to see; but in that same sky the astronomer will call the stars and the planets by their familiar names, and will move amongst them as his friends; and from that same sky the navigator could find the means to bring his ship across the trackless seas to the desired haven. The ordinary person can walk along a country road, and see by the hedgerows nothing but a tangle of weeds and wild flowers and grasses; the trained botanist would see this and that, and call it by name and know its use; and he might even see something of infinite value and rarity because he had eyes to see. Put two men into a room filled with ancient pictures. A man with no knowledge and no skill could not tell an old master from a worthless daub, whereas a trained art critic might well discern a picture worth thousands of pounds in a collection which someone else might dismiss as junk. There are people with filthy minds who can see in any situation material for a prurient snigger and a soiled jest. In every sphere of life we see what we are able to see.

So, says Jesus, it is only the pure in heart who shall see God. It is a warning thing to remember that, as by God's grace we keep our hearts clean, or as by human lust we soil them, we are either fitting or unfitting ourselves some day to see God.

So, then, this sixth beatitude might read:

> O THE BLISS OF THE MAN WHOSE MOTIVES ARE ABSO-
> LUTELY PURE, FOR THAT MAN WILL SOME DAY BE ABLE
> TO SEE GOD!

THE BLISS OF BRINGING MEN TOGETHER

Matthew 5: 9

> Blessed are the peace-makers, for they shall be called the children of God.

WE must begin our study of this beatitude by investigating certain matters of meaning in it.

(i) First, there is the word *peace*. In Greek the word is *eirēnē*, and in Hebrew it is *shalōm*. In Hebrew *peace* is never only a negative state; it never means only the absence of trouble; in Hebrew *peace* always means *everything which makes for a man's highest good*. In the east when one man says to another, *Salaam*—which is the same word—he does not mean that he wishes for the other man only the absence of evil things; he wishes for him the presence of all good things. In the Bible peace means not only freedom from all trouble; it means enjoyment of all good.

(ii) Second, it must carefully be noted what the beatitude is saying. The blessing is on the peace-*makers*, not necessarily on the peace-*lovers*. It very often happens that if a man loves peace in the wrong way, he succeeds in making trouble and not peace. We may, for instance, allow a threatening and dangerous situation to develop, and our defence is that for peace's sake we do not want to take any action. There is many a person who thinks that he is loving peace, when in fact he is piling up trouble for the future, because he refuses to face the situation and to take the action which the situation demands. The peace which the Bible calls blessed does not come from the evasion of issues; it comes from facing them, dealing with them, and conquering them. What this beatitude demands is not the passive acceptance of things because we are afraid of the trouble of doing anything about them, but the active facing of things, and the *making* of peace, even when the way to peace is through struggle.

(iii) The Authorised Version says that the peace-makers shall be called the *children* of God; the Greek more literally is that the peace-makers will be called the *sons* (*huioi*) of God. This is a typical Hebrew way of expression. Hebrew is not rich in adjectives, and often when Hebrew wishes to describe something, it uses, not an adjective, but the phrase *son of* . . . plus an abstract noun. Hence a man may be called *a son of peace* instead of *a peaceful man*. Barnabas is called *a son of consolation* instead of *a consoling and comforting man*. This beatitude says: Blessed are the peacemakers, for they shall be called the sons of God; what it means is: Blessed are the peace-makers, for they shall be doing a God-like work. The man who makes peace is engaged on the very work which the God of peace is doing (*Romans* 15: 33; 2 *Corinthians* 13: 11; 1 *Thessalonians* 5: 23; *Hebrews* 13: 20).

The meaning of this beatitude has been sought along three main lines.

(i) It has been suggested that, since *shalōm* means everything which makes for a man's highest good, this beatitude means: Blessed are those who make this world a better place for all men to live in. Abraham Lincoln once said: " Die when I may, I would like it to be said of me, that I always pulled up a weed and planted a flower where I thought a flower would grow." This then would be the beatitude of those who have lifted the world a little further on.

(ii) Most of the early scholars of the Church took this beatitude in a purely spiritual sense, and held that it meant: Blessed is the man who makes peace in his own heart and in his own soul. In every one of us there is an inner conflict between good and evil; we are always tugged in two directions at once; every man is at least to some extent a walking civil war. Happy indeed is the man who has won through to inner peace, in which the inner warfare is over, and his whole heart is given to God.

(iii) But there is another meaning for this word *peace,* and it is a meaning on which the Jewish Rabbis loved to dwell, and it is almost certainly the meaning which Jesus had in his mind. The Jewish Rabbis held that the highest task which a man can perform is to establish *right relationships* between man and man. That is what Jesus means. There are people who are always storm centres of trouble and bitterness and strife. Wherever they are they are either involved in quarrels themselves or the cause of quarrels between others. They are trouble-makers. There are people like that in almost every society and every Church, and such people are doing the devil's own work. On the other hand—thank God—there are people in whose presence bitterness cannot live, people who bridge the gulfs, and heal the breaches, and sweeten the bitternesses. Such people are doing a godlike work, for it is the great purpose of God to bring peace between men and Himself, and between man and man. The man who divides men is doing the devil's work; the man who unites men is doing a God's work.

So, then, this beatitude might read:

O THE BLISS OF THOSE WHO PRODUCE RIGHT RELATION-
SHIPS BETWEEN MAN AND MAN, FOR THEY ARE DOING
A GODLIKE WORK!

THE BLISS OF THE SUFFERER FOR CHRIST

Matthew 5: 10-12

O the bliss of those who are persecuted for the sake of
righteousness, because the Kingdom of Heaven is
theirs!

Yours is the bliss when men shall heap their insults
on you, and shall persecute you, and shall say in their
lies all kinds of evil things against you for my sake.
Your reward will be great in heaven; for that is the
way in which they persecuted the prophets which were
before you.

ONE of the outstanding qualities of Jesus was His sheer
honesty. He never left men in any doubt what would
happen to them if they chose to follow Him. He was clear
that He had come " not to make life easy, but to make
men great."

It is hard for us to realise what the first Christians had
to suffer. Every department of their life was disrupted.

(i) Their Christianity might well disrupt their *work*.
Suppose a man was a stone-mason. That seems a harmless
enough occupation. But suppose his firm received a contract to build a temple to one of the heathen gods, what
was that man to do? Suppose a man was a tailor, and suppose his firm was asked to produce robes for the heathen
priests, what was that man to do? In a situation such as
that in which the early Christians found themselves there
was hardly any job in which a man might not find a conflict
between his business interests and his loyalty to Jesus
Christ. The Church was in no doubt where a man's duty
lay. More than a hundred years after this a man came to
Tertullian with this very problem. He told of his business
difficulties. He ended by saying, " What can I do? I must

live?" "Must you?" said Tertullian. If it came to a choice between a loyalty and a living, the real Christian never hesitated to choose loyalty.

(ii) Their Christianity would certainly disrupt their *social* life. In the ancient world most feasts were held in the temple of some god. In very few sacrifices was the whole animal burned upon the altar. It might be that only a few hairs from the forehead of the beast were burned as a symbolic sacrifice. Part of the meat went to the priests as their perquisite; and part of the meat was returned to the worshipper. With his share he made a feast for his friends and his relations. One of the gods most commonly worshipped was Serapis. And when the invitations to the feast went out, they would read:

> " I invite you to dine with me at the table of our Lord Serapis."

Could a Christian share in a feast held in the temple of a heathen god? Even an ordinary meal in an ordinary house began with a libation, a cup of wine, poured out in honour of the gods. It was like grace before meat. Could a Christian become a sharer in a heathen act of worship like that? Again the Christian answer was clear. The Christian must cut himself off from his fellows rather than by his presence give approval to such a thing. A man had to be prepared to be lonely in order to be a Christian.

(iii) Worst of all, their Christianity was liable to disrupt their *home* life. It happened again and again that one member of a family became a Christian while the others did not. A wife might become a Christian while her husband did not. A son or a daughter might become a Christian while the rest of the family did not. Immediately there was a split in the family. Often the door was shut for ever in the face of the one who had accepted Christ. Christianity often came to send, not peace, but a sword which divided families in two. It was literally true that a man might have to love Christ more than he loved father or mother, wife, or brother or sister. Christianity often involved in those days a choice between a man's nearest and dearest and Jesus Christ.

Still further, the penalties which a Christian had to suffer were terrible beyond description. All the world knows of the Christians who were flung to the lions or burned at the stake; but these were kindly deaths. Nero wrapped the Christians in pitch and set them alight, and used them as living torches to light his gardens. He sewed them in the skins of wild animals and set his hunting dogs upon them to tear them to death. They were tortured on the rack; they were scraped with pincers; molten lead was poured hissing upon them; red hot brass plates were affixed to the tenderest parts of their bodies; eyes were torn out; parts of their bodies were cut off and roasted before their eyes; their hands and feet were burned while cold water was poured over them to lengthen the agony. These things are not pleasant to think about, but these are the things a man had to be prepared for, if he took his stand with Christ.

We may well ask why the Romans persecuted the Christians. It seems an extraordinary thing that anyone living a Christian life should seem a fit victim for persecution and death. There were two reasons.

(i) There were certain slanders which were spread abroad about the Christians, slanders for which the Jews were in no small measure responsible. (*a*) The Christians were accused of cannibalism. The words of the Last Supper— " This is my body." " This cup is the New Testament in my blood "—were taken and twisted into a story that the Christians sacrificed a child and ate the flesh. (*b*) The Christians were accused of immoral practices, and their meetings were said to be orgies of lust. The Christian weekly meeting was called the *Agapē*, the Love Feast; and the name was grossly misinterpreted. Christians greeted each other with the kiss of peace; and the kiss of peace became a ground on which to build the slanderous accusations. (*c*) The Christians were accused of being incendiaries. It is true that they spoke of the coming end of the world, and they clothed their message in the apocalyptic pictures of the end of the world in flames. Their slanderers took these words and twisted them into threats of political and revolutionary incendiarism. (d) The Christians were accused of tampering with family relationships. Christianity did in fact split families as we have seen; and so Christianity was represented as something which divided man and wife, and disrupted the home. There were slanders enough waiting to be invented by evil-and malicious-minded men.

(ii) But the great ground of persecution was in fact political. Let us think of the situation of the Roman Empire. The Roman Empire included almost the whole known world, from Britain to the Euphrates, and from Germany to North Africa. How could that vast amalgam of nations and peoples be somehow welded into one? Where could a unifying principle be found? At first it was found in the worship of the goddess Roma, the spirit of Rome. This was a worship which the provincial peoples were happy to give, for Rome had brought them peace and good government, and civil order and justice. The roads were cleared of brigands and the seas of pirates; the incalculable despots and tyrants had been banished by impartial Roman justice. The provincial was very willing to sacrifice to the spirit of the Empire which had done so much for him.

But this worship of Roma took a further step. There was one man who personified the Empire, one man in whom Roma might be felt to be incarnated, and that was the Emperor; and so the Emperor came to be regarded as a god, and divine honours came to be paid to him, and temples were raised to his divinity. The Roman government did not begin this worship; at first, in fact, it did all it could to discourage it. Claudius, the Emperor, said that he deprecated divine honours being paid to any human being. But as the years went on the Roman government saw in this Emperor-worship the one thing which could unify the vast Empire of Rome; here was the one centre on which they all could come together. So, in the end, the worship of the Emperor became, not voluntary, but compulsory. Once a year a man had to go and burn a pinch of incense to the godhead of Caesar and say, " Caesar is Lord." And that is precisely what the Christians refused to do. For them Jesus Christ was Lord, and to no man would they give that title which belonged to Christ.

It can be seen at once that Caesar-worship was far more a test of political loyalty than anything else. In actual fact when a man had burned his pinch of incense he received a certificate, a *libellus*, to say that he had done so, and then he could go and worship any god he liked, so long as his worship did not interfere with public order and decency. The Christians refused to conform. Confronted with the choice, " Caesar or Christ? " they uncompromisingly chose Christ. They utterly refused to compromise. The result was that, however good a man, however fine a citizen, a Christian was, he was automatically an outlaw. In the vast Empire Rome could not afford pockets of disloyalty, and that is exactly what every Christian congregation appeared to the Roman authorities to be. A poet has spoken of

" The panting, huddled flock whose crime was Christ."

The only crime of the Christian was that he set Christ above Caesar; and for that supreme loyalty the Christians died in their thousands, and faced torture for the sake of the lonely supremacy of Jesus Christ.

THE BLISS OF THE BLOOD-STAINED WAY

Matthew 5: 10-12 (*continued*)

WHEN we see how persecution arose, we are in a position to see the real glory of the martyr's way. It may seem an extraordinary thing to talk about the bliss of the persecuted; but for him who had eyes to see beyond the immediate present, and a mind to understand the greatness of the issues involved, there must have been a glory in that blood-stained way.

(i) To have to suffer persecution was an opportunity to show one's loyalty to Jesus Christ. One of the most famous of all the martyrs was Polycarp, the aged bishop of Smyrna. The mob dragged him to the tribunal of the Roman magistrate. He was given the inevitable choice—sacrifice to the godhead of Caesar or die. " Eighty and six years," came the immortal reply, " have I served Christ, and He has done me no wrong. How can I blaspheme my King who saved me? " So they brought him to the stake, and he prayed his last prayer: " O Lord God Almighty, the Father of Thy well-beloved and ever-blessed Son, by whom we have received the knowledge of Thee . . . I thank Thee that Thou hast graciously thought me worthy of this day and of this hour." Here was the supreme opportunity to demonstrate his loyalty to Jesus Christ.

In the First World War Rupert Brooke, the poet, was one of those who died too young. Before he went out to the battle he wrote:

> " Now God be thanked Who has matched us with His hour."

There are so many of us who have never in our lives made anything like a real sacrifice for Jesus Christ. The moment when Christianity seems likely to cost us something is the moment when it is open to us to demonstrate our loyalty to Jesus Christ in a way that all the world can see.

(ii) To have to suffer persecution is, as Jesus Himself said, the way to walk the same road as the prophets, and the saints, and the martyrs have walked. To suffer for the right is to gain a share in a great succession. The man who has to suffer something for his faith can throw back his head and say,

> " Brothers we are treading where the saints have trod."

(iii) To have to suffer persecution is to share in the great occasion. There is always something thrilling in even being present on the great occasion, in being there when something memorable and crucial is happening. There is an even greater thrill in having a share, however small, in the actual action of such an occasion. That is the feeling about which Shakespeare wrote so unforgettably in *Henry the Fifth* in the words he put into Henry's mouth before the battle of Agincourt:

> " He that shall live this day and see old age,
> Will yearly on the vigil feast his friends,
> And say, ' Tomorrow is Saint Crispian ':
> Then will he strip his sleeve and show his scars,
> And say, ' These wounds I had on Crispin's day.'
> . . . . . .
> And gentlemen in England now a-bed
> Shall think themselves accurs'd they were not here,
> And hold their manhoods cheap while any speaks
> That fought with us upon Saint Crispin's day."

When a man is called on to suffer something for his Christianity that is always a crucial moment; it is the great occasion; it is the clash between the world and Christ; it is a moment in the drama of eternity. To have a share in such a moment is not a penalty but a glory. " Rejoice at such a moment," says Jesus, " and be exceeding glad." The word for *be exceeding glad* is from the verb *agalliasthai* which has been derived from two Greek words which mean *to leap exceedingly*. It is the joy which leaps for joy. As it has been put, it is the joy of the climber who has reached the summit, and who leaps for joy that the mountain path is conquered.

(iv) To suffer persecution is to make things easier for those who are to follow. To-day we enjoy the blessing of liberty and freedom which we possess because men in the past were willing to buy them for us at the cost of blood, and sweat, and tears. They made it easier for us, and by a steadfast and immovable witness for Christ we may make it easier for others who are still to come. In the great

Boulder Dam scheme in America there were men who lost
their lives in that project which was to bring the water which
was to turn a dust bowl into fertile land. When the scheme
was completed, the names of those who had died were put
on a tablet and the tablet was put into the great wall of
the dam, and on it there was the inscription: " These died
that the desert might rejoice and blossom as the rose."
The man who fights his battle for Christ will always make
things easier for those who follow after. For them there
will be one less struggle to be encountered on the way.

(v) Still further, no man ever suffers persecution alone;
if a man is called upon to bear material loss, the failure of
friends, slander, loneliness, even the death of love for his
principles, he will not be left alone, for Christ will be
nearer to him than at any other time. The old story in
Daniel tells how Shadrach, Meshach and Abed-nego were
thrown into the furnace heated seven times hot because of
their refusal to move from their loyalty to God. The
courtiers watched. " Did we not cast three men, bound,
into the midst of the fire? " they asked. The reply was
that it was indeed so. Then came the astonished answer,
" Lo, I see four men, loose, walking in the midst of the
fire, and they have no hurt; *and the form of the fourth is like
the Son of God* " (*Daniel* 7: 19-25). As Browning had it in
Christmas Eve and Easter Day:

> " I was born sickly, poor and mean,
>   A slave; no misery could screen
>   The holders of the pearl of price
>   From Caesar's envy; therefore twice
>   I fought with beasts, and three times saw
>   My children suffer by his law;
>   At last my own release was earned;
>   I was some time in being burned,
>   But at the close a Hand came through
>   The fire above my head, and drew
>   My soul to Christ, whom now I see.
>   Sergius, a brother, writes for me
>   This testimony on the wall—
>   For me, I have forgot it all."

When a man has to suffer something for his faith, that is the way to the closest possible companionship with Christ.

There remains only one question to ask—why is this persecution so inevitable? It is inevitable because the Church, when it really is the Church, is bound to be the conscience of the nation and the conscience of society. Where there is good the Church must praise; where there is evil the Church must condemn—and inevitably men will try to silence the troublesome voice of conscience. It is not the duty of the individual Christian to find fault, to criticise, to condemn, but it may well be that his every action is a silent condemnation of the unchristian lives of others, and he will not escape their hatred.

It is not likely that death awaits us because of our oyalty to the Christian faith. But insult awaits the man who insists on Christian honour. Mockery awaits the man who practises Christian love and Christian forgiveness. Actual persecution may well await the Christian in industry who insists on doing an honest day's work. Christ still needs his witnesses; He needs those who are prepared, not so much to die for Him, as to live for Him. The Christian struggle and the Christian glory still exist.

THE SALT OF THE EARTH

Matthew 5: 13

> You are the salt of the earth. If the salt has become insipid, how can it regain its saltness? It is no longer good for anything but to be thrown out, and to be trampled on by men.

WHEN Jesus said this, He provided men with an expression which has become the greatest compliment that can be paid to any man. When we wish to stress someone's solid worth and usefulness, we say of him, " People like that are the salt of the earth."

In the ancient world salt was highly valued. The Greeks

called salt *divine* (*theion*). In a phrase, which in Latin is a kind of jingle, the Romans said, " There is nothing more useful than sun and salt." (*Nil utilius sole et sale.*) In the time of Jesus salt was connected in people's minds with three special qualities.

(i) Salt was connected with *purity*. No doubt its glistening whiteness made the connection easy. The Romans said that salt was the purest of all things, because it came from the purest of all things, the sun and the sea. Salt was indeed the most primitive of all offerings to the gods, and to the end of the day the Jewish sacrifices were offered with salt. So then, if the Christian is to be the salt of the earth he must be *an example of purity*. One of the characteristics of the world in which we live is the lowering of standards. Standards of honesty, standards of diligence in work, standards of conscientiousness, moral standards, all tend to be lowered. The Christian must be the person who holds aloft the standard of absolute purity in speech, in conduct, and even in thought. A certain writer dedicated a book to J. Y. Simpson " who makes the best seem easily credible." No Christian can depart from the standards of strict honesty. No Christian can think lightly of the lowering of moral standards in a world where the streets of every great city provide their deliberate enticements to sin. No Christian can allow himself the tarnished and suggestive jests which are so often part of social conversation. The Christian cannot withdraw from the world, but he must, as James said, " keep himself unspotted from the world " (*James* 1: 27).

(ii) In the ancient world salt was the commonest of all *preservatives*. It was used to keep things from going bad and rotten, and to hold decay and putrefaction at bay. Plutarch has a strange way of putting that. He says that meat is a dead body and part of a dead body, and will, if left to itself, go bad; but salt preserves it and keeps it fresh, and is therefore like a new soul inserted into a dead body. So then salt preserves from corruption. If the

Christian is to be the salt of the earth, he must have a certain antiseptic influence on life. We all know that there are certain people in whose company it is easy to be good; and that also there are certain people in whose company it is easy for standards to be relaxed. There are certain people in whose presence a soiled story would be readily told, and there are other people to whom no one would dream of telling such a tale. The Christian must be the cleansing antiseptic in any society in which he happens to be; he must be the person who by his presence defeats corruption and makes it easier for others to be good.

(iii) But the greatest and the most obvious quality of salt is that *salt lends flavour to things*. Food without salt is a sadly insipid and even a sickening thing. Christianity is to life what salt is to food. Christianity lends flavour to life. The tragedy is that so often people have connected Christianity with precisely the opposite. They have connected Christianity with that which takes the flavour out of life. Swinburne had it:

> " Thou hast conquered, O pale Galilaean; the world
> has grown gray from Thy breath."

Even after Constantine had made Christianity the religion of the Roman Empire, there came to the throne another Emperor called Julian, who wished to put the clock back and to bring back the old gods. His complaint, as Ibsen puts it, was:

> " Have you looked at these Christians closely? Hollow-
> eyed, pale-cheeked, flat-breasted all; they brood
> their lives away, unspurred by ambition: the sun
> shines for them, but they do not see it: the earth
> offers them its fulness, but they desire it not; all
> their desire is to renounce and to suffer that they
> may come to die."

As Julian saw it, Christianity took the vividness out of life.

Oliver Wendell Holmes once said, " I might have entered the ministry if certain clergymen I knew had not looked and acted so much like undertakers." Robert Louis

Stevenson once entered in his diary, as if he was recording an extraordinary phenomenon, " I have been to Church to-day, and am not depressed."

Men need to discover the lost radiance of the Christian faith. In a worried world, the Christian should be the only man who remains serene. In a depressed world, the Christian should be the only man who remains full of the joy of life. There should be a sheer sparkle about the Christian life; and too often the Christian dresses like a mourner at a funeral, and talks like a spectre at a feast. Wherever he is, if he is to be the salt of the earth, the Christian must be the diffuser of joy.

Jesus went on to say that, if the salt had become insipid, it was fit only to be thrown out and trodden on by men. This is difficult, because salt does not lose its flavour and its saltness. E. F. F. Bishop in his book *Jesus of Palestine* cites a very likely explanation given by Miss F. E. Newton. In Palestine the ordinary oven is out of doors and is built of stone on a base of tiles. In such ovens " in order to retain the heat a thick bed of salt is laid under the tiled floor. After a certain length of time the salt perishes. The tiles are taken up, the salt removed and thrown on the road outside the door of the oven . . . It has lost its power to heat the tiles and it is thrown out." That may well be the picture here. But the essential point remains whatever the picture, and it is a point which the New Testament makes and remakes again and again—uselessness invites disaster. If a Christian is not fulfilling his purpose as a Christian, then he is on the way to disaster. We are meant to be the salt of the earth, and if we do not bring to life the purity, the antiseptic power, the radiance that we ought, then we invite disaster.

It remains to be noted that sometimes the early Church made a very strange use of this text. In the Synagogue, among the Jews, there was a custom that, if a Jew became an apostate and then returned to the faith, before he was received back into the Synagogue, he must in penitence lie across the door of the Synagogue and invite people to trample upon him as they entered. In certain places the Christian Church took over that custom, and a Christian who had been ejected by discipline from the Church, was compelled, before he was received back, to lie at the door of the Church and to invite people as they entered, "Trample upon me who am the salt which has lost its savour."

THE LIGHT OF THE WORLD

Matthew 5: 14, 15

> You are the light of the world. A city which is situated on the top of a mountain cannot be hidden; nor do people light a lamp and put it under a bushel, but on a lampstand; and it gives light for all who are in the house.

It may well be said that this is the greatest compliment that was ever paid to the individual Christian, for in it Jesus commands the Christian to be what He Himself claimed to be. Jesus said, "As long as I am in the world, I am the light of the world" (*John* 9: 5). When Jesus commanded His followers to be the lights of the world, He demanded nothing less than that they should be like Himself.

When Jesus used this expression, He was using an expression which was quite familiar to the Jews who heard it for the first time. They themselves spoke of Jerusalem as " a light to the Gentiles," and a famous Rabbi was often called " a lamp of Israel." But the way in which the Jews used this expression will give us a key to the way in which Jesus also used it. Of one thing the Jews were very sure— no man kindled his own light. Jerusalem was indeed a light to the Gentiles, but " God lit Israel's lamp." The light with which the nation or the man of God shone was a borrowed light. It must be so with the Christian. It is not the demand of Jesus that we should, as it were, produce our own light.

We must shine with the reflection of His light. The radiance which shines from the Christian is lit by the presence of Christ within the Christian's heart. We often speak about *a radiant bride*, but the radiance which shines from her comes from the love which has been born within her heart.

When Jesus said that the Christian must be the light of the world, what did He mean?

(i) A light is first and foremost something which is meant to be seen. The houses in Palestine were very dark with only one little circular window perhaps not more than eighteen inches across. The lamp was like a sauce-boat filled with oil with the wick floating in it. It was not so easy to rekindle a lamp in the days before matches existed. Normally the lamp stood on the lampstand which would be no more than a roughly shaped branch of wood; but when people went out, for safety's sake, they took the lamp from its stand, and put it under a earthen bushel measure, so that it might burn without risk until they came back. The primary duty of the light of the lamp was to be seen.

So, then, Christianity is something which is meant to be seen. As someone has well said, " There can be no such thing as secret discipleship, for either the secrecy destroys the discipleship, or the discipleship destroys the secrecy." A man's Christianity should be perfectly visible to all men. Further, this Christianity should not be visible only within the Church. A Christianity whose effects stop at the church door is not much use to anyone. It should be even more visible in the ordinary activities of the world. Our Christianity should be visible in the way we treat a shop assistant across the counter, in the way we order a meal in a restaurant, in the way we treat our employees or serve our employer, in the way we play a game or drive or park a motor car, in the daily language we use, in the daily lierature we read. A Christian should be just as mucn a Christian in the factory, the workshop, the shipyard, the mine, the schoolroom, the surgery, the kitchen, the golf course, the playing field as he is in church. Jesus did not say, " You are the light of the *Church* "; He said, " You are the light of the *world*," and in a man's life in the world his Christianity should be evident to all.

(ii) A light is a guide. On the estuary of any river we may see the line of lights which marks the channel for the ships to sail in safety. We know how difficult even the city streets were when there were no lights. A light is something to make clear the way. So then a Christian must make the way clear to others. That is to say, a Christian must of necessity be an example. One of the things which this world needs more than anything else is people who are prepared to be foci of goodness. Suppose there is a group of people, and suppose it is suggested that some questionable thing should be done. Unless someone makes his protest the thing will be done. But if someone rises and says, " I will not be a party to that," another and another and another will rise to say, " Neither will I." But, unless they had been given the lead, they would have remained silent. There are many people in this world who have not the moral strength and courage to take a stand by themselves, but if someone gives them a lead, they will follow; if they have someone strong enough to lean on, they will do the right thing. It is the Christian's duty to take the stand which the weaker brother will support, to give the lead which those with less courage will follow. The world needs its guiding lights; there are people waiting and longing for a lead to take the stand and to do the thing which they do not dare to take and to do by themselves.

(iii) A light can often be a *warning light*. A light is often the warning which tells us to halt when there is danger ahead. It is sometimes the Christian's duty to bring to his fellowmen the necessary warning. That is often difficult, and it is often hard to do it in a way which will not do more harm than good; but one of the most poignant tragedies in life is for someone, especially a young person, to come and say to us, " I would never have been in the situation in which I now find myself, if you had only spoken in time." It was said of Florence Allshorn, the famous teacher and principal, that if she ever had occasion to rebuke her students, she did it " with her arm round about them." If our warnings are given, not in anger, not in irritation, not in criticism, not in condemnation, not in the desire to hurt, but in love, they will be effective.

The light which can be seen, the light which warns, the light which guides, these are the lights which the Christian must be.

SHINING FOR GOD

Matthew 5: 16

> Let your light so shine before men that they may see your good deeds and glorify your Father who is in the heavens.

THERE are two most important things here.

(i) Men are to see our *good* deeds. In Greek there are two words for *good*. There is the word *agathos* which simply defines a thing as good in quality; there is *kalos* which means that a thing is not only good, but that it is also winsome and beautiful and attractive. The word which is used here is *kalos*. The good deeds of the Christian must be not only *good*; they must be also *attractive*. There must be a certain winsomeness in Christian goodness. The tragedy of so much so-called goodness is that in it there is an element of hardness and coldness and austerity. There is a goodness which attracts and a goodness which repels. There is a charm in the Christian goodness which makes it a lovely thing.

(ii) It is further to be noted that our good deeds are meant to draw attention, not to ourselves, but to God. This saying of Jesus is a total prohibition of what someone has called " theatrical goodness." At a conference at which D. L. Moody was present there were also present some young people who took their Christian faith very seriously. One night they held an all night prayer meeting. As they were leaving it in the morning they met Moody, and he asked them what they had been doing. They told him; and then they went on: " Mr. Moody, see how our faces shine." Moody answered very gently: " Moses wist not that his face shone." The goodness which is conscious, which draws attention to itself, is not the Christian goodness.

One of the old historians wrote of Henry the Fifth after the Battle of Agincourt: " Neither would he suffer any ditties to be made and sung by the minstrels of his glorious victory, for that he would wholly have the praise and thanks altogether given to God." The Christian never thinks of what he has done, but of what God has enabled him to do. He never seeks to draw the eyes of men to himself, but always to direct them to God. So long as men are thinking of the praise, the thanks, the prestige which they will get for what they have done, they have not really even begun on the Christian way.

THE ETERNAL LAW

Matthew 5: 17-20

> Do not think that I have come to destroy the Law or the Prophets. I have not come to destroy them but to fulfil them. This is the truth I tell you—until the heaven and the earth shall pass away, the smallest letter or the smallest part of any letter shall not pass away from the Law, until all things in it shall be performed. So then, whoever will break one of the least of these commandments, and will teach others to do so, shall be called least in the Kingdom of the Heavens; but whoever will do them and will teach others to do them, he will be called great in the Kingdom of the Heavens. For I tell you, that you will certainly not enter into the Kingdom of Heaven, unless your righteousness goes beyond that of the Scribes and Pharisees.

At a first reading it might well be held that this is the most astonishing statement that Jesus made in the whole Sermon on the Mount. In this statement Jesus lays down the eternal character of the Law; and yet Paul can say, " Christ is the end of the Law " (*Romans* 10: 4). Again and again Jesus broke what the Jews called the Law. He did not observe the handwashings that the Law laid down; He healed sick people on the Sabbath, although the Law forbade such healings; He was in fact condemned and crucified as a law-breaker; and yet here He seems to speak of the Law with a veneration and a reverence that no Rabbi or Pharisee could exceed. The smallest letter—the letter which the Authorised Version calls the *jot*—was the Hebrew letter *iodh*. In form it was like an apostrophe— ' —; not even a letter not much bigger than a dot was to pass away. The smallest part of the letter—what the Authorised Version calls the *tittle*—is what we call the *serif*, the little projecting part at the foot of a letter, the little line at each side of the foot of, for example, the letter I. Jesus seems to lay it down that the law is so sacred that not the smallest detail of it will ever pass away.

Some people have been so puzzled by this saying that they have come to the conclusion that Jesus could not have said it. They have suggested that, since *Matthew* is the most Jewish of the gospels, and since Matthew wrote it specially to convince Jews, this is a saying which Matthew put into Jesus' mouth, and that this is not a saying of Jesus at all. But that is a weak argument, for this is a saying which is indeed so unlikely that no one would have invented it; it is so unlikely a saying that Jesus must have said it; and when we come to see what it means, we will see that it is inevitable that Jesus should have said it.

The Jews used the expression *The Law* in four different ways. (i) They used it to mean the Ten Commandments. (ii) They used it to mean the first five books of the Bible. That part of the Bible which is known as the *Pentateuch*—which literally means *The Five Rolls*—was to the Jew The

Law *par excellence* and was to them by far the most important part of the Bible. (iii) They used the phrase *The Law
and the Prophets* to mean the whole of Scripture; they used
it as a comprehensive description of what we would call
the whole Old Testament. (iv) They used it to mean the
Oral or the *Scribal Law.*

In the time of Jesus it was the last meaning which was
commonest; and it was in fact this Scribal Law which both
Jesus and Paul so utterly condemned. What, then, was
this Scribal Law?

In the Old Testament itself we find very few rules and
regulations; what we do find is great, broad principles
which a man must himself take and interpret under God's
guidance, and apply to the individual situations in life. In
the Ten Commandments we find no rules and regulations
at all; they are each one of them great principles out of
which a man must find his own rules for life. To the later
Jews these great principles did not seem enough. They held
that the Law was divine, and that in it God had said His
last word, and that therefore everything must be in it.
If a thing was not in the Law *explicitly* it must be there
implicitly. They therefore argued that out of the Law it
must be possible to deduce a rule and a regulation for every
possible man in every possible situation in life. So there
arose a race of men called the Scribes who made it the
business of their lives to reduce the great principles of the
Law to literally thousands upon thousands of rules and
regulations.

We may best see this in action. The Law lays it down
that the Sabbath Day is to be kept holy, and that on it no
work is to be done. That is a great principle. But these
Jewish legalists had a passion for definition. So they
asked: What is work? All kinds of things were classified
as work. For instance, *to carry a burden* on the Sabbath
Day is to work. But next a burden has to be defined. So
the Scribal Law lays it down that a burden is " food equal
in weight to a dried fig, enough wine for mixing in a goblet,

milk enough for one swallow, honey enough to put upon a wound, oil enough to anoint a small member, water enough to moisten an eye-salve, paper enough to write a customs house notice upon, ink enough to write two letters of the alphabet, reed enough to make a pen "—and so on endlessly. So they spent endless hours arguing whether a man could or could not lift a lamp from one place to another on the Sabbath, whether a tailor committed a sin if he went out with a needle in his robe, whether a woman might wear a brooch or false hair, even if a man might go out on the Sabbath with artificial teeth or an artificial limb, if a man might lift his child on the Sabbath Day. These things to them were the essence of religion. Their religion was a legalism of petty rules and regulations.

To write was to work on the Sabbath. But writing has to be defined. So the definition runs: " He who writes two letters of the alphabet with his right or with his left hand, whether of one kind or of two kinds, if they are written with different inks or in different languages, is guilty. Even if he should write two letters from forgetfulness, he is guilty, whether he has written them with ink or with paint, red chalk, vitriol, or anything which makes a permanent mark. Also he that writes on two walls that form an angle, or on two tablets of his account book so that they can be read together is guilty . . . But, if anyone writes with dark fluid, with fruit juice, or in the dust of the road, or in sand, or in anything which does not make a permanent mark, he is not guilty . . . If he writes one letter on the ground, and one on the wall of the house, or on two pages of a book, so that they cannot be read together, he is not guilty." That is a typical passage from the Scribal Law; and that is what the orthodox Jew regarded as true religion and the true service of God.

To heal was to work on the Sabbath. Obviously this has to be defined. Healing was allowed when there was danger to life, and especially in troubles of the ear, nose and throat; but even then, steps could be taken only to keep the patient from becoming worse; no steps might be taken to make him get any better. So a plain bandage might be put on a wound, but no ointment; plain wadding might be put into a sore ear, but not medicated wadding.

The *Scribes* were the men who worked out these rules and regulations. The *Pharisees*, whose name means *The Separated Ones*, were the men who had separated themselves from all the ordinary activities of life to keep all these rules and regulations.

We can see the length to which this went from the following facts. For many generations this Scribal Law was never written down; it was the *oral* law, and it was handed down in the memory of generations of Scribes. In the middle of the third century A.D. a summary of it was made and codified. That summary is known as the *Mishnah*; it contains sixty-three tractates on various subjects of the Law, and in English makes a book of almost eight hundred pages. Later Jewish scholarship busied itself with making commentaries to explain the *Mishnah*. These commentaries are known as the *Talmuds*. Of the Jerusalem *Talmud* there are twelve printed volumes; and of the Babylonian *Talmud* there are sixty printed volumes.

To the strict orthodox Jew, in the time of Jesus' religion, serving God was a matter of keeping thousands of legalistic rules and regulations; they regarded these petty rules and regulations as literally matters of life and death and eternal destiny. Clearly Jesus did not mean that not one of these rules and regulations was to pass away; repeatedly He broke them Himself; and repeatedly He condemned them; that is certainly not what Jesus meant by the Law, for that is the kind of law that both Jesus and Paul condemned.

THE ESSENCE OF THE LAW

Matthew 5: 17-20 (*continued*)

WHAT then did Jesus mean by the Law? He said that He had not come to destroy the Law, but to *fulfil* the Law.

That is to say, He came really to bring out the real meaning of the Law. What was the real meaning of the Law? Even behind the Scribal and Oral Law there was one great principle which the Scribes and the Pharisees had imperfectly and mistakenly grasped. The one great principle was that in all things a man must seek God's will, and that, when he knows it, he must dedicate his whole life to the obeying of it. The Scribes and Pharisees were right in seeking God's will, and profoundly right in dedicating their lives to obeying it; they were wrong in finding that will in their man-made hordes of rules and regulations.

What then is the real principle behind the whole Law, that principle which Jesus came to fulfil, that principle the true meaning of which He came to show?

When we look at the Ten Commandments, which are the essence and the foundation of all law, we can see that their whole meaning can be summed up in one word— *respect*, or even better, *reverence*. Reverence for God and for the name of God, reverence for God's day, respect for parents, respect for life, respect for property, respect for personality, respect for the truth and for another person's good name, respect for oneself so that wrong desires may never master us—these are the fundamental principles behind the Ten Commandments. The foundation principles of the Ten Commandments are reverence for God, and respect for our fellowmen and for ourselves. Without that fundamental reverence and respect there can be no such thing as law. It is on that that all law is based.

It is that reverence and respect which Jesus came to fulfil. He came to show men in actual life what reverence for God and respect for men is like. Justice, said the Greeks, consists in giving to God and to men that which is their due. Jesus came to show men in life what it means to give to God the reverence which is His due, and to give to men the respect which is their due.

That reverence and that respect did not consist in

obeying a multitude of petty rules and regulations. It consisted not in sacrifice, but in mercy; not in legalism but in love; not in prohibitions which demanded that men should not do things, but in commandments which bade them mould their lives on the positive commandment to love.

The reverence and the respect which are the basis of the Ten Comandments can never pass away; they are the permanent stuff of man's relationship to God and to his fellow-men.

THE LAW AND THE GOSPEL

Matthew 5: 17-20 *(continued)*

WHEN Jesus spoke as He did about the Law and the Gospel, He was implicitly laying down certain broad principles.

(i) He was saying that there is a definite continuation between the past and the present. We must never look on life as a kind of battle between the past and the present. The present grows out of the past. After Dunkirk, in the Second World War, there was a tendency on all hands to look for someone to blame for the disaster which had befallen the British forces, and there were many who wished to enter into bitter recriminations with those who had guided things in the past. At that time Mr. Winston Churchill, as he then was, said a very wise thing: " If we open a quarrel between the past and the present, we shall find that we have lost the future."

There had to be the Law before the gospel could come. Men had to learn the difference between right and wrong; men had to learn their own human inability to cope with the demands of the law, and to respond to the commands of God; men had to learn a sense of sin and unworthiness and inadequacy. Men blame the past for many things— and often rightly—but it is equally, and even more, necessary to acknowledge our debt to the past. As Jesus saw it, it is man's duty neither to forget nor to attempt to destroy the past, but to build upon the foundation of the past. We have entered into other men's labours, and we must so labour that other men will enter into ours.

(ii) In this passage Jesus very definitely warns men not to think that Christianity is easy. Men might say, " Christ is the end of the law; now I can do what I like." Men might think that all the duties, all the responsibilities, all the demands are gone. But it is Jesus' warning that the righteousness of the Christian must *exceed* the righteousness of the Scribes and Pharisees. What did He mean by that? The motive under which the Scribes and Pharisees lived was the motive of law; their one aim and their one desire was to satisfy the demands of the Law. Now, at least theoretically, it is perfectly possible to satisfy the demands of the law; in one sense there can come a time when a man can say, " I have done all that the law demands; my duty is discharged; the law has no more claim on me." But the motive under which the Christian lives is the motive of love; the Christian's one desire is to show his wondering gratitude for the love wherewith God has loved him in Jesus Christ. Now, it is not even theoretically possible to satisfy the claims of love. If we love someone with all our hearts, we are bound to feel that if we gave them a lifetime's service and adoration, if we offered them the sun and the moon and the stars, we would still not have offered enough. For love the whole realm of nature is an offering far too small.

The Jew aimed to satisfy the *law* of God; and to the demands of law there is always a limit. The Christian aims to show his gratitude for the *love* of God; and to the claims of love there is no limit in time or in eternity. Jesus set before men, not the law of God, but the love of God. Long ago Augustine said that the Christian life could be summed up in the one phrase: " Love God, and do what you like." But when we realize how God has loved us, the one desire of life is to answer to that love, and that is the greatest task in all the world, for it presents a man with a task the like of which the man who thinks in terms of law never dreams of, and with an obligation more binding than the obligation to any law.

THE NEW AUTHORITY

Matthew 5: 21-48

THIS section of the teaching of Jesus is one of the most important sections in the whole New Testament. Before we deal with it in detail in its sections, there are certain general things about it which we must note.

In it Jesus speaks with an authority which no other man had ever dreamed of using or assuming. The authority which Jesus assumed always amazed those who came into contact with Him. Right at the beginning of His ministry, after He had been teaching in the Synagogue in Capernaum, it is said of His hearers: " They were astonished at His teaching; for He taught them as one that had authority, and not as the Scribes " (*Mark* 1: 22). Matthew concludes his account of the Sermon on the Mount with the words: "And it came to pass when Jesus had ended these sayings, the people were astonished at His teaching; for He taught them as one having authority and not as the Scribes " (*Matthew* 7: 28, 29).

It is difficult for us to realize just how shocking a thing this authority of Jesus must have sounded to the Jews who listened to Him. To the Jew the Law was absolutely holy and absolutely divine; it is impossible to exaggerate the place that the Law had in their reverence. " The Law," said Aristeas, " is holy and has been given by God." " Only Moses' decrees," said Philo, " are everlasting, unchangeable and unshakable, as signed by nature herself with her seal." The Rabbis said, " Those who deny that the Law is from heaven have no part in the world to come." They said, " Even if one says that the Law is from God with the exception of this or that verse, which Moses, not God, spoke from his own mouth, then there applies to him the judgment. He has despised the word of the Lord: he has shown the irreverence which merits the destruction of the soul." The first act of every Synagogue service was the taking of the rolls of the Law from the ark in which they were stored, and the carrying of them round the congregation, that the congregation might show their reverence for them.

That is what the Jews thought of the Law; and now no fewer than five times (*Matthew* 5: 21, 27, 33, 38, 43) Jesus quotes the Law, only to contradict it, and to substitute a teaching of His own. He claimed the right to point out the inadequacies of the most sacred writings in the world, and to correct them out of His own wisdom. The Greeks defined *exousia*, authority, as " the power to add and the power to take away at will." Jesus claimed that power even with regard to that which the Jews believed to be the unchanging and unchangeable word of God. Nor did Jesus argue about this, or seek in any way to justify Himself for so doing, or seek to prove His right to do so. He calmly and without question assumed that right without argument.

No one had ever heard anything like this before. The great Jewish teachers had always had characteristic phrases in their teaching. The characteristic phrase of the prophet was: " Thus saith the Lord." He claimed no personal authority at all; his only claim was that what he spoke God had told him. The characteristic phrase of the Scribe and the Rabbi was: " There is a teaching that . . ." The Scribe or the Rabbi never dared to express even an opinion of his own unless he could buttress it with supporting quotations from the great teachers of the past. Independence was the last quality that he would claim. But to Jesus a statement required no authority other than the fact that He made it. He was His own authority.

Clearly one of two things must be true—either Jesus was mad, or He was unique; either He was a megalomaniac or else He was the Son of God. No ordinary person would dare to claim to take and to overturn that which up to his coming had been regarded as the eternal word of God.

Now the amazing thing about authority is that it is self-evidencing. No sooner does a man begin to teach than we know at once whether or not he has the right to teach. Authority is like an atmosphere about a man. He does not need to claim it; he either has it, or he has not got it. Orchestras which have played under Toscanini, the master conductor, say that as soon as he mounts the rostrum they can feel a wave of authority flowing from him. Julian Duguid tells how he once crossed the Atlantic in the same ship as Sir Wilfred Grenfell, and he says that when Grenfell came into one of the ship's public rooms, he could tell that he had entered the room without even looking around, for a wave of power and authority went out from the man. It was supremely so with Jesus.

Jesus took the highest wisdom of men and corrected it and readjusted it, because He was who He was. He did not need to argue; it was sufficient for Him to speak. No one can honestly face Jesus and honestly listen to Him without feeling that this is God's last word beside which all other words are inadequate, and all other wisdom out of date.

THE NEW STANDARD

Matthew 5: 21-48 (*continued*)

BUT startling as Jesus' accent of authority was, the standard which He put before men was more startling yet. Jesus said that in God's sight it was not only the man who committed murder who was guilty; the man who was angry with his brother was also guilty and liable to judgment. Jesus said that in God's sight it was not only the man who committed adultery who was guilty; the man who allowed the unclean desire to settle in his heart was also guilty. Here was something which was entirely new, something which men have not even yet fully grasped. It was Jesus' teaching that it was not enough not to commit murder; the only thing sufficient was never even to wish to commit murder. It was Jesus' teaching that it was not enough not to commit adultery; the only thing sufficient was never even to wish to commit adultery.

It may be that we have never struck a man; but who can say that he never *wished* to strike a man? It may be that we have never committed adultery; but who can say that he has never experienced the desire for the forbidden thing? It was Jesus' teaching that thoughts are just as important as deeds, and that it is not enough not to commit a sin; the only thing that is enough is not to *wish* to commit it. It was Jesus' teaching that a man is not judged only by his deeds, but that he is judged even more by the desires which never emerged in deeds. By the world's standards a man is a good man, if he never does a forbidden thing; the world is not concerned to judge his thoughts; by Jesus' standards a man is not a good man until he never even desires to do a forbidden thing; Jesus is intensely concerned with a man's thoughts. Three things emerge from this.

(i) Jesus was profoundly right, for Jesus' way is the only way to safety and to security. To some extent every man is a split personality. There is part of him which is attracted to good, and part of him which is attracted to evil. So long as a man is like that, an inner battle is going on inside him. One voice is inciting him to take the forbidden thing; the other voice is forbidding him to take it. Plato likened the soul to a charioteer whose task it was to drive two horses. The one horse was gentle and biddable and obedient to the reins and to the word of command; the other horse was wild and untamed and rebellious. The name of the one horse was reason; the name of the other horse was passion. Life is always a conflict between the demands of the passions and the control of the reason. The reason is the leash which keeps the passions in check. But, *a leash may snap at any time.* Self-control may be for a moment off its guard—

and then what may happen? So long as there is this inner tension, this inner strain, this inner conflict life must be for ever insecure. In such circumstances there can be no such thing as safety. The only way to safety, Jesus said, is to eradicate the desire for the forbidden thing for ever. Then and then alone life is safe.

(ii) If that be so, then God alone can judge men. We see only a man's outward actions; God alone sees the secret of his heart. And there will be many a man, whose outward actions are a model of rectitude, but whose inward thoughts stand condemned before God. There is many a man who can stand the judgment of men, which is bound to be a judgment of externals, but whose goodness collapses before the all-seeing eye of God.

(iii) And if that be so, it means that every one of us is in default; for there is none who can stand this judgment of God. Even if we have lived a life of outward moral perfection, there is none who can say that he never experienced the forbidden desire for the wrong things. For the inner perfection there is only one thing that is enough for a man to be able to say, that he himself is dead and Christ lives in him. " I am crucified with Christ," said Paul. " Nevertheless I live; yet not I, but Christ liveth in me " (*Galatians* 2: 20).

The new standard kills all pride, and forces us to Jesus Christ who alone can enable us to rise to that standard which He Himself has set before us.

THE FORBIDDEN ANGER

Matthew 5: 21, 22

You have heard that it was said by the people of the old days: You shall not kill; and whoever kills is liable to the judgment court. But I say unto you that everyone who is angry with his brother is liable to the judgment court; and he who says to his brother, " You brainless one! " is liable to judgment in the supreme court; and he who says to his brother, " You fool! " is liable to be cast into the Gehenna of fire.

THE GOSPEL OF MATTHEW

HERE is the first example of the new standard which Jesus takes. The ancient law had laid it down: " Thou shalt not kill " (*Exodus* 20: 13); but Jesus lays it down that even anger against a brother is forbidden. It is to be noted in the Authorised Version that the man who is condemned is the man who is angry with his brother *without a cause*, but the words *without a cause* are not found in any of the great manuscripts, and this is nothing less than a total prohibition of anger. It is not enough not to strike a man; the only thing that is enough is not even to wish to strike him; not even to have a hard feeling against him within the heart.

In this passage Jesus is arguing as a Rabbi might argue. He is showing that He was skilful in using the debating methods which the wise men of His time were in the habit of using. There is in this passage a neat gradation of anger, and an answering neat gradation of punishment.

(i) There is first the man who is *angry with his brother*. The verb here used is *orgizesthai*. In Greek there are two words for anger. There is *thumos*, which was described as being like the flame which comes from dried straw. It is the anger which quickly blazes up and which just as quickly dies down. It is an anger which rises speedily and which just as speedily passes. There is *orgē*, which was described as anger become inveterate. It is the long-lived anger; it is the anger of the man who nurses his wrath to keep it warm; it is the anger over which a person broods, and which he will not allow to die.

That anger is liable to *the judgment court*. The judgment court is the local village council which dispensed justice. That court was composed of the local village elders, and varied in number from three in villages of fewer than one hundred and fifty inhabitants, to seven in larger towns and twenty-three in still bigger cities.

So, then, Jesus condemns all selfish anger. The Bible is clear that anger is forbidden. " The wrath of man," said James, " worketh not the righteousness of God " (*James*

135

1: 20). Paul orders his people to put off all " anger, wrath, malice, insulting speaking " (*Colossians* 3: 5). Even the highest pagan thought saw the folly of anger. Cicero said that when anger entered into the scene " nothing could be done rightly and nothing sensibly." In a vivid phrase Seneca called anger " a brief insanity."

So Jesus forbids for ever the anger which broods, the anger which will not forget, the anger which refuses to be pacified, the anger which seeks revenge. If we are to obey Jesus, all anger must be banished from life, and especially that anger which lingers too long. It is a warning thing to remember that no man can call himself a Christian and lose his temper because of any personal wrong which he has suffered.

(ii) Then Jesus goes on to speak of two cases where anger turns into insulting words. The Jewish teachers forbade such anger and such words. They spoke of " oppression in words," and of " the sin of insult." They had a saying, " Three classes go down to Gehenna and return not—the adulterer, he who puts his neighbour openly to shame, and he who gives his neighbour an insulting name." Anger in a man's heart, and anger in a man's speech are equally forbidden.

WORDS OF INSULT

Matthew 5: 21, 22 (continued)

FIRST of all, the man who calls his brother *Raca* is condemned. *Raca* is an almost untranslatable word, because it describes a tone of voice more than anything else. Its whole accent is the accent of *contempt*. To call a man *Raca* was to call him a brainless idiot, a silly fool, an empty-headed blunderer. It is the word of one who despises another with an arrogant contempt. There is a Rabbinic tale of a certain Rabbi, Simon ben Eleazar. He was coming from his teacher's house, and he was feeling uplifted at the thought of his own scholarship and erudition and goodness. A very ill-favoured passer-by gave him a greeting. The Rabbi did not return the greeting, but said, " You Raca! How ugly you are! Are all the men of your town as ugly as you? " " That," said the passer-by, " I do not know. Go and tell the Maker who created me how ugly is the creature He has made." So there the sin of contempt was rebuked.

That sin of contempt is liable to an even severer judgment. It is liable to the judgment of the Sanhedrin (*sunedrion*), the supreme court of the Jews. This of course is not to be taken literally. It is as if Jesus said: " The sin of inveterate anger is bad; the sin of contempt is worse."

There is no sin quite so unchristian as the sin of contempt. There is a contempt which comes from pride of birth, and snobbery is in truth an ugly thing. There is a contempt which comes from place and from money, and pride in material things is also an ugly thing. There is a contempt which comes from knowledge, and of all snobberies intellectual snobbery is the hardest to understand, for no wise man was ever impressed with anything else than his own ignorance. We can never look with contempt on any man for whom Christ died.

(iii) Then Jesus goes on to speak of the man who calls his brother *mōros*. *Mōros* also means *fool*, but the man who is *mōros* is the man who is a *moral fool*. He is the man who is *playing the fool*. The Psalmist spoke of the fool who has said in his heart that there is no God (*Psalm* 14: 1). Such a man was a moral fool, a man who lived an immoral life, and who in wishful thinking said that there was no God. To call a man *mōros* was not to criticise his mental ability; it was to cast aspersions on his moral character; it was to take his name and reputation from him, and to brand him as a loose-living and immoral person.

So Jesus says that he who destroys his brother's name and reputation is liable to the severest judgment of all, the judgment of the *fire of Gehenna*.

Gehenna is a word with a history; often the Authorised Version translates it *hell*. The word was very commonly used by the Jews (*Matthew* 5: 22, 29, 30; 10: 28; 18: 9; 23: 15, 33; *Mark* 9: 43, 45, 47; *Luke* 12: 5; *James* 3: 6). It really means the Valley of Hinnom. The Valley of Hinnom was a valley to the south-west of Jerusalem. It was notorious as the place where Ahaz had introduced into Israel the fire worship of the heathen God Molech, to whom little children were burned in the fire. " He burned incense in the valley of the son of Hinnom, and burned his children in the fire " (2 *Chronicles* 28: 3). Josiah, the reforming king, had stamped out that worship, and had ordered that the valley should be for ever after an accursed place. " He defiled Topheth, which is in the valley of the children of Hinnom, that no man might make his son or daughter to pass the fire to Molech " (2 *Kings* 23: 10). In consequence of this the valley of Hinnom became the place where the refuse of Jerusalem was cast out and destroyed. It was a kind of public incinerator. Always the fire smouldered in it, and a pall of thick smoke lay over it, and it bred a loathsome kind of worm which was hard to kill (*Mark* 9: 44). So Gehenna, the valley of Hinnom, became identified in people's minds with all that was accursed and filthy, as the place where useless and evil things were destroyed. That is why it became a synonym for the place of God's destroying power, for hell.

So, then, Jesus insists that the gravest thing of all is to destroy a man's reputation and to take his good name away. No punishment is too severe for the malicious tale-bearer, or the gossip over the teacups which murders people's reputations. Such conduct, in the most literal sense, is a hell-deserving sin.

As we have said, all these gradations of punishment are not to be taken literally. What Jesus is saying here is this: " In the old days men condemned murder; and truly murder is for ever wrong. But I tell you that not only are a man's outward actions under judgment; his inmost thoughts are also under the scrutiny and the judgment of God. Long-lasting anger is bad; contemptuous speaking is worse, and the careless or the malicious talk which destroys a man's good name is worst of all." The man who is the slave of anger, the man who speaks in the accent of contempt, the man who destroys another's good name, may never have committed a murder in action, but he is a murderer at heart.

THE INSURMOUNTABLE BARRIER

Matthew 5: 23, 24

> So, then, if you bring your gift to the altar, and if you there remember that your brother has something against you, leave your gift there before the altar, and go, and first be reconciled to your brother, and then come and offer your gift.

WHEN Jesus said this, He was doing no more than recall the Jews to a principle which they well knew and ought never to have forgotten. The idea behind sacrifice was quite simple. If a man did a wrong thing, that action disturbed the relationship between him and God, and the sacrifice was meant to be the cure which restored that relationship.

But two most important things have to be noted. First, it was never held that sacrifice could atone for deliberate sin, for what the Jews called " the sins of a high hand." If a man committed a sin unawares, if he was swept into sin in a moment of passion when self-control broke, then sacrifice was effective; but if a man deliberately, defiantly, callously and open-eyed committed sin, then sacrifice was powerless to atone. Second, to be effective, sacrifice had to include confession of sin and true penitence; and true penitence involved the attempt to rectify any consequences sin might have had. The great Day of Atonement was held to make atonement for the sins of the whole nation, but the Jews were quite clear that not even the sacrifices of the Day of Atonement could avail for a man *unless he was first reconciled to his neighbour*. The breach between man and God could not be healed until the breach between man and man was healed. If a man was making a sin-offering, for instance, to atone for a theft, the offering was held to be completely unavailing until the thing stolen had been restored; and, if it was discovered that the thing had not been restored, then the sacrifice had to be destroyed as unclean and burned outside the Temple. The Jews were quite clear that a man had to do his utmost to put things right himself before he could be right with God.

In some sense sacrifice was substitutionary. The symbol of this was that, as the victim was about to be sacrificed, the worshipper placed his hands upon the beast's head, and pressed them down upon it, as if to transfer his own guilt to it. As he did so he said, " I entreat, O Lord; I have sinned, I have done perversely, I have rebelled; I have committed . . . (here the sacrificer specified his sins); but I return in penitence, and let this be for my covering."

If any sacrifice was to be valid, confession and restoration were involved. The picture which Jesus is painting is very vivid. The worshipper, of course, did not make his own sacrifice; he brought it to the priest who offered it on his behalf. The worshipper has entered the Temple; he has passed through its series of courts, the Court of the Gentiles, the Court of the Woman, the Court of the Men. Beyond that there lay the Court of the Priests into which the layman could not go. The worshipper is standing at the rail, ready to hand over his victim to the priest; his hands are on it to confess; and then he remembers his breach with his brother, the wrong done to his brother; if his sacrifice is to avail, he must go back and mend that breach and undo that wrong, or nothing can happen.

Jesus is quite clear about this basic fact—we cannot be right with God until we are right with men; we cannot hope for forgiveness until we have confessed our sin, not only to God, but also to men, and until we have done our

best to remove the practical consequences of it. We sometimes wonder why there is a barrier between us and God;
we sometimes wonder why our prayers seem unavailing.
The reason may well be that we ourselves have erected
that barrier, because we are at variance with our fellow-
men, or because we have wronged someone and have done
nothing to put things right.

MAKE PEACE IN TIME

Matthew **5: 25, 26**

> Get on to good terms again with your opponent, while
> you are still on the road with him, in case your
> opponent hands you over to the judge, and the judge
> hands you over to the court officer, and you be cast
> into prison. This is the truth I tell you—if that
> happens, you certainly will not come out until you
> have paid the last farthing.

HERE Jesus is giving the most practical advice; he is telling
men to get trouble sorted out in time, before it piles up
still worse trouble for the future.

Jesus draws a picture of two opponents on their way
together to the law courts; and He tells them to get things
settled and straightened out before they reach the court,
for, if they do not, and, if the law takes its course, there
will be still worse trouble for one of them at least in the
days to come.

The picture of two opponents on the way to court
together seems to us very strange, and indeed rather
improbable. But in the ancient world it often happened.

Under Greek law there was a process of arrest called
apagōgē, which means *summary arrest*. In it the plaintiff
himself arrested the defendant. He caught him by his robe
at the throat, and held the robe in such a way that, if he
struggled, he would strangle himself. Obviously the causes
for which such an arrest was legal were very few. The
malefactor had to be taken in the act, and caught red-
handed. The crimes for which a man might be summarily

arrested by anyone in this way were thieving, clothes-stealing (clothes-stealers were the curse of the public baths in ancient Greece), picking pockets, house-breaking and kidnapping (the kidnapping of specially gifted and accomplished slaves was very common in ancient Greece). Further, a man might be summarily arrested if he was discovered to be exercising the rights of a citizen when he had been disfranchised, or if he returned to his state or city after being exiled. In view of this custom it was by no means uncommon to see a plaintiff and a defendant on their way to court together in a Greek city.

Clearly it is much more likely that Jesus would be thinking in terms of Jewish law; nor was this situation by any means impossible under Jewish law. This is obviously a case of debt, for, if peace is not made, the last farthing will have to be paid. Such cases were settled by the local council of elders. A time was appointed when plaintiff and defendant had to appear together; in any small town or village there was every likelihood of them finding themselves on the way to the court together. When a man was adjudged guilty, he was handed over to the court officer. Matthew calls the officer the *huperētēs*; Luke calls him, in his version of the saying, by the more common term, *praktōr* (*Luke* 12: 58, 59). It was the duty of the court officer to see that the penalty was duly paid, and, if it was not paid, he had the power to imprison the defaulter, until it was paid. It is no doubt of that situation that Jesus was thinking. Jesus' advice may mean one of two things.

(i) It may be a piece of most practical advice. Again and again it is the experience of life that, if a quarrel, or a difference, or a dispute is not healed immediately, it can go on breeding worse and worse trouble as time goes on. Bitterness breeds bitterness. It has often happened that a quarrel between two people has descended to their families, and has been inherited by future generations, and has in the end succeeded in splitting a church or a society in two.

If at the very beginning one of the parties had had the grace to apologize or to admit fault, a very grievous situation need never have arisen. If ever we are at variance with someone else, we must get the situation put right straight away. It may mean that we must be humble enough to confess that we were wrong and to make apology; it may mean that, even if we were in the right, we have to take the first step towards healing the breach. When personal relations go wrong, in nine cases out of ten immediate action will mend them; but if that immediate action is not taken, they will continue to deteriorate, and the bitterness will spread in an ever-widening circle.

(ii) It may be that in Jesus' mind there was something more ultimate than this. It may be that He is saying, "Put things right with your fellowmen, *while life lasts*, for some day—you know not when—life will finish, and you will go to stand before God, the final Judge of all." The greatest of all Jewish days was the Day of Atonement. Its sacrifices were held to atone for sin known and unknown; but even this day had its limitations. The *Talmud* clearly lays it down: "The Day of Atonement does atone for the offences between man and God. The Day of Atonement does not atone for the offences between a man and his neighbour, unless the man has first put things right with his neighbour." Here again we have the basic fact—a man cannot be right with God unless he is right with his fellow-men. A man must so live that the end will find him at peace with all men.

It may well be that we do not need to choose between these two interpretations of this saying of Jesus. It may well be that both were in the mind of Jesus, and that what Jesus is saying is: "If you want happiness in time, and happiness in eternity, never leave an unreconciled quarrel or an unhealed breach between yourself and your brother man. Act immediately to remove the barriers which anger has raised."

THE FORBIDDEN DESIRE

Matthew 5: 27, 28

> You have heard that it has been said: You must not commit adultery. But I say to you that every one who looks at a woman in such a way as to waken within himself forbidden desires for her has already committed adultery with her within his heart.

HERE is Jesus' second example of the new standard. The Law laid it down: Thou shalt not commit adultery (*Exodus* 20: 14). So serious a view did the Jewish teachers take of adultery that the guilty parties could be punished by nothing less than death (*Leviticus* 20: 10); but once again Jesus lays it down that not only the forbidden action, but also the forbidden thought is guilty in the sight of God,

It is very necessary that we should understand what Jesus is saying here. He is not speaking of the natural, normal desire, which is part of human instinct and human nature. According to the literal meaning of the Greek the man who is condemned is the man who looks at a woman with the deliberate intention of lusting after her. The man who is condemned is the man who deliberately uses his eyes to awaken his lust, the man who looks in such a way that passion is awakened and desire deliberately stimulated.

The Jewish Rabbis well knew the way in which the eyes can be used to excite and to stimulate the wrong desire. They had their sayings. " The eyes and the hand are the two brokers of sin." " Eye and heart are the two handmaids of sin." " Passions lodge only in him who sees." " Woe to him who goes after his eyes for they are adulterous! " As someone has said, " There is an internal desire of which adultery is only the fruit."

In a tempting world there are many things which are deliberately designed to excite and to stimulate desire. There are books, pictures, plays, even advertisements, which are deliberately calculated to awaken and to stimulate desire. The man whom Jesus here condemns is the man who deliberately uses his eyes to stimulate his desires;

the man who finds a strange delight in things which waken the desire for the forbidden thing. To the pure all things are pure. But the man whose heart is defiled can look at any scene and find something in it to titillate, and stimulate, and excite the wrong desire.

THE SURGICAL CURE

Matthew 5: 29, 30

> If your right eye proves a stumbling-block to you, tear it out and throw it away from you; for it is better that one part of your body should be destroyed, than that your whole body should go away to Gehenna. If your right hand proves a stumbling-block to you, cut it off and throw it away from you; for it is better for you that one part of your body should be destroyed than that your whole body should go away to Gehenna.

HERE Jesus makes a great and a surgical demand. He insists that anything which is a cause of, or a seduction to, sin should be completely cut out of life.

The word he uses for a *stumbling-block* is interesting. It is the word *skandalon*. *Skandalon* is a form of the word *skandalēthron*, which means the *bait-stick* in a trap. It was the stick or arm on which the bait was fixed and which operated the trap to catch the animal lured to its own destruction. So the word came to mean *anything which causes a man's destruction*. Behind it there are two pictures. First, there is the picture of a hidden stone in a path against which a man may stumble, or of a cord stretched across a path, deliberately put there to make a man trip. Second, there is the picture of a pit dug in the ground and deceptively covered over with a thin layer of branches or of turf, and so arranged that, when the unwary traveller set his foot on it, he was immediately thrown into the pit. The *skandalon*, the *stumbling-block* is something which trips a man up, something which sends him crashing to destruction, something which lures him to his own ruin.

Of course, the words of Jesus are not to be taken with a crude literalism. What they mean is that anything which helps to seduce us to sin is to be ruthlessly rooted out of life. If in life there is a habit which can be a seduction to sin, if in life there is an association which can be the cause of sin, if in life there is a pleasure which could turn out to be our ruin, then that thing must be surgically excised from life.

Coming as it does immediately after the passage which deals with forbidden thoughts and desires, this passage compels us to ask: How shall we free and liberate ourselves from these unclean desires and defiling thoughts? It is the fact of experience that thoughts and pictures come unbidden into our minds, and it is the hardest thing on earth to shut the door to them.

There is one way in which these forbidden thoughts and desires cannot be dealt with—and that is to sit down and to say, I will not think of these things. The more we say, I will not think of such and such a thing, the more our thoughts are in fact concentrated on it. The outstanding example in history of the wrong way to deal with such thoughts and desires was the hermits and the monks in the desert in the time of the early Church. They were men who wished to free themselves from all earthly things, and especially of the desires of the body. To do so they went away into the Egyptian desert with the idea of living alone and thinking of nothing but God. The most famous of them all was Saint Anthony. He lived the hermit's life; he fasted; he did without sleep; he tortured his body. For thirty-five years he lived in the desert, and these thirty-five years were a non-stop battle, without respite, with his temptations. The story is told in his biography. " First of all the devil tried to lead him away from discipline, whispering to him the remembrance of his wealth, cares for his sister, claims of kindred, love of money, love of glory, the various pleasures of the table, and the other relaxations of life, and, at last, the difficulty of virtue and the labour of it. . .

The one would suggest foul thoughts, and the other counter them with prayers; the one fire him with lust, the other, as one who seemed to blush, fortify his body with prayers, faith and fasting. The devil one night even took upon him the shape of a woman, and imitated all her acts simply to beguile Anthony." So for thirty-five years the struggle went on.

The plain fact is that, if ever anyone was asking for trouble, Anthony and his friends were. It is the inevitable law of human nature that the more a man says he will not think of something, the more that something will present itself to his thoughts. There are only two ways to defeat the forbidden thoughts.

The first way is by Christian action. The best way to defeat such thoughts is to do something, to fill life so full with Christian labour and Christian service that there is no time for these thoughts to enter in, to think so much of others that in the end we entirely forget ourselves, to rid ourselves of a diseased and morbid introspection by concentrating not on ourselves but on other people. The real cure for evil thoughts is good action.

The second way is to fill the mind with good thoughts. There is a famous scene in Barrie's *Peter Pan*. Peter is in the children's bedroom; they have seen him fly; and they wish to fly too. They have tried it from the floor and they have tried it from the beds and the result is failure. " How do you do it? " John said. And Peter answered: " You just think lovely, wonderful thoughts and they lift you up in the air." The only way to defeat evil thoughts is to begin to think of something else.

If any man is harassed by thoughts of the forbidden and unclean things, he will certainly never defeat the evil things by withdrawing from life and saying, I will not think of these things. He can only do so by plunging into Christian action and Christian thought. He will never do it by trying to save his own life; he can only do it by flinging his life away for others.

THE BOND WHICH MUST NOT BE BROKEN

1. *Marriage amongst the Jews*

Matthew 5: 31, 32

It has been said: Let every man who divorces his wife give her a bill of divorcement. But I say to you that every one who divorces his wife for any other cause than fornication causes her to commit adultery; and anyone who marries a woman who has been so divorced himself commits adultery.

WHEN Jesus laid down this law for marriage He laid it down against a very definite situation. There is no time in history when the marriage bond stood in greater peril of almost total destruction than in the days when Christianity first came into this world. At that time the world was in danger of witnessing the break-up of marriage and the collapse of the home. Christianity had a double background. It had the background of the Jewish world, and of the world of the Romans and the Greeks. Let us look at Jesus' teaching against these two backgrounds.

Theoretically no nation ever had a higher ideal of marriage than the Jews had. Marriage was a sacred duty which a man was bound to undertake. He might delay or abstain from marriage for only one reason—to devote his whole time to the study of the Law. If a man refused to marry and to beget children he was said to have broken the positive commandment which bade men to be fruitful and to multiply, and he was said to have " lessened the image of God in the world," and " to have slain his posterity."

Ideally the Jew abhorred divorce. The voice of God had said, " I hate divorce " (*Malachi* 2: 16). The Rabbis had the loveliest sayings. " We find that God is long-suffering to every sin except the sin of unchastity." " Unchastity causes the glory of God to depart." " Every Jew must surrender his life rather than commit idolatry, murder or adultery." " The very altar sheds tears when a man divorces the wife of his youth."

The tragedy was that practice fell so far short of the ideal. One thing vitiated the whole marriage relationship. The woman in the eyes of the law was a thing. She was at the absolute disposal of her father or of her husband. She had to all intents and purposes no legal rights at all. To all intents and purposes a woman could not divorce her husband for any reason, and a man could divorce his wife for any cause at all. "A woman," said the Rabbinic law, "may be divorced with or without her will; but a man only with his will."

The matter was complicated by the fact that the Jewish law of divorce was very simple in its expression and very debatable in its meaning. It is stated in *Deuteronomy* 24: 1: "When a man hath taken a wife and married her, and it comes to pass that she find no favour in his sight, because he hath found some uncleanness in her, let him write her a bill of divorcement, and send her out of his house." The process of divorce was extremely simple. The bill of divorcement simply ran:

> "Let this be from me thy writ of divorce and letter of dismissal and deed of liberation, that thou mayest marry whatsoever man thou wilt."

All that had to be done was to hand that document to the woman in the presence of two witnesses and she stood divorced.

Clearly the crux of this matter lies in the interpretation of the phrase *some uncleanness*. In all matters of Jewish law there were two schools. There was the school of Shammai, which was the strict, severe, austere school; and there was the school of Hillel which was the liberal, broad-minded, generous school. Shammai and his school defined *some uncleanness* as meaning unchastity and nothing but unchastity. "Let a wife be as mischievous as the wife of Ahab," they said, "she cannot be divorced except for adultery." To the school of Shammai there was no possible ground of divorce except only adultery and unchastity. On the other hand the school of Hillel defined *some uncleanness* in the widest possible way. They said that it meant that a man could divorce his wife if she spoiled his dinner by putting too much salt in his food, if she went in public with her head uncovered, if she talked with men in the streets, if she was a brawling woman, if she spoke disrespectfully of her husband's parents in his presence, if she was troublesome or quarrelsome. A certain Rabbi Akiba said that the phrase, if she find no favour in his sight, meant that a man might divorce his wife if he found a woman whom he considered to be more attractive than his wife.

Human nature being such as it is, it is easy to see which school would have the greater influence. In the time of Jesus divorce had grown easier and easier, so that a situation had arisen in which girls were actually unwilling to marry, because marriage was so insecure.

When Jesus said this, He was not speaking as some theoretical idealist; He was speaking as a practical reformer. He was seeking to deal with a situation in which the structure of family life was collapsing, and in which national morals were becoming ever more immoral.

THE BOND THAT CANNOT BE BROKEN

2. Marriage amongst the Greeks

Matthew 5: 31, 32

WE have seen the state of marriage in Palestine in the time of Jesus, but the day was soon to come when Christianity would go out far beyond Palestine, and it is necessary that we should look at the state of marriage in that wider world into which the teachings of Christianity were to go forth.

First then, let us look at marriage amongst the Greeks. Two things vitiated the marriage situation in the Greek world.

A. W. Verrall, the great classical scholar, said that one of the chief diseases from which ancient civilization died was a low view of woman. The first thing which wrecked the

marriage situation among the Greeks was the fact that
relationships outside marriage carried no stigma whatsoever, and were in fact the accepted and the expected thing.
Such relationships brought not the slightest discredit;
they were part of the ordinary routine of life. Demosthenes
laid it down as the accepted practice of life: " We have
courtesans for the sake of pleasure; we have concubines for
the sake of daily cohabitation; we have wives for the
purpose of having children legitimately, and of having a
faithful guardian for all our household affairs." In later
days, when Greek ideas had penetrated into, and had
ruined Roman morality, Cicero in his speech *In defence of
Caelius* says, " If there is anyone who thinks that young
men should be absolutely forbidden the love of courtesans
he is indeed extremely severe. I am not able to deny the
principle that he states. But he is at variance, not only
with the licence of his own age, but also from the customs
and concessions of our ancestors. When indeed was this
not done? When did anyone ever find fault with it? When
was permission denied? When was it that that which is
now lawful was not lawful? " It is Cicero's plea, as it was
the statement of Demosthenes, that relationships outside
marriage were the ordinary and the conventional thing.

The Greek view of marriage was an extraordinary
paradox. The Greek demanded that the respectable woman
should live such a life of seclusion that she could never
even appear on the street alone, and that she did not even
have her meals in the apartments of the men. She had no
part even in social life. From his wife the Greek demanded
the most complete moral purity; for himself he demanded
the utmost immoral licence. To put it bluntly, the Greek
married a wife for domestic security, but he found his
pleasure elsewhere. Even Socrates said, " Is there anyone
to whom you entrust more serious matters than to your
wife, and is there anyone to whom you talk less? " Verus,
the colleague of Marcus Aurelius in the imperial power, was
blamed by his wife for associating with other women. His

answer was that she must remember that the name of wife was a title of dignity, not of pleasure.

So, then, in Greece an extraordinary situation arose. The Temple of Aphrodite at Corinth had a thousand priestesses, who were sacred courtesans; they came down to the streets of Corinth at evening time so that it became a proverb: "Not every man can afford a journey to Corinth." This amazing alliance of religion with prostitution can be seen in an almost incredible way in the fact that Solon was the first to allow the introduction of prostitutes into Athens and the building of brothels, and with the profits of the brothels a new temple was built to Aphrodite the goddess of love. The Greeks saw nothing wrong in the building of a temple with the proceeds of prostitution.

But apart altogether from the practice of common prostitution there arose in Greece an amazing class of women called the *hetairai*. They were the mistresses of famous men; they were easily the most cultured and socially accomplished women of their day; their homes were nothing less than salons; and many of their names go down in history with as much fame as the great men with whom they associated. Thais was the *hetaira* of Alexander the Great; on Alexander's death she married Ptolemy, and became the mother of the Egyptian royal family. Aspasia was the *hetaira* of Pericles, perhaps the greatest ruler and orator Athens ever had; and it is said that she taught Pericles his oratory and wrote his speeches for him. Epicurus, the famous philosopher, had his equally famous Leontinium. Socrates had his Diotima. The way in which these women were regarded can be seen from the visit that Socrates paid to Theodota, as Xenophon tells of it. He went to see if she was as beautiful as she was said to be. He talked kindly to her; he told her that she must shut the door against the insolent; that she must care for her lovers in their sicknesses, and rejoice with them when honour came to them, and that she must tenderly love those who gave their love to her.

Here, then, in Greece we see a whole social system based on relationships outside marriage; we see that these relationships were accepted as natural and normal, and not in the least blameworthy; we see that these relationships could, in fact, become the dominant thing in a man's life. We see an amazing situation in which Greek men kept their wives completely and absolutely secluded in a compulsory purity, while they themselves found their real pleasure and their real life in relationships outside marriage.

The second thing which vitiated the situation in Greece was that divorce required no legal process whatsoever. All that a man had to do was to dismiss his wife in the presence of two witnesses. The one saving clause was that he must return her dowry intact.

It is easy to see what an incredible novelty the Christian teaching regarding chastity and fidelity in marriage was in a civilization like that.

THE BOND THAT CANNOT BE BROKEN

3. Marriage amongst the Romans

Matthew 5: 31, 32 (continued)

The history of the development of the marriage situation amongst the Romans is the history of a tragedy. The whole of Roman religion and society was originally founded on the home. The basis of the whole Roman commonwealth was the *patria potestas*, the father's power; the father had literally the power of life and death over his family. A Roman son never came of age so long as his father was alive. He might be a consul; he might have reached the highest honour and office the state could offer, so long as his father was alive he was still within his father's power. To the Roman the home was everything. The Roman matron was not secluded like her Greek counterpart. She took her full part in life. " Marriage," said Modestinus, the Latin jurist, " is a life-long fellowship of all divine and human rights." Prostitutes, of course, there were, but they were held in contempt and to associate with them was dishonourable. There was, for instance, a Roman magistrate who was assaulted in a house of ill-fame, and who refused to prosecute or to go to law about the case, because to do so would have been to admit that he had been in such a place. So high was the standard of Roman morality that for the first five hundred years of the Roman commonwealth there was not one single recorded case of divorce. The first man to divorce his wife was Spurius Carvilius Ruga in the year 234 B.C., and he did so because she was childless and he desired a child.

Then there came the Greeks. In the military and the imperial sense Rome conquered Greece; but in the moral and the social sense Greece conquered Rome. By the second century B.C. Greek morals had begun to infiltrate into Rome, and the descent was catastrophic. Divorce became as common as marriage. Seneca speaks of women who were married to be divorced and who were divorced to be married. He tells of women who identified the years, not by the names of the consuls, but by the names of their husbands. Juvenal writes: " Is one husband enough for Iberina? Sooner will you prevail upon her to be content with one eye." He cites the case of a woman who had eight husbands in five years. Martial cites the case of a woman who had ten husbands. A Roman orator, Metillus Numidicus, made an extraordinary speech: " If, Romans, it were possible to love without wives, we would be free from trouble; but since it is the law of nature that we can neither live pleasantly with them, nor at all without them, we must take thought for the continuance of the race rather than for our own brief pleasure." Marriage had become nothing more than an unfortunate necessity. There was a cynical Roman jest: " Marriage brings only two happy days—the day when the husband first clasps his wife to his breast, and the day when he lays her in the tomb."

To such a pass did things come that special taxes were levied on the unmarried, and the unmarried were prohibited from entering into inheritances. Special privileges were given to those who had children, for children were regarded as a disaster. The very law was manipulated in an attempt to rescue the necessary institution of marriage.

There lay the Roman tragedy, what Lecky called "that outburst of ungovernable and almost frantic depravity which followed upon the contact with Greece." Again it is easy to see with what a shock the ancient world must have heard the demands of Christian chastity.

We shall leave the discussion of the ideal of Christian marriage until we come to *Matthew* 19: 3-9. At the present we must simply note that with Christianity there had come into the world an ideal of chastity of which men did not dream.

A WORD IS A PLEDGE

Matthew 5: 33-37

> You have heard that it was said by the people of the old days: You shall not take an oath falsely, but you shall pay your oath in full to the Lord. But I say to you: Do not swear at all, neither by heaven, for it is the throne of God, nor by the earth, for it is the footstool of his feet, nor by Jerusalem, for it is the city of the Great King, nor by your head, for you cannot make one hair black or white. When you say, Yes, let it be yes; and when you say, No, let it be no. Anything which goes beyond that has its source in evil.

ONE of the strange things about the Sermon on the Mount is the number of occasions in it when Jesus was recalling to the Jews that which they already knew. The Jewish teachers had always insisted on the paramount obligation of telling the truth. "The world stands fast on three things, on justice, on truth, and on peace." "Four persons are shut out from the presence of God—the scoffer, the hypocrite, the liar, and the retailer of slander." "One who has given his word and who changes it is as bad as an idolater." The school of Shammai was so wedded to the truth that they forbade the ordinary courteous politenesses of society, as, for instance, when a bride was complimented for her charming appearance when in fact she was but ill-favoured!

Still more did the Jewish teachers insist on the truth, if the truth had been guaranteed by an oath. Repeatedly that principle is laid down in the New Testament. The commandment has it: "Thou shalt not take the name of the Lord, Thy God, in vain; for the Lord will not hold him guiltless that taketh His name in vain" (*Exodus* 20: 7). That commandment has nothing to do with swearing in the sense of using bad language; it condemns the man who swears that something is true, or who makes some promise, in the name of God, and who has taken the oath falsely. "If a man vow a vow unto the Lord, or swear an oath to bind his soul with a bond, he shall not break his word, he shall do according to all that proceedeth out of his mouth" (*Numbers* 30: 2). "When thou shalt vow a vow unto the Lord thy God, thou shalt not slack to pay it; for the Lord thy God shall surely require it of thee; and it would be sin in thee" (*Deuteronomy* 23: 21, 22).

But in the time of Jesus there were two unsatisfactory things about taking oaths.

The first was what might be called *frivolous swearing*, taking an oath where no oath was necessary or proper. It had become far too common a custom to introduce a statement by saying, "By thy life," or, "By my head," or, "May I never see the comfort of Israel if . . ." The Rabbis laid it down that to use any form of oath in a simple statement like: "That is an olive tree," was sinful and wrong. "The yes of the righteous is yes," they said, "and their no is no." There is still need of warning here. Far too often people use the most sacred language in the most meaningless way. They take the sacred names and the sacred things upon their lips in the most thoughtless and irreverent way. The sacred names should be kept for sacred things.

The second Jewish custom was in some ways even worse than that; it might be called *evasive swearing*. The Jews divided oaths into two classes, those which were absolutely binding and those which were not. Any oath which contained the name of God was absolutely binding; any oath which succeeded in evading the name of God was held not to be binding. The result was that if a man swore by the name of God in any form, he would rigidly keep that oath; but if he swore by heaven, or by earth, or by Jerusalem, or by his head, he felt quite free to break that oath. The result was that evasion had been brought to a fine art.

The idea behind this was that, if God's name was used, God became a partner in the transaction; whereas if God's name was not used, God had nothing to do with the transaction. The principle which Jesus lays down is quite clear. In effect Jesus is saying that, so far from having to make God a partner in any transaction, no man can keep God out of any transaction. God is already there. The heaven is the throne of God; the earth is the footstool of God; Jerusalem is the city of God; a man's head does not belong to him; he cannot even make a hair white or black; his ife is God's; there is nothing in the world which does not belong to God; and, therefore, whether God is actually named in so many words or not, does not matter. God is there already.

Here is a great eternal truth. Life cannot be divided into compartments in some of which God is involved and in others of which he is not involved; there cannot be one kind of language in the Church and another kind of language in the shipyard or the factory or the office; there cannot be one kind of standard of conduct in the Church and another kind of standard in the business world. The fact is that God does not need to be invited into certain departments of life, and kept out of others. He is everywhere, all through life and every activity of life. He hears not only the words which are spoken in His name; He hears all words; and there cannot be any such thing as a form of words which evades bringing God into any transaction. We will regard all promises as sacred, if we remember that all promises are made in the presence of God.

THE END OF OATHS

Matthew 5: 33-37 (*continued*)

THIS passage concludes with the commandment that when a man has to say yes, he should say yes, and nothing more; and when he has to say no, he should say no, and nothing more.

The ideal is that a man should never need an oath to buttress or guarantee the truth of anything he may say. The man's character should make an oath completely unnecessary. His guarantee and his witness should lie in what he is himself. Isocrates, the great Greek teacher and orator, said, "A man must lead a life which will gain more confidence in him than ever an oath can do." Clement of Alexandria insisted that Christians must lead such a life and demonstrate such a character that no one will ever dream of asking an oath from them. The ideal society is one in which no man's word will ever need an oath to guarantee its truth, and no man's promise ever need an oath to guarantee its fulfilling.

Does this saying of Jesus then forbid a man to take an oath anywhere, for instance, in the witness box? There have been two sets of people who completely refused all oaths. There were the Essenes, an ancient sect of the Jews. Josephus writes of them: " They are eminent for fidelity and are ministers of peace. Whatsoever they say also is firmer than an oath. Swearing is avoided by them and they esteem it worse than perjury. For they say that he who cannot be believed without swearing is already condemned." There were, and still are, the Quakers. The Quakers will not in any situation submit to taking an oath.

The utmost length to which George Fox would go was to use the word *Verily*. He writes: " I never wronged man or woman in all that time (the time that he worked in business). While I was in that service, I used in my dealings the word *Verily*, and it was a common saying, ' If George Fox says *Verily*, there is no altering him.' " In the ancient days the Essenes would not in any circumstances take an oath, and to this day the Quakers are the same.

Are they correct in taking this line in this matter? There were occasions when Paul took an oath, and, as it were, put himself upon oath. " *I call God for a record on my soul*," he writes to the Corinthians, " that to spare you I came not again to Corinth " (2 *Corinthians* 1: 23). " Now the things that I write unto you," he writes to the Galatians, "behold, *before God, I lie not* " (*Galatians* 1: 20). On these occasions Paul is putting himself on oath. Jesus Himself did not protest at being put upon oath. At his trial before the High Priest, the High Priest said to Him: " I adjure you by the living God—I put you on oath by God Himself—that Thou tell us whether Thou be the Christ, the Son of God " (*Matthew* 26: 63). What then is the situation?

Let us look at the last part of this verse. The Authorised Version has it that a man must answer simply yes or no, " for whatsoever is more than these cometh of evil, anything that goes beyond that has its source in evil." What does that mean? It can mean one of two things.

(*a*) If it is necessary to take an oath from a man, that necessity arises from the evil that is in man. If there was no evil in man, no oath would be necessary. That is to say, the fact that it is sometimes necessary to make a man take an oath is a demonstration of the evil in Christless human nature.

(*b*) The fact that it is necessary to put men on oath on certain occasions arises from the fact that this is an evil world. In a perfect world, in a world which was the Kingdom of God, no taking of oaths would ever be necessary. It is necessary only because of the evil of the world.

THE GOSPEL OF MATTHEW

What Jesus is saying is this—the truly good man will never need to take an oath; the truth of his sayings and the reality of his promises need no such guarantee. But the fact that oaths are still sometimes necessary is the proof that men are not good men and that this is not a good world.

So, then, this saying of Jesus leaves two obligations upon us. It leaves upon us the obligation to make ourselves such that men will so see our transparent goodness that they will never ask an oath from us; and it leaves upon us the obligation to seek to make this world such a world that falsehood and infidelity will be so eliminated from it that the necessity for oaths will be abolished.

THE ANCIENT LAW

Matthew 5: 38-42

> You have heard that it has been said: An eye for an eye, and a tooth for a tooth. But I tell you not to resist evil; but if anyone strikes you on the right cheek, turn the other to him also; and if anyone wishes to obtain judgment against you for your tunic, give him your cloak also; and if anyone impresses you into the public service to go a mile, go with him two miles. Give to him who asks you, and do not turn away from him who wishes to borrow from you.

THERE are few passages of the New Testament which have more of the essence of the Christian ethic in them than this passage has. Here is the characteristic ethic of the Christian life, and the conduct which should distinguish the Christian from other men.

Jesus begins by citing the oldest law in the world— an eye for an eye, and a tooth for a tooth. That law is known as the *Lex Talionis*, and it may be described as the law of tit for tat. It appears in the earliest known code of laws, the Code of Hammurabi, who reigned in Babylon from 2285 to 2242 B.C. The Code of Hammurabi makes a curious distinction between the gentleman and the workman. " If a man has caused the loss of a gentleman's eye,

160

THE GOSPEL OF MATTHEW

his eye one shall cause to be lost. If he has shattered a gentleman's limb, one shall shatter his limb. If he has caused a poor man to lose his eye, or shattered a poor man's limb, he shall pay one mina of silver . . . If he has made the tooth of a man who is his equal fall out, one shall make his tooth fall out. If he has made the tooth of a poor man fall out, he shall pay one third of a mina of silver." The principle is clear and apparently simple—if a man has inflicted an injury on any person, an equivalent injury shall be inflicted upon him.

That law became part and parcel of the ethic of the Old Testament. In the Old Testament we find it laid down no fewer than three times. " If any mischief follow, then thou shalt give life for life, eye for eye, tooth for tooth, hand for hand, foot for foot, burning for burning, wound for wound, stripe for stripe " (*Exodus* 21: 23-25). " If a man cause a blemish in his neighbour, as he hath done, so shall it be done unto him, breach for breach, eye for eye, tooth for tooth; as he hath caused a blemish in a man, so it shall be done to him again " (*Leviticus* 24: 19, 20). "And thine eye shall not pity, but life shall go for life, eye for eye, tooth for tooth, hand for hand, foot for foot " (*Deuteronomy* 19: 21). These laws are often quoted as amongst the blood-thirsty, savage and merciless laws of the Old Testament; but before we begin to criticise the Old Testament certain things must be noted.

(i) The *Lex Talionis*, the law of tit for tat, so far from being a savage and bloodthirsty law, is in fact *the beginning of mercy*. Its original aim was definitely *the limitation of vengeance*. In the very earliest days the vendetta and the blood feud were characteristic of tribal society. If a man of one tribe injured a man of another tribe, then at once *all* the members of the tribe of the injured man were out to take vengeance on *all* the members of the tribe of the man who committed the injury; and the vengeance desired was nothing less than death. *This law deliberately limits vengeance.* It lays it down that only the man who com-

THE GOSPEL OF MATTHEW

mitted the injury must be punished, and his punishment
must be no more than the equivalent of the injury he has
inflicted and the damage he has done. Seen against its
historical setting this is not a savage law, but a law of
mercy.

(ii) Further, this was never a law which gave a *private
individual* the right to extract vengeance; it was always a
law which laid down how a *judge* in the law court must
assess punishment and penalty (cp. *Exodus* 19: 18). This
law was never intended to give the individual person the
right to indulge even in the vengeance of tit for tat. It was
always intended as a guide for a judge in the assessment of
the penalty which any violent or unjust deed must receive.

(iii) Still further, this law was never, at least in any
even semi-civilized society, carried out literally. The
Jewish jurists argued rightly that to carry it out literally
might in fact be the reverse of justice, because it obviously
might involve the displacement of a good eye or a good
tooth for a bad eye or a bad tooth. And very soon the
injury done was assessed at a money value; and the
Jewish law in the tractate *Baba Kamma* carefully lays
down how the damage is to be assessed. If a man has
injured another, he is liable on five counts—for injury,
for pain, for healing, for loss of time, for indignity suffered.
In regard to *injury*, the injured man is looked on as a slave
to be sold in the market place. His value *before* and *after*
the injury was assessed, and the man responsible for the
injury had to pay the difference. He was responsible for
the loss in value of the man injured. In regard to *pain*, it
was estimated how much money a man would accept to be
willing to undergo the pain of the injury inflicted, and the
man responsible for the injury had to pay that sum. In
regard to *healing*, the injurer had to pay all the expenses
of the necessary medical attention, until a complete cure
had been effected. In regard to *loss of time*, the injurer had
to pay compensation for the wages lost while the injured
man was unable to work, and he had also to pay compen-

sation if the injured man had held a well paid position, and was now, in consequence of the injury, fit for less well rewarded work. In regard to *indignity*, the injurer had to pay damages for the humiliation and indignity which the injury had inflicted. In actual practice the type of compensation which the *Lex Talionis* laid down is strangely modern.

(iv) And most important of all, it must be remembered that the *Lex Talionis* is by no means the whole of Old Testament ethics. There are glimpses and even splendours of mercy in the Old Testament. " Thou shalt not avenge or bear any grudge against the children of thy people " (*Leviticus* 19: 18). " If thine enemy be hungry, give him bread to eat; and if he be thirsty, give him water to drink " (*Proverbs* 25: 21). " Say not, I will do so to him as he hath done to me " (*Proverbs* 24: 29). " He giveth his cheek to the smiter; he is filled with reproach " (*Lamentations* 3: 30). There is abundant mercy in the Old Testament too.

So, then, ancient ethics were based on the law of tit for tat. It is true that that law was a law of mercy; it is true that it was a law for a judge and not for a private individual; it is true that it was never literally carried out; it is true that there were accents of mercy speaking at the same time. But Jesus obliterated the very principle of that law, because retaliation, however controlled and restricted, has no place in the Christian life.

THE END OF RESENTMENT AND OF RETALIATION

Matthew 5: 38-42 (*continued*)

So, then, for the Christian Jesus abolishes the old law of limited vengeance and introduces the new spirit of non-resentment and of non-retaliation. He goes on to take three examples of the Christian spirit in operation. To take these examples with a crude and ununderstanding literalism is completely to miss their point. It is therefore very necessary to understand what Jesus is saying.

(i) He says that if anyone smites us on the right cheek we must turn to him the other cheek also. There is far more here than meets the eye, far more than a mere matter of blows on the face. Suppose a right-handed man is standing in front of another man, and suppose he wants to slap the other man on the right cheek, how must he do it? Unless he goes through the most complicated contortions, and unless he empties the blow of all force, he can only hit the other man's cheek in one way—*with the back of his hand*. Now according to Jewish Rabbinic law to hit a man with the *back* of the hand was twice as insulting as to hit him with the *flat* of the hand. There is a doubly-insulting contemptuous arrogance about a flick or a blow delivered with the back of the hand. So, then, what Jesus is saying is this: " Even if a man should direct at you the most deadly and calculated insult, you must on no account retaliate, and you must on no account resent it." It will not happen very often, if at all, that anyone will slap us on the face, but time and time again life brings to us insults either great or small; and Jesus is here saying that the true Christian has learned to resent no insult and to seek retaliation for no slight. Jesus Himself was called a gluttonous man and a wine-bibber. He was called the friend of tax-gatherers and harlots, with the implication that He was like the company He kept. The early Christians were called cannibals and incendiaries, and were accused of immorality, gross and shameless, because their service included the Love Feast. When Shaftesbury undertook the cause of the poor and the oppressed he was warned that it would mean that " he would become unpopular with his friends and people of his own class," and that " he would have to give up all hope of ever being a cabinet minister." When Wilberforce began on his crusade to free the slaves the slanderous rumour that he was a cruel husband, a wife-beater, that he was married to a negress was deliberately spread abroad. Time and time again in a church someone is " insulted " because he was

not invited to a platform party, because he was omitted
from a vote of thanks, because in some way he did not get
the place which was due to him. The true Christian has
forgotten what it is to be insulted; he has learned from
his Master to accept any insult and never to resent it, and
never to seek to retaliate.

(ii) Jesus goes on to say that if anyone tries to take away
our tunic in a law suit, we must not only let him have that,
but must offer him our cloak also. Again there is much
more in that than meets the eye. The tunic, *chitōn*, was the
long, sack-like inner garment made of cotton or of linen.
The poorest man would have a change of tunics. The cloak
was the great, blanket-like outer garment which a man
wore as a robe by day, and used as a blanket at night. Of
such garments the Jew would only have one. Now it was
actually the Jewish law that a man's tunic might be taken
as a pledge, but not his cloak. " If thou at all take thy
neighbour's raiment to pledge (his cloak), thou shalt
deliver it unto him by that the sun goeth down; for that is
his covering only, it is his raiment for his skin; wherein
shall he sleep? " (*Exodus* 22: 26, 27). The point is that
by right a man's cloak could not be taken permanently
from him. So, then, what Jesus is saying is this: " The
Christian never stands upon his rights; he never disputes
about his legal rights; he does not consider himself to have
any legal rights at all." There are people who are for ever
standing on their rights, who clutch their privileges to
them and who will not be pried loose from them, who will
militantly go to law rather than suffer what they regard as
the slightest infringement of them. Churches are tragically
full of people like that, officials whose territory has been
invaded, office-bearers who have not had their rights,
courts which do business with a manual of practice and
procedure on the table all the time, lest anyone's rights
should be invaded. People like that have not even begun
to see what Christianity is. The Christian thinks not of his
rights, but of his duties; not of his privileges, but of his

responsibilities. The Christian is a man who has forgotten
that he has any rights at all; and the man who will fight
to the legal death for his rights, inside or outside the
Church, is far from the Christian way.

(iii) Jesus then goes on to speak of being compelled to go
one mile; and says that in such a case the Christian must
willingly go two miles. There is here a picture of which we
know little, for it is a picture from an occupied country.
The word which is used for *to compel* is the verb *aggareuein*,
and *aggareuein* is a word with a history. It comes from the
noun *aggareus*, which is a Persian word meaning a *courier*.
The Persians had an amazing postal system. Each road
was divided into stages lasting one day. At each stage
there was food for the courier and water and fodder for the
horses, and fresh horses for the road. But, if by any chance
there was anything lacking, any private person could be
impressed, compelled into giving food, lodging, horses,
assistance, and even into carrying the message himself for
a stage. The word for such compulsion was *aggareuein*. In
the end the word came to signify any kind of forced
impressment into the service of the occupying power. In
an occupied country citizens could be compelled to supply
food, to provide billets, to carry baggage. Sometimes the
occupying power exercised this right of compulsion in the
most tyrannical and unsympathetic way. Always this
threat of compulsion hung over the citizens. Palestine was
an occupied country. At any moment a Jew might feel the
touch of the flat of a Roman spear on his shoulder, and
know that he was compelled to serve the Romans, it might
be in the most menial way. That, in fact, is what happened
to Simon of Cyrene, when he was compelled (*aggareuein*) to
bear the Cross of Jesus. So, then, what Jesus is saying is:
" Suppose your masters come to you and compel you to be
a guide or a porter for a mile, don't go a mile with bitter and
obvious resentment; go two miles with cheerfulness and
with a good grace." What Jesus is saying is: " Don't be
always thinking of your liberty to do as you like; be

always thinking of your duty and your privilege to be of service to others. When a task is laid on you, even if the task is unreasonable and hateful, don't do it as a grim duty to be resented; do it as a service to be gladly rendered." There are always two ways of doing things. A man can do the irreducible minimum and not a stroke more; he can do it in such a way that he makes it clear that he hates the whole thing; he can do it with the barest minimum of efficiency and no more; or he can do it with a smile, with a gracious courtesy, with a determination, not only to do this thing, but to do it well and graciously. He can do it, not simply as well as he has to, but far better than anyone has any right to expect him to. The inefficient workman, the resentful servant, the ungracious helper has not even begun to have the right idea of the Christian life. The Christian is not concerned to do as he likes; he is concerned only to help, even when the demand for help is discourteous, unreasonable and tyrannical.

So, then, in this passage, under the guise of vivid eastern pictures, Jesus is laying down three great rules—the Christian will never resent or seek retaliation for any insult, however calculated and however deadly; the Christian will never stand upon his legal rights or on any other rights he may believe himself to possess; the Christian will never think of his right to do as he likes, but always of his duty to be of help. The question is: How do we measure up to that?

GRACIOUS GIVING

Matthew 5: 38-42 *(continued)*

FINALLY, it is Jesus' demand that we should give to all who ask and never turn away from him who wishes to borrow. At its highest the Jewish law of giving was a lovely thing. It was based on *Deuteronomy* 15: 7-11:

"And if there be among you a poor man of one of thy brethren within any of thy gates in thy land which the

167

Lord thy God giveth thee, thou shalt not harden thine heart, nor shut thine hand from thy poor brother; but thou shalt open thine hand wide unto him, and shalt surely lend him sufficient for his need, in that which he wanteth. Beware that there be not a thought in thy wicked heart, saying: The seventh year, the year of release is at hand; and thy eye be grudging against thy poor brother, and thou givest him nought; and he cry unto the Lord against thee, and it be sin unto thee. Thou shalt surely give to him, and thine heart shall not be grieved when thou givest unto him; because that for this thing the Lord thy God shall bless thee in all thy works, and in all that thou puttest thine hand unto. For the poor shall never cease out of the land; therefore I command thee saying: Thou shalt open thine hand wide unto thy brother, to thy poor, and to thy needy, in thy land."

The point about the *seventh year* is that in every seventh year there was a cancellation of debts; and the grudging and the calculating man might refuse to lend anything when the seventh year was near, lest the debt be cancelled and he lose what he had given.

It was on that passage that the Jewish law of giving was founded. The Rabbis laid down five principles which ought to govern giving.

(i) Giving must not be refused. " Be careful not to refuse charity, for everyone who refuses charity is put in the same category with idolaters." If a man refuses to give, the day may well come when he has to beg—perhaps from the very people to whom he refused to give.

(ii) Giving must befit the man to whom the gift is given. The law of *Deuteronomy* had said that a man must be given *whatever he lacks*. That is to say, a man must not be given that bare sufficiency which will keep body and soul together; he must be given enough to enable him to retain at least something of the standard and the comfort which once he knew. So, it is said, Hillel arranged that the poverty-stricken son of a noble family should be given, not simply enough to keep him from starvation, but a horse to ride and a slave to run before him; and once, when no slave was available, Hillel himself acted as his slave and ran before him. There is something gracious and lovely in the idea that giving must not only remove actual poverty; it must do something also to remove the humiliation which poverty brings.

(iii) Giving must be carried out privately and secretly. There must be no one else there. In fact, the Rabbis went the length of saying that in the highest kind of giving, the giver must not know to whom he was giving, and the receiver must not know from whom he was receiving. There was a certain place in the Temple to which people secretly came and secretly gave their gifts ; and these secret gifts were used in secrecy to help the impoverished members of once noble families, and to give the daughters of such impoverished ones the dowries without which they could not be married. The Jew would have regarded with abhorrence the gift which was given for the sake of prestige, publicity, or self-glorification.

(iv) The manner of giving must befit the character and the temperament of the recipient. The rule was that if a man had means, but was too miserly to use them, a gift must be given as a gift, but afterwards reclaimed from his estate as a loan. But if a man was too proud to ask for help, Rabbi Ishmael suggested that the giver should go to him and say, " My son, perhaps you need a loan." His self-respect was thus saved, but the loan was never to be asked back, and it was in fact, not a loan, but a gift. It was even laid down that if a man was unable to respond to an appeal for help, his very refusal must be such as to show that, if he could give nothing else, he at least gave sympathy. Even a refusal was to be such that it helped and did not hurt. Giving was to be carried out in such a way that the manner of the giving was to help as much as the gift.

(v) Giving was at once a privilege and an obligation for in reality all giving is nothing less than giving to God. To give to some needy person was not something which a man might *choose* to do; it was something he *must* do; for, if he refused, the refusal was to God. " He who befriends the poor lends to the Lord, and He will repay him for his good deed." " To every one who shows mercy to other men, mercy is shown from heaven; but to him who shows no mercy to other men, no mercy is shown from heaven." The Rabbis loved to point out that loving-kindness was one of the very few things to which the Law appointed no limit at all.

Are we then to say that Jesus urged upon men what can only be called indiscriminate giving? The answer cannot be given without qualification. It is clear that the effect of the giving on the receiver must be taken into account. Giving must never be such as to encourage him in laziness and in shiftlessness, for such giving can only hurt. But at the same time it must be remembered that many people who say that they will only give through official channels, and who refuse to help personal cases, are frequently merely producing an excuse for not giving at all, and are at all times removing the personal element from giving altogether. And it must also be remembered that it is better to help a score of fraudulent beggars than to risk turning away the one man in real need.

CHRISTIAN LOVE

1. *The Meaning of it*

Matthew 5: 43-48

You have heard that it has been said: You shall love your neighbour, and you shall hate your enemy; but I say to you: Love your enemies, and pray for those who persecute you, so that you may become the sons of your Father who is in heaven; for He makes His sun to rise on the evil and the good, and sends rain on the righteous and the unrighteous. If you love those who love you, what reward can you expect? Do not even the tax-gatherers do that? If you greet only your brothers, where is there anything extra about that? Do not even the Gentiles do that? So, then, you must be perfect even as your heavenly Father is perfect.

C. G. Montefiore, the Jewish scholar, calls this "the central and most famous section" of the Sermon on the Mount. It is certainly true that there is no passage of the New Testament which contains such a concentrated expression of the Christian ethic of personal relations as this passage does. To the ordinary person this passage describes essential Christianity in action, and even the person who never darkens the door of the church knows that Jesus said this, and very often condemns the professing Christian for falling so far short of its demands.

When we study this passage we must first try to find out what Jesus was saying, and what He was demanding of His followers. If we are to try to live this out, we must obviously first of all be quite clear as to what it is demanding. What does Jesus mean by *loving our enemies*?

Greek is a language which is rich in synonyms; it has words with shades of meaning which English does not possess. In Greek there are four different words for *love*.

(i) There is the noun *storgē* with its accompanying verb *stergein*. These words are the characteristic words of *family love*. They are the words which describe the love of a parent for a child and a child for a parent. "A child," said Plato *"loves (stergein)* and is loved by those who brought him into the world." "Sweet is a father to his children," said Philemon, "if he has *love (storgē).*" These words describe family affection.

(ii) There is the noun *erōs* and the accompanying verb *eran*. These words describe the love of a man for a maid; there is always passion in them; and there is always sexual love. Sophocles described *erōs* as "the terrible longing." In these words there is nothing essentially bad; they simply describe the passion of human love; but as time went on they began to be tinged with the idea of lust rather than love, and they never occur in the New Testament at all.

(iii) There is *philia* with its accompanying verb *philein.* This is the warmest and the best Greek word for love. It describes real love, real affection. *Hoi philountes*, the present participle, is the word which describes a man's closest and nearest and truest friends. It is the word which is used in the famous saying of Menander: "Whom the gods *love*, dies young." *Philein* can mean to *fondle* or to *kiss*. It is the word of warm, tender affection, the highest kind of love.

(iv) There is *agapē* with its accompanying verb *agapan*. *Agapē* is the word which is used here. The real meaning of *agapē* is *unconquerable benevolence, invincible goodwill*. If we regard a person with *agapē*, it means that no matter what that person does to us, no matter how he treats us, no matter if he insults us or injures us or grieves us, we will never allow any bitterness against him to invade our hearts, but we will regard him with that unconquerable benevolence and goodwill which will seek nothing but his highest good. From this certain things emerge.

(i) Jesus never asked us to love our enemies in the same was as we love our loved ones, our nearest and our dearest. The very word is different; to love our enemies in the same way as we love our nearest and our dearest would neither be possible or right. This is a different kind of love.

(ii) Wherein does the main difference lie? In the case of our nearest and our dearest we cannot help loving them; we speak of *falling in love*; it is something which comes to us quite unsought; it is something which is born of the emotions of the heart. But in the case of our enemies, love is not only something of the *heart*; it is also something of the *will*. It is not something which we cannot help; it is something which we have to will ourselves into doing. It is in fact a victory and a conquest over that which comes instinctively to the natural man. *Agapē* does not mean a feeling of the heart, which we cannot help, and which comes unbidden and unsought; it means a determination of the mind, whereby we achieve this unconquerable goodwill even to those who hurt and injure us. *Agapē*, someone has said, is the power to love those whom we do not

like and who do not like us. In point of fact we can only
have *agapē* when Jesus Christ enables us to conquer our
natural tendency to anger and to bitterness, and to achieve
this invincible goodwill to all men.

(iii) It is then quite obvious that the last thing *agapē*,
Christian love, means is that we allow people to do absolutely as they like, and that we leave them quite unchecked.
No one would say that a parent really loves his child if he
lets the child do as he likes. If we regard a person with
invincible goodwill, it will often mean that we must punish
him, that we must restrain him, that we must discipline
him, that we must protect him against himself. But it will
also mean that we do not punish him to satisfy our desire
for revenge, but in order to make him a better man. It
will always mean that all Christian discipline and all
Christian punishment must be aimed, not at vengeance,
but at cure. Punishment will never be merely retributive;
it will always be remedial.

(iv) It must be noted that Jesus laid this love down as
a basis for *personal relationships*. People use this passage
as a basis for pacifism and as a text on which to speak about
international relationships. Of course, it includes that, but
first and foremost it deals with our personal relationships
with our family and our neighbours and the people we
meet with every day in life. It is very much easier to go
about declaring that there should be no such thing as war
between nation and nation, than to live a life in which we
personally never allow any such thing as bitterness to
invade our relationships with those we meet with every
day. First and foremost, this commandment of Jesus deals
with personal relationship. This is a commandment of
which we should say first and foremost: " This means me."

(v) We must note that this is a commandment which is
only possible for a Christian. Only the grace of Jesus
Christ can enable a man to have this unconquerable benevolence and this invincible goodwill in his personal relationships with other people. It is only when Christ lives in our

173

hearts that this bitterness will die and this love spring to life. It is often said that this world would be perfect if only people would live according to the principles of the Sermon on the Mount; but the plain fact is that no one can even begin to live according to these principles without the help of Jesus Christ. We need Christ to enable us to obey Christ's command.

(vi) Lastly—and it may be most important of all—we must note that this commandment does not only involve allowing people to do as they like to us; it also involves that we should do something for them. *We are bidden to pray for them.* No man can pray for another man and still hate him. When he takes himself and the man whom he is tempted to hate both to God, something happens. We cannot go on hating another man in the presence of God. The surest way of killing bitterness is to pray for the man we are tempted to hate.

CHRISTIAN LOVE
2. *The Reason for it*

Matthew 5: 43-48 *(continued)*

WE have seen what Jesus meant when He commanded us to have this Christian love; and now we must go on to see why He demanded that we should have it. Why does Jesus demand that a man should have this love, this unconquerable benevolence, this invincible goodwill? The reason is very simple and very tremendous—it is that such a love makes a man like God.

Jesus pointed to the action of God in the world, and that action is the action of unconquerable benevolence. God makes His sun to rise on the good and the evil; He sends His rain on the just and the unjust. Rabbi Joshua ben Nehemiah used to say, " Have you ever noticed that the rain fell on the field of A, who was righteous, and not on the field of B, who was wicked? Or that the sun rose and shone on Israel, who was righteous, and not upon the Gentiles, who were wicked? God causes the sun to shine both on Israel and on the nations, for the Lord is good to all." Even the Jewish Rabbi was moved and impressed with the sheer benevolence of God to saint and sinner alike. There is a rabbinic tale which tells of the destruction of the Egyptians in the Red Sea. When the Egyptians were drowned, so the tale runs, the angels began a paean of praise, but God said sorrowfully: " The work of my hands are sunk in the sea, and you would sing before me! " The love of God is such that He can never take pleasure in the destruction of any of the creatures whom His hands have made. The Psalmist had it: " The eyes of *all* wait upon Thee; and Thou givest them their meat in due season. Thou openest Thine hand, and satisfiest the desire of *every living thing* " (*Psalm* 145: 15). In God there is this universal benevolence even towards men who have broken His law and broken His heart.

Jesus says that we must have this love that we may become " the sons of our Father who is in heaven." Hebrew is not rich in adjectives; and for that reason Hebrew often uses *son of* . . . with an abstract noun, where we would use an adjective. For instance *a son of peace* is *a peaceful man; a son of consolation* is *a consoling man.* So, then, *a son of God* is *a godlike man.* The reason why we must have this unconquerable benevolence and goodwill is that God has it; and, if we have it, we become nothing less than *sons of God, godlike men.*

Here we have the key to one of the most difficult sentences in the New Testament, the sentence with which this passage finishes. Jesus said: " You must be perfect even as your heavenly Father is perfect." On the face of it that sounds like a commandment which cannot possibly have anything to do with us. There is none of us who would even faintly connect ourselves with perfection. The Greek word for *perfect* is *teleios.* This word is often used in Greek in a very special way. It has nothing to do with what we might call abstract, philosophical, metaphysical perfection.

A victim which is fit for a sacrifice to God, that is a victim which is without blemish, is *teleios*. A man who has reached his full-grown stature is *teleios* in contradistinction to a half-grown lad. A student who has reached a mature knowledge of his subject is *teleios* as opposed to a learner who is just beginning, and who as yet has no grasp of things. To put it in another way, the Greek idea of perfection is *functional*. A thing is perfect if it fully realises the purpose for which it was planned, and designed, and made. In point of fact, that meaning is involved in the derivation of the word. *Teleios* is the adjective formed from the noun *telos*. *Telos* means an *end*, a *purpose*, an *aim*, a *goal*. A thing is *teleios*, if it realises the purpose for which it was planned; a man is perfect if he realises the purpose for which he was created and sent into the world.

Let us take a very simple analogy. Suppose in my house there is a screw loose, and I want to tighten and adjust this screw. I go out to the ironmongers and I buy a screw-driver. I find that the screw-driver exactly fits the grip of my hand; it is neither too large nor too small, too rough or too smooth. I lay the screw-driver on the slot of the screw, and I find that it exactly fits. I then turn the screw and the screw is fixed. In the Greek sense, and especially in the New Testament sense, that screw-driver is *teleios*, because it exactly fulfilled the purpose for which I desired and bought it.

So, then, a man will be *teleios* if he fulfils the purpose for which he was created. For what purpose was man created? The Bible leaves us in no doubt as to that. In the old creation story we find God saying, " Let us make man in our image and after our likeness " (*Genesis* I: 26). *Man was created to be like God.* The characteristic of God is this universal benevolence, this unconquerable goodwill, this constant seeking of the highest good of every man. The great characteristic of God is love to saint and to sinner alike. No matter what men do to Him, God seeks nothing but their highest good. The hymn has it of Jesus:

" Thy foes might hate, despise, revile,
  Thy friends unfaithful prove;
Unwearied in forgiveness still,
  Thy heart could only love."

It is when man reproduces in his life the unwearied, forgiving, sacrificial benevolence of God that he becomes like
God, and is therefore *perfect* in the New Testament sense
of the word. To put it at its simplest, the man who cares
most for men is the most perfect man.

It is the whole teaching of the Bible that we only realise
our manhood by becoming godlike. The one thing which
makes us like God is the love which never ceases to care
for men, no matter what men do to it. We realize our
manhood, we enter upon Christian perfection, when we
learn to forgive as God forgives, and to love as God loves.

MATTHEW 6: 1-18

THE REWARD MOTIVE IN THE CHRISTIAN
LIFE

WHEN we study the opening verses of *Matthew* 6, we are
immediately confronted with one most important question
—What is the place of the reward motive in the Christian
life? Three times in this section Jesus speaks of God
rewarding those who have given to Him the kind of service
which He desires (*Matthew* 6: 4, 6, 18). This question is so
important that we will do well to pause to examine it
before we go on to study this chapter in detail.

It is very often stated that the reward motive has no
place whatsoever in the Christian life. It is held that we
must be good for the sake of being good, that virtue is its
own reward, and that the whole conception of reward
must be banished from the Christian life. There was an
old saint who used to say that he would wish to quench all

the fires of hell with water, and to burn up all the joys of heaven with fire, in order that men might seek for goodness for nothing but goodness' sake, and in order that the idea of reward and punishment might be totally eliminated from life.

On the face of it that point of view is very fine and noble; but it is not the point of view which Jesus held. We have already seen that three times in this passage Jesus speaks about reward. The right kind of almsgiving, the right kind of prayer, and the right kind of fasting will all have their reward. Nor is this an isolated instance of the idea of reward in the teaching of Jesus. He says of those who loyally bear persecution, who suffer insult without bitterness, that their reward will be great in heaven (*Matthew* 5: 12). He says that whoever gives to one of these little ones a cup of cold water in the name of a disciple will not lose his reward (*Matthew* 10: 41). At least part of the teaching of the parable of the talents is that faithful service will receive its reward (*Matthew* 25: 14-30). In the parable of the last judgment the plain teaching is that there is reward and punishment in accordance with our reaction to the needs of our fellow-men (*Matthew* 25: 31-46). It is abundantly clear that Jesus did not hesitate to speak in terms of rewards and punishments. And it may well be that we ought to be careful that we do not try to be more spiritual than Jesus was in our thinking about this matter of reward. There are certain obvious facts which we must note.

(i) It is an obvious rule of life that any action which achieves nothing is futile and meaningless. A goodness which achieves no end would be a meaningless goodness. As has been very truly said: " Unless a thing is good for something, it is good for nothing." Unless the Christian life has an aim and a goal which it is a joy to obtain, it becomes largely without meaning. He who believes in the Christian way and the Christian promise cannot believe that goodness can have no result beyond itself.

(ii) To banish all rewards and punishments from the idea of religion is in effect to say that injustice has the last word. It cannot reasonably be held that the end of the good man and the end of the bad man are one and the same. That would simply mean that God does not care whether men are good or not. It would mean, to put it crudely and bluntly, that there is no point in being good, and no special reason why a man should live one kind of life instead of another. To eliminate all rewards and punishments is really to say that in God there is neither justice nor love.

Rewards and punishments are necessary in order to make sense of life. A. E. Housman wrote:

" Yonder, on the morning blink,
The sun is up, and so must I,
To wash and dress and eat and drink
And look at things and talk and think
And work, and God knows why.

And often have I washed and dressed,
And what's to show for all my pain?
Let me lie abed and rest;
Ten thousand times I've done my best,
And all's to do again."

If there are no rewards and no punishments, then that poem's view of life is true. Action is meaningless and all effort goes unavailingly whistling down the wind.

(i) The Christian Idea of Reward

BUT having gone this length with the idea of reward in the Christian life, there are certain things about which we must be clear.

(i) When Jesus spoke of reward, He was very definitely *not* thinking in terms of material reward. It is quite true that in the Old Testament the idea of goodness and prosperity are closely connected. If a man prospered, if his fields were fertile and his harvest great, if his children were many and his fortune large, it was taken as a proof that he was a good man. That is precisely the problem at the back of the *Book of Job*. Job is in misfortune; his friends come to him to argue that that misfortune must be the result of his own sin; and Job most vehemently denies that charge. " Remember, I pray thee," said Eliphaz, " who ever perished, being innocent? " (*Job* 4: 7). " If thou wert pure and upright," said Bildad, " surely now He would awake for thee, and make the habitation of thy righteousness prosperous " (*Job* 8: 6). " Thou hast said, My doctrine is pure, and I am clean in thine eyes," said Zophar, " but oh that God would speak and open His lips against thee " (*Job* 11: 4). The very idea that the *Book of Job* was written to contradict is that goodness and material prosperity go hand in hand.

" I have been young, and now am old," said the Psalmist, " yet have I not seen the righteous forsaken, nor his seed begging bread " (*Psalm* 37: 25). " A thousand shall fall at thy side," said the Psalmist " and ten thousand at thy right hand; but it shall not come nigh thee. Only with thine eyes shalt thou behold and see the reward of the wicked. Because thou hast made the Lord, which is thy refuge, even the most High, thy habitation, there shall no evil befall thee, neither shall any plague come nigh thy dwelling " (*Psalm* 90: 7-10). These are things that Jesus could never have said. It was certainly not material prosperity which Jesus promised His disciples. He in fact promised them trial and tribulation, suffering, persecution and death. Quite certainly Jesus did not think in terms of material rewards.

(ii) The second thing which it is necessary to remember is that the highest reward never comes to him who is seeking reward. If a man is always seeking reward, if he is always reckoning up that which he believes himself to be earning, then he will in fact miss the reward for which he is seeking. And he will miss it because he is looking at God and looking at life in the wrong way. A man who is always calculating his reward is thinking of God in terms of a judge or an accountant, and above all he is thinking of life in terms of *law*. He is thinking of doing so much and earning so much. He is thinking of life in terms of a credit and debit balance sheet. He is thinking of presenting an account to God and of saying, " I have done so much. Now I claim my reward."

The basic mistake of this point of view is that it thinks of life in terms of law, instead of *love*. If we love a person deeply and passionately, humbly and selflessly, we will be quite sure that if we give that person all we have to give, we will still be in default, that if we give that person the sun, the moon and the stars, we will still be in debt. He who is in love is always in debt; the last thing that enters his mind is that he has earned a reward. If a man has a *legal* view of life, he may think constantly in terms of reward that he has won; if a man has a *loving* view of life, the idea of reward will never enter his mind.

The great paradox of Christian reward is this—the person who looks for reward, and who calculates that it is due to him, does not receive it; the person whose only motive is love, and who never thinks that he has deserved any reward, does, in fact, receive it. The strange fact is that reward is at one and the same time the by-product and the ultimate end of the Christian life.

(ii) *The Christian Reward*

WE must now go on to ask: What are the rewards of the Christian life?

(i) We must begin by noting one basic and general truth. We have already seen that Jesus Christ does not think in terms of material reward at all. *The rewards of the Christian life are rewards which are only rewards to a spiritually minded person.* To the materially minded person they would not be rewards at all. The Christian rewards are rewards only to a Christian.

(ii) The first of the Christian rewards is *satisfaction*. The doing of the right thing, obedience to Jesus Christ, the taking of His way, whatever else it may or may not bring, always brings satisfaction. It may well be that, if a man does the right thing, and obeys Jesus Christ, he may lose his fortune and his position, he may end in gaol or on the scaffold, he may finish up in unpopularity, loneliness and disrepute, but he will still possess that inner satisfaction, which is greater than all the rest put together. No price-ticket can be put upon this; this is not to be evaluated in terms of earthly currency, but there is nothing like it in all the world. It brings that contentment which is the crown of life.

The poet, George Herbert, was a member of a little group of friends who used to meet to play their musical instruments together like a little orchestra. Once he was on his way to a meeting of this group, when he passed a carter whose cart was stuck in the mud of the ditch. George Herbert laid aside his instrument and went to the help of the man. It was a long job to get the cart out, and he finished covered with mud. When he arrived at the house of his friends, it was too late for music. He told them what had detained him on the way. One said: " You have missed all the music." George Herbert smiled. " Yes," he said, " but I will have songs at midnight." He had the satisfaction of having done the Christlike thing.

Godfrey Winn tells of a man who was the greatest plastic surgeon in Britain. During the war, he gave up a private practice, which brought him in £10,000 a year, to devote all his time to remoulding the faces and the bodies of airmen who had been burned and mutilated in battle. Godfrey Winn said to him, " What's your ambition, Mac? " Back came the answer, " I want to be a good craftsman." The £10,000 a year was nothing compared with the satisfaction of a selfless job well done.

Once a woman stopped Dale of Birmingham on the street. " God bless you, Dr. Dale," she said. She absolutely refused to give her name. She only thanked him and blessed him and passed on. Dale at the moment had been

THE GOSPEL OF MATTHEW

much depressed. " But," he said, " the mist broke, the
sunlight came; I breathed the free air of the mountains of
God." In material things he was not one penny the richer,
but in the deep satisfaction, which comes to the preacher
who discovers he has helped someone, he had gained
wealth untold.

The first Christian reward is the satisfaction which no
money on earth can buy.

(iii) The second reward of the Christian life is *still more
work to do*. It is the paradox of the Christian idea of reward
that a task well done does not bring rest and comfort and
ease; it brings still greater demands and still more strenu-
ous endeavours. In the parable of the talents the reward of
the faithful servants was still greater responsibility (*Matthew*
25: 14-30). When a teacher gets a really brilliant and able
scholar, he does not exempt him from work; he gives him
harder work than is given to anyone else. The brilliant
young musician is given, not easier, but harder music to
master. The lad who has played well in the second eleven
is not put into the third eleven, where he could walk
through the game without breaking sweat; he is put into
the first eleven where he has to play his heart out. The
Jews had a curious saying. They said that a wise teacher
will treat the pupil " like a young heifer whose burden is
increased daily." The Christian reward is the reverse of
the world's reward. The world's reward would be an
easier time; the reward of the Christian is that God lays
still more and more upon a man to do for Him and for his
fellow-men. The harder the work we are given to do, the
greater the reward.

(iv) The third, and the final, Christian reward is what men
all through the ages have called *the vision of God*. For the
worldly man, who has never given a thought to God, to
be confronted with God would be a terror and not a joy.
If a man takes his own way, he drifts farther and farther
from God; the gulf between him and God becomes ever
wider, until in the end God becomes a grim stranger, whom

he only wishes to avoid. But, if a man all his life has sought to walk with God, if he has sought to obey his Lord, if goodness has been his quest through all his days, then all his life he has been growing closer and closer to God, until in the end he passes into God's nearer presence, without fear and with radiant joy—and that is the greatest reward of all.

RIGHT THINGS FROM THE WRONG MOTIVE

Matthew 6: 1

> Take care not to try to demonstrate how good you are in the presence of men, in order to be seen by them. If you do, you have no reward with your Father in heaven.

To the Jew there were three great cardinal works of the religious life, three great pillars on which the good life was based—*almsgiving, prayer* and *fasting*. Jesus would not for a moment have disputed that; what troubled Him was that so often in human life the finest things were done from the wrong motives.

It is the strange fact that these three great cardinal good works readily lend themselves to wrong motives. It was Jesus warning that, when these things were done with the sole intention of bringing glory to the doer, they lost by far the most important part of their value. A man may give alms, not really to help the person to whom he gives, but simply to demonstrate his own generosity, and to bask in the warmth of some one's gratitude and all men's praise. A man may pray in such a way that his prayer is not really addressed to God, but to his fellow-men. His praying may simply be an attempt to demonstrate his exceptional piety in such a way that no one can fail to see it. A man may fast, not really for the good of his own soul, not really to humble himself in the sight of God, but simply to show the world what a splendidly self-disciplined character he is

THE GOSPEL OF MATTHEW

A man may practise good works simply to win praise from men, to increase his own prestige, and to show the world how good he is.

As Jesus saw it, there is no doubt at all that that kind of thing does receive a certain kind of reward. Three times Jesus uses the phrase, as the Authorised Version has it: " Verily I say unto you, they have their reward " (*Matthew* 6: 2, 5, 16). It would be better to translate it: " They have received payment in full." The word that is used in the Greek is the verb *apechein*, which was the technical business and commercial word for receiving payment in full. It was the word which was used on receipted accounts. For instance, one man signs a receipt given to another man: " I have received (*apechō*) from you the rent of the olive press which you have on hire." A tax collector gives a receipt, saying, " I have received (*apechō*) from you the tax which is due." A man sells a slave and gives a receipt, saying, " I have received (*apechō*) the whole price due to me."

What Jesus is saying is this: " If you give alms to demonstrate your own generosity, you will get the admiration of men—but that is all you will ever get. That is your payment in full. If you pray in such a way as to flaunt your piety in the face of men, you will gain the reputation of being an extremely devout man—but that is all you will ever get. That is your payment in full. If you fast in such a way that all men know that you are fasting, you will become known as an extremely abstemious and ascetic man—but that is all you will ever get. That is your payment in full." Jesus is saying, " If your one aim is to get yourself the world's rewards, no doubt you will get them—but you must not look for the rewards which God alone can give." And he would be a sadly short-sighted creature who grasped the rewards of time, and let the rewards of eternity go.

HOW NOT TO GIVE

Matthew 6: 2-4

So, when you give alms, do not sound a trumpet before you, as the hypocrites do in the synagogues and in the streets, that they may be praised by men. This is the truth I tell you—they are paid in full. But when you give alms, your left hand must not know what your right hand is doing, so that your alms-giving may be in secret, and your Father who sees what happens in secret will give you your reward in full.

To the Jew almsgiving was the most sacred of all religious duties. How sacred it was may be seen from the fact that the Jews used the same word—*tzedakah*—both for *righteousness* and *almsgiving*. To give alms and to be righteous were one and the same thing. To give alms was to gain merit in the sight of God, and was even to win atonement and forgiveness for past sins. " It is better to give alms than to lay up gold; almsgiving doth deliver from death, and it purges away all sin " (*Tobit* 12: 8).

> " Almsgiving to a father shall not be blotted out,
> And as a substitute for sins it shall stand firmly planted.
> In the day of affliction it shall be remembered to thy credit.
> It shall obliterate thine iniquities as the heat, the hoar-frost."
>
> (*Ecclesiasticus* 3: 14, 15).

There was a rabbinic saying: " Greater is he who gives alms than he who offers all sacrifices." Almsgiving stood first in the catalogue of good works.

It was then natural and inevitable that the man who desired to be good should concentrate on almsgiving. The highest teaching of the Rabbis was exactly the same as the teaching of Jesus. They too forbade ostentatious alms-giving. " He who gives alms in secret," they said, " is greater than Moses." The almsgiving which saves from death is that " when the recipient does not know from

186

THE GOSPEL OF MATTHEW

whom he gets it, and when the giver does not know to whom he gives it." There was a Rabbi who, when he wished to give alms, dropped money behind him, so that he would not see who picked it up. " It were better," they said, " to give a man nothing, than to give him something, and to put him to shame." There was one particularly lovely custom connected with the Temple. In the Temple there was a room called The Chamber of the Silent. People who wished to make atonement for some sin placed money there; and poor people from good families who had come down in the world were secretly helped by these contributions.

But as in so many other things practice fell far short of precept. Too often the giver gave in such a way that all men might see the gift, and gave far more to bring glory to himself than to bring help to someone else. During the Synagogue services, offerings were taken for the poor, and there were those who took good care that others should see how much they gave. J. J. Wetstein quotes an eastern custom from the ancient days: " In the east water is so scarce that sometimes it had to be bought. When a man wanted to do a good act, and to bring blessing on his family, he went to a water-carrier with a good voice, and instructed him: ' Give the thirsty a drink.' The water-carrier filled his skin and went to the market-place. ' O thirsty ones,' he cried, ' come to drink the offering.' And the giver stood by him and said, ' Bless me, who gave you this drink.' " That is precisely the kind of thing that Jesus condemns. He talks about the *hypocrites* who do things like that. The word *hupokritēs* is the Greek word for an actor. People like that put on an act of giving which is designed only to glorify themselves.

THE MOTIVES OF GIVING
Matthew 6: 2-4 (continued)
LET us now look at some of the motives which lie behind the act of giving.

(i) **A man may give from *a sense of duty*.** He may give
not because he wishes to give, but because he feels that
giving is a duty which he cannot well escape. It may even
be that a man can come—perhaps unconsciously—to regard
the poor as being in the world to allow him to carry out
this duty, and thus to acquire merit in the sight of God.
Catherine Carswell in her autobiography, *Lying Awake*,
tells of her early days in Glasgow: " The poor, one might
say, were our pets. Decidedly they were always with us.
In our particular ark we were taught to love, honour and
entertain the poor." The key-note, as she looked back
upon it, was superiority and condescension. Giving was
regarded as a duty, but often with the giving there was a
moral lecture which provided a smug pleasure for the man
who gave it. In those days Glasgow was a drunken city on
a Saturday night. She writes: " Every Sunday afternoon,
for some years, my father went a round of the cells of the
police station, bailing out the week-end drunks with half-
crowns, so that they might not lose their jobs on Monday
morning. He asked each one to sign the pledge, and to
return his half-crown out of the next week's wages." No
doubt he was perfectly right, but he gave from a smug
eminence of respectability, and included a moral lecture
in the giving. He clearly felt himself to be in a quite
different moral category from those to whom he gave. It
was said of a great, but superior man: " With all his
giving he never gives himself." When a man gives, as it
were, from a pedestal, when he gives always with a certain
calculation, when he gives from a sense of duty, even a
sense of Christian duty, he may give generously of things,
but the one thing he never gives is himself, and therefore
the giving is incomplete.

(ii) **A man may give from *motives of prestige*.** He may
give to get to himself the glory of giving. The chances are
that, if no one is to know about it, or, if there is no publicity
attached to it, he would not give at all. Unless he is duly
thanked and praised and honoured, he is sadly disgruntled

and discontented. He gives, not to the glory of God, but to the glory of himself. He gives, not primarily to help the poor person, but to gratify his own vanity and his own sense of power.

(iii) A man may give simply *because he has to.* He may give simply because the overflowing love and kindliness in his heart will allow him to do no other. He may give because, try as he may, he cannot rid himself of a sense of responsibility for the man in need. There was a kind of vast kindliness about Dr. Johnson. There was a poverty-stricken creature called Robert Levett. Levett in his day had been a waiter in Paris and a doctor in the poorer parts of London. He had an appearance and manners, as Johnson said himself, such as to disgust the rich and to terrify the poor. Somehow or other he became a member of Johson's household. Boswell was amazed at the whole business, but Goldsmith knew Johnson better. He said of Levett: " He is poor and honest which is recommendation enough for Johnson. He is now become miserable, and that insures the protection of Johnson." Misfortune was a passport to Johnson's heart. Boswell tells this story of Johnson. " Coming home late one night he found a poor woman lying on the street, so much exhausted that she could not walk: he took her upon his back and carried her to his house, where he discovered that she was one of these wretched females, who had fallen into the lowest state of vice, poverty and disease. Instead of harshly upbraiding her, he had her taken care of with all tenderness for a long time, at considerable expense, till she was restored to health, and endeavoured to put her in a virtuous way of living." All that Johnson got out of that was unworthy suspicions about his own character, but the heart of the man demanded that he should give. Surely one of the loveliest pictures in literary history is the picture of Johnson, in his own days of poverty, coming home in the small hours of the morning, and, as he walked along the Strand, slipping pennies into the hands of the waifs and strays who were sleeping in the doorways because they had nowhere else to go. Hawkins tells that one asked him how he could bear to have his house filled with " necessitous and undeserving people." Johnson answered: " If I did not assist them no one else would, and they must not be lost for want." There you have real giving, the giving which is the upsurge of love in the heart of a man, the giving which is a kind of overflow of the love of God.

We have the pattern of this perfect giving in Jesus Christ Himself. Paul wrote to his friends at Corinth: " Ye know the grace of our Lord Jesus Christ, that, though He was rich, yet for your sakes He became poor, that ye through His poverty might be rich " (2 *Corinthians* 8: 9). Our giving must never be the grim and self-righteous outcome of a sense of duty, still less must it be done to enhance our own glory and prestige among men; it must be the instinctive outflow of the loving heart; we must give to others as Jesus Christ gave Himself to us.

HOW NOT TO PRAY

Matthew 6: 5-8

> And when you pray, you must not be like the hypocrites, for they are fond of praying standing in the synagogues and at the corners of the streets, so that they may be seen by people. This is the truth I tell you—they are paid in full. But when you pray, go into your private room, and shut the door, and pray to your Father who is in secret; and your Father who sees what happens in secret will give you your reward in full.

> When you pray, do not pile up meaningless phrases, as the Gentiles do, for their idea is that they will be heard because of the length of their words. So, then, do not be like them, for your Father knows the things you need before you ask Him.

No nation ever had a higher ideal of prayer than the Jews had; and no religion ever ranked prayer higher in the scale of priorities than the Jews did. " Great is prayer," said the Rabbis, " greater than all good works." One of the loveliest things that was ever said about family worship is the Rabbinic saying, " He who prays within his house surrounds it with a wall that is stronger than iron." The only regret of the Rabbis was that it was not possible to pray all the day long.

But certain faults had crept into the Jewish habits of prayer. It is to be noted that these faults are by no means peculiar to Jewish ideas of prayer; they can and do occur anywhere. And it is to be noted that they could only occur in a community where prayer was taken with the greatest seriousness. They are not the faults of neglect; they are the faults of misguided devotion.

(i) Prayer tended to become formalized. There were two things the daily use of which was prescribed for every Jew. The first was the *Shema*, which consists of three short passages of scripture—*Deuteronomy* 6: 4-9; 11: 13-21; *Numbers* 15: 37-41. *Shema* is the imperative of the Hebrew word *to hear*, and the *Shema* takes its name from the verse which was the essence and centre of the whole matter: " Hear, O Israel, the Lord our God is one Lord." The full *Shema* had to be recited by every Jew every morning and every evening. It had to be said as early as possible. It had to be said as soon as the light was strong enough to enable a man to distinguish between blue and white, or, as Rabbi Eliezer said, between blue and green. In any event it had to be said before the third hour, that is, 9 a.m.; and in the evening it had to be said before 9 p.m. If the last possible moment for the saying of the *Shema* had come, no matter where a man found himself, at home, in the street, at work, in the synagogue, he must stop and say it. There were many who loved the *Shema*, and who repeated it with reverence and adoration and love; but inevitably there were still more who gabbled their way through it, and went their way. The *Shema* had every chance of becoming a vain repetition, which men mumbled through

like some spell or incantation. We Christians are but ill-
qualified to criticise, for everything that has been said
about formally gabbling through the *Shema* can be said
about grace before meat in many a family.

The second thing which every Jew must daily repeat
was called the *Shemonēh 'esreh*, which means *The Eighteen*.
It consisted of eighteen prayers, and was, and still is, an
essential part of the synagogue service. In time the prayers
became nineteen, but the old name remains. Most of these
prayers are quite short, and nearly all of them are very
lovely. The twelfth runs:

> " Let Thy mercy, O Lord, be showed upon the up-
> right, the humble, the elders of Thy people Israel,
> and the rest of its teachers; be favourable to the
> pious strangers amongst us, and to us all. Give
> Thou a good reward to those who sincerely trust in Thy
> name, that our lot may be cast among them in
> the world to come, that our hope be not deceived.
> Praised be Thou, O Lord, who art the hope and
> confidence of the faithful."

The fifth runs:

> "Bring us back to Thy law, O our Father; bring us
> back, O King, to Thy service; bring us back to Thee
> by true repentance. Praised be Thou, O Lord, who
> dost accept our repentance."

No Church possesses a more beautiful liturgy than the
Shemonēh 'esreh. The law was that the Jew must recite it
three times a day, once in the morning, once in the afternoon, and once in the evening. The same thing happened
again. The devout Jew prayed it with loving devotion;
but there were many to whom this series of lovely prayers
became a gabbled formula. There was even a summary
supplied which a man might pray, if he had not the time or
the memory to repeat the whole eighteen. The repetition
of the *Shemonēh 'esreh* became nothing more than the
superstitious incantation of a spell. Again, we Christians
are ill-qualified to criticise, for there are many occasions

when we do precisely the same with the prayer which Jesus taught us to pray.

HOW NOT TO PRAY

Matthew 6: 5-8 *(continued)*

(ii) STILL further, the Jewish liturgy supplied stated prayers for all occasions. There was hardly an event or a sight in life which had not its stated formula of prayer. There was prayer before and after each meal; there were prayers in connection with the light, the fire, the lightning, on seeing the new moon, comets, rain, tempest, at the sight of the sea, lakes, rivers, on receiving good news, on using new furniture, on entering or leaving a city. Everything had its prayer. Clearly there is something infinitely lovely here. It was the intention that every happening in life should be brought into the presence of God. But just because the prayers were so meticulously prescribed and stated, the whole system lent itself to formalism, and the tendency was for the prayers to slip off the tongue with very little meaning. The tendency was glibly to repeat the right prayer at the right time. The great Rabbis knew that and tried to guard against it. " If a man," they said, " says his prayers, as if to get through a set task, that is no prayer." " Do not look on prayer as a formal duty, but as an act of humility by which to obtain the mercy of God." Rabbi Eliezer was so impressed with the danger of formalism that it was his custom to compose one new prayer every day, that his prayer might be always fresh. It is quite clear that this kind of danger is not confined to Jewish religion. Even quiet times which began in devotion can end in the formalism of a rigid and ritualistic time-table.

(iii) Still further, the devout Jew had set times for prayer. The hours were the third, the sixth and the ninth hours, that is, 9 a.m., 12 midday and 3 p.m. In whatever place a man found himself he was bound to pray. Clearly he might be genuinely remembering God, or he might be carrying out an habitual formality. The Mohammedans have the same custom. There is a story of a Mohammedan who was pursuing an enemy with drawn knife to kill him. The muezzin rang out; he stopped, unrolled his prayer mat, knelt and raced through his prayer; and then rose to continue his murderous pursuit. It is a lovely thing that three times a day a man should remember God, but there is a very real danger that three times a day a man might gabble his prayers without a thought of God.

(iv) There was a tendency to connect prayer with certain places, and especially with the synagogue. It is undeniably true that there are certain places where God seems very near, but there were certain Rabbis who went the length of saying that prayer was efficacious only if it was offered in the Temple or in the synagogue. So there grew up the custom of going to the Temple at the hours of prayer. In the first days of the Christian Church, even the disciples of Jesus thought in terms like these, for we read of Peter and John going up to the Temple at the hour of prayer (*Acts* 3: 1). There was a danger here, the danger that a man might come to think of God as being confined to certain holy places and that he might forget that the whole earth is the temple of God. The wisest of the Rabbis saw this danger. They said, " God says to Israel, pray in the synagogue of your city; if you cannot, pray in the field; if you cannot, pray in your house; if you cannot, pray on your bed; if you cannot, commune with your own heart upon your bed, and be still."

The trouble about any system lies, not in the system, but in the men who use it. A man may make any system of prayer an instrument of devotion or a formality, glibly and unthinkingly to be gone through.

(v) There was amongst the Jews an undoubted tendency towards long prayers. That was a tendency by no means confined to the Jews. In 18th century worship in Scotland length meant devotion. In such a Scottish service there was a verse by verse lecture on scripture which lasted for an hour, and a sermon which lasted for another hour. Prayers were lengthy and extempore. Dr. W. D. Maxwell writes, " The efficacy of prayer was measured by its ardour and its fluency, and not least by its fervid lengthiness." Rabbi Levi said, " Whoever is long in prayer is heard." Another saying has it: " Whenever the righteous make their prayer long, their prayer is heard." There was— and still is—a kind of subconscious idea that if men batter long enough at God's door, He will answer; that God can be talked, and even pestered, into condescension. The wisest Rabbis were well aware of this danger. One of them said, " It is forbidden to lengthen out the praise of the Holy One. It says in the *Psalms: ' Who can* recite the mighty deeds of the Lord, *who can* proclaim His praise?' (*Psalm* 106: 2). There only *he who can* may lengthen out and tell His praise—*but no one can.*" " Let a man's words before God always be few, as it is said, ' Be not rash with thy mouth, and let not thy heart be hasty to utter a word before God; for God is in heaven, and thou on earth, therefore let thy words be few.' " (*Ecclesiastes* 5: 1, 2). " The best adoration consists in keeping silence." It is easy to confound verbosity with piety, and fluency with devotion, and into that mistake many of the Jews fell.

HOW NOT TO PRAY

Matthew 6: 5-8 (*continued*)

(vi) THERE were certain other forms of repetition, which the Jews, like all eastern peoples, were apt to use and to overuse. The eastern peoples had a habit of hypnotising themselves by the endless repetition of one phrase or even of one word. In I *Kings* 18: 26 we read how the prophets of Baal cried out, " O Baal hear us," for the space of half a day. In *Acts* 19: 34 we read how the Ephesian mob, for two hours, kept shouting, " Great is Diana of the Ephesians." The Mohammedans will go on repeating the sacred syllable *HE* for hours on end, running round in circles, until they drive themselves to ecstasy, and finally fall down unconscious in total exhaustion. The Jews did that with the *Shema*. It is a kind of substitution of self-hypnotism for prayer.

There was another way in which Jewish prayer used repetition. There was an attempt to pile up every possible title and adjective in the address of the prayer to God. One famous prayer begins:

" Blessed, praised, and glorified, exalted, extolled and honoured, magnified and lauded be the name of the Holy One."

There is one Jewish prayer which actually begins with sixteen different adjectives attached to the name of God. There was a kind of intoxication with words. When a man begins to think more of how he is praying than of what he is praying, his prayer dies upon his lips.

(vii) The final fault which Jesus found with certain of the Jews was that they prayed to be seen of men. The Jewish system of prayer made ostentation very easy. The Jew prayed standing, with hands stretched out, palms upwards, and with head bowed. Prayer had to be said at 9 a.m., 12 midday, and 3 p.m. It had to be said wherever a man might be, and it was easy for a man to make sure that at these hours he was at a busy street corner, or in a crowded city square, so that all the world might see with what devotion he prayed. It was easy for a man to halt on the top step of the entrance to the synagogue, and there pray lengthily and demonstratively, so that all men might admire his exceptional piety. It was easy to put on an act of prayer which all the world might see. The wisest of the Jewish Rabbis fully understood and unsparingly condemned this attitude. " A man in whom is hypocrisy brings wrath upon the world, and his prayer is not heard." " Four classes of men do not receive the face of the glory of God—the mockers, the hypocrites, the liars, and the slanderers." The Rabbis said that no man could pray at all, unless his heart was attuned to pray. They laid it down that for perfect prayer there were necessary an hour of private preparation beforehand, and an hour of meditation afterwards. But the Jewish system of prayer did lend itself to ostentation, if in a man's heart there was pride.

In effect, Jesus lays down two great rules for prayer.

(i) He insists that all true prayer must be offered to God. The real fault of the people whom Jesus was criticising was that they were praying to men and not to God. A certain great preacher once described an ornate and elaborate prayer offered in a Boston Church as " the most eloquent prayer ever offered to a Boston audience." The preacher was much more concerned with impressing the congregation than with making contact with God. Whether in public or in private prayer, a man should have no thought in his mind and no desire in his heart but God.

(ii) He insists that we must always remember that the God to whom we pray is a God of love who is more ready to answer than we are to pray. His gifts and His grace have not to be unwillingly extracted from Him. We do not come to a God who has to be coaxed, or pestered, or battered into answering our prayers. We come to one whose one desire is to give. When we remember that, it is surely sufficient to go to God with the sigh of desire in our hearts, and on our lips the words, " Thy will be done."

THE DISCIPLE'S PRAYER

Matthew 6: 9-15

> So, then, pray in this way:
> Our Father in heaven, let your name be held holy:
> Let your Kingdom come:
> Let your will be done, as in heaven, so upon earth:
> Give us to-day bread for the coming day:
> Forgive us our debts as we forgive our debtors:

And lead us not into temptation, but deliver us from
the Evil One.
For, if you forgive men their trespasses, your heavenly
Father will forgive you too; but if you do not forgive
men their trespasses, neither will your Father forgive
your trespasses.

BEFORE we begin to think about the Lord's Prayer in
detail there are certain general facts which we will do well
to remember about it.

We must note, first of all, that this is a prayer which
Jesus taught His *disciples* to pray. Both Matthew and Luke
are clear about that. Matthew sets the whole Sermon on
the Mount in the context of the disciples (*Matthew* 5: 1);
and Luke tells us that Jesus taught this prayer in response
to the request of one of His disciples (*Luke* 11: 1). The
first thing to remember about the Lord's Prayer is that it
is a prayer which only a disciple can pray; it is a prayer
which only one who is pledged and committed to Jesus
Christ can take upon his lips with any meaning. The Lord's
Prayer is not a child's prayer, as it is so often regarded;
it is, in fact, not meaningful for a child. The Lord's Prayer
is not the Family Prayer as it is sometimes called, unless
by the word *family* we mean *the family of the Church*. The
Lord's Prayer is specifically and definitely stated to be the
disciple's prayer; and only on the lips of a disciple has the
prayer its full meaning. To put it in another way, the
Lord's Prayer can only really be prayed when the man
who prays it knows what he is saying, and he cannot know
that until he has entered into discipleship.

We must note the *order* of the petitions in the Lord's
Prayer. The first three petitions have to do with God and
with the glory of God; the second three petitions have to
do with our needs and our necessities. That is to say, God
is first given His supreme place, and then, and only then,
we turn to ourselves and our needs and desires. It is only
when God is given His proper place that all things fall into
their proper places. Prayer must never be an attempt to

bend the will of God to our desires; prayer is always an attempt to submit our wills to the will of God.

The second part of the prayer, the part of it which deals with our needs and our necessities, is a marvellously wrought unity. It deals with the three essential needs of man, and the three spheres of time within which man moves. First, it asks for *bread*, thereby asking for that which is necessary for the *maintenance of life*, and thereby bringing the needs of the *present* to the throne of God. Second, it asks for *forgiveness*, thereby bringing the *past* into the presence of God, and of God's forgiving grace. Third, it asks for *help in temptation*, thereby committing all the future into the hands of God. In these three brief petitions, we are taught to lay the present, the past, and the future, all before the footstool of the grace of God.

But not only is this carefully wrought prayer a prayer which lays the whole of life in the presence of God; it is also a prayer which brings the whole of God to our lives. When we ask for *bread* to sustain our earthly lives, that request immediately directs our thoughts to God *the Father*, the Creator and the Sustainer of all life. When we ask for *forgiveness*, that request immediately directs our thoughts to God *the Son*, Jesus Christ our Saviour and Redeemer. When we ask for help for future temptation, that request immediately directs our thoughts to God *the Holy Spirit*, the Comforter, the Strengthener, the Illuminator, the Guide and the Guardian of our way.

In the most amazing way this brief second part of the Lord's Prayer takes the present, the past, and the future, the whole of man's life, and presents them to God the Father, God the Son and God the Holy Spirit, to God in all His fulness. In the Lord's Prayer Jesus teaches us to bring the whole of life to the whole of God, and to bring the whole of God to the whole of life.

THE FATHER IN HEAVEN

Matthew 6: 9

Our Father in Heaven.

It might well be said that the word *Father* used of God is
a compact summary of the Christian faith. The great
value of this word *Father* is that it settles all the relationships of this life.

(i) *It settles our relationship to the unseen world.* Mission-
aries tell us that one of the greatest reliefs which Christianity brings to the heathen mind and heart is the certainty
that there is only one God. It is the heathen belief that
there are hordes of gods, that every stream and river, and
tree and valley, and hill and wood, and every natural
force has its own god. The heathen lives in a world crowded
with gods. Still further, all these gods are jealous, and
grudging, and hostile. They must all be placated, and a
man can never be sure that he has not omitted the honour
due to some of these gods. The consequence is that the
heathen lives in terror of the gods; he is " haunted and
not helped by his religion."

The most significant Greek legend of the gods is the
legend of Prometheus. Prometheus was a god. It was in
the days before men possessed fire; and life without fire
was a cheerless and a comfortless thing. In pity Prometheus took fire from heaven and gave it as a gift to men.
Zeus, the king of the gods, was mightily angry that men
should receive this gift. So he took Prometheus and he
chained him to a rock in the middle of the Adriatic Sea,
where he was tortured with the heat and the thirst of the
day, and the cold of the night. Even more, Zeus prepared
a vulture to tear out Prometheus' liver, which always grew
again, only to be torn out again. That is what happened
to the god who tried to help men. The whole conception
is that the gods are jealous, and vengeful, and grudging;
that the last thing the gods wish to do is to help men.
That is the heathen idea of the attitude of the unseen

world to men. The heathen is haunted by the fear of a horde of jealous and grudging gods. So, then, when we discover that the God to whom we pray has the name and the heart of a *father* it makes literally all the difference in the world. We need no longer shiver before a horde of jealous gods; we can rest in a father's love.

(ii) *It settles our relationship to the seen world,* to this world of space and time in which we live. It is easy to think of this world as a hostile world. There are the chances and the changes of life; there are the iron laws of the universe which we break at our peril; there is suffering and death; but if we can be sure that behind this world there is, not a capricious, jealous, mocking god, but a God whose name is Father, then much may still remain dark, but all is bearable because behind all is love. It will always help us if we regard this world as organized, not for our comfort but for our training. Take, for instance, *pain.* Pain might seem a bad thing, but pain has its place in the order of God. It sometimes happens that a person is so abnormally constituted that he is incapable of feeling pain. Such a person is a danger to himself and a problem to everyone else. If there were no such thing as pain, we would never know that we were ill, and often we would die before steps could be taken to deal with any disease or illness. That is not to say that pain cannot *become* a bad thing, but it is to say that times without number pain is God's red light to tell us that there is danger ahead.

Lessing used to say that if he had one question to ask the Sphinx, it would be: " Is this a friendly universe? " If we can be certain that the name of the God who created this world is *Father,* then we can also be certain that fundamentally this is a friendly universe. To call God *Father* is to settle our relationship to the world in which we live.

THE FATHER IN HEAVEN

Matthew 6: 9 (*continued*)

(iii) IF we believe that God is Father, *it settles our relationship to our fellow-men*. If God is Father, He is Father of all men. The Lord's Prayer does not teach us to pray *My Father;* it teaches us to pray *Our Father*. It is very significant that in the Lord's Prayer the word *I, me, my,* and *mine* never occur; it is true to say that Jesus came to take these words out of life and to put in their place *we, us,* and *ours*. God is not any man's exclusive possession. The very phrase *Our Father* involves *the elimination of self.* The fatherhood of God is the only possible basis of the brotherhood of man.

(iv) If we believe that God is Father, *it settles our relationship to ourselves*. There are times in life when every man despises and hates himself. He knows himself to be lower than the lowest thing that crawls upon the earth. The heart knows its own bitterness, and no one knows a man's unworthiness better than that man himself. Mark Rutherford wished to add a new beatitude: " Blessed are those who heal us of our self-despisings." Blessed are those who give us back our self-respect. That is precisely what God does. In these grim, bleak, terrible moments we can still remind ourselves that, even if we matter to no one else, we matter to God; that in the infinite mercy of God we are of royal lineage, children of the King of kings.

(v) If we believe that God is Father, *it settles our relationship to God*. It is not that it removes the might, majesty and power of God. It is not that it makes God any the less God; but it makes that might, and majesty, and power, approachable for us. There is an old Roman story which tells how a Roman Emperor was enjoying a triumph. He had the privilege, which Rome gave to her great victors, of marching his troops through the streets of Rome, with all his captured trophies and his prisoners in his train. So the Emperor was on the march with his troops. The streets were lined with cheering people. The tall legionaries lined the streets' edges to keep the people in their places. At one point on the triumphal route there was a little platform where the Empress and her family were sitting to watch the Emperor go by in all the pride of his triumph. On the platform with his mother there was the Emperor's youngest son, a little boy. As the Emperor came near the little boy jumped off the platform, burrowed through the crowd, tried to dodge between the legs of a legionary, and to run out on to the road to meet his father's chariot. The legionary stooped down and stopped him. He swung him up in his arms: " You can't do that, boy," he said. " Don't you know who that is in the chariot? That's the Emperor. You can't run out to his chariot." And the little lad laughed down. " He may be your Emperor," he said, " but he's my father." That is exactly the way in which the Christian feels towards God. The might, and the majesty, and the power are the might, and the majesty, and the power of one whom Jesus Christ taught us to call *Our Father*.

THE FATHER IN HEAVEN

Matthew 6: 9 (continued)

So far we have been thinking of the first two words of this address to God—*Our Father;* but God is not only *Our Father*, He is Our Father *who is in heaven*. The last words are of primary importance. They conserve two great truths.

(i) They remind us of the *holiness* of God. It is very easy to cheapen and to sentimentalize the whole idea of the fatherhood of God, and to make it an excuse for an easy-going, comfortable religion. " He's a good fellow and all will be well." As Heine said of God: " God will forgive. It is His trade." If we were to say *Our Father,* and stop there, there might be some excuse for that; but it is Our Father *in heaven* to whom we pray. The love is there, but the holiness is there, too.

One of the extraordinary things is how seldom Jesus used the word Father in regard to God. Mark's gospel is the earliest gospel, and is therefore the nearest thing we will ever have to an actual report of all that Jesus said and did; and in Mark's gospel Jesus calls God *Father* only six times, and never outside the circle of the disciples. To Jesus the word *Father* was so sacred that He could hardly bear to use it; and He could never use it except, amongst those who had grasped something of what it meant. We must never use the word *Father* in regard to God cheaply, easily, and sentimentally. God is not an easy-going parent who tolerantly shuts His eyes to all sins and faults and mistakes. This God, whom we can call Father, is the God whom we must still approach with reverence and adoration, and awe and wonder. God is our Father in heaven, and in God there is *love* and *holiness* combined.

(ii) They remind us of the *power* of God. In human love there is so often the tragedy of frustration. We may love a person and yet be quite unable to help that person to achieve something, or to stop him doing something. Human love can be intense—and quite helpless. Any parent with an erring child, or any lover with a wandering loved one knows that. But when we say *Our Father—in heaven* we place two things side by side. We place side by side the *love* of God and the *power* of God. We tell ourselves that the power of God is always motivated by the love of God, and can never be exercised for anything but our good; we tell ourselves that the love of God is backed by the power of God, and that therefore its purposes can never be ultimately frustrated or defeated. It is love of which we think, but it is the love of God. When we pray *Our Father in heaven* we must ever remember the holiness of God, and we must ever remember the power which moves in love, and the love which has behind it the undefeatable power of God.

THE GOSPEL OF MATTHEW

THE HALLOWING OF THE NAME

Matthew 6: 9

Let your name be held holy.

" HALLOWED be Thy name "—it is probably true to say that of all the petitions of the Lord's Prayer this is the one the meaning of which we would find it most difficult to express. If we were asked, what does this petition actually mean? not a few of us would find some difficulty in answering. First, then, let us concentrate on the actual meaning of the words.

The word which is translated *hallowed* is a part of the Greek verb *hagiazesthai*. The Greek verb *hagiazesthai* is connected with the adjective *hagios*, and means *to treat a person or a thing as hagios*. *Hagios* is the word which is usually translated *holy*; but the basic meaning of *hagios* is *different* or *separate*. A thing which is *hagios* is *different* from other things. A person who is *hagios* is *separate* from other people. So a temple is *hagios* because it is *different* from other buildings. An altar is *hagios* because it exists for a purpose *different* from the purpose of ordinary things. God's day is *hagios* because it is *different* from other days. A priest is *hagios* because he is *separate* from other men. So, then, this petition means, " Let God's name be treated differently from all other names; let God's name be given a position which is absolutely unique."

But there is something to add to this. In Hebrew the *name* does not mean simply the name by which a person is called—John or James, or whatever the name may be. In Hebrew the *name* means the *nature*, the *character*, the *personality* of the person in so far as it is known or revealed to us. That becomes clear when we see how the Bible writers use the expression the *name*. The Psalmist says, " They that know Thy *name* will trust in Thee " (*Psalm* 9: 10). Quite clearly that does not mean that those who know that God is called Jehovah will trust in Him. It means that those who know what God is like, those who know the nature and the character of God will put their trust in Him. The Psalmist says, " Some trust in chariots and some in horses, but we will remember the *name* of Jehovah our God " (*Psalm* 20: 7). Quite clearly that does not mean that in a time of difficulty the Psalmist will remember that God is called Jehovah. It means that at such a time some will put their trust in human and material aids and defences, but the Psalmist will remember the nature and the character of God; he will remember what God is like, and that memory will give him confidence.

So, then, let us take these two things and put them together. *Hagiazesthai*, which is translated to *hallow*, means *to regard as different*, to give a unique and special place to. The *name* is the *nature*, the *character*, the *personality* of the person in so far as it is known and revealed to us. Therefore, when we pray " Hallowed be Thy name," it means, " Enable us to give to Thee the unique place which Thy nature and character deserve and demand." This is a prayer that we should be enabled to give to God the unique place which His nature demands.

THE PRAYER FOR REVERENCE

Matthew 6: 9 (*continued*)

Is there, then, one word in English for giving to God the unique place which His nature and character demand? There is such a word, and the word is *reverence*. This petition is a prayer that we should be enabled to reverence God as God deserves to be reverenced. In all true reverence of God there are four essentials.

(i) In order to reverence God we must believe that God exists. We cannot reverence someone who does not exist; we must begin by being sure of the existence of God. To the modern mind it is strange that the Bible nowhere attempts to prove the existence of God. For the Bible God is an axiom. An axiom is a self-evident fact which is not itself proved, but which is the basis of all other proofs. For instance, A straight line is the shortest distance between two points, and, Parallel lines, however far produced, will never meet, are axioms. The Bible writers would have said that it was superfluous to prove the existence of God, because they *experienced* the presence of God every moment of their lives. They would have said that a man no more needed to prove that God exists than he needs to prove that his wife exists. He meets his wife every day, and he meets God every day. But suppose we did need to try to prove that God exists, using our own minds to do so, how would we begin? We can begin from *the world in which we live*. Paley's old argument is not yet completely outdated. Suppose there was a man walking along the road. He strikes his foot against a watch lying in the dust. He has never in his life seen a watch before; he does not know what it is. He picks it up; he sees that it consists of a metal case, and inside the case a complicated arrangement of wheels, levers, springs and jewels. He sees that the whole thing is moving and working in the most orderly way. He sees further that the hands are moving round the dial in an obviously predetermined routine. What then does he say? Does he say: " All these metals and jewels came together from the ends of the earth by chance, by chance made themselves into wheels and levers and springs, by chance assembled themselves into this mechanism, by chance wound themselves up and set themselves going, by chance acquired their obvious orderly working "? No. He says, " I have found a watch; somewhere there must be a watch-maker." Order presupposes mind. We look at the world; we see a vast machine which is working in order. Suns rise and set in an unvarying succession. Tides ebb and flow to a timetable. Seasons follow each other in an order. We look at the world, and we are bound to say, " Somewhere there there must be a world-maker." The fact of the world drives us to God. As Sir James Jeans has said, " No astronomer can be an atheist." The order of the world demands the mind of God behind it. We can begin from *ourselves*. The one thing man has never created is life. Man can alter and rearrange and change things; but he cannot create a living thing. Where then did we get our life? From our parents. Yes, but where did they get theirs? From their parents. But where did all this begin? At some time life must have come into the world; and it must have come from outside the world for man cannot create life; and once again we are driven back to God.

When we look in upon ourselves and out upon the world we are driven to God. As Kant said long ago, "the moral law within us, and the starry heavens above us," drive us to God.

(ii) Before we can reverence God, we must not only believe that God is, we must also know the kind of God God is. No one could reverence the Greek gods with their loves and wars, their hates and their adulteries, their trickeries and their knaveries. No one can reverence capricious, immoral, impure gods. But in God as we know Him there are three great qualities. There is *holiness;* there is *justice;* and there is *love.* We must reverence God, not only because God exists, but because God is the God whom we know Him to be.

(iii) But a man might believe that God is; he might be intellectually convinced that God is holy, just and loving; and still he might not have reverence. For reverence there is necessary *a constant awareness of God.* To reverence God means to live in a God-filled world, to live a life in which we never forget God. This awareness is not confined to the Church or to so-called holy places; it must be an awareness which exists everywhere and at all times. Wordsworth spoke of it in *Lines composed near Tintern Abbey:*

" And I have felt
A presence that disturbs me with the joy
Of elevated thoughts; a sense sublime
Of something far more deeply interfused,
Whose dwelling is the light of setting suns,
And the round ocean, and the living air,
And the blue sky, and in the mind of man:
A motion and a spirit, that impels
All thinking things, all objects of all thought,
And rolls through all things."

One of the finest of modern devotional poets is Henry
Ernest Hardy who wrote under the name of Father Andrew.
In *The Mystic Beauty* he writes:

" O London town has many moods,
And mingled 'mongst its many broods
A leavening of saints,

And ever up and down its streets,
If one has eyes to see one meets
Stuff that an artist paints.

I've seen a back street bathed in blue,
Such as the soul of Whistler knew:
A smudge of amber light,

Where some fried fish-shop plied its trade,
A perfect note of colour made—
Oh, it was exquisite!

I once came through St. James's Park
Betwixt the sunset and the dark,
And oh the mystery

Of grey and green and violet!
I would I never might forget
That evening harmony.

I hold it true that God is there
If beauty breaks through anywhere;
And His most blessed feet,

Who once life's roughest roadway trod,
Who came as man to show us God,
Still pass along the street."

God in the back street, God in St. James's Park, God in
the fried fish shop—that is reverence. The trouble with

most people is that their awareness of God is spasmodic, acute at certain times and places, totally absent at others. Reverence means the constant awareness of God.

(iv) There remains one further ingredient in reverence. We must believe that God exists; we must know what kind of a God God is; we must be constantly aware of God. But a man might have all these things and still not have reverence. To all these things must be added obedience and submission to God. Reverence is knowledge plus submission. In his catechism Luther asks, " How is God's name hallowed amongst us? " and his answer is, " When both our life and doctrine are truly Christian," that is to say, when our intellectual convictions, and our practical actions, are in full submission to the will of God

To know that God is, to know what kind of a God God is, to be constantly aware of God, and to be constantly obedient to Him—that is reverence, that is what we pray for when we pray: " Hallowed be Thy name." Let God be given the reverence which His nature and character deserve.

GOD'S KINGDOM AND GOD'S WILL

Matthew 6: 10, 11

> Let your Kingdom come:
> Let your will be done, as in heaven, so also on earth.

THE phrase *The Kingdom of God* is characteristic of the whole New Testament. There is no phrase which is used oftener in prayer and in preaching and in Christian literature. It is, therefore, of primary importance that we should be clear as to what it means.

It is quite clear that the Kingdom of God was central to the message of Jesus. The first emergence of Jesus on the scene of history was when He came into Galilee preaching the good news of the Kingdom of God (*Mark* 1: 14). Jesus Himself described the preaching of the Kingdom as an obligation laid upon him: " I must preach the Kingdom of God to other cities also, for therefore am I sent " (*Luke* 4: 43; *Mark* I: 38). Luke's description of Jesus' activity is that He went through every city and village preaching and showing the good news of the Kingdom of God (*Luke* 8: I). Clearly the meaning of the Kingdom of Heaven is something which we are bound to try to understand.

When we do try to understand the meaning of this phrase we meet with certain puzzling facts. We find that Jesus spoke of the Kingdom in three different ways. He spoke of the Kingdom as existing in the *past*. He said that Abraham, Isaac and Jacob, and all the prophets were in the Kingdom (*Luke* 13: 28; *Matthew* 8: II). Clearly therefore the Kingdom goes far back into history. He spoke of the Kingdom as *present*. " The Kingdom of God," He said, " is within you, or, it may be, among you " *Luke* 17: 21). The Kingdom of God is therefore a present reality here and now. He spoke of the Kingdom of God as *future*, for He taught men to pray for the coming of the Kingdom in this His own prayer. How then can the Kingdom be past, present and future all at the one time? How can the Kingdom be at one and the same time something which existed, which exists, and for which it is our duty to pray?

We will find the key to this problem in this double petition of the Lord's Prayer. One of the commonest characteristics of Hebrew style is what is technically known as *parallellism*. The Hebrew tended to say everything twice. He said it in one way, and then he said it in another way which repeats or amplifies or explains the first way. Almost any verse of the *Psalms* will show this parallellism in action. Almost every verse of the *Psalms* divides in two in the middle; and the second half repeats or amplifies or explains the first half. Let us take some examples and the thing will become clear:

" God is our refuge and strength—a very present help in trouble " (*Psalm* 46: I).

" The Lord of Hosts is with us—the God of Jacob is our refuge " (*Psalm* 46: 7).

" The Lord is my shepherd—I shall not want.
He maketh me to lie down in green pastures—He leadeth me beside the still waters " (*Psalm* 23: 1, 2).

Let us apply this principle to these two petitions of the Lord's Prayer. Let us set them down side by side:

" Thy Kingdom come—Thy will be done in earth as it is in heaven."

Let us assume that the second petition explains, and amplifies, and defines the first. We then have the perfect definition of the Kingdom of God—*The Kingdom of God is a society upon earth where God's will is as perfectly done as it is in heaven.* Here we have the explanation of how the Kingdom can be past, present and future all at the one time. Any man who at any time in history perfectly did God's will was within the Kingdom; any man who perfectly does God's will is within the Kingdom; but since the world is very far from being a place where God's will is perfectly and universally done, the consummation of the Kingdom is still in the future and is still something for which we must pray.

To be in the Kingdom is to obey the will of God. Immediately we see that, we see that the Kingdom is not something which primarily has to do with nations and peoples and countries. It is something which has to do with each one of us. The Kingdom is in fact the most personal thing in the world. The Kingdom demands the submission of *my* will, *my* heart, *my* life. It is only when each one of us makes the personal decision and submission that the Kingdom comes.

The Chinese Christian prayed the well-known prayer, " Lord, revive Thy Church, beginning with me," and we might well paraphrase that and say, " Lord, bring in Thy Kingdom, beginning with me." To pray for the Kingdom of Heaven is to pray that *we* may submit our wills entirely to the will of God.

GOD'S KINGDOM AND GOD'S WILL

Matthew 6: 10, 11 (continued)

FROM what we have already seen it becomes clear that the most important thing in the world is to obey the will of God; the most important words in the world are the words: " Thy will be done." But it is equally clear that the frame of mind and the tone of voice in which these words are spoken will make a world of difference.

(i) A man can say, " Thy will be done," in a tone of defeated resignation. He may say it, not because he wishes to say it, but because he has accepted the fact that he cannot possibly say anything else; he may say it because he has accepted the fact that God is too strong for him, and that it is useless to batter his head against the walls of the universe. He may say it thinking only of the ineluctable power of God which has him in its grip. As Omar Khayyam had it:

" But helpless Pieces of the Game He plays
Upon this Chequer-board of Nights and Days;
Hither and thither moves, and checks, and slays,
And one by one back in the closet lays.

The Ball no question makes of Ayes and Noes,
But Here or There as strikes the Player goes;
And He that toss'd you down into the Field,
He knows about it all—He knows—HE knows ! "

A man can accept the will of God for no other reason than that he has realized that he cannot do anything else.

(ii) A man may say, " Thy will be done," in a tone of bitter resentment. Swinburne spoke of men feeling the trampling of the iron feet of God. He speaks of the supreme evil, God. Beethoven died all alone; and it is said that when they found his body his lips were drawn back in a snarl and his fists were clenched as if he were shaking his fists in the very face of God and of high heaven. A man may feel that God is his enemy, and yet an enemy so strong that he cannot resist. He may therefore accept God's will, but he may accept it with bitter resentment and smouldering anger.

(iii) A man may say, " Thy will be done," in perfect love and trust. He may say it gladly and willingly, no matter what that will may be. It should be easy for the Christian to say, " Thy will be done," like that; for the Christian can be very sure of two things about God.

(a) He can be sure of the *wisdom* of God. Sometimes when we want something built or constructed, or altered or repaired, we take it to the craftsman and consult him about it. He makes some suggestion, and we often end up by saying, " Well, do what you think best. You are the expert." God is the expert in life, and his guidance can never lead anyone astray. When Richard Cameron, the Scottish Covenanter was killed, his head and his hands were cut off by one Murray and taken to Edinburgh. " His father being in prison for the same cause, the enemy carried them to him, to add grief unto his former sorrow, and inquired at him if he knew them. Taking his son's head and hands, which were very fair (being a man of fair complexion like himself), he kissed them and said, ' I know them—I know them. They are my son's—my own dear son's. It is the Lord. Good is the will of the Lord, who cannot wrong me or mine, but hath made goodness and mercy to follow us all our days.' " When a man can speak like that, when he is quite sure that his times are in the hands of the infinite wisdom of God, it is easy to say, " Thy will be done."

(b) He can be sure of the *love* of God. We do not believe in a mocking and a capricious God, or in a blind and iron determinism. Thomas Hardy finishes his novel *Tess* with the grim words: " The President of the Immortals had finished his sport with Tess." We believe in a God whose name is love. As Whittier had it:

" I know not where His islands lift
    Their fronded palms in air.
I only know I cannot drift
    Beyond His love and care."

As Browning triumphantly declared his faith:

" God, Thou art love! I build my faith on that . . .
I know Thee who has kept my path and made
Light for me in the darkness, tempering sorrow
So that it reached me like a solemn joy.
It were too strange that I should doubt Thy love."

And as Paul had it: " He that spared not His own Son, but delivered Him up for us all, how shall He not with Him also freely give us all things? " (*Romans* 8: 32). No man can look at the Cross and doubt the love of God, and when we are sure of the love of God, it is easy to say, " Thy will be done."

OUR DAILY BREAD
Matthew 6: 12

Give us to-day bread for the coming day.

One would have thought that this is the one petition of the Lord's Prayer about the meaning of which there could have been no possible doubt. It seems on the face of it to be the simplest and the most direct of them all. But it is the fact that many interpreters have offered many interpretations of it. Before we think of its simple and obvious meaning, let us look at some of the other explanations which have been offered.

(i) The bread has been identified with the bread of the Lord's Supper. From the very beginning the Lord's Prayer has been closely connected with the Lord's Table. In the very first orders of service which we possess it is always laid down that the Lord's Prayer should be prayed at the

Lord's Table, and some have taken this petition as a prayer to be granted the daily privilege of sitting at the Table of our Lord, and of eating the spiritual food which a man receives there.

(ii) The bread has been identified with the spiritual food of the word of God. We sometimes sing the hymn:

> " Break Thou the bread of life,
>   Dear Lord, to me,
> As Thou didst break the loaves
>   Beside the sea.
> Beyond the sacred page
>   I seek Thee, Lord,
> My spirit pants for Thee,
>   O living word."

So this petition has been taken to be a prayer for the true teaching, the true doctrine, the essential truth, which are in the scriptures and the word of God, and which are indeed food for a man's mind and heart and soul.

(iii) The bread has been taken to stand for Jesus Himself. Jesus called Himself *the bread of life* (*John* 6: 33-35), and this has been taken to be a prayer that daily we may be fed on Him who is the living bread. It was in that way that Matthew Arnold used the phrase, when he wrote his poem about the saint of God he met in the east end of London one suffocating day:

> " 'Twas August, and the fierce sun overhead
> Smote on the squalid streets of Bethnal Green,
> And the pale weaver, through his windows seen,
> In Spitalfields, look'd thrice dispirited.
>
> I met a preacher there I knew and said:
> ' Ill and o'er worked, how fare you in this scene? '
> ' Bravely! ' said he, ' for I of late have been
> Much cheer'd with thoughts of Christ, the living
>   bread.' "

So then this petition has been taken as a prayer that we too might be cheered and strengthened with Christ the living bread.

(iv) This petition has been taken in a purely Jewish

sense. The bread has been taken to be the bread of the heavenly kingdom. Luke tells how one of the bystanders said to Jesus: " Blessed is he who shall eat bread in the Kingdom of God " (*Luke* 14: 15). The Jews had a strange yet vivid idea. They held that when the Messiah came, and when the golden age dawned, there would be what they called the Messianic banquet, at which the chosen ones of God would sit down. The slain bodies of the monsters Behemoth and Leviathan would provide the meat and the fish courses of the banquet. It would be a kind of reception feast given by God to His own people. So, then, this has been taken to be a petition for a place at the final Messianic banquet of the people of God.

Although we need not agree that any one of these explanations is the main meaning of this petition, we need not reject any of them as false. They all have their own truth and their own relevance.

The difficulty of interpreting this petition was increased by the fact that there was very considerable doubt as to the meaning of the word *epiousios*, which is the word which the Authorised Version translates *daily*. The extraordinary fact was that, until a short time ago, there was no other known occurence of this word in the whole of Greek literature. Origen knew this, and indeed held that Matthew had invented the word. It was therefore not possible to be sure what it precisely meant. But not very long ago a papyrus fragment turned up with this word on it; and the papyrus fragment was actually a woman's shopping list! And against an item on it was the word *epiousios*. It was a note to remind her to buy supplies of a certain food for the coming day. So, very simply, what this petition means is: " Give me the things we need to eat for this coming day. Help me to get the things I've got on my shopping list when I go out this morning. Give me the things we need to eat when the children come in from school, and the men folk come in from work. Grant that

the table be not bare when we sit down together to-day."
This is a simple prayer that God will supply us with the
things we need for the coming day.

OUR DAILY BREAD

Matthew 6: 12 (*continued*)

WHEN we see that this petition is a simple petition for the
needs of the everyday, there are certain tremendous
truths which emerge from it.

(i) It tells us that God cares for our bodies. Jesus showed
us that; He spent so much time healing men's diseases and
satisfying their physical hunger. He was anxious when He
thought that the crowd who had followed Him out into
the lonely places had a long road home, and no food to eat
before they set out upon it. We do well to remember that
God is interested in our bodies. Any teaching which
belittles, and despises, and slanders the body is wrong. We
can see what God thinks of our human bodies, when we
remember that He Himself in Jesus Christ took that body
upon Him. It is not simply *soul* salvation, it is *whole*
salvation, the salvation of body, mind and spirit, at which
Christianity aims.

(ii) This petition teaches us to pray for our *daily* bread,
for bread *for the coming day*. It teaches us to live one day at
a time, and not to worry and be anxious about the distant
and the unknown future. When Jesus taught His disciples
to pray this petition, there is little doubt that His mind
was going back to the story of the manna in the wilderness
(*Exodus* 16: 1-21). The children of Israel were starving
in the wilderness, and God sent them the manna, the food
from heaven; but there was one condition—they must
gather only enough for their immediate needs. If they
tried to gather too much, and to store it up, it went bad
and rotten. They had to be satisfied with enough for the
day. As one Rabbi put it: " The portion of a day in its

day, because He who created the day created sustenance for the day." And as another Rabbi had it: " He who possesses what he can eat to-day, and says, ' What shall I eat to-morrow? ' is a man of little faith." This petition tells us to live one day at a time. It forbids the anxious worry which is so characteristic of the life which has not learned to trust God.

(iii) By implication this petition gives God His proper place. It admits that it is from God we receive the food which is necessary to support life. No man has ever created a seed which will grow. The scientist can analyse a seed into its constituent elements, but no synthetic seed would ever grow. All living things come from God. Our food is the direct gift of God.

(iv) This petition very wisely reminds us of how prayer works. If a man prayed this prayer, and then sat back and waited for bread to fall into his hands, he would certainly starve. It reminds us that prayer and work go hand in hand, that when we pray we must go on to work to make our prayers come true. It is true that the living seed comes from God, but it is equally true that it is man's task to grow and to cultivate that seed. Dick Sheppard used to love a certain story. There was a man who had an allotment; he had with great toil reclaimed a piece of ground, clearing away the stones, eradicating the rank growth of weeds, enriching and feeding the ground, until it produced the loveliest flowers and vegetables. One evening he was showing a pious friend around his allotment. The pious friend said, " It's wonderful what God can do with a bit of ground like this, isn't it? " " Yes," said the man who had put in such toil, " but you should have seen this bit of ground when God had it to Himself! " God's bounty and man's toil must combine. Prayer, like faith, without works is dead. When we pray this petition we are recognizing two basic truths—that without God we can do nothing, and that without our effort and co-operation God can do nothing for us.

(v) We must note that Jesus did not teach us to pray:
" Give *me my* daily bread." He taught us to pray: " Give
us our daily bread." The problem of the world is not that
there is not enough to go round; there is enough and to
spare. In America granaries overflow with corn; in Brazil
they fire locomotives with blocks of surplus coffee. The
problem is not the *supply* of life's essentials; it is the
distribution of them. This prayer teaches us never to be
selfish in our prayers. It is a prayer which we can help God
to answer by giving to others who are less fortunate than
we are. This prayer is not only a prayer that we may
receive our daily bread; it is also a prayer that we may
share our daily bread with others.

FORGIVENESS HUMAN AND DIVINE

Matthew 6: 12, 14, 15

> Forgive us our debts as we forgive our debtors . . . For
> if you forgive men their trespasses, your heavenly
> Father will forgive you too; but, if you do not forgive
> men their trespasses, neither will your Father forgive
> your trespasses.

BEFORE a man can truly and honestly pray this petition
of the Lord's Prayer he must realize that he needs to pray
it. That is to say, before a man can pray this petition he
must have a sense of sin. Sin is not nowadays a popular
word. Men and women rather resent being called, or
treated as, hell-deserving sinners. The trouble is that most
people have a wrong conception of sin. They would readily
agree that the burglar, the drunkard, the murderer, the
adulterer, the foul-mouthed person is a sinner; but they
are guilty of none of these sins; they live decent, ordinary,
respectable lives, and have never even been in danger of
appearing in court, or going to prison, or getting their
names into the newspapers. They therefore feel that sin
has nothing to do with them. The New Testament uses
five different words for *sin.*

(i) The commonest word is the word *hamartia*. *Hamartia* was originally a shooting word and means *a missing of the target*. To fail to hit the target was *hamartia*. Therefore *sin is the failure to be what we might have been and could have been*. Charles Lamb has a picture of a man named Samuel le Grice. Le Grice was a brilliant youth who never fulfilled his promise. Lamb says that there were three stages in his career. There was a time when people said, " He will do something." There was a time when people said, " He could do something if he would." There was a time when people said, " He might have done something, if he had liked." Edwin Muir writes in his *Autobiography:* " After a certain age all of us, good and bad, are grief stricken because of powers within us which have never been realized: because, in other words, we are not what we should be." That precisely is *hamartia;* and that is precisely the situation in which we are all involved. Are we as good a husband or as good a wife as we could be? Are we as good a son or as good a daughter as we could be? Are we as good a workman or as good an employer as we could be? Is there anyone who will dare to claim that he is all he might have been, and has done all he could have done? When we realise that sin means the failure to hit the target, the failure to be all that we might have been and could have been, then it is clear that every one of us is a sinner.

(ii) The second word for sin is *parabasis*, which literally means a *stepping across*. *Sin is the stepping across the line which is drawn between right and wrong.* Do we always stay on the right side of the line which divides honesty and dishonesty? Is there never any such thing as a petty dishonesty in our lives? Do we always stay on the right side of the line which divides truth and falsehood? Do we never, by word or by silence, twist or evade or distort the truth? Do we always stay on the right side of the line which divides kindness and courtesy from selfishness and harshness? Is there never an unkind action or a discourteous word in our lives? When we think of it in this way, there can be none who can claim always to have remained on the right side of the dividing line.

(iii) The third word for sin is *paraptōma*, which means a *slipping across*. It is the kind of slip which a man might make on a slippery or an icy road. It is not so deliberate as *parabasis*. Again and again we speak of words slipping out; again and again we are swept away by some impulse or passion, which has momentarily gained control of us, and which has made us lose our self-control. The best of us can slip into sin when for the moment we are off our guard.

(iv) The fourth word for sin is *anomia*, which means *lawlessness*. *Anomia* is the sin of the man who knows the right, and who yet does the wrong; the sin of the man who knows the law, and who breaks the law. The first of all the human instincts is the instinct to do what we like; and therefore there come into any man's life times when he wishes to kick over the traces, and to defy the law, and to do or to take the forbidden thing. In *Mandalay*, Kipling makes the old soldier say:

" Ship me somewheres east of Suez, where the best is
    like the worst,
        Where there aren't no Ten Commandments, an' a
    man can raise a thirst."

Even if there are some who can say that they have never broken any of the Ten Commandments, there are none who can say that they have never wished to break them.

(v) The fifth word for sin is the word *opheilēma* which is the word used in the body of the Lord's Prayer; and *opheilēma* means a *debt*. It means *a failure to pay that which is due*, a failure in duty. There can be no man who will ever dare to claim that he has perfectly fulfilled his duty to man and to God. Such perfection does not exist among men.

So, then, when we come to see what sin really is we come to see that it is a universal disease in which every man is involved. Outward respectability in the sight of man, and inward sin in the sight of God may well go hand in hand. This, in fact, is the petition of the Lord's Prayer which every man needs to pray.

FORGIVENESS HUMAN AND DIVINE

Matthew 6: 12, 14, 15 (continued)

NOT only does a man need to realize that he needs to pray this petition of the Lord's Prayer; he also needs to realize what he is doing when he prays it. Of all petitions of the Lord's Prayer this is the most frightening. " Forgive us our debts as we forgive our debtors." The literal meaning is: " Forgive us our sins *in proportion as* we forgive those who have sinned against us." Matthew goes on in verses 14 and 15 to make that quite clear by showing us that Jesus says in the plainest possible language that if we forgive others, God will forgive us; but if we refuse to forgive others, God will refuse to forgive us. It is, therefore, quite clear that, if we pray this petition with an unhealed breach, an unsettled quarrel in our lives, we are asking God *not* to forgive us. If we say, " I will never forgive so-and-so for what he or she has done to me," if we say, " I will never forget what so-and-so did to me," and then go and take this petition on our lips, we are quite deliberately asking God not to forgive us. As someone has put it: " Forgiveness, like peace, is one and indivisible." Human forgiveness and divine forgiveness are inextricably intercombined. Our forgiveness of our fellow-men and God's forgiveness of us cannot be separated; they are interlinked and interdependent. If we remembered what we are doing when we take this petition on our lips, there would be times when we would not dare to pray it.

When Robert Louis Stevenson lived in the South Sea Islands he used always to conduct family worship in the mornings for his household. It always concluded with the Lord's Prayer. One morning in the middle of the Lord's

Prayer he rose from his knees and left the room. His health was always precarious, and his wife followed him thinking that he was ill. " Is there anything wrong? " she said. " Only this," said Stevenson, " I am not fit to pray the Lord's Prayer to-day." No one is fit to pray the Lord's Prayer so long as the unforgiving spirit holds sway within his heart. If a man has not put things right with his fellow-men, he cannot put things right with God.

If we are to have this Christian forgiveness in our lives, three things are necessary.

(i) We must learn *to understand*. There is always a reason why a person does something. If he is boorish and impolite and cross-tempered, maybe he is worried and in pain. If he treats us with suspicion and dislike, maybe he has mis-understood, or has been misinformed about something we have said or done. Maybe the man is the victim of his own environment or his own heredity. Maybe his temperament is such that life is difficult and human relations a problem for him. Forgiveness would be very much easier for us, if we tried to understand before we allow ourselves to condemn.

(ii) We must learn *to forget*. So long as we remember and brood upon a slight or an injury, there is no hope that we will forgive. We so often say, " I can't forget what so-and-so did to me," " I will never forget how I was treated by such-and-such a person or in such-and-such a place." These are dangerous sayings, because we can in the end make it humanly impossible for us to forget. We can print the memory indelibly upon our minds. Once the famous Scottish man of letters, Andrew Lang, wrote and published a very kind review of a book by a young man. The young man repaid him with a bitter, insolent, and insulting attack. About three years later Andrew Lang was staying with Robert Bridges, the Poet Laureate. Bridges saw Lang reading a certain book. " Why," he said, " that's another book by that ungrateful young cub who behaved so shamefully to you." To his astonishment he found that

Andrew Lang's mind was a blank on the whole affair. He had completely forgotten the bitter and insulting attack. To forgive, said Bridges, was the sign of a great man, but to forget was sublime. Nothing but the cleansing spirit of Christ can take from these memories of ours the old bitterness that we must forget.

(iii) We must learn *to love*. We have already seen that Christian love, *agapē*, is that unconquerable benevolence, that undefeatable good-will, which will never seek anything but the highest good of others, no matter what they do to us, and no matter how they treat us. That love can come to us only when Christ, who is that love, comes to dwell within our hearts—and He cannot come unless we invite Him.

To be forgiven we must forgive, and that is a condition of forgiveness which only the power of Christ can enable us to fulfil.

THE ORDEAL OF TEMPTATION

Matthew 6: 13

> And lead us not into temptation, but deliver us from the Evil One.

THERE are two matters of meaning at which we must look before we begin to study this petition in detail.

(i) To modern ears the word *tempt* is always a bad word; it always means *to seek to seduce into evil*. But in the Bible the verb *peirazein* is often better translated by the word *test* than by the word *tempt*. In its New Testament usage to *tempt* a person is not so much to seek to seduce him into sin, as it is to test his strength and his loyalty and his ability for service. In the Old Testament we read the story of how God tested the loyalty of Abraham by seeming to demand the sacrifice of his only son Isaac. The story begins: " And it came to pass that God did *tempt* Abraham " (Genesis 22: 1). Very obviously the word *tempt* cannot there mean to seek to seduce into sin, for that is something that God would never do. It means rather to submit to a test of loyalty and obedience. When we read the story of the temptations of Jesus, it begins: " Then was Jesus lead up of the Spirit into the wilderness to be *tempted* of the devil " (*Matthew* 3: 1). If we take the word *tempt* there simply in the sense of to seduce into sin, then it makes the Holy Spirit a partner in an attempt to compel Jesus to sin. Time and again in the Bible we will find that the word *tempt* has the idea of *testing* in it, at least as much as the idea of seeking to lead into sin.

Here, then, is one of the great and precious truths about temptation. Temptation is not designed to make us fall. Temptation is designed to make us stronger and better men and women. Temptation is not designed to make us sinners. It is designed to make us good. We may fail in the test, but we were not meant to. We were meant to emerge stronger and finer. In one sense temptation is not so much the *penalty* of being a man; it is the *glory* of being a man. If metal is to be used in a great engineering project, it is tested at stresses and strains far beyond those which it is ever likely to have to bear. So a man has to be tested before God can use him greatly in his service.

(i) All that is true; but it is also true that the Bible is never in any doubt that there is a power of evil in this world. The Bible is not a speculative book, and it does not discuss the origin of that power of evil, but it knows that it is there. Quite certainly this petition of the Lord's Prayer should be translated not, " Deliver us from evil," but, " Deliver us from the Evil One." The Bible does not think of evil as an abstract principle or force, but as an active, personal power in opposition to God.

The development of the idea of Satan in the Bible is of the greatest interest. In Hebrew the word *Satan* simply means an *adversary*. It can often be used of men. A man's adversary is his *Satan*. The Philistines are afraid that David may turn out to be their *Satan* (*I Samuel* 29: 4). Solomon declares that God has given him such peace and prosperity that there is no *Satan* left to oppose him (*I Kings* 5: 4). David regards Abishai as his *Satan* (*II Samuel* 19: 22). In all these cases *Satan* means an *adversary* or *opponent*. From that the word Satan goes on to mean *one who pleads a case against someone*. Then the word leaves earth and, as it were, enters heaven. The Jews had the idea that in heaven there was an angel whose charge it was to state the case against a man, a kind of prosecuting angel; and that became the function of *Satan*. At that stage Satan is not an evil power; he is part of the judgment apparatus of heaven. In *Job* 1: 6, Satan is numbered among the sons of God: " Now there came a day when the sons of God came to present themselves before the Lord, and Satan came also among them." At this stage Satan is the divine prosecutor of man.

But it is not so very far a step from *stating* a case against a man to *making up a case* against a man. And that is the next step. The other name of Satan is the Devil; and *Devil* comes from the Greek word *Diabolos*, which is the regular word for a *slanderer*. So *Satan* becomes the *Devil*, the slanderer *par excellence*, the adversary of mankind, the power who is out to frustrate the purposes of God and to ruin mankind. Satan comes to stand for everything which is anti-man and anti-God. It is from that ruining power that Jesus teaches us to pray to be delivered. The origin of that power is not discussed; there are no speculations. As someone has put it: " If a man wakes up and finds his house on fire, he does not sit down in a chair and write or read a treatise on the origin of fires in private houses; he sets to to try to extinguish the fire and to save his house." So the Bible wastes no time in speculations about the origin of evil. It equips man to fight the battle against the evil, which is unquestionably there.

THE GOSPEL OF MATTHEW

THE ATTACK OF TEMPTATION

Matthew 6: 13 (*continued*)

LIFE is always under attack from temptation, but no enemy can launch an invasion until he finds a bridgehead. Where then does temptation find its bridgehead? Where do our temptations come from? To be forewarned is to be forearmed, and, if we know whence the attack is likely to come, we will have a better chance to overcome and to defeat it.

(i) Sometimes the attack of temptation comes from outside us. There are people whose influence is bad. There are people in whose company it would be very difficult even to suggest doing a dishonourable thing, and there are people in whose company it is easy to do the wrong things. When Robert Burns was a young man he went to Irvine to learn flax-dressing. There he fell in with a certain Robert Brown, who was a man who had seen much of the world, and who had a fascinating and a dominating personality. Burns tells us that he admired him and strove to imitate him. Burns goes on: " He was the only man I ever saw who was a greater fool than myself when Woman was the guiding star. . . . He spoke of a certain fashionable failing with levity, which hitherto I had regarded with horror. . . . Here his friendship did me a mischief." There are friendships and associations which can do us a mischief. In a tempting world a man should be very careful in his choice of friends and of the society in which he will move. He should give the temptations which come from outside as little chance as possible.

(ii) It is one of the tragic facts of life that temptations can come to us from those who love us; and of all kinds of temptation this is the hardest to fight against. It comes from people who love us and who have not the slightest intention of harming us. The kind of thing that happens is this. A man may know that he ought to take a certain course of action; he may feel divinely drawn to a certain

228

career; but to follow that course of action may involve unpopularity and risk; to accept that career may be to give up all that the world calls a career. It may well be that in such circumstances those who love him will seek to dissuade him from the course of action he knows he ought to take, and they will do so just because they love him. They counsel caution, prudence, worldly wisdom; they want to see the one they love do well in a worldly sense; they do not wish to see him throw his chances away; and so they seek to stop him doing what he knows to be right for him. In *Gareth and Lynette* Tennyson tells the story of Gareth, the youngest son of Lot and Bellicent. Gareth wishes to join his brothers in the service of King Arthur. Bellicent his mother does not wish him to go. " Hast thou no pity on my loneliness? " she asks. His father Lot is old and lies " like a log all but smouldered out." Both his brothers have gone to Arthur's court. Must he go too? If he will stay at home, she will arrange the hunt, and find him a princess for his bride, and make him happy. It was because she loved him that she wished to keep him; the tempter was speaking with the very voice of love. But Gareth answers:

> " O mother,
> How can you keep me tethered to you—shame.
> Man am I grown, and man's work must I do.
> Follow the deer? Follow the Christ, the King.
> Live pure, speak true, right wrong, follow the King—
> Else, wherefore born? "

The lad went out, but the voice of love tempted him to stay.

That was what happened to Jesus. " A man's foes," said Jesus, " shall be they of his own household " (*Matthew* 10: 36). They came and they tried to take Him home, because they said that He was mad (*Mark* 3: 21). To them He seemed to be throwing his life and His career away; to them He seemed to be making a fool of Himself; and they tried to stop Him. Sometimes the bitterest of all temptations come to us from the voice of love.

(iii) There is one very odd way in which temptation can come to us, especially to younger people. There is in most of us a queer streak, which, at least in certain company, makes us wish to appear worse than we are. We do not wish to appear to be soft and pious, and namby-pamby and holy. We would rather be thought to be daredevil, swashbuckling adventurers, men of the world and not innocents. Augustine has a famous passage in his confessions: " Among my equals I was ashamed of being less shameless than others, when I heard them boast of their wickedness. . . . And I took pleasure not only in the pleasure of the deed but in the praise. . . . I made myself worse than I was, that I might not be reproached, and when in anything I had not sinned as the most abandoned ones, I would say that I had done what I had not done, that I might not seem contemptible." Many a man has begun on some indulgence, or introduced himself to some habit, because he did not wish to appear less experienced in worldliness than the company in which he happened to be. One of the great defences against temptation is simply the courage to be good.

THE ATTACK OF TEMPTATION

Matthew 6: 13 *(continued)*

(iv) BUT temptation comes not only from outside us; it comes from inside us too. If there was nothing in us to which temptation could appeal, then temptation would be helpless to defeat us. In every one of us there is some weak spot; and at that weak spot temptation launches its attack. The point of vulnerability differs in all of us. What is a violent temptation to one man, leaves another man quite unmoved; and what leaves one man quite unmoved may be an irresistible temptation to another. Sir James Barrie has a play called *The Will*. Mr. Devizes, the lawyer, noticed that an old clerk, who had been in his

service for many years, was looking very ill. He asked him
if anything was the matter. The old man told him that his
doctor had informed him that he was suffering from a
fatal and incurable disease.

Mr Devizes [*uncomfortably*]: I'm sure it's not—what
you fear. Any specialist would tell you so.

Surtees [*without looking up*]: I've been to one, sir—
yesterday.

Mr Devizes: Well?

Surtees: It's——that, sir.

Mr Devizes: He couldn't be sure.

Surtees: Yes, sir.

Mr Devizes: An operation——

Surtees: Too late for that, he said. If I had been
operated on long ago, I might have had a chance.

Mr Devizes: But you didn't have it long ago.

Surtees: Not to my knowledge, sir; but he says it was
there all the same, always in me, a black spot, not
as big as a pin's head, but waiting to spread and
destroy me in the fulness of time.

Mr Devizes [*helpless*]: It seems damnably unfair.

Surtees [*humbly*]: I don't know, sir. He says there is a
spot of that kind in pretty nigh all of us, and, if we
don't look out, it does for us in the end.

Mr Devizes: No. No. No.

Surtees: He called it the accursed thing. I think he
meant we should know of it, and be on the watch.

In every man there is the weak spot, which, if he is not
on the watch, can ruin him. Somewhere in every man there
is the flaw, some fault of temperament which can ruin life,
some instinct or passion so strong that it may at any time
snap the leash, some quirk in our make-up that makes
what is a pleasure to someone else a menace to us. We
should realize it, and be on the watch.

(v) But, strangely enough, temptation comes sometimes,
not from our weakest point, but from our strongest point.
If there is one thing of which we are in the habit of saying,
" That is one thing anyway which I would never do," it

is just there that we should be upon the watch. History is full of the stories of castles which were taken just at the point where the defenders thought them so strong that no guard was necessary. Nothing gives temptation its chance like over-confidence. At our weakest and at our strongest points we must be upon the watch.

THE DEFENCE AGAINST TEMPTATION

Matthew 6: 13 *(continued)*

WE have thought of the attack of temptation; let us now assemble our defences against temptation.

(i) There is the simple defence of *self-respect*. When Nehemiah's life was in danger, it was suggested that he should quit his work and shut himself in the Temple until the danger was past. His answer was: " Should such a man as I flee? And who is there that, being such as I am, would go into the Temple to save his life? I will not go in " (*Nehemiah* 6: 11). A man may escape many things, but he cannot escape himself. He must live with his memories, and if he has lost his self-respect life becomes intolerable. Once President Garfield was urged to take a profitable, but dishonourable, course of action. It was said, " No one will ever know." His answer was, " President Garfield will know—and I've got to sleep with him." When a man is tempted, he may well defend himself by saying, " Is a man like me going to do a thing like that? "

(ii) There is the defence of *tradition*. No man can lightly fail the traditions and the heritage into which he has entered, and which have taken generations to build up. When Pericles, the greatest of the statesmen of Athens, was going to address the Athenian Assembly, he always whispered to himself: " Pericles, remember that you are an Athenian and that you go to speak to Athenians." One of the epics of the war was the defence of Tobruk. The Coldstream Guards cut their way out of Tobruk, and only

a handful of them survived, and even these were only
shadows of men. Two hundred survivors out of two
battalions were being cared for by the R.A.F. A Coldstream Guards officer was in the mess. Another officer
said to him, " After all, as Foot Guards, you had no option
but to have a go." And a R.A.F. man standing there
said, " It must be pretty tough to be in the Brigade of
Guards, because tradition compels you to carry on irres-
pective of circumstances." The power of a tradition is one
of the greatest things in life. We belong to a country, a
school, a family, a Church. What we do affects that to
which we belong. We cannot lightly betray the traditions
into which we have entered.

(iii) There is the defence of *those whom we love and those
who love us.* Many a man would sin, if the only penalty he
had to bear was the penalty he would have to bear himself;
but he is saved from sin because he could not meet the pain
in someone's eyes, if he made shipwreck of life. Laura
Richards has a parable like this:

" A man sat by the door of his house smoking his pipe,
and his neighbour sat beside him and tempted him.
' You are poor,' said the neighbour, ' and you are out
of work and here is a way of bettering yourself. It will
be an easy job and it will bring in money, and it is no
more dishonest than things that are done every day
by respectable people. You will be a fool to throw
away such a chance as this. Come with me and we
will settle the matter at once.' And the man listened.
Just then his young wife came to the door of the
cottage and she had her baby in her arms. ' Will you
hold the baby for a minute,' she said, ' He is fretful
and I must hang out the clothes to dry.' The man took
the baby and held him on his knees. And as he held
him, the child looked up, and the eyes of the child
spoke: ' I am flesh of your flesh,' said the child's eyes.
' I am soul of your soul. Where you lead I shall follow.
Lead the way, father. My feet come after yours.'
Then said the man to his neighbour: ' Go, and come
here no more.' "

A man might be perfectly willing to pay the price of sin, if that price affected only himself. But if he remembers that his sin will break someone else's heart, he will have a strong defence against temptation.

(iv) There is the defence of *the presence of Jesus Christ.* Jesus is not a figure in a book; He is a living presence. Sometimes we ask, " What would you do, if you suddenly found Christ standing beside you? How would you live, if Jesus Christ was a guest in your house? " But the whole point of the Christian faith is that Jesus Christ *is* beside us, and He *is* a guest in every home. His is the inescapable presence, and, therefore, we must make all life fit for Him to see. We have a strong defence against temptation in the memory of the continual presence of Jesus Christ.

HOW NOT TO FAST

Matthew 6: 16-18

> When you fast, don't put on a sad face, as the hypo-crites do, for they disfigure their faces, so that all men may see that they are fasting. This is the truth I tell you—they are paid in full. But when you fast, anoint your head and wash your face, so that to men you may not look as if you were fasting, but to your Father who is in secret; and your Father, who sees what happens in secret, will give you your reward in full.

To this day fasting is an essential part of the religious life in the east. The Mohammedan strictly keeps the fast of Ramadan, which falls in the ninth month of the Moham-medan year, and which commemorates the first revelation which came to Mohammed. The fast lasts from dawn—when it is light enough to distinguish a white thread from a black thread—until sunset. Bathing, drinking, smoking, smelling perfumes, eating, every unnecessary indulgence is forbidden. Nurses and pregnant women are exempt. Soldiers and those on a journey are excused, but must at some other time fast for an equivalent number of days. If for health's sake a man must have food, he must make good his breach of the law of fasting by giving alms to the poor. The Jewish fasting customs were exactly the same. It is to be noted that, as we have said, fasting lasted from dawn to sunset; outside that time normal meals could be eaten. For the Jew, in the time of Jesus, there was only one compulsory fast, the fast on the Day of Atonement. On that day from morning to evening, all men had " to afflict their souls " (*Leviticus* 16: 31). The Jewish scribal law lays it down: " On the Day of Atonement it is forbidden to eat, or to drink, or to bathe, or to anoint oneself, or to wear sandals, or to indulge in conjugal intercourse." Even young children had to be trained to some measure of fasting on the Day of Atonement so that, when they grew up, they would be prepared to accept the national fast.

But, although there was only the one compulsory, universal day of fasting, the Jews made great use of private fasting.

There was *the fasting which was connected with mourning*. Between the time of death and burial mourners must abstain from all flesh and wine. There was fasting *to expiate some sin*. It was said, for instance, that Reuben fasted for seven years for his share in the selling of Joseph: " He drank no wine or other liquor; no flesh passed his lips, and he ate no appetising food " (*The Testament of Reuben* 1: 10). For the same reason, " Simeon afflicted his soul with fasting for two years, because he had hated Joseph " (*The Testimony of Simon* 3: 4). In repentance of his sin with Tamar, it was said that Judah to his old age " took neither wine nor flesh, and saw no pleasure " (*The Testament of Judah* 15: 4). It is fair to say that Jewish thought saw no value in fasting apart from repentance. The fast was only designed to be the outer expression of an inward sorrow. The writer of *Ecclesiasticus* (31: 30) says, " A man who fasts to get rid of his sins, and goes again and does the same thing—who will listen to his prayer, and what profit is there in his humbling himself? "

In many cases fasting was an act of *national penitence*. So the whole nation fasted after the disaster of the civil war with Benjamin (*Judges* 20: 26). Samuel made the people fast because they had strayed away after Baal (*I Samuel* 7: 6). Nehemiah made the people fast and confess their sins (*Nehemiah* 9: 1). Again and again the nation fasted as a sign of national penitence before God.

Sometimes fasting was *a preparation for revelation*. Moses in the mountain fasted for forty days and forty nights (*Exodus* 24: 15). Daniel fasted as he awaited God's word (*Daniel* 9: 3). Jesus Himself fasted as He awaited the ordeal of temptation (*Matthew* 4: 3). This was a sound principle, for when the body is most disciplined, the mental and the spiritual faculties are most alert. Sometimes fasting was *an appeal to God*. If, for instance, the rains failed and the harvest was in jeopardy, a national fast would be called as an appeal to God.

In Jewish fasting there were really three main ideas in the minds of men.

(i) Fasting was a deliberate attempt *to draw the attention of God* to the person who fasted. This was a very primitive idea. The fasting was designed to attract God's attention, and to make Him notice the person who thus afflicted himself.

(ii) Fasting was a deliberate attempt *to prove that penitence was real*. Fasting was a guarantee of the sincerity of words and prayers; it was designed to be a proof that penitence was real. It is easy to see that there was a danger here, for that which was meant to be a *proof* of repentance could very easily come to be regarded as a *substitute* for repentance.

(iii) A great deal of fasting was *vicarious*. It was not designed to save a man's own soul so much as to move God to liberate the nation from its distresses. It was as if specially devoted people said, " Ordinary people cannot do this. They are too involved in work and in the world.

We will do this extra thing to counterbalance the necessary deficiency of piety in others."

Such then was the Jewish theory and practice of fasting.

HOW NOT TO FAST

Matthew 6: 16-18 (continued)

HIGH as the ideal of fasting might be, the practice of it involved certain inevitable dangers. The great danger was that a man might fast as a sign of superior piety, that his fasting might be a deliberate demonstration, not to God, but to men, of how devoted and disciplined a person he was. That is precisely what Jesus was condemning. He was condemning fasting when it was used as an ostentatious parade of piety. The Jewish days of fasting were Monday and Thursday. These were market days, and into the towns and villages, and especially into Jerusalem, there crowded the people from the country; the result was that those who were ostentatiously fasting would on those days have a bigger audience to see and admire their piety. There were many who took deliberate steps to see that others could not miss the fact that they were fasting. They walked through the streets with hair deliberately unkempt and dishevelled, with clothes deliberately soiled and disarrayed. They even went the length of deliberately whitening their faces to accentuate their paleness. This was no act of humility; it was a deliberate act of spiritual pride and ostentation.

The wisest of the Rabbis would have condemned this as unsparingly as Jesus did. They were quite clear that fasting for its own sake was valueless. They said that a vow of abstinence was like an iron collar which prisoners had to wear; and he who imposed on himself such a vow was said to be like a man who found such a collar lying about, and who misguidedly stuck his head into it, thereby voluntarily undertaking a useless slavery. One of the finest things ever said is the Rabbinic saying, " A man will have to give an account on the judgment day for every good thing which he might have enjoyed, and did not."

Dr. Boreham has a story which is a commentary on the wrong idea of fasting. A traveller in the Rocky mountains fell in with an old Roman Catholic priest; he was amazed to find so aged a man struggling amidst the rocks and the precipices and the steep passes. The traveller asked the priest, " What are you doing here? " The old man answered, " I am seeking the beauty of the world." " But," said the traveller, " surely you have left it very late in life? " So the old man told his story. He had spent nearly all his life in a monastery; he had never been further outside it than the cloisters. He fell seriously ill, and in his illness he had a vision. He saw an angel stand beside his bed. " What have you come for? " he asked the angel. " To lead you home," the angel said. " And is it a very beautiful world to which I am going? " asked the old man. " It is a very beautiful world you are leaving," said the angel. " And then," said the old man, " I remembered that I had seen nothing of it except the fields and the trees around the monastery." So he said to the angel, " But I have seen very little of the world which I am leaving." " Then," said the angel, " I fear you will see very little beauty in the world to which you are going." " I was in trouble," said the old man, " and I begged that I might stay for just two more years. My prayer was granted, and I am spending all my little hoard of gold, and all the time I have, in exploring the world's loveliness— and I find it very wonderful ! " It is the duty of a man to accept and to enjoy the world's loveliness, and not to refuse and to reject it. There is no religious value in fasting undertaken for its own sake, or as an ostentatious demonstration of superior piety.

THE TRUE FASTING

Matthew 6: 16-18 (*continued*)

ALTHOUGH Jesus condemned the wrong kind of fasting, His words imply that there is a wise fasting, in which He expected that the Christian would take part. This is a thing of which few of us ever think. There are very few ordinary people in whose lives fasting plays any part at all. And yet there are many reasons why a wise fasting is an excellent thing.

(i) Fasting is *good for health*. Many of us live a life in which it is easy to get soft and flabby. It is even possible for a man to reach the stage when he lives to eat instead of eating to live. It would do a great many people a great deal of physical good to practise fasting far more than they do.

(ii) Fasting is *good for self-discipline*. It is easy to become almost completely self-indulgent. It is easy to come to a stage when we deny ourselves nothing which it is in our power to have or to pay for. It would do most people a great deal of good to cease for some time each week to make their wishes and their desires their master, and to exercise a stringent and an antiseptic self-discipline.

(iii) Fasting preserves us from becoming *the slaves of a habit*. There are not a few of us who indulge in certain habits because we find it impossible to stop them. They have become so essential that we cannot break them; we develop such a craving for certain things that that which ought to be a pleasure has become a necessity; and to be cut off from the thing which we have learned so to desire can be a purgatory. If we practised a wise fasting no pleasure would become a chain, and no habit would become a master. We would be masters of our pleasures, and not our pleasures masters of us.

(iv) Fasting preserves *the ability to do without things*. One of the great tests of any man's life is the number of things which he has come to regard as essential. Clearly, the fewer things we regard as essentials, the more independent we will be. When all kinds of things become essentials, we are at the mercy of the luxuries of life. It is no bad thing for a man to walk down a street of shop windows, and to look in at them, and remind himself of all the things that he can do without. Some kind of fasting preserves the ability to do without the things which should never be allowed to become essentials.

(v) Fasting makes us *appreciate things all the more*. It may be that there was a time in life when some pleasure came so seldom that we really and truly enjoyed it when it did come. It may be that nowadays the appetite is blunted; the palate is dulled; the edge is gone off it. What was once a sharp pleasure has become simply a drug which we cannot do without. Fasting keeps the thrill in pleasure by keeping pleasure always fresh and new.

Fasting has gone almost completely out of the life of the ordinary person. Jesus condemned the wrong kind of fasting, but He never meant that fasting should be completely eliminated from life and living. We would do well to practise it in our own way and according to our own need. And the reason for practising it is,

" So that earth's bliss may be our guide,
    And not our chain."

THE TRUE TREASURE

Matthew 6: 19-21

Do not lay up for yourselves treasures upon earth, where moth and rust destroy them, and where thieves dig through and steal. Lay up for yourselves treasures in heaven, where moth and rust do not destroy them, and where thieves do not dig through and steal. For where your treasure is, there will your heart be also.

In the ordinary, everyday management of life it is simple wisdom to get to oneself only these things which will last. Whether we are buying a suit of clothes, a motor car, a carpet for the floor, a suite of furniture, it is common sense to avoid shoddy goods, and to buy the things which have solidity and permanence and craftsmanship wrought into them. That is exactly what Jesus is saying here; He is telling us to concentrate on the things which will last.

Jesus calls up three pictures from the three great sources of wealth in Palestine.

(i) He tells men to avoid the things that *the moth can destroy*. In the east, part of a man's wealth often consisted in fine and elaborate clothes. When Gehazi, the servant of Elisha, wished to make some forbidden profit out of Naaman, after his master had cured him, he asked him for a talent of silver and *two changes of garments* 2 Kings 5: 22). One of the things which tempted Achan to sin was *a goodly Babylonish garment* (*Joshua* 7: 21). But such things were foolish things to set the heart upon, for the moths got at them, when they were stored away, and all their beauty and their value might be destroyed. There was no permanence about possessions like that.

(ii) He tells men, as the Authorised Version has it, to avoid the things that *rust can destroy*. The word translated *rust* is *brōsis*. It literally means an *eating away*, but it is nowhere else used to mean *rust*. Most likely the picture is this. In the east many a man's wealth consisted in the corn and the grain that he had stored away in his great barns. But into that corn and grain there could come the worms which would eat it away; there could come the rats and the mice which could invade it, until the store was polluted and destroyed. In all probability the reference is to the way in which rats, and mice, and worms, and other vermin could get into a granary and eat away the grain. There was no permanence about possessions like that.

(iii) He tells men to avoid the treasures *which thieves can steal by digging through*. The word which is used for *to dig through*—the Authorised Version has *to break through*—is *diorussein*. In Palestine the walls of many of the houses were made of nothing stronger than baked clay; and burglars did effect an entry by literally digging through the wall. The reference here is to the man who had hoarded up in his house a little store of gold, only to find, when he comes home one day, that the burglars have dug through his flimsy walls and that his treasure is gone. There is no permanency about a treasure which is at the mercy of any enterprising thief.

So Jesus warns men against three kinds of pleasures and possessions.

(i) He warns them against the pleasures which will wear out like an old suit of clothes. The finest garment in the world, moths or no moths, will in the end disintegrate. All purely physical pleasures have a way of wearing out. At each successive enjoyment of them the thrill becomes less thrilling. It requires more of them to produce the same effect. They are like a drug which loses its initial potency and which becomes increasingly less effective. A man is a foolish man who finds his pleasures in things which are bound to offer diminishing returns.

(ii) He warns against the pleasures which can be eroded away. The grain store is the inevitable prey of the marauding rats and mice who nibble and gnaw away the grain. There are certain pleasures which inevitably lose their attraction as a man grows older. It may be that he is physically less able to enjoy them; it may be that as his mind matures they cease in any sense to satisfy him. In life a man should never give his heart to the joys the years can take away; he should find his delight in the things the thrill of which time is powerless to erode.

(iii) He warns against the pleasures which can be stolen way. All material things are like that; not one of them is secure; and if a man builds his happiness on them, he is building on a most insecure basis. Suppose a man arranges his life in such a way that his happiness depends on his possession of money; then suppose a crash comes and he wakes up to find his money gone; then with his wealth his happiness has gone. If any man is wise, he will build his happiness on things which he cannot lose, things which

are independent of the chances and the changes of this life.
Burns wrote of the fleeting things:

> " But pleasures are like poppies spread:
> You seize the flower, its bloom is shed;
> Or like the snow falls in the river,
> A moment white—then melts for ever."

Any one whose happiness depends on things like that is
doomed to disappointment. Any man whose treasure is in
things is bound to lose his treasure, for in things there is no
permanence, and there is no thing which lasts forever.

TREASURE IN HEAVEN

Matthew 6: 19-21 (continued)

THE Jews were very familiar with the phrase *treasure in
heaven*. They identified such treasure with two things in
particular.

(i) They said that the deeds of kindness which a man did
upon earth became his treasure in heaven. The Jews had
a famous story about a certain King Monobaz of Adiabēne
who became a convert to Judaism. " Monobaz distributed
all his treasures to the poor in the year of famine. His
brothers sent to him and said, ' Thy fathers gathered
treasures, and added to those of their fathers, but thou
hast dispersed yours and theirs.' He said to them, ' My
fathers gathered treasures for below, I have gathered
treasures for above; they stored treasures in a place over
which the hand of man can rule, but I have stored treasures
in a place over which the hand of man cannot rule; my
fathers collected treasures which bear no interest, I have
gathered treasures which bear interest; my fathers gathered
treasures of money, I have gathered treasures in souls; my
fathers gathered treasures for others, I have gathered
treasures for myself; my fathers gathered treasures in this
world, I have gathered treasures for the world to come. ' "
Both Jesus and the Jewish Rabbis were sure that that which

is selfishly hoarded is lost, but that that which is generously given away brings treasure in heaven.

That was also the principle of the Christian Church in the days to come. The Early Church always lovingly cared for the poor, and the sick, and the distressed, and the helpless, and those for whom no one else cared. In the days of the terrible Decian persecution in Rome, the Roman authorities broke into a Christian Church. They were out to loot the treasures which they believed the Church to possess. The Roman prefect demanded from Laurentius, the deacon: " Show me your treasures at once." Laurentius pointed at the widows and orphans who were being fed, the sick who were being nursed, the poor whose needs were being supplied, " These," he said, " are the treasures of the Church." The Church has always believed that " what we keep, we lose, and what we spend, we have."

(ii) The Jews always connected the phrase *treasure in heaven* with *character*. When Rabbi Yose ben Kisma was asked if he would dwell in a heathen city on condition of receiving very high pay for his services, he replied that he would not dwell anywhere except in a home of the Law, " for," he said, " in the hour of a man's departure neither silver, nor gold, nor precious stones accompany him, but only his knowledge of the Law, and his good works." As the grim Spanish proverb has it, " There are no pockets in a shroud." The only thing which a man can take out of this world into the world beyond is himself; and the finer the self he brings, the greater his treasure in heaven will be.

(iii) Jesus ends this section by stating the truth that where a man's treasure is, his heart is there also. If everything that a man values and sets his heart upon is on earth, then all his interest will be upon earth, and he will have no interest in any world beyond this world. If all through his life a man's eyes are on eternity, then he will evaluate lightly the things of this world. If everything which a man counts valuable is on this earth, then he will leave this

earth reluctantly and grudgingly; if a man's thoughts
have been ever in the world beyond, he will leave this
world with gladness, because he goes at last to God. Once
Dr. Johnson was shown through a noble castle and its
grounds; when he had seen round it he turned to his
companions and said, " These are the things which make
it difficult to die." Jesus never said that this world was
unimportant; but He said and implied over and over again
that its importance is not in itself, but in that to which it
leads. This world is not the end of life, it is a stage on the
way; and therefore a man should never lose his heart to
this world and to the things of this world, for his eyes
ought to be for ever fixed on the goal beyond.

THE DISTORTED VISION

Matthew 6: 22, 23

> The light of the body is the eye. So then, if your eye
> is generous, the whole body will be full of light; but
> if your eye is grudging, your whole body will be in the
> dark. If, then, the light which is in you is darkness,
> how great is that darkness!

THE idea behind this passage is one of childlike simplicity.
The eye is regarded as the window by which the light gets
into the whole body. The colour and state of a window
decide what light gets into a room. If the window is clear,
clean, and undistorted, the light will come flooding into
the room, and will illuminate every corner of it. If the
glass of the window is coloured or frosted, distorted, dirty,
or obscure, the light will be hindered, and the room will
not be lit up. The amount of light which gets into any
room depends on the state of the window through which it
has to pass. So, then, says Jesus, the light which gets into
any man's heart and soul and being depends on the
spiritual state of the eye through which it has to pass, for
the eye is the window of the whole body. The view we take
of people depends on the kind of eye we have. There are

certain obvious things which can blind our eyes and distort our vision.

(i) *Prejudice* can distort our vision. There is nothing which so destroys a man's judgment as prejudice does. It prevents him from forming the clear, reasonable and logical judgment which it is the duty of any man to form. It blinds him alike to the facts and to the significance of the facts. Almost all new discoveries have had to fight their way against unreasonable prejudice. When Sir James Simpson discovered the virtues of chloroform he had to fight against the prejudice of the medical and religious world of his day. One of his biographers writes: " Prejudice, the crippling determination to walk only in time-worn paths, and to eschew new ways, rose up against it, and did their best to smother the new-found blessing." " Many of the clergy held that to try to remove the primal curse on women was to fight against divine law." One of the most necessary things in life is the fearless self-examination which will enable us to see when we are acting on principle and when we are the victims of our own unreasonable and unreasoning prejudices. In any man who is swayed by prejudice the eye is darkened and the vision distorted.

(ii) *Jealousy* can distort our vision. Shakespeare gave us the classic example of that in the tragedy of *Othello*. Othello, the Moor, won fame by his heroic exploits and married Desdemona, who loved him with utter devotion and complete fidelity. As general of the army of Venice, Othello promoted Cassio and passed over Iago. Iago was consumed with jealousy. By careful plotting and the manipulation of facts Iago sowed in Othello's mind the suspicion that Cassio and Desdemona were carrying on an intrigue. He manufactured evidence to prove it, and moved Othello to such a passion of jealousy that he finally murdered Desdemona by smothering her with a pillow. A. C. Bradley writes, " Such jealousy as Othello's converts human nature into chaos, and liberates the beast in man."

Many a marriage, many a friendship has been wrecked on the rock of a jealousy which distorted perfectly innocent incidents into guilty actions, and which blinded the eye to truth and fact.

(iii) *Self-conceit* can distort our vision. In her biography of Mark Rutherford, Catherine Macdonald Maclean has a curiously caustic sentence about John Chapman, the book-seller and publisher, who was at one time Mark Ruther-ford's employer: " Handsome in the Byronic fahion, and pleasant-mannered, he was exceedingly attractive to women, and he thought himself even more attractive to them than he actually was." Self-conceit doubly affects a man's vision, for it renders him incapable of seeing himself as he really is, and incapable of seeing others as they really are. If a man is convinced of his own surpassing wisdom, he will never be able to realise his own foolishness; and if he is blind to everything except his own virtues, he will never be aware of his own faults. Whenever he com-pares himself with others, he will do so to his own advantage, and to their disadvantage. He will be for ever incapable of self-criticism, and therefore for ever incapable of self-improvement. The light in which he should see himself and see others will be darkness.

THE NECESSITY OF THE GENEROUS EYE

Matthew 6: 22, 23 *(continued)*

BUT here Jesus speaks of one special virtue which fills the eye with light, and one special fault which fills the eye with darkness. The Authorised Version speaks here about the eye being *single* and the eye being *evil*. Certainly that is the literal meaning of the Greek, but the words *single* and *evil* are here used in a special way which is common enough in the Greek in which scripture is written.

The word for *single* is *haplous*, and its corresponding noun is *haplotēs*. Regularly in the Greek of the Bible these words mean *generous* and *generosity*. James speaks of God who gives *liberally* (*James* I: 5), and the adverb he uses is *haplōs*. Similarly in *Romans* 12: 8. Paul urges his friends to give *liberally* (*haplōs*). In this instance the margin of the Authorised Version gives the correct translation. Paul reminds the Corinthian Church of the *liberality* (*haplotēs*) of the Churches in Macedonia, and talks about their own *liberal* (*haplous*) distribution to all men (2 *Corinthians* 9: 31). To get the real meaning of this we must translate *haplous*, not *single*, but *generous*; it is the *generous eye* which Jesus is commending.

The word which is in the Authorised Version translated *evil* is *ponēros*. Certainly that is the normal meaning of the word; but both in the New Testament and in the Septuagint *ponēros* regularly means *niggardly* or *grudging*. *Deuteronomy* speaks of the duty of lending to a brother who is in need. But the matter was complicated by the fact that every seventh year was a year of release when debts were cancelled. It might, therefore, very well happen that, if the seventh year was near, a cautious man might refuse to help, lest the person helped might take advantage of the seventh year never to repay his debt. So the law lays it down: " Beware that there be not a thought in thy wicked heart saying, the seventh year, the year of release is at hand; and thine eye be *evil* (*ponēros*) against thy poor brother and thou givest him nought " (*Deuteronomy* 15: 9). Clearly *ponēros* there means *niggardly, grudging* and *ungenerous*. It is the advice of the proverb: " Eat not the bread of him that hath an *evil* eye " (*Proverbs* 23: 6). That is to say, " Don't be a guest in the house of a man who grudges you every bite you eat." Another proverb has it: " He that hath an *evil* eye hasteth after riches " (*Proverbs* 28: 22). That is to say, " The grudging and the ungenerous man is always out for what he can get." To get the real meaning of this passage we must translate *ponēros*, not *evil*, but *grudging* and *ungenerous*.

So Jesus is saying, " There is nothing like generosity for

giving you a clear and undistorted view of life and of people; and there is nothing like the grudging and ungenerous spirit for distorting your view of life and of people."

(i) We must be generous in our *judgments of others*. It is characteristic of human nature to think the worst, and to find a malignant delight in repeating the worst. Every day in life the reputations of perfectly innocent people are murdered over the tea-cups by gossiping groups whose judgments are dipped in poison. The world would be saved a great deal of heartbreak, if we would put the best, and not the worst, construction on the actions of other people.

(ii) We must be generous in our *actions*. In her biography of Mark Rutherford, Catherine Macdonald Maclean speaks of the days when Mark Rutherford came to work in London: " It was about this time that there can be noted in him the beginning of that ' cherishing pity for the souls of men ' which was to become habitual with him. . . . The burning question with him, haunted as he was at times by the fate of many in the district in which he lived, was, ' What can I do? Wherein can I help them? ' It seemed to him then, as always, that any kind of action was of more value than the most vehement indignation that spent itself in talk." When Mark Rutherford was with Chapman the publisher, George Eliot, or Maria Evans as her real name was, lived and worked in the same place. One thing impressed him about her: " She was poor. She had only a small income of her own; and, although she hoped to earn a livelihood as a woman of letters, her future was very uncertain. But she was fantastically generous. She was always helping lame dogs over stiles, and the poverty of others pressed on her more than her own. She wept more bitterly because she could not adequately relieve a sister's poverty than because of any of her own privations." It is when we begin to feel like that that we begin to see people and things clearly. It is then that our eye becomes full of light.

There are three great evils of the ungenerous spirit, of the eye that is grudging.

(i) It makes it *impossible to live with ourselves.* If a man is for ever envying another his success, grudging another his happiness, shutting his heart against another's need, he becomes that most pitiable of creatures—a man with a grudge. There grows within him a bitterness and a resentment which robs him of his happiness, steals away his peace, and destroys his content.

(ii) It makes it *impossible to live with other people.* The mean man is the man abhorred by all; the man whom all men despise is the man with the miser's heart. Charity covers a multitude of sins, but the grudging spirit makes useless a multitude of virtues. However bad the generous man may be, there are those who will love him; and however good the mean man may be, all men will detest him.

(iii) It makes it *impossible to live with God.* There is no one so generous as God, and, in the last analysis, there can be no fellowship between two people who guide their lives by diametrically opposite principles. There can be no fellowship between the God whose heart is afire with love, and the man whose heart is frozen with meanness.

The grudging eye distorts our vision; the generous eye alone sees clearly, for it alone sees as God sees.

THE EXCLUSIVE SERVICE

Matthew 6: 24

No man can be a slave to two owners; for either he will hate the one and love the other, or he will cleave to the one and despise the other. You cannot be a slave to God and to material things.

To one brought up in the ancient world this is an even more vivid saying than it is to us. The Authorised Version translates it: No man can serve two masters. But that is not nearly strong enough. The word which the Authorised

Version translates "serve" is *douleuein*; *doulos* is a slave; and *douleuein* means *to be a slave to*. The word that the Authorised Version translates *master* is *kurios*, and *kurios* is the word which denotes *absolute ownership*. We get the meaning far better, if we translate it: No man can be a slave to two owners.

To understand all that this means and implies we must remember two things about the slave in the ancient world. First, the slave in the eyes of the law was not a person but a thing. He had absolutely no rights of his own; his master could do with him absolutely as he liked. In the eyes of the law the slave was a *living tool*. His master could sell him, beat him, throw him out, and even kill him. His master possessed him as completely as he possessed any of his material possessions. Second, in the ancient world a slave had literally no time which was his own. Every moment of his life belonged to his master. Under modern conditions a man has certain hours of work, and outside these hours of work his time is his own. It is indeed often possible for a man nowadays to find his real interest in life outside his hours of work. He may be a clerk in an office during the day and play the violin in an orchestra at night; and it may be that it is in his music that he finds his real life. He may work in a shipyard or in a factory during the day and run a youth club at night, and it may be that it is in the youth club that he finds his real delight and the real expression of his personality. But it was far otherwise with the slave. The slave had literally no moment of time which belonged to himself. Every moment belonged to his owner and was at his owner's disposal.

Here, then, is our relationship to God. In regard to God we have no rights of our own; God must be undisputed master of our lives. We can never ask, " What do I wish to do? " We must always ask, " What does God wish me to do?" We have no time which is our own. We cannot sometimes say, " I will do what God wishes me to do," and, at other times say, " I will do what I like." The Christian has no time off from being a Christian; there is no time when he can relax his Christian standards, as if he was off duty. A partial or a spasmodic service of God is not enough. Being a Christian is a whole-time job. Nowhere in the Bible is the exclusive service which God demands more clearly set forth.

Jesus goes on to say, " You cannot serve God and mamon." The correct spelling is with one *m*. *Mamon* was a Hebrew word for *material possessions*. Originally it was not a bad word at all. The Rabbis, for instance, had a saying, " Let the *mamon* of thy neighbour be as dear to thee as thine own." That is to say, a man should regard his neighbour's material possessions as being as sacrosanct as his own. But the word *mamon* had a most curious and a most revealing history. It comes from a root which means *to entrust;* and *mamon* was that which a man entrusted to a banker or to a safe deposit of some kind. *Mamon* was the wealth which a man entrusted to someone to keep safe for him. But as the years went on *mamon* came to mean, not *that which is entrusted,* but *that in which a man puts his trust.* The end of the process was that *mamon* came to be spelled with a capital M and came to be regarded as nothing less than a god.

The history of that word shows vividly how material possessions can usurp a place in life which they were never meant to have. Originally a man's material possessions were the things which he entrusted to someone else for safe-keeping; in the end they came to be the things in which a man puts his trust. Surely there is no better description of a man's god, than to say that his god is the power in whom he trusts; and when a man puts his trust in material things, then material things have become, not his support, but his god.

THE PLACE OF MATERIAL POSSESSIONS

Matthew 6: 24 (continued)

THIS saying of Jesus is bound to turn our thoughts to the place which material possessions should have in life. At the basis of Jesus' teaching about possessions there are three great principles.

(i) In the last analysis *all things belong to God*. Scripture makes that abundantly clear. " The earth is the Lord's and the fulness thereof; the world and they that dwell therein " (*Psalm* 24: 1). " For every beast of the forest is mine, and the cattle upon a thousand hills. . . . If I were hungry I would not tell thee, for the world is mine and the fulness thereof " (*Psalm* 50: 10, 12). In Jesus' teaching it is the master who gives his servants the talents (*Matthew* 25: 15), and the owner who gives the husbandmen the vineyard (*Matthew* 21: 33). This principle has far-reaching consequences. Men can buy and sell things; men can to some extent alter and rearrange things; but man cannot create things. The ultimate ownership of all things belongs to God. There is nothing in this world of which a man can say, " This is mine." Of all things he can only say, " This belongs to God, and God has given me the use of it." Therefore this basic principle of life emerges. There is nothing in this world of which any man can say, " This is mine, and I will therefore do what I like with it." Of everything he *must* say, " This is God's, and I must use it as its owner would have it to be used." There is a story of a city child who was taken for a day in the country. For the first time in her life she saw a drift of bluebells. She turned to her teacher and said, " Do you think God would mind, if I picked one of His flowers? " That is the correct attitude to life and all things in the world.

(ii) The second basic principle is that *people are always more important than things*. If possessions have to be acquired, if money has to be amassed, if wealth has to be accumulated at the expense of treating people as things, then all such riches are wrong. Whenever and wherever that principle is forgotten, or neglected, or defied, far-reaching disaster is certain to follow. In this country we are to this day suffering in the world of industrial relationships from the fact that in the days of the industrial revolution people were treated as things. Sir Arthur Bryant in *English Saga* tells of some of the things which happened in those days. Children of seven and eight years of age—there is actually a case of a child of three—were employed in the mines. Some of them dragged trucks along galleries on all fours; some of them pumped out water standing knee deep in the water for twelve hours a day; some of them, called trappers, opened and shut the ventilating doors of the shafts, and were shut into little ventilating chambers for as much as sixteen hours a day. In 1815 children were working in the mills from 5 a.m. to 8 p.m. without even a Saturday half-holiday, and with half an hour off for breakfast and half an hour off for dinner. In 1833 there were 84,000 children under fourteen in the factories. There is actually a case recorded in which the children whose labour was no longer required were taken to a common and turned adrift. The owners objected to the expression " turned adrift." They said that the children had been set at liberty. They agreed that the children might find things hard. " They would have to beg their way or something of that sort." In 1842 the weavers of Burnley were being paid 7½d. a day, and the miners of Staffordshire 2s. 6d. a day. There were those who saw the criminal folly of all this. Carlyle thundered, " If the cotton industry is founded on the bodies of rickety children, it must go; if the devil gets in your cotton-mill, shut the mill." It was pleaded that cheap labour was necessary to keep costs down. Coleridge answered, " You talk about making this article cheaper by reducing its price in the market from 8d. to 6d. But suppose in so doing you have rendered your country weaker against a foreign foe; suppose you have demoralized thousands of your fellow-countrymen, and have sown discontent between one class of society and another, your article is tolerably dear, I take it, after all." It is perfectly true that things are very different nowadays. But there is such a thing as racial memory. Deep in the unconscious memory of people the impression of these bad days is indelibly impressed. Whenever people are treated as things, as machines, as instruments for producing so much labour and for enriching those who employ them, then as certainly as the night follows the day disaster follows. A nation forgets at its peril the principle that people are always more important than things.

(iii) The third principle is that *wealth is always a subordinate good*. The Bible does not say that, " Money is the root of all evil," it says that " *The love of money* is the root of all evil " (*I Timothy* 6: 10). It is quite possible to find in material things what someone has called " a rival salvation." A man may think that, because he is wealthy, he can buy anything, that he can buy his way out of any situation. Wealth can become his measuring-rod; wealth can become his one desire; wealth can become the one weapon with which he faces life. If a man desires material things for an honourable independence, to help his family and to do something for his fellow-men, that is good; but if he desires it simply to heap pleasure upon pleasure, and to add luxury to luxury, if wealth has become the thing he lives for and lives by, then wealth has ceased to be a subordinate good, and has usurped the place in life which only God should occupy.

One thing emerges from all this—the possession of wealth, money, material things is not a sin, but it is a grave *responsibility*. If a man owns many material things it is not so much a matter for congratulation as it is a matter for prayer, that he may use them as God would have him to do.

THE TWO GREAT QUESTIONS ABOUT
POSSESSIONS

Matthew 6: 24 *(continued)*

THERE are two great questions about possessions, and on the answer to these questions everything depends.

(i) *How did a man gain his possessions?* Did he gain them in a way that he would be glad that Jesus Christ should see, or did he gain them in a way that he would wish to hide from Jesus Christ? *A man may gain his possessions at the expense of honesty and honour.* George Macdonald tells of a village shop-keeper who grew very rich. Whenever he was measuring cloth, he measured it with his two thumbs inside the measure so that he always gave short measure. George Macdonald says of him, " He took from his soul, and he put it in his siller-bag." A man can enrich his bank account at the expense of impoverishing his soul. *A man may gain his possessions by deliberately smashing some weaker rival.* Many a man's success is founded on someone else's failure. Many a man's advancement has been gained by pushing someone else out of the way. It is hard to see how a man who prospers in such a way can sleep at nights. *A man may gain his possessions at the expense of still higher duties.* Robertson Nicoll, the great editor, was born in a manse in the north-east of Scotland. His father had one passion, to buy and to read books. He was a minister and he never had more than £200 a year. But he amassed the greatest private library in Scotland amounting to 17,000 books. He did not use them in his sermons; he was simply consumed to own and to read them. When he was forty he married a girl of twenty-four. In eight years she was dead of tuberculosis; of a family of five only two lived to be over twenty. That cancerous growth of books filled every room and every passage in the manse. It may have delighted the owner of the books, but it killed his wife and family. There are possessions which can be acquired at too great a cost. A man must ask himself: " How do I acquire the things which I possess? "

(ii) *How does a man use his possessions?* There are various ways in which a man may use the things he has acquired. *He may not use them at all.* He may have the miser's acquisitiveness which delights simply in possession. His possessions may be quite useless—and uselessness always invites disaster. *He may use them completely selfishly.* A man may desire a bigger pay for no other reason than that he wants a bigger car, a new television set, a more expensive holiday. He may think of possessions simply and solely in terms of what they can do for him. *He may use them malignantly.* A man can use his possessions to persuade someone else to do things he has no right to do, or to sell things he has no right to sell. Many a young person has been bribed or dazzled into sin by someone else's money. Wealth gives power, and a corrupt man can use his possessions to corrupt others—and that in the sight of God is a very terrible sin. *A man may use his possessions for his own independence and for the happiness of others.* It does not need great wealth to do that, for a man can be just as generous with half a crown as with a thousand pounds. A man will not go far wrong, if he uses his possessions to see how much happiness he can bring to others. Paul remembered a saying of Jesus which everyone else had forgotten: " It is a happier thing to give than to get " (*Acts* 20: 35). It is characteristic of God to give, and, if in our lives giving always ranks above getting, we will use aright what we possess, however much or however little it may be.

THE FORBIDDEN WORRY

Matthew 6: 25-34

I tell you, therefore, do not worry about your life, about what you are to eat, or what you are to drink;

and do not worry about your body, about what you are to wear. Is not your life more than food, and your body more than clothes? Look at the birds of the air, and see that they do not sow, or reap, or gather things into store-houses, and yet your heavenly Father feeds them. Are you not better than they? Who of you can add one span to his life by worrying about it? And why do you worry about clothes? Learn a lesson from the lilies of the field, from the way in which they grow. They do not toil or spin; but I tell you that not even Solomon in all his glory was clothed like one of these. If God so clothes the grass of the field, which exists to-day, and which is thrown into the oven to-morrow, shall He not much more clothe you, O you of little faith? So then do not worry, saying, What are we to eat? or, What are we to drink? or, What are we to wear? The Gentiles seek after all these things. But seek first His Kingdom and His righteousness, and all these things will come to you in addition. So, then, do not worry about to-morrow; to-morrow will worry about itself. Its own troubles are quite enough for the day.

WE must begin our study of this passage by making sure that we understand what Jesus is forbidding and what He is demanding. The Authorised Version translates Jesus' commandment: Take no thought for the morrow. Strange to say, the Authorised Version was the first translation to translate it in that way. Wyclif had it: " Be not busy to your life." Tyndale, Granmer and the Geneva Version all had: " Be not careful for your life." They used the word *careful* in the literal sense of *full of care*. The older versions were in fact more accurate. It is not ordinary, prudent foresight, such as becomes a man, that Jesus forbids; it is *worry*. Jesus is not advocating a shiftless, thriftless, reckless, thoughtless, improvident attitude to life; He is forbidding a care-worn, worried fear, which takes all the joy out of life.

The word which is used is the word *merimnan*, which means *to worry anxiously*. Its corresponding noun is *merimna*, which means *worry*. In a papyrus letter a wife writes to her absent husband: " I cannot sleep at night or by day, because of the *worry* (*merimna*) I have about your welfare." A mother, on hearing of her son's good health and prosperity writes back: "That is all my prayer and all my *anxiety* (*merimna*)." Anacreon, the poet, writes: "When I drink wine, my worries (*merimnai*) go to sleep." In Greek the word is the characteristic word for anxiety, and worry, and care.

The Jews themselves were very familiar with this attitude to life. It was the teaching of the great Rabbis that a man ought to meet life with a combination of prudence and serenity. They insisted, for instance, that every man must teach his son a trade, for, they said, not to teach him a trade was to teach him to steal. That is to say, they believed in taking all the necessary steps for the prudent handling of life. But at the same time, they said, " He who has a loaf in his basket, and who says, ' What will I eat to-morrow? ' is a man of little faith."

Jesus is here teaching a lesson which His countrymen well knew—the lesson of prudence and forethought and serenity and trust combined.

WORRY AND ITS CURE
Matthew 6: 25-34 (continued)

In these ten verses Jesus sets out seven different arguments and defences against worry.

(i) He begins by pointing out (verse 25) that God gave us life, and, if He gave us life, surely we can trust Him for the lesser things. If God gave us life, surely we can trust Him to give us food to sustain that life. If God gave us bodies, surely we can trust Him for raiment to clothe these bodies. If anyone gives us a gift which is beyond price, surely we can be certain that such a giver will not be mean, and stingy, and niggardly, and careless, and forgetful about much less costly gifts. So, then, the first argument is that, if God gave us life, we can trust Him for the things which are necessary to support life.

(ii) Jesus goes on to speak about the birds (verse 26). There is no worry in their lives, no attempt to pile up goods for an unforeseen and unforeseeable future; and yet their lives go on. More than one Jewish Rabbi was fascinated by the way in which the animals live. " In my life," said Rabbi Simeon, " I have never seen a stag as a dryer of figs, or a lion as a porter, or a fox as a merchant, yet they are all nourished without worry. If they, who are created to serve me, are nourished without worry, how much more ought I, who am created to serve my Maker, to be nourished without worry; but I have corrupted my ways, and so I have impaired my substance." The point that Jesus is making is not that the birds do not work; it has been said that no one works harder than the average sparrow to make a living; the point that He is making is that they do not worry. There is not to be found in them man's straining to see a future which he cannot see, and man's seeking to find security in things stored up and accumulated against the future.

(iii) In verse 27, Jesus goes on to prove that worry is in any event useless. The verse can bear two meanings. It can mean that no man by worrying can add a cubit to his height; but a cubit is eighteen inches, and no man surely would ever contemplate adding eighteen inches to his height! It can mean that no man by worrying can add the shortest space to his life; and that meaning is more likely. It is Jesus' argument that worry is pointless anyway.

(iv) Jesus goes on to speak about the flowers (verses 28-30), and He speaks about them as one who loved them. The lilies of the field were the scarlet poppies and anemones. They bloomed one day on the hillsides of Palestine; and yet in their brief life they were clothed with a beauty which surpassed the beauty of the robes of kings. When they died they were used for nothing better than for burning. The point is this. The Palestinian oven was made of clay. It was like a clay box set on bricks over the fire. When it was desired to raise the temperature of it especially quickly, some handfuls of dried grasses and wild flowers were flung *inside* the oven and set alight. The flowers had but one day of life; and then they were set alight to help a woman to heat an oven when she was baking in a hurry; and yet God clothes them with a beauty which is beyond man's power to imitate. If God gives such beauty to a short-lived flower, how much more will He care for man? Surely the generosity which is so lavish to the flower of a day will not be forgetful of man, the crown of creation.

(v) Jesus goes on to advance a very fundamental argument against worry. Worry, He says, is characteristic of a heathen, and not of one who knows what God is like (verse 32). Worry is essentially distrust of God. Such a distrust may be understandable in a heathen who believes in a jealous, capricious, unpredictable god; but it is beyond comprehension in one who has learned to call God by the name of Father. The Christian cannot worry because he believes in the love of God.

(vi) Jesus goes on to advance two ways in which to defeat worry. The first is to seek first, to concentrate upon, the Kingdom of God. We have seen that to be in the Kingdom and to do the will of God is one and the same thing (*Matthew* 6: 10). To concentrate on the doing of, and the acceptance of, God's will is the way to defeat worry. We know how in our own lives a great love can drive out every other concern. Such a love can inspire a man's work, intensify his study, purify his life, dominate his whole being. It was Jesus' conviction that worry is banished when God becomes the dominating power of our lives.

(vii) Lastly, Jesus says that worry can be defeated when we acquire the art of living one day at a time (verse 34). The Jews had a saying: " Do not worry over to-morrow's evils, for you know not what to-day will bring forth. Perhaps to-morrow you will not be alive, and you will have worried for a world which will not be yours." If each day is lived as it comes, if each task is done as it appears, then the sum of all the days is bound to be good. It is Jesus' advice that we should handle the demands of each day as it comes, without worrying about the unknown future and the things which may never happen.

THE FOLLY OF WORRY

Matthew 6: 25-34 (continued)

LET us now see if we can gather up Jesus' arguments against worry.

(i) *Worry is needless, useless and even actively injurious.* Worry cannot affect the past, for the past is past. Omar Khayyam was grimly right:

> " The moving finger writes, and, having writ,
> Moves on; nor all thy piety nor wit
> Shall lure it back to cancel half a line,
> Nor all thy tears wash out a word of it."

The past is past. It is not that a man can or ought to dissociate himself from his past; but he ought to use his past as a spur and a guide for better action in the future, and not as something about which he broods until he has worried himself into a paralysis of action.

Equally, worry about the future is useless. Alistair MacLean in one of his sermons tells of a story which he had read. A London doctor was the hero. " He was paralysed and bed-ridden, but almost outrageously cheerful, and his smile so brave and radiant that everyone forgot to be sorry for him. His children adored him, and when one of his boys was leaving the nest and starting forth upon life's adventure, Dr. Greatheart gave him good advice: ' Johnny,' he said, ' the thing to do, my lad, is to hold your own end up, and to do it like a gentleman, and please remember the biggest troubles you have got to face are those that never come.' " Worry about the future is wasted effort, and the future of reality is seldom as bad as the future of our fears.

But worry is worse than useless; it is often actively injurious. The two typical diseases of modern life are the stomach ulcer and the coronary thrombosis, and in many cases both are the result of worry. It is a medical fact that he who laughs most lives longest. The worry which wears out the mind wears out the body along with it. Worry affects a man's judgment, lessens his powers of decision, and renders him progressively incapable of dealing with life. Let a man give his best to every situation—he cannot give more—and let him leave the rest to God.

(ii) *Worry is blind.* Worry refuses to learn the lesson of *nature.* Jesus bids men to look at the birds, and to see the bounty which is behind nature, and to trust the love that lies behind that bounty. Worry refuses to learn the lesson of *history.* There was a Psalmist who cheered himself with the memory of history. " O my God," he cries, " my soul is cast down within me." And then he goes on: " *Therefore* will I remember Thee, from the land of Jordan, and of the Hermonites, from the hill Mizar " (*Psalm* 42: 6; cp. *Deuteronomy* 3: 9). When he was up against it, he comforted himself with the memory of what God had done. The man who feeds his heart on the record of what God has done in the past will never worry about the future. Worry refuses to learn the lesson of *life.* We are still alive and our heads are still above water; and yet if someone had told us that we would have to go through what we have actually gone through, we would have said that it was impossible. The lesson of life is that somehow we have been enabled to bear the unbearable and to do the undoable and to pass the breaking-point and not to break. The lesson of life is that worry is unnecessary.

(iii) *Worry is essentially irreligious.* Worry is not caused by external circumstances. In the same circumstances one man can be absolutely serene, and another man can be worried to death. Both worry and peace come, not from circumstances, but from the heart. Alistair MacLean quotes a story from Tauler, the German mystic. One day

Tauler met a beggar. " God give you a good day, my friend." he said. The beggar answered, " I thank God I never had a bad one." Then Tauler said, " God give you a happy life, my friend." " I thank God," said the beggar, " I am never unhappy." Tauler in amazement said, " What do you mean? " " Well," said the beggar, " when it is fine, I thank God; when it rains, I thank God; when I have plenty, I thank God; when I am hungry, I thank God; and since God's will is my will, and whatever pleases Him pleases me, why should I say I am unhappy when I am not? " Tauler looked at the man in astonishment. " Who are you? " he asked. " I am a king," said the beggar. " Where then is your kingdom? " asked Tauler. And the beggar answered quietly: " *In my heart*." Isaiah said it long ago: " Thou wilt keep him in perfect peace, whose mind is stayed on Thee: because he trusteth in Thee " (*Isaiah* 26: 3). As the north country woman had it: " I am always happy, and my secret is always to sail the seas, and ever to keep the heart in port."

There may be greater sins than worry, but very certainly there is no more disabling sin. " Take no anxious thought for the morrow "—that is the commandment of Jesus, and it is the way, not only to peace, but also to power.

THE ERROR OF JUDGMENT

Matthew 7: 1-5

Do not judge others, in order that you may not be judged; for with the standard of judgment with which you judge you will be judged; and with the measure you measure to others it will be measured to you. Why do you look for the speck of dust in your brother's eye, and never notice the plank that is in your own eye? or, how will you say to your brother: " Let me remove the speck of dust from your eye," and, see, there is a plank in your own eye. Hypocrite! first remove the plank from your own eye; then you will see clearly to remove the speck of dust from your brother's eye.

WHEN Jesus spoke like this, as so often in the Sermon on the Mount, He was using words and ideas which were quite familiar to the highest thoughts of the Jews. Many a time the Rabbis warned people against judging others. " He who judges his neighbour favourably," they said, " will be judged favourably by God." They laid it down that there were six great works which brought a man credit in this world and profit in the world to come—study, visiting the sick, hospitality, devotion in prayer, the education of children in the Law, and *thinking the best of other people.* The Jews, too, knew that kindliness in judgment is nothing less than a sacred duty.

One would have thought that this would have been a commandment which it would have been easy to obey, for history is strewn with the record of the most amazing misjudgments. There have been so many misjudgments that one would have thought it would be a warning to men not to judge at all. It has been so in literature. In the *Edinburgh Review* of November, 1814, Lord Jeffrey wrote a review of Wordsworth's newly published poem *The Excursion,* in which he delivered the now famous, or infamous, verdict: " This will never do." In a review of Keats *Endymion, The Quarterly* patronisingly noted " a certain amount of talent which deserves to be put in the right way."

Again and again men and women who became famous have been dismissed as nonentities. In his autobiography Gilbert Frankau tells how in the Victorian days his mother's house was a salon where the most brilliant people met. His mother arranged for the entertainment of her guests. Once she engaged a young Australian soprano to sing. After she had sung, Gilbert Frankau's mother said, " What an appalling voice! She ought to be muzzled and allowed to sing no more! " The young singer's name was Nellie Melba. Gilbert Frankau himself was producing a play. He sent to a theatrical agency for a young male actor to play the leading male part. The young man was interviewed and tested. After the test Gilbert Frankau telephoned to the agent. " This man," he said, " will never do. He cannot act, and he never will be able to act, and you had better tell him to look for some other profession before he starves. By the way, tell me his name again so that I can cross him off my list." The actor's name was Ronald Colman who was to become one of the most famous actors the screen has ever known.

Again and again people have been guilty of the most notorious moral misjudgments. Collie Knox tells of what happened to himself and a friend. Collie Knox himself had been badly smashed up in a flying accident while he was serving in the Royal Flying Corps. The friend had that very day been decorated for gallantry at Buckingham Palace. They had changed from their service dress into civilian clothes, and they were lunching together at a famous London restaurant, when a girl came up to them and handed to each of them a white feather—the badge of cowardice.

There is hardly anyone who has not been guilty of some grave misjudgment; there is hardly anyone who has not suffered from someone else's misjudgment. And yet the strange fact is that there is hardly any commandment of Jesus which is more consistently broken and neglected.

NO MAN CAN JUDGE

Matthew 7: 1-5

THERE are three great reasons why no man can judge another.

(i) *We never know the whole facts or the whole person.* Long ago Hillel the famous Rabbi said, " Do not judge a man until you yourself have come into his circumstances or situation." No man knows the strength of another man's temptations. The man with the placid and equable temperament knows nothing of the temptations of the man whose blood is afire and whose passions are on a hair-trigger. The man brought up in a good home and in Christian surroundings knows nothing of the temptation of the man brought up in a slum, or in a place where evil stalks abroad. The man blessed with fine parents knows nothing of the temptations of the man who has the load of a bad heredity upon his back. The fact is that if we realized what some people have to go through, so far from condemning them, we would be amazed that they have succeeded in being as good as they are.

No more do we know the whole person. In one set of circumstances a person may be unlovely and graceless; in another that same person may be a tower of strength and beauty. In one of his novels Mark Rutherford tells of a man who married for the second time. His wife had also been married before, and she had a daughter in her teens. The daughter seemed a sullen and unlovely creature, without a grain of attractiveness in her. The man could make nothing of her. Then, unexpectedly, the mother fell ill. At once the daughter was transformed. She became the perfect nurse, the embodiment of service and tireless devotion. Her sullenness was lit by a sudden radiance, and there appeared in her a person no one would ever have dreamed was there. There is a kind of crystal called Labrador spar. At first sight it is dull and without lustre; but if it is turned round and round, and here and there, it will suddenly come into a position where the light strikes it in a certain way and it will sparkle with flashing beauty. People are like that. They may seem to be unlovely, but that is because we do not know the whole person. Everyone has something good in him or her. Our task is not to condemn, and to judge by, the superficial unloveliness, but to look for the underlying beauty. That is what we would have others do to us, and that is what we must do to others.

(ii) *It is almost impossible for any man to be strictly impartial in his judgment.* Again and again we are swayed by our instinctive and unreasoning reactions to people.

Our judgments come not from judgment at all, but simply from a quite unreasonable and illogical reaction. It is told that sometimes, when the Greeks held a particularly important and difficult trial, they held it in the dark so that judge and jury would not even see the man on trial, and so would be influenced by nothing but the facts of the case. Montaigne has a grim tale in one of his essays. There was a Persian judge who had given a biased verdict, and he had given it under the influence of bribery. When Cambysses, the king, discovered what had happened, he ordered the judge to be executed. Then he had the skin flayed from the dead body and preserved; and with the skin he covered the seat of the chair on which judges sat in judgment, that it might be a grim reminder to them never to allow prejudice to affect their verdicts. Only a completely impartial person has a right to judge. It is not in human nature to be completely impartial. Only God can judge.

(iii) But it was Jesus who stated the supreme reason why we should not judge others. *No man is good enough to judge any other man.* Jesus drew a vivid picture of a man with a plank in his own eye trying to extract a speck of dust from someone else's eye. The humour of the picture would raise a laugh which would drive the lesson home. Only the faultless has a right to look for faults in others. No man has a right to criticize another man unless he is prepared at least to try to do the thing he criticizes better. Every Saturday the football terracings are full of people who are violent critics, and who would yet make a pretty poor show if they themselves were to descend to the arena. Every association and every Church is full of people who are prepared to criticize from the body of the hall, or even from an arm-chair, but who would never even dream of taking office themselves. The world is full of people who claim the right to be extremely vocal in criticism and extremely exempt from action. No man has a right to criticize others unless he is prepared to venture himself in the same situation. No man is good enough to criticize his fellow-men.

We have quite enough to do to rectify our own lives without seeking censoriously to rectify the lives of others. We would do well to concentrate on our own faults, and to leave the faults of others to God.

THE TRUTH AND THE HEARER

Matthew 7: 6

> Do not give that which is holy to the dogs, and do not cast your pearls before pigs, lest they trample upon them with their feet, and turn and rend you.

THIS is obviously a very difficult saying of Jesus for, on the face of it, it seems to demand an exclusiveness which is the very reverse of the Christian message. It was, in fact, a saying which was used in two special ways in the early Church.

(i) It was used by the Jews who believed that God's gifts and God's grace were for Jews alone. It was used by those Jews who were the enemies of Paul, and who argued that a gentile must become circumcized and must accept the Law, and must become a Jew before he could become a Christian. It was indeed a text which could be used—or misused—in the interests of Jewish exclusiveness.

(ii) The early Church used this text in a special way. The early Church was under a double threat. It was under the threat which came from *outside*. The early Church was an island of Christian purity in a surrounding sea of gentile immorality; and it was always supremely liable to be infected with the taint of the world. It was under the threat which came from *inside*. In those early days men were thinking things out, and it was inevitable that there would be those whose speculations would wander into the pathways of heresy; there were those who tried to effect a compromise between Christian and pagan thought, and to arrive at some synthesis of belief which would satisfy both. If the Christian Church was to survive, it had to defend itself alike from the threat from outside and from inside, or it would have become simply another of these many religions which competed within the Roman Empire. In particular the early Church was very careful about whom it admitted to the Lord's Table, and this text became associated with the Lord's Table. The Lord's Supper began with the announcement: " Holy things for holy people." Theodoret quotes what he says is an unwritten saying of Jesus: " My mysteries are for myself and for my people." *The Apostolic Constitutions* lay it down that at the beginning of the Lord's Supper the deacon shall say, " Let none of the catechumens (that is, those still under instruction), let none of the hearers (that is, those who had come to the service because they were interested in Christianity), let none of the unbelievers, let none of the heretics, stay here." There was a fencing of the Table against all but pledged Christians. The *Didachē*, or, to give it its full name, *The Teaching of the Twelve Apostles*, which dates back to A.D. 100 and which is the first service order book of the Christian Church, lays it down: " Let no one eat or drink of your Eucharist except those baptised into the name of the Lord; for, as regards this, the Lord has said, ' Give not that which is holy unto dogs.' " It is Tertullian's complaint that the heretics allow all kinds of people, even the heathen, into the Lord's Supper, and by so doing, " That which is holy they will cast to the dogs, and pearls (although, to be sure, they are not real ones) to swine " (*De Praescriptione* 41). In all these instances this text is used as a basis of exclusiveness. It was not that the Church was not missionary-minded; the Church in the early days was consumed with the desire to win everyone; but the Church was desperately aware of the utter necessity of maintaining the purity of the faith, lest Christianity should be gradually assimilated to and ultimately swallowed up in, the surrounding sea of paganism.

It is easy to see the *temporary* meaning of this text; but we must try to see its *permanent* meaning as well.

REACHING THOSE WHO ARE UNFIT TO HEAR

Matthew 7: 6 (*continued*)

IT is just possible that this saying of Jesus has become altered accidentally in its transmission. It is a good example of the Hebrew habit of parallelism which we have already met (*Matthew* 6: 10). Let us set it down in its parallel clauses:

" Give not that which is holy unto the dogs;
 Neither cast ye your pearls before swine."

With the exception of one word the parallelism is complete. *Give* is parallelled by *cast*; *dogs* by *swine*; but *holy* is not really balanced by *pearls*. There the parallelism breaks down. It so happens that there are two Hebrew words which are very like each other, especially when we remember that Hebrew has no written vowels. The word for *holy* is *kadosh* (*K D SH*); and the Aramaic word for an ear-ring is *kadasha* (*K D SH*). The consonants are exactly the same, and in primitive written Hebrew the words would look exactly the same. Still further, in the *Talmud*, " an ear-ring in a swine's snout " is a proverbial phrase for something which is entirely incongruous and out of place. It is by no means impossible that the original phrase ran:

" Give not an ear-ring to the dogs;
 Neither cast ye your pearls before swine,"

in which case the parallelism would be perfect.

If that is the real meaning of the phrase, it would simply mean that there are certain people who are not fit, not able, to receive the Christian message which the Church is so willing to give. It would not then be a statement of exclusiveness; it would be the statement of a practical difficulty of communication which meets the preacher in every age. It is quite true that there are certain people to whom it is impossible to impart truth. Something has to happen to them before they can be taught. There is actually a rabbinic saying, " Even as a treasure must not be shown to everyone, so with the words of the Law; one must not go deeply into them, except in the presence of suitable people."

This is in fact a universal truth. It is not to everyone that we can talk of everything. Within a group of friends we may sit and talk about our faith; we may allow our minds to question and adventure; we may talk about the things which puzzle and perplex; and we may allow our minds to go out on the roads of speculation. But if into that group there comes a person of rigid and unsympathetic orthodoxy, he might well brand us as a set of dangerous heretics; or if there entered a simple and an unquestioning soul, his faith might well be shocked and shaken. A medical film might well be to one person an eye-opening, a revealing, a valuable, and a salutary experience; while to another it might equally produce a prurient and prying obscenity. It is told that once Dr. Johnson and a group of friends were talking and jesting as only old friends can. Johnson saw an unpleasant creature coming. " Let us be silent," he said, " a fool is coming."

So, then, there are some people who cannot receive Christian truth. It may be that their minds are shut; it may be that their minds are brutalised and covered over with a film of filth; it may be that they have lived a life which has obscured their ability to see the truth; it may be that they are constitutional mockers of all things holy; it may be, as sometimes happens, that we and they have absolutely no common ground on which we can argue. A man can only understand what he is fit to understand. It is not to everyone that we can lay bare the secrets of our hearts. There are always those to whom the preaching of Christ will be foolishness, and in whose minds the truth, when expressed in words, will meet an insuperable barrier.

What is to be done with these people? Are they to be abandoned as hopeless? Is the Christian message simply to be withdrawn from them? What Christian words cannot do, a Christian life can often do. A man may be blind and impervious to any Christian argument in words; he can have no answer to the demonstration of a Christian life. Cecil Northcott in *A Modern Epiphany* tells of a discussion in a camp of young people where representatives of many nations were living together. " One wet night the campers were discussing various ways of telling people about Christ. They turned to the girl from Africa. ' Maria,' they asked, ' what do you do in your country?' ' Oh,' said Maria, ' we don't have missions or give pamphlets away. We just *send* one or two Christian families to live and work in a village, and when people see what Christians are like, then they want to be Christians too.'" In the end the only all-conquering argument is the argument of a Christian life.

It is often impossible to talk to some people about Jesus Christ. Their insensitiveness, their moral blindness, their intellectual pride, their cynical mockery, the tarnishing film, may make them impervious to words about Christ. But it is always possible to show men Christ; and the weakness of the Church lies not in lack of Christian arguments, but in lack of Christian lives.

THE CHARTER OF PRAYER

Matthew 7: 7-11

> Keep on asking, and it will be given you;
> Keep on seeking, and you will find;
> Keep on knocking, and it will be opened to you.
> For everyone that asks receives;
> And he who seeks finds;
> And to him who knocks it will be opened.

> What man is there, who, if his son will ask him for bread, will give him a stone? Or, if he will ask for a fish, will he give him a serpent? If, then, you, who are grudging, know how to give good gifts to your children, how much more will your Father in heaven give good things to them that ask Him?

ANY man who prays is bound to want to know to what kind of God he is praying. He wants to know in what kind of atmosphere his prayers will be heard. Is he praying to a grudging God out of whom every gift has to be squeezed and coerced? Is he praying to a mocking God whose gifts may well be double-edged? Is he praying to a God whose heart is so kind that He is more ready to give than we are to ask?

Jesus came from a nation which loved prayer. The Jewish Rabbis said the loveliest things about prayer. " God is as near to His creatures as the ear to the mouth." " Human beings can hardly hear two people talking at once, but God, if all the world calls to Him at the one time, hears their cry." " A man is annoyed by being worried by the requests of his friends, but with God, all the time a man puts his needs and requests before Him, God loves him all the more." Jesus had been brought up to love prayer; and in this passage He gives us the Christian charter of prayer.

Jesus' argument is very simple. One of the Jewish Rabbis asked, " Is there a man who ever hates his son? " Jesus' argument is that no father ever refused the request of his son; and God the great Father will never refuse the requests of His children.

Jesus' examples are carefully chosen. He takes three examples, for *Luke* adds a third to the two *Matthew* gives. If a son asks bread, will his father give him a stone? If a son asks a fish, will his father give him a serpent? If a son asks an egg, will his father give him a scorpion? (*Luke* 11: 12). The point is that in each case the two things cited bear a close resemblance. The little, round, limestone

stones on the seashore were exactly the shape and the
colour of little loaves. If a son asks bread will his father
mock him by offering him a stone, which looks like bread
but which is impossible to eat? If a son asks a fish, will
his father give him a serpent? Almost certainly the *serpent*
is an *eel*. According to the Jewish food laws an eel could
not be eaten, because an eel was an unclean fish. " Whatsoever has no fins or scales in the water, that is an abomin-
ation unto you " (*Leviticus* 11: 12). That regulation ruled
out the eel as an article of diet. If a son asks for a fish, will
his father indeed give him a fish, but a fish which it is
forbidden to eat, and which is useless to eat? Would a
father mock his son's hunger like that? If the son asks
for an egg, will his father give him a scorpion? The scorpion
is a dangerous little animal. In action it is rather like a
small lobster, with claws with which it clutches its victim.
Its sting is in its tail, and it brings its tail up over its back
to strike its victim. The sting can be exceedingly painful,
and sometimes even fatal. When the scorpion is at rest
its claws and tail are folded in, and there is a pale kind of
scorpion, which, when folded up, would look exactly like
an egg. If a son asks for an egg, will his father mock him
by handing him a biting scorpion?

God will never refuse our prayers; and God will never
mock our prayers. The Greeks had their stories about the
gods who answered men's prayers, but the answer was an
answer with a barb in it, a double-edged gift. Aurora, the
goddess of the dawn, fell in love with Tithonus a mortal
youth, so the Greek story ran. Zeus, the king of the gods,
offered her any gift that she might choose for her mortal
lover. Aurora very naturally chose that Tithonus might
live for ever; but she had forgotten to ask that Tithonus
might remain for ever young; and so Tithonus grew older
and older and older, and could never die, and the gift
became a curse.

There is a lesson here; God will always answer our
prayers; *but He will answer them in His way*, and His way

will be the way of perfect wisdom and of perfect love. Often if He answered our prayers as we at the moment desire, it would be the worst thing possible for us, for in our ignorance we often ask for gifts which would be our ruin. This saying of Jesus tells us, not only that God will answer, but that God will answer in wisdom and in love.

But although this is the charter of prayer, it lays certain obligations upon us. In Greek there are two kinds of imperative; there is the *aorist* imperative which issues one definite command. "Shut the door behind you," would be an *aorist* imperative. There is the *present* imperative which issues a command that a man should always do something or should go on doing something. "Always shut doors behind you," would be a present imperative. The imperatives here are *present* imperatives; therefore Jesus is saying, "Go on asking; go on seeking; go on knocking." He is telling us to persist in prayer; He is telling us never to be discouraged in prayer. Clearly therein lies the test of our sincerity. Do we really want a thing? Is a thing such that we can bring it repeatedly into the presence of God, for the biggest test of any desire is: Can I pray about it? Jesus here lays down the twin facts that God will always answer our prayers *in His way*, in wisdom and in love; and that we must bring to God an undiscouraged life of prayer, which tests the rightness of the things we pray for, and which tests our own sincerity in asking for them.

THE EVEREST OF ETHICS

Matthew 7: 12

> So, then, all the things which you wish that men should do to you, so do you too do to them; for this is the Law and the prophets.

THIS is very probably the most universally famous thing that Jesus ever said. With this commandment the Sermon on the Mount reaches its summit and its peak. This saying of Jesus has been called " the capstone of the whole discourse." This saying is the topmost peak of social ethics, and the Everest of all ethical teaching.

It is possible to quote rabbinic parallels for almost everything that Jesus said in the Sermon on the Mount; but there is no real parallel to this saying. This is something which had never been said before. It is new teaching, and a new view of life and of life's obligations.

It is not difficult to find many parallels to this saying in its negative form. As we have seen, there were two most famous Jewish teachers. There was Shammai who was famous for his stern and rigid austerity; there was Hillel who was famous for his sweet graciousness. The Jews had a story like this: " A heathen came to Shammai and said, ' I am prepared to be received as a proselyte on the condition that you teach me the whole Law while I am standing on one leg.' Shammai drove him away with a foot-rule which he had in his hand. He went to Hillel who received him as a proselyte. He said to him, ' *What is hateful to yourself, do to no other*; that is the whole Law, and the rest is commentary. Go and learn.' " There is the Golden Rule in its negative form. In the *Book of Tobit* there is a passage in which the aged Tobias teaches his son all that is necessary for life. One of his maxims is: " What thou thyself hatest, to no man do " (*Tobit* 4: 16). There is a Jewish work called *The Letter to Aristeas*, which purports to be an account of the Jewish scholars who went to Alexandria to translate the Hebrew scriptures into Greek, and who produced the Septuagint. The Egyptian king gave them a banquet at which he asked them certain difficult questions. " What is the teaching of wisdom? " he asked. A Jewish scholar answered, " As you wish that no evil should befall you, but to be a partaker of all good things, so you should act on the same principle towards your subjects and offenders, and you should mildly admonish the noble and the good. For God draws all men unto Himself by his benignity " (*The Letter to Aristeas* 207). Rabbi Eliezer came nearer to Jesus' way of putting it when he said, " Let the honour of thy friend be as dear unto thee as thine own." The Psalmist again had the negative form when he said that only the man who does no evil to his neighbour can approach God (*Psalm* 15: 3). It is not difficult to find this rule in Jewish teaching in its *negative* form; but there is no parallel to the *positive* form in which Jesus put it.

The same is true of the teaching of other religions. The negative form is one of the basic principles of Confucius. Tsze-Kung asked him, " Is there one word which may serve as a rule of practice for all one's life? " Confucius said, " Is not *reciprocity* such a word? What you do not want done to yourself, do not do to others."

There are certain beautiful lines in the Buddhist *Hymns of the Faith* which come very near the Christian teaching:

" All men tremble at the rod, all men fear death;
Putting oneself in the place of others, kill not, nor
  cause to kill.
All men tremble at the rod, unto all men life is dear;
Doing as one would be done by, kill not nor cause to
  kill."

With the Greeks and the Romans it is the same. Isocrates tells how King Nicocles advised his subordinate officials: " Do not do to others the things which make you angry when you experience them at the hands of other people." Epictetus condemned slavery on the principle: " What you avoid suffering yourselves, seek not to inflict upon others." The Stoics had as one of their basic maxims: ' What you do not wish to be done to you, do not do to anyone else." And it is told that the Emperor Alexander Severus had that sentence engraved upon the walls of his palace that he might never forget it as a rule of life.

In its negative form this rule is in fact the basis of all ethical teaching, but no one but Jesus ever put it in its positive form. Many voices had said, " Do not do to

others what you would not have them do to you," but no
voice had ever said, " Do to others what you would have
them do to you."

THE GOLDEN RULE OF JESUS

Matthew 7 : 12 *(continued)*

LET us see just how the positive form of the golden rule
differs from the negative form; and let us see just how
much more Jesus was demanding than any teacher had
ever demanded before.

When this rule is put in its negative form, when we are
told that we must refrain from doing to others that which
we would not wish them to do to us, it is not an essentially
religious rule at all. It is simply a common-sense statement
without which no social intercourse at all would be possible.
Sir Thomas Browne once said, " We are beholden to every
man we meet that he doth not kill us." In a sense that is
true, but, if we could not assume that the conduct and the
behaviour of other people to us would conform to the
accepted standards of civilized life, then life would be
intolerable. The negative form of the golden rule is not in
any sense an extra; it is something without which life
could not go on at all.

Further, the negative form of the rule involves nothing
more than *not* doing certain things; it means refraining
from certain actions. It is never very difficult *not* to do
things. That we must not do injury to other people is not
a specially religious principle; it is rather a legal principle.
It is the kind of principle that could well be kept by a man
who has no belief and no interest in religion at all. A man
might for ever refrain from doing any injury to any one
else, and yet be a quite useless citizen to his fellow-men.
A man could satisfy the negative form of the rule by simple
inaction; if he consistently did nothing he would never
break it. And a goodness which consists in doing nothing

would be a contradiction of everything that Christian goodness means.

When this rule is put positively, when we are told that we must actively do to others what we would have them do to us, a new principle enters into life, and a new attitude to our fellow-men. It is one thing to say, " I must not injure people; I must not do to them what I would object to their doing to me." That, the law can compel us to do. It is quite another thing to say, " I must go out of my way to help other people and to be kind to them, as I would wish them to help and to be kind to me." That, only love can compel us to do. The attitude which says, " I must do no harm to people," is quite different from the attitude which says, " I must do my best to help people." To take a very simple analogy—if a man has a motor car the law can compel him to drive it in such a way that he does not injure anyone else on the road, but no law can compel him to stop and to give a weary and a foot-sore traveller a lift along the road. It is quite a simple thing to refrain from hurting and injuring people; it is not so very difficult to respect their principles and their feelings; it is a far harder thing to make it the chosen and deliberate policy of life to go out of our way to be as kind to them as we would wish them to be to us.

And yet it is just that new attitude which makes life beautiful. Jane Stoddart quotes an incident from the life of W. H. Smith. " When Smith was at the War Office, his private secretary, Mr. Fleetwood Wilson, noticed that at the end of a week's work, when his chief was preparing to leave for Greenlands on a Saturday afternoon, he used to pack a despatch-box with the papers he required to take with him, and carry it himself on his journey. Mr. Wilson remarked that Mr. Smith would save himself much trouble, if he did as was the practice of other ministers— leave the papers to be put in an office ' pouch ' and sent by post. Mr. Smith looked rather ashamed for a moment, and then looking up at his secretary said, ' Well, my dear

Wilson, the fact is this: our postman who brings the letters from Henley, has plenty to carry. I watched him one morning coming up the approach with my heavy pouch in addition to his usual load, and I determined to save him as much as I could.' " An action like that shows a certain attitude to one's fellow-men. It is the attitude which believes that we should treat our fellow-men, not as the law allows, but as love demands.

It is perfectly possible for a man of the world to observe the negative form of the golden rule. He could without very serious difficulty so discipline his life that he would not do to others what he did not wish them to do to him; but the only man who can even begin to satisfy the positive form of the rule is the man who has the love of Christ within his heart. He will try to forgive as he would wish to be forgiven, to help as he would wish to be helped, to praise as he would wish to be praised, to understand as he would wish to be understood. He will never seek to avoid doing things; he will always look for things to do. Clearly this will make life much more complicated; clearly he will have much less time to spend on his own desires and his own activities, for time and time again he will have to stop what he is doing to help someone else. It will be a principle which will dominate his life at home, in the factory, in the bus, in the office, in the street, in the train, at his games, everywhere. He can never do it until self withers and dies within his heart. To obey this command-ment a man must become a new man with a new centre to his life; and if the world was composed of people who sought to obey this rule, it would be a new world.

LIFE AT THE CROSS-ROADS

Matthew 7: 13, 14

> Go in through the narrow gate; for wide is the gate and broad is the road which leads to ruin, and there are many who go in through it. Narrow is the gate and hard is the way that leads to life, and those who find it are few.

THE GOSPEL OF MATTHEW

THERE is always a certain dramatic quality about life, for, as it has been said, " all life concentrates on man at the cross-roads." In every action of life man is confronted with a choice; and he can never evade the choice, because he can never stand still. He must always take one way or the other. Because of that, it has always been one of the supreme functions of the great men of history that they should confront men with that inevitable choice. As the end drew near, Moses spoke to the people: " See, I have set before thee this day life and good, and death and evil. . . . Therefore choose life, that thou and thy seed may live " (*Deuteronomy* 30: 15-20). When Joshua was laying down the leadership of the nation at the end of his life, he presented them with the same choice: " Choose you this day whom you will serve " (*Joshua* 24: 15). Jeremiah heard the voice of God saying to him, " Unto this people shalt thou say, Thus saith the Lord: Behold I have set before you the way of life and the way of death " (*Jeremiah* 21: 8). John Oxenham wrote:

> " To every man there openeth
> A way and ways and a way;
> And the high soul treads the high way,
> And the low soul gropes the low;
> And in between on the misty flats
> The rest drift to and fro;
> But to every man there openeth
> A high way and a low;
> And every man decideth
> The way his soul shall go."

That is the choice with which Jesus is confronting men in this passage. There is a broad and an easy way, and there are many who take it; but the end of it is ruin. There is a narrow and a hard way, and there are few who take it; but the end of it is life. Cebes, the disciple of Socrates, writes in the *Tabula*: " Dost thou see a little door, and a way in front of the door, which is not much crowded, but the travellers are few? That is the way that leadeth to true instruction." Let us examine the difference between the two ways.

(i) It is the difference between *the hard and the easy way.* There is never any easy way to greatness; greatness is always the product of toil. Hesiod, the old Greek poet, writes, "Wickedness can be had in abundance easily; smooth is the road, and very nigh she dwells; but in front of virtue the gods immortal have put sweat." Epicharmus said, "The gods demand of us toil as the price of all good things." "Knave," he warns, "yearn not for the soft things, lest thou earn the hard."

Once Edmund Burke made a great speech in the House of Commons. Afterwards his brother Richard Burke was observed deep in thought. He was asked what he was thinking about, and answered, "I have been wondering how it has come about that Ned has contrived to monopolise all the talents of our family; but then again I remember that, when we were at play, he was always at work." Even when a thing is done with an appearance of ease, that ease is the product of unremitting toil. The skill of the master executant on the piano, or the champion player on the golf course did not come without sweat. There never has been any other way to greatness than the way of toil, and anything else which promises such a way is a delusion and a snare.

(ii) It is *the difference between the long and the short way.* Very rarely something may emerge complete and perfect in a flash, but far oftener greatness is the result of long labour and constant attention to detail. Horace in *The Art of Poetry* advises Piso, when he has written something, to keep it beside him for nine years before he publishes it. He tells how a pupil used to take exercises to Quintilius, the famous critic. Quintilius would say, "Scratch it out; the work has been badly turned; send it back to the fire and the anvil." Virgil's *Aeneid* occupied the last ten years of Virgil's life; and, as he was dying, he would have destroyed it, because he thought it so imperfect, if his friends had not stopped him. Plato's *Republic* begins with a simple sentence: " I went down to the Piraeus yesterday with Glaucon, the son of Ariston, that I might offer up prayer to the goddess." On Plato's own manuscript, in his own handwriting, there were no fewer than thirteen different versions of that opening sentence. The master writer had laboured at arrangement after arrangement that he might get the cadences exactly right. Thomas Gray's *Elegy wrote in a Country Churchyard* is one of the immortal poems. It was begun in the summer of 1742; it was finally privately circulated on 12th June, 1750. Its lapidary perfection had taken eight years to produce. No one ever arrived at a masterpiece by a short-cut. In this world we are constantly faced with the short way, which promises immediate results, and the long way, of which the results are in the far distance. But the lasting things never come quickly; the long way is the best way in the end.

(iii) It is the difference between *the disciplined and the undisciplined way*. Nothing was ever achieved without discipline; and many an athlete and many a man has been ruined because he abandoned discipline and let himself grow slack. Coleridge is the supreme tragedy of indiscipline. Never did so great a mind produce so little. He left Cambridge University to join the army; he left the army because, in spite of all his erudition, he could not rub down a horse; he returned to Oxford and left without a degree. He began a paper called *The Watchman* which lived for ten numbers and then died. It has been said of him: " He lost himself in visions of work to be done, that always remained to be done. Coleridge had every poetic gift but one—the gift of sustained and concentrated effort." In his head and in his mind he had all kinds of books, as he said, himself, " completed save for transcription." " I am on the eve," he says, " of sending to the press two octavo volumes." But the books were never composed outside Coleridge's mind, because he would not face the discipline of sitting down to write them out. No one ever reached any eminence, and no one having reached it ever maintained it, without discipline.

(iv) It is the *difference between the thoughtful and the thoughtless way*. Here we come to the heart of the matter. No one would ever take the easy, the short, the undisciplined way, if he only thought. Everything in this world has two aspects—how it looks at the moment, and how it will look in the time to come. The easy way may look very inviting at the moment, and the hard way may look very daunting. The only way to get our values right is to see, not the beginning, but the end of the way, to see things, not in the light of time, but in the light of eternity.

THE FALSE PROPHETS

Matthew 7: 15-20

> Beware of false prophets, who come to you in sheeps' clothing, but who within are rapacious wolves. You will recognize them from their fruits. Surely men do not gather grapes from thorns, and figs from thistles? So every good tree produces fine fruit; but every rotten tree produces bad fruit. A good tree cannot produce bad fruit, nor can a rotten tree produce fine fruit. Every tree which does not produce fine fruit is cut down and thrown into the fire. So then you will recognize them from their fruits.

ALMOST every phrase and word in this section would ring an answering bell in the minds of the Jews who heard it for the first time.

The Jews knew all about *false prophets*. Jeremiah, for instance, had his conflict with the prophets who said, " Peace, peace, when there was no peace " (*Jeremiah* 6: 14; 8: 11). *Wolves* was the very name by which false rulers and false prophets were called. In the bad days Ezekiel had said, " Her princes in the midst thereof are like wolves ravening the prey, to shed blood and to destroy souls, to get dishonest gain " (*Ezekiel* 22: 27). Zephaniah drew a grim picture of the state of things in Israel, when, " Her

THE GOSPEL OF MATTHEW

princes within her are roaring lions; her judges are evening
wolves; they gnaw not the bones till morning. Her prophets are light and treacherous persons " (*Zephaniah* 3: 3).
When Paul was warning the elders of Ephesus of dangers
to come, as he took a last farewell of them, he said,
" Grievous wolves shall enter in among you, not sparing
the flock " (*Acts* 20: 29). Jesus said that He was sending
out His disciples as sheep in the midst of wolves (*Matthew*
10: 16); and He told of the Good Shepherd who protected
the flock from the wolves with his life (*John* 10: 12). Here
indeed was a picture which everyone could recognize and
understand.

He said that the false prophets were like wolves in
sheeps' clothing. When the shepherd watched his flocks
upon the hillside, his garment was a sheepskin, worn with
the skin outside and the fleece inside. But a man might
wear a shepherd's dress and still not be a shepherd. The
prophets had acquired a conventional dress. Elijah had
a mantle (I *Kings* 19: 13, 19), and that mantle had been
a hairy cloak (2 *Kings* 1: 8). That sheepskin mantle had
become the uniform of the prophets, just as the Greek
philosophers had worn the philosopher's robe. It was by
that mantle that the prophet could be distinguished from
other men. But sometimes that garb was worn by those
who had no right to wear it, for Zechariah in his picture
of the great days to come says, " Neither shall they wear
a rough garment to deceive " (*Zechariah* 13: 4). There were
those who wore a prophet's cloak, but who lived anything
but a prophet's life.

There were false prophets in the ancient days, but there
were also false prophets in New Testament times. *Matthew*
was written about A.D. 85, and at that time prophets were
still an institution in the Church. They were men with no
fixed abode, men who had given up everything to wander
throughout the country, bringing to the Churches a message

which they believed to come direct from God. At their best the prophets were the inspiration of the Church, for they were men who had abandoned everything to serve God and the Church of God. But the office of prophet was singularly liable to abuse. There were men who used it to gain prestige, and to impose on the generosity of local congregations, and so live a life of comfortable, and even pampered, idleness. The *Didachē* is the first order book of the Christian Church; it dates to about A.D. 100; and its regulations concerning these wandering prophets are very illuminating. A true prophet was to be held in the highest honour; he was to be welcomed; his word must never be disregarded, and his freedom must never be curtailed; but " He shall remain one day, and, if necessary, another day also; but if he remain three days, he is a false prophet." He must never ask for anything but bread. " If he asks for money, he is a false prophet." Prophets all claim to speak in the Spirit, but there is one acid test: " By their characters a true and a false prophet shall be known." " Every prophet that teacheth the truth, if he do not what he teacheth, is a false prophet." If a prophet, claiming to speak in the Spirit, orders a table and a meal to be set before him he is a false prophet. " Whosoever shall say in the Spirit: Give me money or any other things, ye shall not hear him; but if he tell you to give in the matter of others who have need, let no one judge him." If a wanderer comes to a congregation, and wishes to settle there, if he has a trade, " let him work and eat." If he has no trade, " consider in your wisdom how he may not live with you as a Christian in idleness. . . . But if he will not do this, he is a trafficker in Christ. Beware of such " (*Didachē*, chapters 11 and 12).

Past history and present events made the words of Jesus meaningful to those who heard them for the first time, and to those to whom Matthew transmitted them.

KNOWN BY THEIR FRUITS

Matthew 7: 15-20 (continued)

THE Jews, the Greeks and the Romans all used the idea that a tree is to be judged by its fruits. "Like root, like fruit," ran the proverb. Epictetus was later to say, "How can a vine grow not like a vine but like an olive, or, how can an olive grow not like an olive but like a vine" (Epictetus, *Discourses* 2: 20). Seneca declared that good cannot grow from evil any more than a fig tree can from an olive.

But there is more in this than meets the eye. "Do men," asked Jesus, "gather grapes off thorns?" There was a certain thorn, the buckthorn, which had little black berries which closely resembled little grapes. "Do men," asked Jesus, "gather figs off thistles?" There was a certain thistle, which had a flower, which, at least at a distance, might well be taken for a fig. The point is real, and relevant, and salutary. There may be a superficial resemblance between the true and the false prophet. The false prophet may wear the right clothes and use the right language; but you cannot sustain life with the berries of a buckthorn or the flowers of a thistle; and the life of the soul can never be sustained with the food which a false prophet offers. The real test of any teaching is: Does it strengthen a man to bear the burdens of life, and to walk in the way wherein he ought to go? Let us then look at the false prophets and see their characteristics. If the way is difficult and the gate is so narrow that it is hard to find, then we must be very careful to get to ourselves teachers who will help us to find it, and not teachers who will lure us away from it.

The basic fault of the false prophet is *self-interest*. The true shepherd cares for the flock more than he cares for his life; the wolf cares for nothing but to satisfy his own gluttony and his own greed. The false prophet is in the business of teaching, not for what he can give to others, but for what he can get to himself. The Jews were alive to this danger. The Rabbis were the Jewish teachers, but it was a cardinal principle of Jewish Law that a Rabbi must have a trade by which he earned his living, and must on no account accept any payment for teaching. Rabbi Zadok said, "Make the knowledge of the Law neither a crown wherewith to make a show, nor a spade wherewith to dig." Hillel said, "He who uses the crown of the Law for external aims fades away." The Jews knew all about the teacher who used his teaching self-interestedly, for no other reason than to make a profit for himself. There are three ways in which a teacher can be dominated by self interest.

(i) He may teach solely for *gain*. It is told that there was trouble in the Church at Ecclefechan, where Thomas Carlyle's father was an elder. It was a dispute between the congregation and the minister on a matter of money and of salary. When much had been said on both sides, Carlyle's father rose and uttered one devastating sentence: "Give the hireling his wages, and let him go." No man can live on nothing, and few men can do their best work when the pressure of material things is too fiercely on them, but the great privilege of teaching is not the pay it offers, but the thrill of opening the minds of boys and girls, and young men and maidens, and men and women to the truth.

(ii) He may teach solely for *prestige*. A man may teach in order to help others, or he may teach to show how clever he is. Denney once said a savage thing: "No man can at one and the same time prove that he is clever and that Christ is wonderful." Prestige is the last thing that the great teachers desire. J. P. Struthers was a saint of God. He spent all his life in the service of the little Reformed Presbyterian Church when he could have occupied any pulpit in Britain. Men loved him, and the better they knew him the more they loved him. Two men were talking of him. One man knew all that Struthers had done, but did not know Struthers personally. Remembering Struthers saintly ministry, he said, "Struthers will have a front seat in the Kingdom of Heaven." The other had known

Struthers personally and his answer was: " Struthers would be miserable in a front seat anywhere." There is a kind of teacher and preacher who uses his message as a setting for himself. The false prophet is interested in self-display; the true prophet desires self-obliteration.

(iii) He may teach solely *to transmit his own ideas.* The false prophet is out to disseminate his version of the truth; the true prophet is out to publish abroad God's truth. It is quite true that every man must think things out for himself; but it was said of John Brown of Haddington that, when he preached, ever and again he used to pause " as if listening for a voice." The true prophet listens to God before he speaks to men. He never forgets that he is nothing more than a voice to speak for God and a channel through which God's grace can come to men. It is a teacher's duty and a preacher's duty to bring to men, not his private idea of the truth, but the truth as it is in Jesus Christ.

THE FRUITS OF FALSENESS

Matthew 7: 15-20 (*continued*)

THIS passage has much to say about the evil fruits of the false prophets. What are the false effects, the evil fruits, which a false prophet may produce?

(i) Teaching is false if it produces *a religion which consists solely or mainly in the observance of externals.* That is what was wrong with the Scribes and Pharisees. To them religion consisted in the observance of the ceremonial law. If a man went through the correct procedure of hand-washing, if on the Sabbath he never carried anything weighing more than two figs, if he never walked on the Sabbath farther than the prescribed distance, if he was meticulous in giving tithes of everything down to the herbs of his kitchen garden, then he was a good man. It is easy to confuse religion with religious practices. It is possible—and indeed not uncommon—to teach that religion consists in going to Church, observing the Lord's Day, fulfilling one's financial obligations to the Church, reading one's Bible. A man might do all these things and be far off from being a Christian, for Christianity is an attitude of the heart to God and to man.

(ii) Teaching is false if it produces *a religion which consists in prohibitions*. Any religion which is based on a series of " thou shalt nots " is a false religion. There is a type of teacher who says to a person who has set out on the Christian way: " From now on you will no longer go to the cinema; from now on you will no longer dance; from now on you will no longer smoke or use make-up; from now on you will no longer read a novel or a Sunday newspaper; from now on you will never enter a theatre." If a man could become a Christian simply by abstaining from doing things Christianity would be a much easier religion than it is. But the whole essence of Christianity is that it does not consist in *not* doing things; it consists in doing things. A negative Christianity on our part can never answer the positive love of God.

(iii) Teaching is false if it produces *an easy religion*. There were false teachers in the days of Paul, an echo of whose teaching we can hear in *Romans* 6. They said to Paul: " You believe that God's grace is the biggest thing in the universe? " " Yes." " You believe that God's grace is wide enough to cover every sin? " " Yes." " Well then, if that be so, let us go on sinning to our hearts' content. God will forgive. And, after all, our sin is simply giving God's wonderful grace an opportunity to operate." A religion like that is a travesty of religion because it is an insult to the love of God. Any teaching which takes the iron out of religion, any teaching which takes the Cross out of Christianity, any teaching which eliminates the threat from the voice of Christ, any teaching which pushes judgment into the background and makes men think lightly of sin, is false teaching.

(iv) Teaching is false *if it divorces religion and life.* **Any** teaching which removes the Christian from the life and activity of the world is false. That was the mistake the monks and the hermits made. It was their belief that to live the Christian life they must retire to a desert or to a monastery, that they must cut themselves off from the engrossing and tempting life of the world, that they could only be truly Christian by ceasing to live in the world. Jesus said, as He prayed for His disciples, " I pray not that Thou shouldest take them out of the world, but that Thou shouldest keep them from the evil " (*John* 17: 15). We have heard, for instance, of a journalist who found it hard to maintain her Christian principles in the life of a daily newspaper, and who left it to take up work on a purely religious journal. No man can be a good soldier by running away, and the Christian is the soldier of Christ. How shall the leaven ever work if the leaven refuses to be inserted into the mass? What is witness worth unless it is witness to those who do not believe? Any teaching which encourages a man to take what John Mackay called " the balcony view of life " is wrong. The Christian is not a spectator from the balcony; he is involved in the warfare of life.

(v) Teaching is false if it produces *a religion which is arrogant and separatist.* Any teaching which encourages a man to withdraw into a narrow sect, and to regard the rest of the world as sinners, is false teaching. The function of religion is not to erect middle walls of partition but to tear them down. It is the dream of Jesus Christ that there shall be one flock and one shepherd (*John* 10: 16). Exclusiveness is not a religious quality; it is an irreligious quality. Fosdick quotes four lines of doggerel:

" We are God's chosen few,
All others will be damned;
There is no room in heaven for you;
We can't have heaven crammed."

Religion is meant to bring men closer together, not to drive men apart. Religion is meant to gather men into one family, not to split them up into hostile groups. The teaching which declares that any Church or any sect has a monopoly of the grace of God is false teaching, for Christ is not the Christ who divides, He is the Christ who unites.

ON FALSE PRETENCES

Matthew 7: 21-23

> Not everyone that says to me: " Lord, Lord " will enter into the Kingdom of Heaven, but he who does the will of my father who is in heaven. Many will say to me on that day: " Lord, Lord, did we not prophesy in your name, and in your name did we not cast out devils, and in your name did we not do many deeds of power? " Then will I publicly announce to them: " I never knew you. Depart from me you doers of iniquity."

THERE is an apparently surprising feature about this passage. Jesus is quite ready to concede that many of the false prophets will do and say wonderful and impressive things. We must remember what the ancient world was like. Miracles were common events. The frequency of miracles came from the ancient idea of illness. In the ancient world all illness was held to be the work of demons. A man was ill because a demon had succeeded in exercising some malign influence over him, or in winning a way into some part of his body. Cures were therefore wrought by exorcism. The result of all this was that a great deal of illness was what we would call psychological, as were a great many cures. If a man succeeded in convincing—or deluding himself—into a belief that a demon was in him or had him in his power, that man would undoubtedly be ill. And if someone could convince him that the hold of the demon was broken, then quite certainly that man would be cured. In the ancient world a man could *believe* that he was demon-possessed, and therefore he could be ill; he could *believe* that the demon was exorcised and therefore could be cured. The leaders of the Church never denied heathen miracles. In answer to the miracles of Christ, Celsus quoted the miracles attributed to Aesculapius and Apollo. Origen, who met his arguments, did not for a moment deny these miracles. He simply answered, " Such curative power is of itself neither good nor bad, but within the reach of godless as well as of honest people " (Origen, *Against Celsus* 3: 22). Even in the New Testament we read of Jewish exorcists who added the name of Jesus to their repertoire, and who banished devils by its aid (*Acts* 19: 13). There was many a charlatan who rendered a lip service to Jesus Christ, and who used His name to produce wonderful effects on demon-possessed people. What Jesus is saying is that if any man uses His name on false pretences, the day of reckoning will come. His real motives will be exposed, and he will be banished from the presence of God.

There are two great permanent truths within this passage. There is only one way in which a man's sincerity can be proved, and that is by his practice. Fine words can never be a substitute for fine deeds. There is only one proof of love, and that proof is obedience. There is no point in saying that we love a person, and then doing things which break that person's heart. When we were young maybe we used sometimes to say to our mothers, " Mother, I love you." And maybe the mother sometimes smiled a little wistfully and said, " I wish you would show it a little more in the way you behave." So often we confess God with our lips and deny Him with our lives. It is not difficult to recite a creed, but it is difficult to live the Christian life. Faith without practice is a contradiction in terms, and love without obedience is an impossibility.

At the back of this passage is the idea of judgment. All through it there runs the certainty that the day of reckoning comes. A man may succeed for long in maintaining the pretences and the disguises, but there comes a day when the pretences are shown for what they are, and the disguises are stripped away. We may deceive men with our words, but we cannot deceive God. " Thou understandest my thought afar off," said the Psalmist (*Psalm* 139: 2). No man can ultimately deceive the God who sees the heart.

THE ONLY TRUE FOUNDATION

Matthew 7: 24-27

> So, then, everyone who hears these words of mine and does them will be likened to a wise man who built his house upon the rock. And the rain came down, and the rivers swelled, and the wind blew, and fell upon that house, and it did not fall, for it was founded upon the rock. And everyone who hears these words of mine and does not do them will be likened to a foolish man who built his house upon the sand. And the rain came down, and the rivers swelled, and the winds blew and beat upon that house, and it fell; and its fall was great.
>
> And when Jesus had ended these words, the people were astonished at His teaching, for He was teaching them as one who had authority, and not as their Scribes.

JESUS was in a double sense an expert. He was an expert in scripture. The writer of *Proverbs* gave Him the hint for His picture: " As the whirlwind passeth, so is the wicked no more; but the righteous is an everlasting foundation " (*Proverbs* 10: 25). Here is the germ of the picture which Jesus drew of the two houses and the two builders. But Jesus was also an expert in life. He was the craftsman who knew all about the building of houses, and when He spoke about the foundations of a house He knew what He was talking about. This is no illustration formed by a scholar in his study; this is the illustration of a practical man.

Nor is this a far-fetched illustration; it is a story of the kind of thing which could well happen. In Palestine the builder must think ahead. There is many a gulley which in summer is a pleasant sandy hollow, but which in winter

L

is a raging torrent of rushing water. A man might be looking for a house; he might find a pleasantly sheltered sandy hollow; and he might think that this was a very suitable place. But, if he was a short-sighted man, he might well have built his house in the dried-up bed of a river, and, when the winter came, his house would disintegrate. Even on an ordinary site it was tempting to begin building on the smoothed over sand, and not to bother digging down to the shelf of rock below; but that way disaster lay ahead. Only a house whose foundations are firm can withstand the storm; and only a life whose foundations are sure can stand the test. Jesus demanded two things.

(i) He demanded that men should *listen*. One of the great difficulties which face us to-day is the simple fact that men often do not know what Jesus said or what the Church teaches. In fact the matter is worse. They have often a quite mistaken notion of what Jesus said and of what the Church teaches. It is no part of the duty of an honourable man to condemn either a person, or an institution, unheard—and that to-day is precisely what so many do. The first step to the Christian life is simply to give Jesus Christ a chance to be heard.

(ii) He demanded that men should *do*. Knowledge only becomes relevant when it is translated into action. It would be perfectly possible for a man to pass an examination in Christian Ethics with the highest distinction, and yet not to be a Christian. Knowledge must become action; theory must become practice; theology must become life. There is little point in going to a doctor, unless we are prepared to do the things we hear him say to us. There is little point in going to an expert, unless we are prepared to act upon his advice. And yet there are thousands of people who listen to the teaching of Jesus Christ every Sunday, and who have a very good knowledge of what Jesus taught, and who yet make little or no deliberate attempt to put it into practice. If we are to be in any sense followers of Jesus, we must *hear* and *do*.

Is there any word in which *hearing* and *doing* are summed up? There is such a word, and that word is *obedience*. Jesus demands our implicit obedience. To learn to obey is the most important thing in life. Some time ago there was a report of the case of a sailor in the Royal Navy who was very severely punished for a breach of discipline. So severe was the punishment that in certain civilian quarters it was thought to be far too severe. A newspaper asked its readers to express their opinions about the severity of the punishment. One who answered was a man who himself had served for years in the Royal Navy. In his view the punishment was not too severe. He held that discipline was absolutely essential, for the purpose of discipline was to condition a man automatically and unquestioningly to obey orders, and on such obedience a man's life might well depend. He cited a case from his own experience. He was in a launch which was towing a much heavier vessel in a rough sea. The vessel was attached to the launch by a wire hawser. Suddenly in the midst of the wind and the spray there came a single, insistent word of command from the officer in charge of the launch. " Down! " he shouted. On the spot the crew of the launch flung themselves down. Just at that moment the wire towing-hawser snapped, and the broken parts of it whipped about like a maddened steel snake. If any man had been struck by it he would have been instantly killed. But the whole crew automatically obeyed and no one was injured. If anyone had stopped to argue, or to ask why, he would have been a dead man. Obedience saved lives.

It is such obedience that Jesus demands. It is Jesus' claim that obedience to Him is the only sure foundation for life; and it is His promise that the life which is founded on obedience to him is safe, no matter what storms may come.

THE GOSPEL OF MATTHEW

LOVE IN ACTION

Of all the gospel writers Matthew is the most orderly. He never sets out his material haphazardly. If in *Matthew* one thing follows another in a certain sequence, there is always a reason for that sequence; and it is so here. In chapters 5, 6 and 7 Matthew has given us the Sermon on the Mount. That is to say, in these chapters he has given us his account of the *words* of Jesus; and now in chapter 8 he gives us an account of the *deeds* of Jesus. Chapters 5, 6, 7 show us the divine wisdom in words; chapter 8 shows us the divine love in action. Chapter 8 is a chapter of miracles. Let us look at these miracles as a whole, before we proceed to deal with them in detail. In the chapter there are seven miraculous happenings.

(i) There is the healing of the leper (verses 1-4). Here we see Jesus touching the untouchable. The leper was banished from the society of men; to touch him, and even to approach him, was to break the Law. Here we see the man who was kept at arm's length by all men wrapped around with the pity and the compassion of the love of God.

(ii) There is the healing of the centurion's servant (verses 5-13). The centurion was a Gentile, and therefore the strict orthodox Jew would have said that he was merely fuel for the fires of hell; he was the servant of a foreign government and of an occupying power and therefore the nationalistic Jew would have said that he was a candidate for assassination and not for assistance; the servant was a slave and a slave was no more than a living tool. Here we see the love of God going out to help the man whom all men hated and the slave whom all men despised.

(iii) There is the healing of Peter's wife's mother (verses 14 and 15). This miracle took place in a humble cottage in a humble home in Palestine. There was no publicity; there was no admiring audience; there was only Jesus and

298

the family circle. Here we see the infinite love of the God of all the universe displaying all its power when there was none but the circle of the family to see.

(iv) There was the healing of all the sick who were brought to the doors at evening time (verses 16 and 17). Here we see the sheer universality of the love of God in action. To Jesus no one was ever a nuisance; He had no hours when He was on duty and hours when He was off duty. Any man could come to Him at any time and receive the willing, gracious help of the love of God.

(v) There was the reaction of the scribe (verses 18-22). On the face of it this little section appears to be out of place in a chapter on miracles; but this is the miracle of personality. That any scribe should be moved to follow Jesus is nothing less than a miracle. Somehow this scribe had forgotten his devotion to the Scribal Law; somehow although Jesus contradicted all the things to which he had dedicated his life, he saw in Jesus not an enemy but a friend, not an opponent but a master. It must have been an instinctive reaction. Negley Farson writes of his old grandfather. When Farson was a boy, he did not know his grandfather's history and all that he had done, but, he says, " All I knew was that he made other men around him look like mongrel dogs." That scribe saw in Jesus a splendour and a magnificence he had never seen in any other man. The miracle happened, and the scribe's heart ran out to Jesus Christ.

(vi) There is the miracle of the calming of the storm (verses 23-27). Here we see Jesus dealing with the waves and the billows which threaten to engulf a man. As Pusey had it when his wife died, " All through that time it was as if there was a hand beneath my chin to bear me up." Here is the love of God bringing peace and serenity into tumult and confusion.

(vii) There is the healing of the Gerasene demoniac (verses 28-34). In the ancient world people believed that all illness was due to the action of devils. Here we see the power of God dealing with the power of the devil; here we see God's goodness invading earth's evil, God's love going out against evil's malignancy and malevolence. Here we see the goodness and the love which save men triumphantly overcoming the evil and the hatred which ruin men.

THE LIVING DEATH

Matthew 8: 1-4

> When Jesus had come down from the mountain, great crowds followed Him; and, look you, a leper came to Him, and remained kneeling before Him. " Lord," he said, " you can cleanse me, if you are willing to do so." Jesus stretched out His hand and touched him. " I am willing," He said, " be cleansed." And immediately his leprosy was cleansed. And Jesus said to him: " See that you tell no one; but go, show yourself to the priest, and bring the gift which Moses ordered, so that they will be convinced that you are cured."

IN the ancient world leprosy was the most terrible of all diseases. E. W. G. Masterman writes: " No other disease reduces a human being for so many years to so hideous a wreck." It might begin with little nodules which go on to ulcerate. The ulcers develop a foul discharge; the eyebrows fall out; the eyes become staring; the vocal chords become ulcerated, and the voice becomes hoarse, and the breath wheezes. The hands and feet always ulcerate. Slowly the sufferer becomes a mass of ulcerated growths. The average course of that kind of leprosy is nine years, and it ends in mental decay, coma and ultimately death. Leprosy might begin with the loss of all sensation in some part of the body; the nerve trunks are affected; the muscles waste away; the tendons contract until the hands are like claws. There follows ulceration of the hands and feet. Then comes the progressive loss of fingers and toes, until in the end a whole hand or a whole foot may drop off. The duration of that kind of leprosy is anything from twenty to thirty years. It is a kind of terrible progressive death in which a man dies by inches.

The physical condition of the leper was terrible; but there was something which made it worse. Josephus tells us that lepers were treated " as if they were, in effect, dead men." Immediately leprosy was diagnosed, the leper was absolutely and completely banished from human society. " All the days wherein the plague shall be in him he shall be defiled; he is unclean; he shall dwell alone; outside the camp shall his habitation be " (*Leviticus* 13: 46). The leper had to go with rent clothes, dishevelled hair, with a covering upon his upper lip, and, as he went, he had to cry: " Unclean, unclean " (*Leviticus* 13: 45). In the middle ages, if a man became a leper, the priest donned his stole and took his crucifix, and brought the man into the church, and read the burial service over him. For all human purposes the man was dead.

In Palestine in the time of Jesus the leper was barred from Jerusalem and from all walled towns. In the Synagogue there was provided for him a little isolated chamber, ten feet high and six feet wide, called the *Mechitsah*. The Law enumerated sixty-one different contacts which could defile, and the defilement involved in contact with a leper was second only to the defilement involved in contact with a dead body. If a leper so much as put his head into a house, that house became unclean even to the roof beams. Even in an open place it was illegal to greet a leper. No one might come nearer to a leper than four cubits —a cubit is eighteen inches. If the wind was blowing towards a person from a leper, the leper must stand at least one hundred cubits away. One Rabbi would not even eat an egg bought in a street where a leper had passed by. Another Rabbi actually boasted that he flung stones at lepers to keep them away. Other Rabbis hid themselves, or took to their heels, at the sight of a leper even in the

distance. There never has been any disease which so
separated a man from his fellow-men as leprosy did. And
this was the man whom Jesus touched. To a Jew there
would be no more amazing sentence in the New Testament
than the simple statement: " And Jesus put forth His
hand and touched the leper."

COMPASSION BEYOND THE LAW

Matthew 8: 1-4 (*continued*)

IN this story we must note two things—the leper's *approach*
and Jesus' *response*. In the leper's approach there were
three elements.

(i) The leper came with *confidence*. He had no doubt
that, if Jesus willed, Jesus could make him clean. Here
there was faith. No leper would ever have come near an
orthodox scribe or Rabbi; he knew too well that he would
be stoned away; but this man came to Jesus. He had
perfect confidence in Jesus' willingness to welcome the
man everyone else would have driven away. No man need
ever feel himself too unclean to come to Jesus Christ.
He had perfect confidence in Jesus' power. Leprosy was
the one disease for which there was no prescribed
rabbinic remedy. But this man was sure that Jesus could
do what no one else could do. No man need ever feel
himself incurable in body or unforgivable in soul while
Jesus Christ exists.

(ii) The leper came with *humility*. He did not demand
healing; he only said, " *If you will,* you can cleanse me."
It was as if he said, " I know I don't matter; I know that
other men will flee from me and will have nothing to do
with me; I know that I have no claim on you; but perhaps
in your divine condescension you will give your power
even to such as I am." It is the humble heart which is
conscious of nothing but its need which finds its way to
Christ.

(iii) The leper came with *reverence*. The Authorized Version says that he *worshipped* Jesus. The Greek verb is *proskunein*, and that word is never used of anything but *worship of the gods*; it always describes a man's feeling and action in presence of the divine. That leper could never have told anyone what he thought Jesus was; but he knew that in the presence of Jesus he was in the presence of God. We do not need to put this into theological or philosophical terms; it is enough to be convinced that when we are confronted with Jesus Christ, we are confronted with the love and the power of Almighty God.

So to this approach of the leper there came the reaction of Jesus. First and foremost, that reaction was *compassion*. The Law said that Jesus must not touch that man; the Law threatened Him with terrible uncleanness if He allowed the leper to come within six feet of Him; but Jesus stretched out His hand and touched him. The medical knowledge of the day would have said that Jesus was running a desperate risk of a ghastly infection; but Jesus stretched out His hand and touched this man. For Jesus there was only one obligation in life—and that was to help. There was only one law—and that law was love. The duty of compassion, the obligation of love took precedence over all other rules and laws and regulations; it made Him defy all physical risks. To a good doctor a man sick of a loathsome disease is not a disgusting spectacle; he is a human being who needs his skill. To a doctor a child sick of an infectious disease is not a menace; he is a child who needs to be helped. Jesus was like that: God is like that: we must be like that. The true Christian will break any convention and will take any risk to help a fellow-man in need.

TRUE PRUDENCE

Matthew 8: 1-4 (*continued*)

BUT there remain two things in this incident which show that, while Jesus would defy the Law and risk any infection

to help, He was not senselessly reckless, nor did He forget
the demands of true prudence.

(i) He ordered the man to keep silence, and not to publish
abroad what He had done for him. This injunction to
silence is common on Jesus' lips (*Matthew* 9: 30; 12: 16;
17: 9; *Mark* 1: 34; 5: 43; 7: 36; 8: 26). Why should
Jesus command this silence? Palestine was an occupied
country, and the Jews were a proud race. They never
forgot that they were God's chosen people. They dreamed
of the day when their divine deliverer would come. But
for the most part they dreamed of that day in terms of
military conquest and political power. For that reason
Palestine was the most inflammable country in the world.
It lived amidst revolutions. Leader after leader arose,
and had his moment of glory and was then eliminated
by the might of Rome. Now, if this leper had gone out and
published abroad what Jesus had done for him, there
would have been a rush to instal a man with powers such
as Jesus had as a political leader and a military commander.
Before Jesus could have stopped it another red rebellion
would be on the way. Jesus had to educate men's minds;
He had to change their ideas; He had somehow to enable
them to see that His power was love and not force of arms.
He had to work almost in secrecy until men knew Him
for what He was, the lover and not the destroyer of the
lives of men. Jesus enjoined silence upon those He helped
lest men should use Him to make their dreams come true
instead of waiting on the dream of God. They had to be
silent until they had learned the right things to say about
Him.

(ii) Jesus sent this leper to the priests to make the correct
offering and to receive a certificate that he was clean.
The Jews were so terrified of the infection of leprosy that
there was a prescribed ritual in the very unlikely event
of a cure. The ritual is described in *Leviticus* 14. The leper
was examined by a priest. Two birds were taken, and one
was killed over running water. In addition there were

taken cedar, scarlet and hyssop. These things were taken, together with the living bird, and dipped in the blood of the dead bird, and then the living bird was allowed to go free. The man washed himself and his clothes, and shaved himself. Seven days were allowed to pass, and then he was re-examined. He must then shave his hair, his head and his eye-brows. Certain sacrifices were then made consisting of two male lambs without blemish, and one ewe lamb; three-tenths of a deal of fine flour mingled with oil; and one log of oil. The restored leper was touched on the tip of the right ear, the right thumb, and the right great toe with blood and oil. He was finally examined for the last time, and, if the cure was real, he was allowed to go with a certificate that he was cleansed.

Jesus told this man to go through that process. There is guidance here. Jesus was telling that man not to neglect the treatment that was available for him in those days. We do not receive miracles by neglecting the medical and scientific treatment that are open to us. Men must do all man can do before God's power will co-operate with our efforts. A miracle does not come by a lazy waiting upon God to do it all; it comes from the co-operation of the faith-filled effort of man with the illimitable grace of God.

A GOOD MAN'S PLEA

Matthew 8: 5-13

When Jesus had come into Capernaum, a centurion came to Him. "Lord," he appealed to Him, "my servant lies at home, paralysed, suffering terribly." He said to him: "Am I to come and cure him?" "Lord," answered the centurion, "I am not worthy that you should enter my house; but, only speak a word, and my servant will be cured. For even I am a man under authority, and I have soldiers under me. I say to one soldier, 'Go!' and he goes, and to another, 'Do this!' and he does it." Jesus was amazed when

He heard this, and said to those who were following Him, "This is the truth I tell you—not even in Israel have I found so great a faith. I tell you that many will come from the east and west and will sit down at table with Abraham and Isaac and Jacob in the Kingdom of Heaven; but the sons of the Kingdom will be cast into outer darkness. There will be weeping and gnashing of teeth there." And Jesus said to the centurion, "Go; let it be done for you as you have believed." And his servant was healed at that hour.

EVEN in the brief appearance that he makes on the stage of the New Testament story this centurion is one of the most attractive characters in the gospels. The centurions were the backbone of the Roman army. In a Roman legion there were 6,000 men; the legion was divided into sixty centuries, each containing 100 men, and in command of each century there was a centurion. These centurions were the long service, regular soldiers of the Roman army; they were responsible for the discipline of the regiment, and they were the cement which held the army together. In peace and in war alike the morale of the Roman army depended on them. In his description of the Roman army Polybius describes what a centurion should be: "They must not be so much venturesome seekers after danger as men who can command, steady in action, and reliable; they ought not to be over-anxious to rush into the fight, but when hard pressed, they must be ready to hold their ground, and die at their posts." The centurions were the finest men in the Roman army.

It is interesting to note that every centurion mentioned in the New Testament is mentioned with honour. There was the centurion who recognized Jesus on the Cross as the Son of God; there was Cornelius, the first Gentile convert to the Christian Church; there was the centurion who suddenly discovered that Paul was a Roman citizen, and who rescued him from the fury of the rioting mob; there was the centurion who was informed that the Jews had planned to murder Paul between Jerusalem and

Caesarea, and who took steps to foil their plans; there was the centurion whom Felix ordered to look after Paul; there was the centurion who was with Paul on his last journey to Rome, and who treated Paul with every courtesy, and accepted him as leader when the storm struck the ship (*Matthew* 27: 34: *Acts* 10: 22; 26; 23: 17; 23: 24; 24: 23; 27: 43).

But there was something very special about this centurion at Capernaum, and that was his attitude to his servant. This servant of his would be a slave, but this centurion was grieved that his servant was ill and was determined to do everything in his power to save him. That was the reverse of the normal attitude of a master to a slave. In the Roman Empire slaves did not matter. It was a matter of no importance to anyone if they suffered, and whether they lived or died. Aristotle is talking about the friendships which are possible in life, and he writes: " There can be no friendship nor justice towards inanimate things; indeed, not even towards a horse or an ox, nor yet towards a slave as a slave. For master and slave have nothing in common; a slave is a living tool, just as a tool is an inanimate slave." A slave was no better than a thing. A slave had no legal rights whatsoever; his master was free to treat him, or maltreat him, as he liked. Gaius, the Roman legal expert, lays it down in his *Institutes*: " We may note that it is universally accepted that the master possesses the power of life and death over the slave." Varro, the Roman writer on agriculture, has a grim passage in which he divides the instruments of agriculture into three classes—the articulate, the inarticulate and the mute, " the articulate comprising the slaves, the inarticulate comprising the cattle, and the mute comprising the vehicles." The only difference between a slave and a beast or a cart was that the slave could speak. Cato, another Roman writer on agriculture, has a passage which shows how unusual the attitude of this centurion was. He is giving advice to a man taking over a farm: " Look over the livestock, and hold a sale. Sell your oil, if the price is satisfactory, and sell the surplus of your wine and grain. Sell worn-out oxen, blemished cattle, blemished sheep, wool, hides, an old wagon, old tools, an old slave, a sickly slave, and whatever else is superfluous." Carro's blunt advice is to throw out the slave who is sick. Peter Chrysologus sums the matter up: " Whatever a master does to a slave, undeservedly, in anger, willingly, unwillingly, in forgetfulness, after careful thought, knowingly, unknowingly, is judgment, justice and law."

It is quite clear that this centurion was an extraordinary man, for he loved his slave. It may well be that it was this totally unusual and unexpected gentleness and love which so moved Jesus when this centurion first came to Him. Love always covers a multitude of sins; the man who cares for men is always near to Jesus Christ.

THE PASSPORT OF FAITH

Matthew 8: 5-13 (*continued*)

NOT only was this centurion quite extraordinary in his attitude to his servant; he was also a man of a most extraordinary faith. He wished for Jesus' power to help and to heal his servant; but there was one problem. He was a Gentile and Jesus was a Jew, and, according to the Jewish law, a Jew could not enter the house of a Gentile for all Gentile dwelling-places were unclean. The *Mishnah* lays it down: " The dwelling-places of Gentiles are unclean." It is to that that Jesus refers when He puts the question: " Am I to come and heal him? " It was not that this law of uncleanness meant anything to Jesus; it was not that He would have refused to enter any man's dwelling; it was simply that Jesus was testing and trying the centurion's faith. It was then that the centurion's faith reached its peak. As a soldier he well knew what it was to give a command and to have that command instantly and unquestioningly carried out; so he said to Jesus, "You don't need to come to my house; I am not fit for you to enter my house; all you have to do is to speak the word of command, and that command will be obeyed." There spoke the voice of faith, and Jesus laid it down that faith is the only passport to the bliss and the blessedness of God.

Here Jesus uses a famous and a vivid Jewish picture. The Jews believed that when the Messiah came there would be a great banquet at which all Jews would sit down to feast. Behemoth, the greatest of the land beasts, and leviathan, the greatest of the denizens of the sea, would provide the fare for the banqueters. "Thou hast reserved them to be devoured by whom Thou wilt and when" (4 *Ezra* 6: 52). "And behemoth shall be revealed from his place, and leviathan shall ascend from the sea, those two great monsters which I created on the fifth day of creation, and shall have kept until that time; and then shall they be food for all that are left" (2 *Baruch* 29: 4). The Jews looked forward with all their hearts to this Messianic banquet; but it never for a moment crossed their minds that any Gentile would ever sit down at it. By that time the Gentiles would have been destroyed. "The nation and kingdom that will not serve thee shall perish; yea those nations shall be utterly wasted" (*Isaiah* 60: 12); and here is Jesus saying that many shall come from the east and from the west, and sit down at table at that banquet. Still worse, He says that many of the sons of the kingdom will be shut out. A son is an heir; therefore the son of the kingdom is the man who is to inherit the kingdom, for the son is always heir; but the Jews are to lose their inheritance. Always in Jewish thought "the inheritance of sinners is darkness" (*Psalms of Solomon* 15: 11). The rabbis had a saying, "The sinners in Gehenna will be covered with darkness." To the Jew the extraordinary and the shattering thing about all this was that the Gentile, whom he expected to be absolutely shut out, was to be a guest at the Messianic banquet, and the Jew, whom he expected to be welcomed with open arms, is to be shut out in the outer darkness. The tables were to be turned, and all expectations were to be reversed.

The Jew had to learn that the passport to God's presence is not membership of any nation; it is faith. The Jew believed that he belonged to the chosen people and that because he was a Jew he was therefore dear to God. He belonged to God's *herrenvolk*, and that was enough automatically to gain him salvation. Jesus taught that the only aristocracy in the Kingdom of God is the aristocracy of faith. Jesus Christ is not the possession of any race of men; Jesus Christ is the possession of every man in every race in whose heart there is faith.

THE POWER WHICH ANNIHILATES DISTANCE

Matthew 8: 5-13 (continued)

So Jesus spoke the word and the servant of the centurion was healed. Not so very long ago this would have been a miracle at which the minds of most people would have staggered. It is not so very difficult to think of Jesus healing when He and the sufferer were in actual contact; but to think of Jesus healing at a distance, healing with a word a man he had never seen and never touched, seemed a thing almost, if not completely, beyond belief. But the strange thing is that science itself has come to see that there are forces which are working in a way which is still mysterious, but which is undeniable.

Again and again men have been confronted by a power which does not travel by the ordinary contacts, and the ordinary routes and the ordinary channels. One of the classic instances of this comes from the life of Emanuel Swedenborg. In 1759 Swedenborg was in Gotenborg. He described a fire occurring in Stockholm 300 miles away. He gave an account of the fire to the city authorities.

He told them when it began, where it began, the name of the owner of the house, and when it was put out, and subsequent research proved him correct in every detail. Knowledge had come to him by a route which was not any of the routes known to men. W. B. Yeats, the famous Irish poet, had experiences like this. He had certain symbols for certain things, and he experimented, not so much scientifically, but in every day life, in the transmission of these symbols to other people by what might be called the sheer power of thought. He had an uncle in Sligo, who was by no means a mystical or devotional or spiritual man. He used to visit him each summer. " There are some high sandhills and low cliffs, and I adopted the practice of walking by the seashore while he walked on the cliffs of sandhills; I, without speaking, would imagine the symbol, and he would notice what passed before his mind's eye, and in a short time he would practically never fail of the appropriate vision." Yeats tells of an incident at a London dinner party, where all the guests were intimate friends: " I had written upon a piece of paper: ' In five minutes York Powell will talk of a burning house,' thrust the paper under my neighbour's plate, and imagined my fire symbol, and waited in silence. Powell shifted the conversation from topic to topic, and within the five minutes was describing a fire he had seen as a young man."

Men have always quoted things like that; but within our own generation Dr. J. B. Rhine began upon definite scientific experiments in what he called Extra-Sensory Perception, a phenomenon which has become so much discussed that it is commonly called by its initial letters, ESP. Dr. Rhine has carried out, in Duke University in America, thousands of experiments which go to show that men can become aware of things by other means than the ordinary senses. A pack of twenty-five cards marked with certain symbols is used. A person is asked to name the cards as they are dealt without seeing them. One of the students who participated in these experiments was called Hubert Pearce. On the first five thousand trials—a trial is a run through the whole pack of cards—he averaged ten correct out of twenty-five, when the laws of chance would say that four correct could be expected. On one occasion, in conditions of special concentration, he named the whole twenty-five cards correctly. The mathematical odds against this feat being pure chance are 298,023,223, 876,953,125 to 1. An experimenter called Brugman carried out another experiment. He selected two subjects. He put the sender of the messages in an upstairs room and the receiver below. Between the rooms there was an opening covered by two layers of glass with an air space between, so that the sending of any message based on sound was quite impossible. Through the glass panel the sender looked at the hands of the receiver. In front of the receiver was a table with forty-eight squares. The receiver was blindfolded. Between him and the squared table was a thick curtain. He held a pointer which passed through the curtain on to the table. The experiment was that the sender had to will the receiver to move the pointer to a certain square. According to the laws of chance the receiver should have been right in four out of one hundred and eighty results. In point of fact he was right in sixty. It is difficult to avoid the conclusion that the mind of the sender was influencing the mind of the receiver. It is a definitely proved fact that a certain Dr. Janet in eighteen out of twenty-five cases was able to hypnotise subjects at a distance, and he was partially successful in four other cases.

There is no doubt that mind can act on mind across the distances in a way which we are beginning to see, although yet we are far from understanding. If human minds can get to this length, how much more the mind of Jesus? The strange thing about this miracle is that modern thought, instead of making it harder, has made it easier to believe it.

THE GOSPEL OF MATTHEW

A MIRACLE IN A COTTAGE

Matthew 8: 14, 15

> And when Jesus had come into Peter's house, He
> saw Peter's mother-in-law lying in bed, ill with a
> fever. So He touched her hand and the fever left her.
> And she rose, and busied herself serving them.

WHEN we compare Mark's narrative of events with that
of Matthew, we see that this incident happened in Capernaum, on the Sabbath day, after Jesus had worshipped
in the synagogue. When Jesus was in Capernaum, His
headquarters were in the house of Peter, for Jesus never
had any home of His own. Peter was married, and legend
has it that in the after days Peter's wife was his helper
in the work of the gospel. Clement of Alexandria (*Stromateis*
7: 6) tells us that Peter and his wife were martyred
together. Peter, so the story runs, had the grim ordeal
of seeing his wife suffer before he suffered himself. " On
seeing his wife led to death, Peter rejoiced on account
of her call and her conveyance home, and called very
encouragingly and comfortingly, addressing her by name,
' Remember thou the Lord.' "

On this occasion Peter's wife's mother was ill with a
fever. There were three kinds of fever which were common
in Palestine. There was a fever which was called Malta
fever, and which was marked by weakness, anaemia and
wasting away, and which lasted for months, and often
ended in a decline which finished in death. There was what
was called intermittent fever, which may well have been
very like typhoid fever. And above all there was malaria.
In the regions where the Jordan River entered and
left the Sea of Galilee there was marshy ground; there
the malarial mosquitos bred and flourished, and both
Capernaum and Tiberias were areas where malaria was
very prevalent. It was often accompanied by jaundice
and ague, and was a most wretched and miserable experience for the sufferer from it. It was most likely malaria
from which Peter's wife's mother was suffering.

This miracle tells us much about Jesus, and not a little about the woman whom He cured.

(i) Jesus had come from the synagogue; there He had dealt with and had cured the demon-possessed man (*Mark* 1: 21-28). As *Matthew* has it, He had healed the centurion's servant on the way home. Miracles did not cost Jesus nothing; virtue went out of Him with every healing; and beyond a doubt He would be tired. It would be for rest that He came into Peter's house, and yet no sooner was He in it than there came still another demand on Him for help and healing. Here was no publicity; here there was no crowd to look and to admire and to be astonished. Here there was only a simple cottage and a poor woman tossing with a common fever. And yet in those circumstances Jesus put forth all His power. Jesus was never too tired to help; the demands of human need never came to Him as an intolerable nuisance. Jesus was not one of these people who are at their best in public and at their worst in private. No situation was too humble for Him to help. He did not need an admiring audience to be at His best. In a crowd or in a cottage His love and His power were at the disposal of anyone who needed Him.

(ii) But this miracle also tells us something about the woman whom Jesus healed. No sooner had He healed her than she busied herself in attending to His needs and to the needs of the other guests. She clearly regarded herself as " saved to serve." He had healed her; and her one desire was to use her new-found health to be of use and of service to Him and to others. How do we use the gifts of Christ? Once Oscar Wilde wrote what he himself called " the best short story in the world." W. B. Yeats quotes it in his autobiography in all of what he calls " its terrible beauty." Yeats quotes it in its original simplicity before it had been decorated and spoiled by the literary devices of its final form:

" Christ came from a white plain to a purple city, and, as He passed through the first street, He heard voices overhead, and saw a young man lying drunk upon a window-sill. ' Why do you waste your soul in drunkenness?' He said. He said, ' Lord, I was a leper, and you healed me, what else can I do?' A little farther through the town He saw a young man following a harlot, and said, ' Why do you dissolve your soul in debauchery?' And the young man answered, ' Lord, I was blind and you healed me, what else can I do?' At last, in the middle of the city, He saw an old man crouching, weeping on the ground, and, when He asked why he wept, the old man answered, ' Lord, I was dead, and you raised me into life, what else can I do but weep?' "

That is a terrible parable of how men use the gifts of Christ and the mercy of God. Peter's wife's mother used the gift of her health restored to serve Jesus and to serve others. That is the way in which we should use every gift of God.

MIRACLES IN A CROWD

Matthew 8: 16, 17

And, when it was late in the day, they brought to Him many who were in the power of evil spirits, and He cast out the spirits with a word, and healed all those who were ill. This happened that the saying spoken through the prophet Isaiah might be fulfilled: " He took our weaknesses and carried our sins."

As we have already seen, Mark's account of this series of incidents makes it clear that they happened on the Sabbath day (*Mark* 1: 21-34). That explains why this scene happened late in the day, at the evening time. According to the Sabbath Law, which forbade all work on the Sabbath day, it was illegal to heal on the Sabbath. Steps could be taken to prevent a person from getting any worse, but no steps might be taken to make him any better. The general law was that on the Sabbath medical attention might only be given to those whose lives were actually in danger. Further, it was illegal to carry a burden on the Sabbath day, and a burden was anything which weighed more than two dried figs. It was, therefore, illegal to carry a sick person from place to place on a stretcher or in one's arms or on one's shoulders, for to do so would have been to carry a burden. Officially the Sabbath ended when two stars could be seen in the sky, for there were no clocks to tell the time in those days. That is why the crowd in Capernaum waited until the evening time to come to Jesus for the healing which they knew that He could give.

But we must think of what Jesus had been doing on that Sabbath day. He had been in the synagogue and had healed the demon-possessed man. He had sent healing to the centurion's servant. He had healed Peter's wife's mother. No doubt He had preached and taught all day; and no doubt He had encountered those who were bitter in their opposition to Him. Now it was evening. God gave to men the day for work, and the evening for rest. The evening is the time of quiet when work is laid aside. But it was not so for Jesus. At the time when He might have expected rest, He was surrounded by the insistent demands of human need—and selflessly and uncomplainingly and with a divine generosity He met them all. So long as there was a soul in need there was no rest for Jesus Christ.

That scene called to Matthew's mind the saying of Isaiah (*Isaiah* 53: 4) where it is said of the servant of the Lord that he bore our weaknesses and carried our sins.

The follower of Christ cannot seek for rest while there are others to be helped and healed; and the strange thing is that he will find his own weariness refreshed and his own weakness strengthened in the service of others. Somehow he will find that as the demands come, strength also comes; and somehow he will find that he is able to go on for the sake of others when he feels that he cannot take another step for himself.

THE SUMMONS TO COUNT THE COST

Matthew 8: 18-22

> When Jesus saw the great crowds surrounding Him,
> He gave orders to go away, across to the other side.
> A scribe came to Him. " Teacher," he said, " I will
> follow you wherever you may be going." Jesus said
> to him: " The foxes have lairs, and the birds of the
> sky have places where they may lodge, but the Son
> of Man has nowhere where He may lay His head."
> Another of His disciples said: " Lord, let me first
> go away and bury my father." Jesus said to him:
> " Follow me, and let the dead bury their dead."

AT first sight this section seems out of place in this chapter.
The chapter is a chapter of miracles, and at first sight these
verses do not seem to fit into a chapter which tells of a
series of miraculous events. Why then does Matthew put
it here?

It has been suggested that Matthew inserted this passage
here because his thoughts were running on Jesus as the
Suffering Servant. He has just quoted *Isaiah* 53: 4:
" He took our weaknesses and carried our sins " (*Matthew*
8: 17), and very naturally, it is said, that picture led on in
Matthew's thoughts to the picture of the one who had
nowhere to lay his head. As Plummer has it, " Jesus'
life began in a borrowed stable and ended in a borrowed
tomb." So it is suggested that Matthew inserted this
passage here because both it and the immediately preceding
verses show Jesus as the Suffering Servant of God.

It may be so, but it is even more likely that Matthew
inserted this passage in this chapter of miracles because
he saw a miracle in it. It was a scribe who wished to follow
Jesus. He gave Jesus the highest title of honour that
he knew. " Teacher " he called Him; the Greek is *didas-
kalos*, which is the normal translation of the Hebrew word
Rabbi. To him Jesus was the greatest teacher to whom
he had ever listened and whom he had ever seen. It was
indeed a miracle that any scribe should give to Jesus that
title, and should wish to follow Him. Jesus stood for the

destruction and the end of all that narrow legalism on which scribal religion was built; and it was indeed a miracle that a scribe should come to see anything lovely or anything desirable in Jesus. This is the miracle of the impact of the personality of Jesus Christ on men. The impact of one personality on another can indeed produce the most wonderful effects. Very often a man has been launched on a career of scholarship by the impact of the personality of a great teacher upon him; many a man has been moved to the Christian way and to a life of Christian service by the impact of a great Christian personality on his life. Preaching itself has been described and defined as " truth through personality." W. H. Elliott in his autobiography *Undiscovered Ends* tells a thing about Edith Evans, the great actress: " When her husband died, she came to us, full of grief. . . . In our drawing room at Chester Square she poured out her feelings about it for an hour or so, and they were feelings that came from springs that were very deep. Her personality filled the room. The room was not big enough! . . . For days that room of ours was ' electric,' as I expressed it then. The strong vibrations had not gone." This story is the story of the impact of the personality of Jesus on the life of a Jewish scribe. It remains true that to this day what is needed most of all is not so much to talk to men about Jesus as to confront them with Jesus, and to allow the personality of Jesus to do the rest.

But there is more than that. No sooner had this scribe undergone this reaction than Jesus told him that the foxes have their lairs and the birds of the sky have a place in the trees to rest, but the Son of Man has no place on earth to lay His head. It is as if Jesus said to this man: " Before you follow me—*think what you are doing*. Before you follow me—*count the cost*." Jesus did not want followers who were swept away by a moment of emotion, which quickly blazed and just as quickly died. He did not want men who were carried away by a tide of mere feeling, which quickly flowed and just as quickly ebbed. He wanted men who knew what they were doing. He talked about taking up a cross (*Matthew* 10: 38); He talked about setting Himself above the dearest relationships in life (*Luke* 14: 26); He talked about giving away everything to the poor (*Matthew* 19: 21). He was always saying to men: " Yes, I know that your heart is running out to me, but— *do you love me enough for that?* "

In any sphere of life men must be confronted with the facts. If a young man expresses a desire for scholarship, we must say to him: " Good, but are you prepared to scorn delights and live laborious days? " When an explorer is building up his team, he will be inundated with people offering their services, but he must weed out the romantics and the realists by saying, " Good, but are you prepared for the snow and the ice, or the swamps and the heat, for the exhaustion and the weariness of it all? " When a young person wishes to become an athlete, the trainer must say, " Good, but are you prepared for the self-denial, the self-discipline that alone will win you the eminence of which you dream? " This is not to discourage enthusiasm, but it is to say that enthusiasm which has not faced the facts will soon be dead ashes instead of a flame. No man could ever say that he followed Jesus on false pretences. Jesus was uncompromisingly honest. We do Jesus a grave dis-service, if ever we lead people to believe that the Christian way is an easy way. There is no thrill like the way of Christ, and there is no glory like the end of that way; but Jesus Christ never said it was an easy way. The way to glory always involved a cross.

THE TRAGEDY OF THE UNSEIZED MOMENT

Matthew 8: 18-22 (*continued*)

BUT there was another man who wished to follow Jesus. He said he would follow Jesus, if he was first allowed

THE GOSPEL OF MATTHEW

to go and bury his father. Jesus' answer was: " Follow me; and let the dead bury their dead." At first sight that seems a hard saying. To the Jew it was a sacred duty to ensure decent burial for a dead parent. When Jacob died, Joseph asked permission from Pharaoh to go and bury his father: " My father made me swear, saying, Lo, I die; in my grave which I have digged for me in the land of Canaan, there shalt thou bury me. Now therefore let me go up, I pray thee, and bury my father, and I will come again " (*Genesis* 50: 5). Because of the apparently stern and unsympathetic character of this saying different explanations have been given of it.

It has been suggested that in the translation of the Aramaic which Jesus used into the Greek of the gospels there has been a mistake; and that Jesus is saying that the man can well leave the burying of his father to the official buriers. There is a strange verse in *Ezekiel* 39: 15: " And the passengers that pass through the land, when any seeth a man's bone, then shall he set up a sign by it, till the buriers have buried it in the valley of Hamon-gog." That seems to imply a kind of official called a *burier*; and it has been suggested that Jesus is saying that the man can leave the burial to these officials. That does not seem a very likely explanation.

It has been suggested that this is indeed a hard saying, and that Jesus is saying bluntly that the society in which this man is living is dead in sin, and he must get out of it as quickly as possible, even if it means leaving his father still unburied, that nothing, not even the most sacred duty, must delay his embarkation on the Christian way.

But the true explanation undoubtedly lies in the way in which the Jews used this phrase—" I must bury my father "—and in the way in which it is still used in the east. Wendt quotes an incident related by a Syrian missionary, M. Waldmeier. This missionary was friendly with an intelligent and rich young Turk. He advised him to make a tour of Europe at the close of his education, so that his education would be completed and his mind broadened. The Turk answered, " I must first of all bury my father." The missionary expressed his sympathy and sorrow that the young man's father had died. But the young Turk explained that his father was still very much alive, and that what he meant was that he must fulfil all his duties to his parents and to his relatives, before he could leave them to go on the suggested tour, that, in fact, he could not leave home until after his father's death, which might not happen for many years. That is undoubtedly what the man in this gospel incident meant. He meant, " I will follow you some day, when my father is dead, and when I am free to go." He was in fact putting off his following of Jesus for many years to come.

Jesus was wise: Jesus knew the human heart; and Jesus knew well that, if that man did not follow Him on the moment, he never would. Again and again there come to us moments of impulse when we are moved to the higher things; and again and again we let them pass without acting upon them. The tragedy of life is so often the tragedy of the unseized moment. We are moved to some fine action, we are moved to the abandoning of some weakness or habit, we are moved to say something to someone, some word of sympathy, of warning, or encouragement; but the moment passes, and the thing is never done, the evil thing is never conquered, and the word is never spoken. In the best of us there is a certain lethargy and inertia; there is a certain habit of procrastination and of putting things off; there is a certain fear and indecision; and the moment is never turned into action and into fact.

Jesus was saying to this man: " You are feeling at the moment that you must get out of that dead society in which you move; you say you will get out when the years have passed and your father has died; get out now—or you will never get out at all."

In his autobiography H. G. Wells told of a crucial moment in his life. He was apprenticed to a draper, and there seemed to be little or no future in life. There came to him one day what he called " an inward and prophetic voice: ' Get out of this trade before it is too late; at any cost get out of it.' " He did not wait; he got out; and that is why he became H. G. Wells. May God give to us that strength of decision which will save us from the tragedy of the unseized moment.

THE PEACE OF THE PRESENCE

Matthew 8: 23-27

> When He embarked on the boat, His disciples followed Him. And, look you, a great upheaval arose on the sea, so that the boat was hidden by the waves; and He was sleeping. They came and wakened Him. " Lord," they said, " save us; we are perishing." He said to them, " Why are you such cowards, you whose faith is little? " Then, when He had been roused from sleep, He rebuked the winds and the sea, and there was a great calm. The men were amazed. " What kind of man is this," they said, " for the winds and the sea obey Him? "

IN one sense this was a very ordinary scene on the Sea of Galilee. The Sea of Galilee is small; it is only thirteen miles from north to south and eight miles from east to west at its widest. The Jordan valley makes a deep cleft in the surface of the earth, and the Sea of Galilee is part of that cleft. It is 680 feet below sea level. That gives it a climate which is warm and gracious, but it also gives it its dangers. On the west side there are mountains with valleys and gulleys; and, when a cold wind comes from the west, these valleys and gulleys act like gigantic funnels. The wind, as it were, becomes compressed in them, and rushes down upon the lake with savage violence and with startling suddenness, so that the calm of one moment can become the raging storm of the next. The storms on the Sea of Galilee combine suddenness and violence in a unique way.

W. M. Thomson in the *Land and the Book* describes his experience on the shores of the Sea of Galilee:

> " On the occasion referred to, we subsequently pitched our tents at the shore, and remained for three days and nights exposed to this tremendous wind. We had to double-pin all the tent-ropes, and frequently were obliged to hang with our whole weight upon them to keep the quivering tabernacle from being carried up bodily into the air. . . . The whole lake, as we had it, was lashed into fury; the waves repeatedly rolled up to our tent door, tumbling over the ropes with such violence as to carry away the tent-pins. And, moreover, these winds are not only violent, but they come down suddenly, and often when the sky is perfectly clear. I once went to swim near the hot baths, and, before I was aware, a wind came rushing over the cliffs with such force that it was with great difficulty that I could regain the shore."

Dr. W. M. Christie, who spent many years in Galileee describes his experience. He says that during these storms the winds seem to blow from all the directions at the same time, for they rush down the narrow gorges in the hills and strike the water at an angle. He tells of an occasion when

> " A company of visitors were standing on the shore at Tiberias, and, noting the glassy surface of the water and the smallness of the lake, they expressed doubts as to the possibility of such storms as those described in the gospels. Almost immediately the wind sprang up. In twenty minutes the sea was white with foam-crested waves. Great billows broke over the towers at the corner of the city walls, and the visitors were compelled to seek shelter from the blinding spray, though now two hundred yards from the lakeside."

In less than half an hour the placid sunshine had become a raging storm.

That is what happened to Jesus and His disciples. The words in the Greek are very vivid. The storm is called a *seismos*, which is the word for an *earthquake*. The waves were so high that the boat was hidden (*kalup-*

testhat) in the trough as the crest of the waves towered over them. Jesus was asleep. If we read the narrative in Mark 4: 1, 35, we see that before they had set out He had been using the boat as a pulpit to address the people and no doubt He was exhausted. And then in their moment of terror the disciples awoke Him, and the storm became a calm.

CALM AMIDST THE STORM

Matthew 8: 23-27 (*continued*)

IN this story there is something very much more than the calming of a storm at sea. Suppose that Jesus did in actual physical fact still a raging storm on the Sea of Galilee somewhere round about A.D. 28, that would in truth be a very wonderful thing; but it would have very little to do with us. It would be the story of an isolated wonder, which had no relevance for us in the twentieth century. If that is all the story means, we may well ask: " Why does he not do it now? Why does He allow those who love Him nowadays to be drowned in the raging of the sea without intervening to save them? " If we take the story simply as the story of the stilling of a weather storm, then it actually produces problems which for some of us break the heart.

But the meaning of this story is far greater than that— the meaning of this story is not that Jesus stopped a storm in Galilee; the meaning is that *wherever Jesus is the storms of life become a calm*. It means that in the presence of Jesus the most terrible of tempests turns to peace. It means that in His presence there is peace, whatever storms may blow.

When the cold, bleak wind of sorrow blows, there is calm and comfort in the presence of Jesus Christ. When the hot blast of passion blows, there is peace and security in the presence of Jesus Christ. When the storms of doubt seek to uproot the very foundations of the faith, there is a steady safety in the presence of Jesus Christ. In every storm that shakes the human heart there is peace with Jesus Christ.

Margaret Avery tells a wonderful story. In a little village school in the hill country a teacher had been telling the children of the stilling of the storm at sea. Shortly afterwards there came a terrible blizzard and snowstorm to the hills. When the school closed for the day, the teacher had almost to drag the little children bodily through the tempest. They were in very real danger. In the midst of it all she heard a little boy say as if to himself: " We could be doing with that chap Jesus here now." The child had got it right; that teacher must have been a wonderful teacher. The lesson of this story, the meaning of this story, the fact of this story, is that when the storms of life shake our souls Jesus Christ is there, and in His presence the raging of the storm turns to the peace that no storm can ever take away.

THE DEMON-HAUNTED UNIVERSE

Matthew 8: 28-34

And, when He had come to the other side, to the territory of the Gadarenes, two demon-possessed men met Him, as they emerged from the tombs. They were very fierce, so that no one was able to pass by that road. And, look you, they shouted: " What have we to do with you, you Son of God? Have you come to torture us before the proper time? " A good distance away from them a herd of many pigs was grazing. The devils urged Jesus: " If you cast us out, send us into the herd of pigs." He said to them: " Begone." They came out and went into the herd of pigs. And, look you, the whole herd rushed down the cliff into the sea, and died in the waters. Those who were herding them fled, and went away into the town and related the whole story, and told of the things which had happened to the demon-possessed men. And, look you, the whole town came out to meet Jesus: and when they saw Him, they urged Him to depart from their districts.

BEFORE we begin to study this passage in detail, we may stop to try to clear up one difficulty which meets the student of the gospels. There was clearly some uncertainty in the mind of the gospel writers as to where this incident actually happened. That uncertainty is reflected in the differences between the three gospels. In the Authorized Version Matthew says that this happened in the country of the *Gergesenes* (*Matthew* 8: 28); Mark and Luke say that it happened in the country of the *Gadarenes* (*Mark* 5: 1; *Luke* 8: 26). There is even very considerable differences between the different manuscripts of each gospel. In the American Revized Standard Version, which follows the best manuscripts, and which makes use of the most up-to-date scholarship, in *Matthew* the incident is said to happen in the country of the *Gadarenes*; and in *Mark* and *Luke* in the country of the *Gerasenes*. The difficulty is that no one has ever really succeeded in identifying this place beyond doubt. *Gerasa* can hardly be right, for the only Gerasa of which we have any information was thirty-six miles inland, south-east of the lake, in Gilead; and it is certain that Jesus did not voyage thirty-six miles inland. *Gadara* is almost certainly right, because Gadara was a town six miles inland from the shores of the lake, and it would be very natural for the town burying-place and the town grazing-place to be some distance outside the town. *Gergesa* is very likely due to the conjecture of Origen, the great third century Alexandrian scholar. He knew that Gerasa was impossible; he doubted that Gadara was possible; and he actually knew of a village called Gergesa which was on the eastern shores of the lake, and so he conjectured that Gergesa must be the place. The differences are simply due to the fact that those who copied the manuscripts did not know Palestine well enough to be sure where this incident actually happened.

This miracle confronts us with the idea of demon-possession which is so common in the gospels. The ancient world believed unquestioningly and intensely in demons and evil spirits. The air was so full of these spirits that it was not even possible to insert into it the point of a needle without coming against one. Some said that there were seven and a half million of them; there were ten thousand of them on a man's right hand and ten thousand on his left; and all were waiting to work men harm. They lived in unclean places such as tombs, and places where no cleansing water was to be found. They lived in the deserts where their howling could be heard. We still speak of a *howling* desert. They were specially dangerous to the lonely traveller, to the woman in childbirth, to the newly married bride and bridegroom, to children who were out after dark, and to voyagers by night. They were specially dangerous in the midday heat, and between sunset and sunrise. The male demons were called *shedim*, and the female *lilin* after Lilith. The female demons had long hair, and were specially dangerous to children; that was why children had their guardian angels (cp. *Matthew* 18: 10).

As to the origin of the demons different views were held. Some held that they had been there since the beginning of the world. Some held that they were the spirits of wicked, malignant people, who had died, and who even after their death still carried on their evil work. Most commonly of all they were connected with the strange old story in *Genesis* 6: 1-8. That story tells how the sinning angels came to earth and seduced mortal women. The demons were held to be the descendants of the children produced by that evil union.

To these demons all illness was ascribed. They were held to be responsible, not only for diseases like epilepsy and mental illness, but also for physical illness. The Egyptians held that the body had thirty-six different parts, and that every one could be occupied by a demon.

One of their favourite ways of gaining an entry into a man's body was to lurk beside him while he ate, and so to settle on his food.

It may seem fantastic to us; but the ancient peoples believed implicitly in demons. If a man gained the idea that he was possessed by a demon, he would easily go on to produce all the symptoms of demon-possession. He could genuinely convince himself that there was a demon inside him. To this day anyone can think himself into having a pain or into the idea that he is ill; that could happen even more easily in days when there was much of what we would call superstition, and when men's knowledge was much more primitive than it is now. Even if there are no such things as demons, a man could only be cured by the assumption that for him at least the demons were the realest of all things.

THE DEFEAT OF THE DEMONS

Matthew 8: 28-34 (continued)

WHEN Jesus came to the other side of the lake, He was confronted by two demon-possessed men, who dwelt in the tombs, for the tombs were the natural place for the demons to inhabit. These men were so fierce that they were a danger to passers-by, and the prudent traveller would give them a very wide berth indeed. W. M. Thomson in the *Land and the Book* tells us that he himself, in the nineteenth century, saw men who were exactly like these two demon-possessed men in the tombs at Gadara:

> " There are some very similar cases at the present day—furious and dangerous maniacs, who wander about the mountains and sleep in caves and tombs. In their worst paroxysms they are quite unmanageable, and prodigiously strong. . . . And it is one of the most common traits of this madness that the victims refuse to wear clothes. I have often seen them absolutely naked in the crowded streets of Beirut and Sidon. There are also cases in which they run wildly about the country and frighten the whole neighbourhood."

Apart from anything else, Jesus showed a most unusual courage in stopping to speak to these two men at all.

If we really want the details of this story we have to go to *Mark*. Mark's narrative (*Mark* 5: 1-19) is much longer, and what Matthew gives us is only a summary. This is a miracle story which has caused much discussion, and the discussion has centred round the destruction of the herd of pigs. Many have found it strange and have considered it heartless that Jesus should destroy a herd of animals like this. But it is almost certain that Jesus did not in fact deliberately destroy the pigs. We must try to visualize what happened. The men were shouting and shrieking (*Mark* 5: 7; *Luke* 8: 28). We must remember that the men were completely convinced that they were occupied by demons. Now it was normal and orthodox belief, shared by everyone, that when the Messiah and the time of judgment came, the demons would be destroyed and annihilated. That is what the men meant when they asked Jesus why He had come to torture them before the proper time. These men were so convinced that they were possessed by demons that nothing in this world could have rid them of that conviction other than ocular and visible demonstration that the demons had gone out of them. Something had to be done which to them would be unanswerable proof. Almost certainly what happened was that their shouting and shrieking alarmed the herd of pigs; and in their terror the pigs took to flight and plunged into the lake. Water was fatal to demons. Thereupon Jesus seized the chance which had come to Him. " Look," He said. " Look at these swine; they are gone into the depths of the lake and your demons are gone with them for ever." Jesus knew that in no other way could He ever convince these two men that they were in fact cured. If that be so, Jesus did not deliberately destroy the herd of swine; He used their stampede to help these two poor sufferers to believe in their cure.

Even if Jesus did deliberately work the destruction of this herd of pigs, it could surely never be held against Him. There is such a thing as being over-fastidious. T. R. Glover spoke of people who think they are being religious when in fact they are being fastidious. Surely we could never compare the value of a herd of swine with the value of a man's immortal soul. It is unlikely that we refuse to eat bacon for breakfast or pork for dinner. Our sympathy with the pigs does not extend far enough to prevent us eating them; are we then to complain if Jesus did restore sanity to two men's minds at the cost of a herd of pigs? No one need say that this is to encourage or even to condone cruelty to animals. It is simply to say that we must preserve a sense of proportion in life.

The supreme tragedy of this story lies in its conclusion. Those who were herding the pigs ran back to the town and told what had happened; and the result was that the people of the town besought Jesus to leave their territory at once. Here is human selfishness at its worst. It did not matter to these people that two men had been given back their reason; all that mattered to them was that their pigs had perished. It is so often the case that people in effect say, " I don't care what happens to anyone else, if my profits and my comfort and my ease are preserved." We may be amazed at the callousness of these people of Gadara, but we must have a care that we too do not resent any help of others which reduces our own privileges.

THE GROWTH OF OPPOSITION

WE have repeatedly seen that in Matthew's gospel there is nothing haphazard. The gospel is carefully planned and carefully designed. In chapter 9 we see another example of this careful planning, for in it we see the first shadows of the gathering storm. We see the opposition beginning to grow ; we hear the first hint of the charges which are going to be levelled against Jesus, and which are finally going to bring about His death. In this chapter four charges are made against Jesus.

(i) He is accused of *blasphemy*. In *Matthew* 9: 1-8 we see Jesus curing the paralytic by forgiving his sins; and we hear the scribes accusing Him of blasphemy because He claimed to do what only God can do. Jesus was accused of blasphemy because He spoke with the voice of God. *Blasphēmia* literally means *insult* or *slander*; and Jesus' enemies accused Him of insulting God because He arrogated to Himself the very powers of God.

(ii) He is accused of *immorality*. In *Matthew* 9: 10-13 we see Jesus at the feast at which He sat with tax-gatherers and sinners. The Pharisees demanded to know the reason why He ate with such people. The implication was that He was like the company He kept. Jesus was in effect accused of being an immoral character because He kept company with immoral characters. Once a man is disliked, it is the easiest thing in the world to twist and to misinterpret and to misrepresent everything he does, and to attribute to him motives which he never had. Mr. Harold Nicolson tells of a talk he had with Mr. Stanley Baldwin, as he then was. Nicolson was at the time starting out on a political career and he went to ask Mr. Baldwin, a political veteran, for any advice he might care to give. Mr. Baldwin said something like this: " You are going to begin to try to be a statesman, and to handle the affairs of the country. Well, I have had a long experience of such a life, and I will give you three rules which you would do well to follow. First, if you are a subscriber to a press-cutting agency, cancel your subscription at once. Second, never laugh at your opponents' mistakes. Third, *steel yourself to the attribution of false motives*." One of the favourite weapons of any public man's enemies is the attribution of false motives to him; that is what His enemies did to Jesus.

(iii) He is accused of slackness in *piety*. In *Matthew* 9: 14-17 we see the disciples of John demanding of Jesus' disciples why their Master does not fast. He was not going through the orthodox motions of religion, and therefore the orthodox were suspicious of Him. Any man who breaks the conventions will suffer for it; and any man who breaks the religious conventions will suffer especially for it. Jesus broke the orthodox conventions of ecclesiastical piety, and He was criticized for it.

(iv) He is accused of being *in league with the devil*. In *Matthew* 9: 31-34 we see Him curing a dumb man, and His enemies ascribe the cure to the fact that He is in league with the devil. Whenever a new power comes into life—it has been said, for instance, of spiritual healing—there are those who will say, " We must be cautious; this may well be the work of the devil and not of God." It is the strange fact that when people meet something which they do not like, and which they do not understand, and which cuts across their preconceived notions, they very often ascribe it to the devil and not to God.

Here then we see the beginning of the campaign against Jesus. The slanderers are at work; the whispering tongues are poisoning truth; the wrong motives are being ascribed. The drive to eliminate this disturbing Jesus has begun.

GET RIGHT WITH GOD

Matthew 9: 1-8

Jesus embarked on the boat, and crossed to the other side, and came to His own town. And, look you, they brought to Him a paralysed man lying on a bed. When Jesus saw their faith, He said to the paralysed man, " Courage, child, your sins are forgiven." And, look you, some of the scribes said to themselves, " This fellow is blaspheming." Jesus knew their thoughts. " Why," He said, " do you think evil thoughts in your hearts? Which is easier—to say, ' Your sins are forgiven,' or, to say, ' Rise and walk'? But to let you understand that the Son of Man has authority on earth to forgive sins— " then He said to the paralysed man, " Rise: lift your bed; and go to your house." And he rose and went away to his house. When the crowds saw this, they were moved to awe, and glorified God because He had given such power to men.

FROM *Mark* 2: 1 we learn that this incident took place in Capernaum; and it is interesting to note that by this time Jesus had become so identified with Capernaum that it could be called His own town. At this stage in His ministry Capernaum was the centre of His work.

A paralysed man was brought to Him, carried on a bed by his friends. Here is a wonderful picture of a man who was saved by the faith of his friends. Had it not been for his friends this man would never have reached the healing presence of Jesus at all. It may well be that he had become dully resigned and defeatedly hopeless, and that his friends had carried him almost against his will to Jesus. However that may be, this man was certainly saved by the faith of his friends. W. B. Yeats in his play *The Cat and the Moon* has a sentence: " Did you ever know a holy man but a wicked man for his comrade, and his heart's darling? " It is the very characteristic of a really holy man that he clings to a really bad or an entirely thoughtless man, until he has brought that man into the presence of Jesus Christ. If any man has a friend who does not know Christ, or who does not care for Christ, or who is even hostile to Christ, it is his Christian duty not to let that man go until he has brought him into the presence of Jesus Christ. We cannot force a man against his will to accept Jesus Christ. Coventry Patmore once said that we cannot teach another religious truth; we can only point out to him a way whereby he may find it for himself. We cannot make a man a Christian, but we can do everything possible to bring that man into the presence of Jesus Christ.

It might seem that Jesus' approach to this man was astonishing. He began by telling him that his sins were forgiven. There was a double reason for that. In Palestine it was a universal belief that *all* sickness was the result of sin, and that no sickness could ever be cured until sin was forgiven. Rabbi Ami said, " There is no death without sin, and no pains without some transgression." Rabbi Alexander said, " The sick arises not from his sickness, until his sins are forgiven." Rabbi Chija ben Abba said, " No sick person is cured from sickness, until all his sins are forgiven him." This unbreakable connection between suffering and sin was part of the orthodox Jewish belief of the time of Jesus. For that reason there is no doubt at all that this man could never have been cured at all, until he was convinced that his sins had been forgiven. It is most probable that this man had indeed been a sinner, and that he was convinced that his illness was the result of his sin, as it may very well have been; and without the assurance of forgiveness healing could never have come to him.

In point of fact modern medicine would agree whole-heartedly that the mind can and does influence the physical condition of the body, and that a person can never have a healthy body when his mind is not in a healthy state. Paul Tournier in *A Doctor's Case Book* quotes an actual example of that: " There was, for example, the girl whom one of my friends had been treating for several months for anaemia, without much success. As a last resort my colleague decided to send her to the medical officer of the district in which she worked in order to get his permission to send her into a mountain sanatorium. A week later the patient brought word back from the medical officer. He proved to be a good fellow and he had granted the permit, but he added, ' On analysing the blood, however, I do not arrive at anything like the figures you quote.' My friend, somewhat put out, at once took a fresh sample of the blood, and rushed to his laboratory. Sure ʼnough the

334

blood count had suddenly changed. ' If I had not been the kind of person who keeps carefully to laboratory routine,' my friend's story goes on, ' and if I had not previously checked my figures at each of my patient's visits, I might have thought that I had made a mistake.' He returned to the patient and asked her, ' Has anything out of the ordinary happened in your life since your last visit?' ' Yes, something has happened,' she replied. ' I have suddenly been able to forgive someone against whom I bore a nasty grudge; and all at once I felt I could at last say, yes, to life! ' " Her mental attitude was changed, and the very state of her blood was changed along with it. Her mind was cured, and her body was well on the way to being cured.

This man in the gospel story knew that he was a sinner; because he was a sinner, he was certain that God was his enemy; because God was his enemy, he was paralysed and ill. Once Jesus had brought to him the forgiveness of God, he knew that he was right with God; he knew that God was not his enemy, but his friend, and therefore he was cured.

But it was the very manner of the cure which scandalized the scribes. Jesus had dared to forgive sin; to forgive sin is the prerogative of God; therefore Jesus had insulted God. Jesus did not stop to argue. He joined issue with them on their own ground. " Whether," he demanded, " is it easier to say, ' Your sins are forgiven,' or to say, ' Get up and walk'? " Now remember that these scribes believed that no one could get up and walk unless his sins were forgiven. If Jesus was able to make this man get up and walk, then that was unanswerable proof that the man's sins were forgiven, and that Jesus' claim was true. So Jesus demonstrated that He was able to bring forgiveness to a man's soul and health to a man's body. And it remains eternally true that we can never be right physically until we are right spiritually, that health in body and peace with God go hand in hand.

THE MAN WHOM ALL MEN HATED

Matthew 9: 9

> As Jesus passed on from there, He saw a man called
> Matthew seated at the tax-collector's table. " Follow
> me," He said to him; and he arose and followed Him.

THERE was never a more unlikely candidate for the office
of apostle than Matthew. Matthew was what the Authorized
Version calls a *publican*; the *publicani* were tax-gatherers,
and were so called because they dealt with public money
and with public funds.

The problem of the Roman government was to devise
a system whereby the taxes could be collected as efficiently
and as cheaply as possible. They had done so by auctioning
the right to collect taxes in a certain area. A man bought
the right to collect the taxes within a certain district;
he was responsible to the Roman government for an
agreed sum; anything he could raise over and above
that he was allowed to keep as commission. Obviously
this system lent itself to grave abuses. People did not
really know how much they ought to pay in the days before
newspapers and wireless announcements and the widespread diffusion of news; nor had they any right of appeal
against the tax-collector. The consequence was that many
a tax-collector became a wealthy man through his illegal
extortion. This system had led to so many abuses that
in Palestine it had been brought to an end before the time
of Jesus, but taxes still had to be paid, and there were
still abuses.

There were three great stated taxes. There was a ground
tax by which a man had to pay one-tenth of his grain and
one-fifth of his fruit and vine to the government either
in cash or in kind. There was income tax, which was
one per cent of a man's income. There was a poll-tax
which had to be paid by every male from the age of fourteen
to the age of sixty-five, and by every female from the age
of twelve to sixty-five. These were statutory taxes and

could not well be used by tax-collectors for private profit. But in addition to these taxes there were all sorts of other taxes. There was a duty of anything from 2½ per cent to 12½ per cent on all goods imported and exported. A tax had to be paid to travel on main roads, to cross bridges, to enter market-places and towns or harbours. There was a tax on pack animals, and a tax on the wheels and axles of carts. There were purchase taxes on goods bought and sold. There were certain commodities which were government monopolies. For instance, in Egypt the trade in nitrate, beer, and papyrus was entirely in government control. Although the old method of auctioning the taxes had been stopped, all kinds of people were needed to collect these taxes. The people who collected them were drawn from the provincials themselves. Often they were volunteers. Usually in any district one person was responsible for one tax, and it was not difficult for such a person to line his own pockets in addition to collecting the taxes which were legally due.

These tax-gatherers were universally hated. They had entered the service of their country's conquerors, and they amassed their fortunes at the expense of their country's misfortunes. To use a modern term, they were quislings. They were notoriously dishonest. Not only did they fleece their own countrymen, but they also did their best to swindle the government, and they made a flourishing income by taking bribes from rich people who wished to avoid taxes which they should have paid. Every country hates its tax-gatherers, but the hatred of the Jews for them was doubly violent. The Jews were fanatical nationalists. But what roused the Jews more than anything else was their religious conviction that God alone was king, and that to pay any taxes to any mortal ruler was an infringement of God's rights and an insult to His majesty. By Jewish law a tax-gatherer was debarred from the synagogue; he was included with things and beasts unclean, and *Leviticus* 20: 5 was applied to them; he was forbidden to be a witness in any case; " robbers, murderers and tax-gatherers " were classed together. When Jesus called Matthew He called a man whom all men hated. Here is one of the greatest instances in the New Testament of Jesus' power to see in a man, not only what he was, but also that which he could be. No one ever had such faith in the possibilities of human nature as Jesus had.

A CHALLENGE ISSUED AND RECEIVED

Matthew 9: 9 (continued)

CAPERNAUM was in the territory of Herod Antipas, and in all probability Matthew was not directly in the service of the Romans. He was in the service of Herod. Capernaum was a great meeting place of roads. In particular the great road from Egypt to Damascus, the Way of the Sea, passed through Capernaum. It was there that it entered the dominion of Herod for business purposes; and no doubt Matthew was one of these customs officers who exacted the duty on all goods and commodities as they entered and left the territory of Herod.

It is not to be thought that Matthew had never seen Jesus before. No doubt Matthew had heard about this young Galilean who came with a message which was breathtakingly new, who spoke with an authority the like of which no one had ever heard before, and who numbered amongst His friends men and women from whom the orthodox good people of the day would have shrunk in loathing. No doubt Matthew had listened on the outskirts of the crowd, and had felt his heart stir within him. Perhaps Matthew had wondered wistfully if even yet it was not too late to set sail and to seek a newer world, to leave his old life and his old shame and to begin again. So he found Jesus standing before him; so he heard Jesus issue His challenge; and Matthew accepted that challenge and rose up and left all and followed Him.

We must note *what Matthew lost and what Matthew found.*
He lost a comfortable job, but he found a destiny. He
lost a good income, but he found honour. He lost a comfortable security, but he found an adventure the like of which
he had never dreamed. It may be that if we accept the
challenge of Christ, we shall find ourselves poorer in
material things. It may be that the worldly ambitions
will have to go. But beyond doubt we will find a peace
and a joy and a thrill in life that we never knew before.
In Jesus Christ a man finds a wealth beyond anything
that he may have to abandon for the sake of Christ.

We must note *what Matthew left and what Matthew took.*
He left his tax-collector's table; but from it he took one
thing with him—his pen. Here is a shining example of
how Jesus can use whatever gift a man may bring to him.
It is not likely that the others of the Twelve were handy
with a pen. Galilean fishermen would not have much
skill in writing or in putting words together. But Matthew
had; and this man, whose trade had taught him to use a
pen, used that pen to compose the first handbook of the
teaching of Jesus, which must rank as one of the most
important books the world has ever read.

When Matthew left that tax-collector's table that day,
he gave up much in the material sense, but in the spiritual
sense he became heir to a fortune.

WHERE THE NEED IS GREATEST

Matthew 9: 10-13

He was sitting at table in the house, and, look you,
many tax-gatherers and sinners came and sat at
table with Jesus and His disciples. When the Pharisees
saw this, they said to His disciples, "Why does
your teacher eat with tax-gatherers and sinners?"
He heard this. "Those who are well," He said, "do
not need a doctor, but those who are ill. Go and learn
what the saying means: 'It is mercy I wish, and not
sacrifice.' For I did not come to invite the righteous,
but sinners."

JESUS did not only call Matthew to be His man and His follower; He actually sat at table with men and women like Matthew, with tax-gatherers and sinners. A very interesting question arises here—where was this meal where Jesus ate with tax-gatherers and sinners? It is only Luke who definitely says that the meal was in the house of Matthew or Levi (cp. *Matthew* 9: 10-13; *Mark* 2: 14-17; *Luke* 5: 27-32). As far as the narrative in *Matthew* and *Mark* goes, this meal could well have been in *Jesus'* house, or in the house where Jesus was staying. If the meal was in Jesus' house, Jesus' saying becomes even more pointed. Jesus said, " I did not come to invite the righteous, but sinners." The word that is used for to *invite* is the Greek word *kalein*, which is in fact the technical Greek word for inviting a guest to a house or to a meal. In the Parable of the Great Feast (*Matthew* 22: 1-10; *Luke* 14: 15-24) we well remember how the invited guests refused their invitation, and how the poor, and the lame, and the halt, and the blind were gathered together from the highways and the byways and the hedgerows to sit at the table of the King. It may well be that Jesus is saying, " When you make a feast you invite the coldly orthodox and the piously self-righteous; when I make a feast I invite those who are most conscious of their sin and those whose need of God is greatest." However that may be, whether this meal was in the house of Matthew or in the house where Jesus was staying, it was to the orthodox Scribes and Pharisees a most shocking proceeding. Broadly speaking, in Palestine people were divided into two sections. There were the orthodox who rigidly kept the Law in every petty detail and regulation; and there were the people who did not keep the petty regulations of the Law. The second were classed as *the people of the land*; and it was forbidden to the orthodox to go on a journey with them, to do any business with them, to give anything to them or to receive anything from them, to entertain them as guests or to be guests in their houses. By companying with people like this Jesus was doing something which the pious people of His day would never have done.

Jesus' defence was perfectly simple; He simply said that He went where the need was greatest. He would be a poor doctor who visited only houses where people enjoyed good health; the doctor's place is the house of those who are ill; it is his glory and his task to go to those who need him. Diogenes was one of the great teachers of ancient Greece. He was a man who loved virtue, and a man with a caustic tongue. He was never tired of comparing the decadence of Athens, where he spent most of his time, with the strong simplicities of Sparta. One day someone said to him, " If you think so much of Sparta and so little of Athens, who don't you leave Athens and go and stay in Sparta? " His answer was, " Whatever I may wish to do, I must stay where men need me most." It was sinners who needed Jesus, and amongst sinners He would move.

When Jesus said, " I did not come to invite the righteous, but sinners," we must understand what He was saying. He was not saying that there were some people who were so good that they had no need of anything which He could give; still less was He saying that He was not interested in people who were good. This is a highly compressed saying. Jesus was saying, " I did not come to invite people who are so self-satisfied that they are convinced of their own goodness and that they do not need anyone's help; I came to invite people who are very conscious of their sin and desperately aware of their need for a saviour." He was saying, " It is only those who know how much they need me who can accept my invitation."

These Scribes and Pharisees had a view of religion which is by no means dead.

(i) They were more concerned with the preservation of their own holiness than with the helping of another's sin. They were like doctors who refused to visit the sick lest they should be injured by some infection. They shrank away in fastidious disgust from the sinner; they did not want anything to do with people like that. Essentially their religion was selfish; they were much more concerned to save their own souls than to save the souls of others. And they had forgotten that that was the surest way to lose their own souls.

(ii) They were more concerned with criticism than with encouragement. They were far more concerned to point out the faults of other people than to help them to conquer these faults. When a doctor sees some particularly loathesome disease, which would turn the stomach of anyone else to look at, he is not filled with disgust; he is filled with the desire to help. Our first instinct should never be to condemn the sinner; our first instinct should be to help him.

(iii) They practised a goodness which issued in condemnation rather than in forgiveness and in sympathy. They would rather leave a man in the gutter than give him a hand to get out of it. They were like doctors who were very much concerned to diagnose and to recognize disease, but who were not in the least concerned to help to cure it. They were much more concerned to look down with contempt rather than to help in sympathy.

(iv) They practised a religion which consisted of outward orthodoxy rather than in practical help. Jesus loved that saying from *Hosea* 6: 6 which said that God desired mercy and not sacrifice, for He quoted it more than once (cp. *Matthew* 12: 7). A man may diligently go through all the motions of orthodox piety, but if his hand is never stretched out to help the sinner and the man in need, he is not a religious man.

PRESENT JOY AND FUTURE SORROW

Matthew 9: 14, 15

Then the disciples of John came to Him. " Why," they said, " do we and the Pharisees fast frequently, while your disciples do not fast? " Jesus said to them, " Surely the bridegroom's closest friends cannot mourn while the bridegroom is with them? But the days will come when the bridegroom will be taken away from them, and then they will fast."

To the Jew almsgiving, prayer and fasting were the three great works of the religious life. We have already fully described Jewish fasting when we were dealing with *Matthew* 6: 16-18. A. H. McNeile suggests that this incident may have taken place when the autumn rains had not fallen, and when a public fast had been ordained.

When Jesus was asked why He and His disciples did not practise fasting, He answered with a vivid picture. The Authorised Version speaks of the *children of the bride-chamber*, which is a correct literal translation of the Greek. A Jewish wedding was a time of special festivity. The unique feature of it was that the couple who were married did not go away for a honeymoon; they stayed at home for a honeymoon. For a week after the wedding open house was kept; the bride and bridegroom were treated as, and even addressed as, a king and queen. And during that week their closest friends shared all the joy and all the festivities with them; these closest friends were called *the children of the bridechamber*. On such an occasion there came into the lives of poor and simple people a joy, a rejoicing, a festivity, a plenty that might come only once in a lifetime. So Jesus compares Himself to the bridegroom and His disciples to the bridegroom's closest friends. How could a company like that be sad and grim? That was no time for fasting, but for the rejoicing of a lifetime. There are great things in this passage.

(i) It tells us that to be with Jesus is a thing of joy; it tells us that in the presence of Jesus there is a sheer thrilling effervesence in life, that a gloom-encompassed Christianity is an impossibility. The man who walks with Christ walks in radiance of joy.

(ii) But it also tells us that no joy lasts for ever. For

John's disciples the time of sorrow had come, for John was already in prison; for Jesus' disciples that time of sorrow would most certainly come. It is one of the great inevitabilities of life that the dearest joy must come to an end. Epictetus said grimly: " When you are kissing your child, say to yourself: ' One day you must die.' " That is why we must know God and Jesus Christ. Jesus alone is the same yesterday, today and for ever; God alone abides amidst all the chances and the changes of life. The dearest human relationships must some day come to an end; it is only the joy of heaven which lasts for ever, and if we have it in our hearts, nothing can take it away.

(iii) But this also is a challenge. It may be that at the moment the disciples did not see it, but Jesus is saying to them: " You have experienced the joy that following me can bring; can you also go through the trouble, the hardship, the suffering of a Christian's cross? " The Christian way brings its joy; but the Christian way also brings its blood and sweat and tears, which cannot take the joy away, but which, none the less, must be faced. So Jesus says, " Are you ready for both—the Christian joy and the Christian cross? "

(iv) Here enshrined in this saying is the courage of Jesus. Jesus was never under any illusions; clearly at the end of the road He saw awaiting Him the Cross. Here the curtain is lifted, and there is a glimpse into the mind of Jesus. He knew that for Him the way of life was the way of the Cross, and yet He did not swerve one step aside from His appointed way. Here is the courage of the man who knows what God's way costs, and who yet goes on.

THE PROBLEM OF THE NEW IDEA

Matthew 9: 16, 17

" No one puts a patch of unshrunken cloth on an old garment, for, if he does, the patch which he uses to fill n the hole tears the garment apart, and the rent is worse than ever. No one puts new wine into old wine-skins. If he does, the wine-skins burst, and the wine is spilled, and the skins perish; but they put new wine into new skins, and both are preserved."

JESUS was perfectly conscious that He came to men with new ideas and with a new conception of the truth, and He was well aware how difficult it is to get a new idea into men's minds at all. So He used two pictures which any Jew would understand.

(i) " No one," He said, " takes a piece of new and unshrunken cloth to patch an old garment. If he does, on the first occasion the garment becomes wet, the new patch shrinks, and as it shrinks, it tears the cloth apart, and the rent in the garment gapes wider than ever." The Jews were passionately attached to things as they were. The Law was to them God's last and final word; to add one word to it, or to subtract one word from it, was a deadly sin. It was the avowed object of the Scribes and Pharisees " to build a fence around the Law." To them a new idea was not so much a mistake as a sin. That spirit is by no means dead. Very often in a church, if a new idea or a new method or any change is suggested, the objection is promptly raised, " We never did that before." I once heard two theologians talking together. One was a younger man who was intensely interested in all that the new thinkers have to say; the other was an older man of a rigid and conventional orthodoxy. The older man heard the younger man with a kind of half-contemptuous tolerance, and finally closed the conversation by saying, " The old is better." Throughout all its history the Church has clung to the old. What Jesus is saying is that there comes a time when patching is folly, and when the only thing to do is to scrap something entirely and to begin again. There are forms of church government, there are forms of church service, there are forms of words which express our beliefs, which we so often try to adjust and to tinker with in order to bring them up to date;

we try to patch them. No one would willingly, or recklessly, or callously abandon that which has stood the test of time and of the years, that in which former generations have found their comfort and put their trust; but the fact remains that this is a growing and an expanding universe; and there comes a time when patches are useless, and when a man and a church has to accept the adventure of the new, or to withdraw into a backwater, where it worships, not God, but its own past.

(ii) No one, said Jesus, tries to put new wine into old wine-skins. In the old days men stored their wine in skins, and not in bottles. When new wine was put into a skin, the wine was still fermenting. The gases it gave off exerted pressure on the skin. In a new skin there was a certain elasticity, and no harm was done because the skin gave with the pressure. But an old skin had grown hard, and had lost all its elasticity, and, if new and fermenting wine was put into it, it could not give to the pressure of the gases; it could only burst.

To put this into modern terms: our minds must be elastic enough to receive and to contain new ideas. The history of progress is the history of the overcoming of the prejudices of the shut mind. Every new idea has had to fight for its existence against the instinctive opposition of the human mind. The motor car, the railway train, the aeroplane were in the beginning regarded with suspicion. Simpson had to fight to introduce chloroform, and Lister had to struggle to introduce antiseptics into the work of the doctor and the surgeon. Copernicus was compelled to retract his statement that the earth went round the sun, and not the sun round the earth. Even Jonas Hanway, who brought the umbrella to this country, had to suffer a barrage of missiles and insults when he first walked down a street with an umbrella. In our own day automation is regarded with resentment and suspicion because it is new.

This dislike of the new enters into every sphere of life. Norman Marlow is a writer who is an expert on railways, and who has made many journeys on the footplate of locomotives. He tells of a journey he made not long after the amalgamation of the railways in his book *Footplate and Signal Cabin*. At that, locomotives which had been used on one of the branches of the railways were being tested out on other lines. He was on the footplate of a Manchester to Penzance express. The locomotive was a " Jubilee " class 4-6-0. The driver was a Great Western Railway driver who had been used to driving locomotives of the " Castle " class. " The driver did nothing but discourse with moody eloquence on the wretchedness of the engine he was driving " as compared with the " Castle " engines. He refused to use the technique necessary for the new engine, although he had been instructed in it, and knew it perfectly well. He insisted on driving his " Jubilee " as if it had been a " Castle," and grumbled all the way that he could not get better speed than 50 miles an hour. He was used to " Castles " and with him nothing else had a chance. At Crewe a new driver took over, a man who was quite prepared to adopt the necessary new technique, and soon he had the " Jubilee " travelling at 80 miles per hour. Even in engine-driving men resent new ideas.

Within the Church this resentment of the new is chronic, and the attempt to pour new things into old moulds is almost universal. We attempt to pour the activities of a modern congregation into an ancient church building which was never meant for them. We attempt to pour the truth of new discoveries into creeds which are based on Greek metaphystics. We attempt to pour modern instruction into outworn language which cannot express it. We read God's word to twentieth century men and women in Elizabethan English, and seek to present the needs of the twentieth century man and woman to God in prayer language which is four hundred years old.

It may be that we would do well to remember that when any living thing stops growing, it starts dying. It may be that we need to pray that God would deliver us from the shut mind and give us the open mind. It so happens that we are living in an age of rapid and tremendous changes. Viscount Samuel was born in 1870, and he begins his autobiography with a description of the London of his childhood. " We had no motor-cars, or motor-buses, or taxis, or tube railways; there were no bicycles—except the high ' penny-farthings '; there were no electric light or telephones, no cinemas or broadcasts." That was less than ninety years ago. We are living in a changing and an expanding and a growing world. It is Jesus' warning that the Church dare not be the only institution which still lives in the past.

THE IMPERFECT FAITH AND THE PERFECT POWER

Matthew 9: 18-31

BEFORE we deal with this passage in detail, we must look at is as a whole; for in it there is something very wonderful.

This passage has three miracle stories in it, the healing of the ruler's daughter (verses 18, 19, 23-26); the healing of the woman with the issue of blood (verses 20-22); and the healing of the two blind men (verses 27-31). Each of these stories has something in common. Let us look at them one by one.

(i) Beyond a doubt the ruler came to Jesus when everything else had failed. He was, as we shall see, a ruler of the synagogue; that is to say, he was a pillar of Jewish orthodoxy. He was one of the men who despised and hated Jesus, and who would have been glad to see Him eliminated. No doubt he tried every kind of doctor, and every kind of cure; and only in sheer desperation, and as a last resort, did he come to Jesus at all. That is to say, *the ruler came to Jesus from a very inadequate motive.* He did not come to Jesus as a result of an outflow of the love of his heart; he came to Jesus because he had tried everything and everyone else, and because there was nowhere else to go. Faber somewhere makes God say of a straying child of God:

" If goodness lead him not,
Then weariness may toss him to my breast."

This man came to Jesus simply because desperation drove him to Jesus.

(ii) The woman with the issue of blood crept up behind Jesus in the crowd and touched the hem of His cloak. Suppose we were reading that story with a detached and critical faculty awake, what would we say that woman showed? We would say that she showed nothing other than superstition. To touch the edge of Jesus' cloak is the same kind of thing as to look for healing power in the relics and the handkerchiefs of saints. *This woman came to Jesus with what we would call a very inadequate faith.* If we regard this with the eyes of criticism, we see in it something which is much more like superstition than faith.

(iii) The two blind men came to Jesus, crying out: " Have pity on us, you Son of David." *Son of David* was not a title that Jesus desired; *Son of David* was the kind of title that a Jewish nationalist might use. So many of the Jews were waiting for a great leader and commander of the line of David who would be the conquering and victorious general who would lead them to military and political triumph over their Roman masters. That is the idea which lies behind this title *Son of David.* So the *these blind men came to Jesus with a very inadequate conception of who He was.* They saw in Him no more than the conquering hero of David's line.

Here is an astonishing thing. The ruler came to Jesus with an *inadequate motive*; the woman came to Jesus with an *inadequate faith*; the blind men came to Jesus with an *inadequate conception* of who He was, or, if we like to put it so, with an *inadequate theology*; and yet they found His love and power waiting for their needs. Here we see a tremendous thing. It does not matter how we come to Christ, if we only come. No matter how inadequately and how imperfectly we come, His love and His arms are open to receive us. There is a double lesson here. It means that we do not wait to ask the help of Christ for life until our motives, our faith, our theology is perfect; we can come to Him exactly as we are. And it means that we have no right to criticize others whose motives we suspect, whose faith we question, and whose theology we believe to be mistaken. It is not how we come to Christ that matters; it is that we should come at all, for He is willing to accept us as we are, and He is able to make us what we ought to be.

THE AWAKENING TOUCH

Matthew 9: 18, 19, 23-26

> While He was saying these things, look you, a ruler came and knelt before Him in worship; " My daughter," he said, " has just died. But come and lay your hand upon her, and she will live." Jesus rose and went with him, and His disciples came too. . . . And Jesus came to the house of the ruler, and He saw the flute-players and the tumult of the crowd. " Leave us," He said, " for the maid is not dead; she is asleep." And they laughed at Him. When the crowd had been put out, He went in and took her hand, and the maid arose. And the report of this went out to the whole country.

MATTHEW tells this story much more briefly than the other gospel writers do. If we want further details of it we must read it in *Mark* 5: 21-43 and in *Luke* 8: 40-56. There we discover that the ruler's name was Jairus, and that he was a ruler of the synagogue (*Mark* 5: 22; *Luke* 8: 41). The ruler of the synagogue was a very important person. He was elected from among the elders. He was not a teaching or a preaching official; he had " the care of the external order in public worship, and the supervision of the concerns of the synagogue in general." He appointed those who were to read and to pray in the service, and invited those who were to preach. It was his duty to see that nothing unfitting took place within the synagogue; and the care of the synagogue buildings were in his oversight. The whole practical administration of the synagogue was in his hands.

It is clear that such a man would only come to Jesus as a last resort. He would be one of these strictly orthodox Jews who regarded Jesus as a dangerous heretic; and it was only when everything else had failed that he would turn in desperation to Jesus. Jesus might well have said to this man, " When things were going well with you, you wanted to kill me; now that things are going ill with you, you are appealing for my help." And Jesus might well have refused help to a man who came like that. But Jesus bore no grudge; here was a man who needed Him, and Jesus' one desire was to help. Injured pride and the unforgiving spirit had no part in the mind of Jesus.

So Jesus went with the ruler of the synagogue to his house; and there He would find a scene like pandemonium. The Jews set very high the obligation of mourning over the dead. " Whoever is remiss," they said, " in mourning over the death of a wise man deserves to be burned alive." There were three mourning customs which characterized every Jewish household of grief.

There was the *rending of garments*. There were no fewer than thirty-nine different rules and regulations which laid down how garments should be rent. The rent was to be made standing. Clothes were to be rent to the heart so that the skin was exposed. For a father or mother the rent was exactly over the heart; for others it was on the right side. The rent must be big enough for a fist to be inserted into it. For seven days the rent must be left gaping open; for the next thirty days it must be loosely stitched so that it could still be seen; only then could it be permanently repaired. It would obviously have been improper for women to rend their garments in such a way that the breast was exposed. So it was laid down that a woman must rend her inner garment in private; she must then reverse the garment so that she wore it back to front; and then in public she must rend her outer garment.

There was *wailing for the dead*. In a house of grief an incessant wailing was kept up. The wailing was done by professional wailing women. They still exist in the east and W. M. Thomson in *The Land and the Book* describes them: " There are in every city and community women exceedingly cunning in this business. They are always sent for and kept in readiness. When a fresh company of sympathisers comes in, these women make haste to take up a wailing, that the newly-come may the more easily unite their tears with the mourners. They know the domestic history of every person, and immediately strike up an impromptu lamentation, in which they introduce the names of their relatives who have recently died, touching some tender chord in every heart; and thus each one weeps for his own dead, and the performance, which would otherwise be difficult or impossible, comes easy and natural." The shrill incessant wailing of the professional mourners would be filling the house of Jairus that day.

There were *the flute-players*. The music of the flute was especially associated with death. The *Talmud* lays it down: " The husband is bound to bury his dead wife, and to make lamentations and mourning for her, according to the custom of all countries. And also the very poorest amongst the Israelites will not allow her less than two flutes and one wailing woman; but, if he be rich, let all things be done according to his qualities." Even in Rome the flute-players were a feature of days of grief. There were flute-players at the funeral of the Roman Emperor Claudius, and Seneca tells us that they made such a shrilling that even Claudius himself, dead though he was, might have heard them. So insistent and so emotionally exciting was the wailing of the flute that Roman law limited the number of flute-players at any funeral to ten.

We can then picture the scene in the house of the ruler of the synagogue. The garments would be being rent; the wailing women would be uttering their shrieks in an abandonment of synthetic grief; the flutes would be shrilling their eerie sound. In that house there would be all the pandemonium of eastern grief.

Into that excited and hysterical atmosphere came Jesus. Authoritatively He put them all out. Quietly He told them that the maid was not dead but only asleep, and they laughed Him to scorn. It is a strangely human touch this. These mourners were so luxuriating in their grief that they even resented hope. It is very probable that when Jesus said that the maid was asleep, He meant exactly what He said. In Greek as in English a dead person was often said to be asleep. In fact the word *cemetery* comes from the Greek word *koimētērion,* and means *a place where people sleep.* In Greek there are two words for *to sleep;* the one is *koimasthai,* which is very commonly used both of natural sleep and of the sleep of death; the other is *katheudein,* which is not used nearly so frequently of the sleep of death, but which much more usually means natural sleep. It is *katheudein* which is used in this passage. In the east cataleptic coma was by no means uncommon. Burial in the east follows death very quickly, because the climate makes that necessary. Tristram writes: " Interments always take place at latest on the evening of the day of death, and frequently at night, if the deceased have lived till after sunset." Because of the commonness of this state of coma, and because of the commonness of speedy burial, not infrequently people were buried alive, as the evidence of the tombs shows. It may well be that here we have an example, not so much of divine healing as of divine diagnosis; and that Jesus saved this girl from a very dreadful and a very terrible death. One thing is true, Jesus that day in Capernaum rescued a Jewish maid from the grasp of death.

ALL HEAVEN'S POWER FOR ONE

Matthew 9: 20-22

> And, look you, a woman who had had a haemorrhage for twelve years came up behind Him, and touched the tassel of His cloak. For she said to herself, " If I only touch His cloak, I will be cured." Jesus turned and saw her. " Courage, daughter! " He said. " Your faith has brought you healing." And the woman was cured from that hour.

FROM the Jewish point of view this woman could not have suffered from any more terrible and humiliating disease than an issue of blood. It was a trouble which was very common in Palestine. The *Talmud* sets out no fewer than eleven different cures for it. Some of them were tonics and astringents which may well have been effective; others were merely superstitious remedies. One was to carry the ashes of an ostrich-egg in a linen bag in summer, and in a cotton bag in winter; another was to carry about a barleycorn which had been found in the dung of a white she-ass. When Mark tells this story, he makes it clear that this woman had tried everything, and had gone to every available doctor, and was worse instead of better (*Mark* 5: 26).

The horror of this disease was that it rendered the sufferer from it unclean. The Law laid it down: " If a woman have an issue of blood many days out of the time of her separation, or if it run beyond the time of her separation, all the days of the issue of her uncleanness shall be as the days of her separation; she shall be unclean. Every bed whereon she lieth all the days of her issue shall be unto her as the bed of her separation; and whatsoever she sitteth upon shall be unclean, as the uncleanness of her separation. And whosoever toucheth these things shall be unclean, and shall wash his clothes and bathe himself in water, and be unclean until the even " (*Leviticus* 15: 25-27). That is to say, a woman with an issue of blood was unclean; everything and everyone she touched was infected with that uncleanness. She was absolutely shut off from the worship of God and from the fellowship of other men and women. This woman should not even have been in that crowd surrounding Jesus, for, if they had known it, she was infecting with her uncleanness everyone whom she touched. There is little wonder that this woman was desperately eager to try anything which would rescue her from this life of isolation and of humiliation.

So she slipped up behind Jesus and touched what the Authorized Version calls the *hem* of His garment; the Greek word is *kraspedon*. In the Old Testament this word is translated *fringe*; in Hebrew the word is *zizith*. These fringes were four tassels of hyacinth blue worn by a Jew on the corners of his outer garment. They were worn in obedience to the injunction of the Law in *Numbers* 15: 37-41 and *Deuteronomy* 22: 12. Matthew again refers to them in 14: 36 and 23: 5. They consisted of four threads passing through the four corners of the garment and meeting in eight. One of the threads was longer than the others. It was twisted seven times round the others, and a double knot formed; then eight times, then eleven times, then thirteen times. The thread and the knots stood for the five books of the Law. The idea of the fringe was two-fold. It was meant to identify a Jew as a Jew, and as a member of the chosen people, no matter where he was; and it was meant to remind a Jew every time he put on and took off his clothes that he belonged to God. In later times, when the Jews were universally persecuted, the tassels were worn on the undergarment, and today they are worn on the prayer-shawl which a devout Jew wears when he prays. It was the tassel on the robe of Jesus that this woman touched.

When she touched it, it was as if time stood still. It is as if we were looking at a motion picture, a film, and suddenly the picture stopped, and left us looking at one scene. The extraordinary, and the movingly beautiful thing, about this scene is that suddenly amidst that crowd Jesus stopped, and for the moment it seemed that for Him no one but that woman and nothing but her need existed. She was not simply a poor woman who was lost in the crowd; she was someone to whom Jesus gave the whole of Himself. For Jesus no one is ever lost in the crowd, because Jesus is like God. W. B. Yeats once wrote in one of his moments of mystical beauty: " The love of God is infinite for every human soul, because every human soul is unique; no other can satisfy the same need in God." God gives all of Himself to each individual person.

The world is not like that. The world is very apt to divide people into those who are important and those who are unimportant. In *A Night to Remember* Walter Lord tells in detail the story of the sinking of the *Titanic* in April, 1912. There was an appalling loss of life, when that new and supposedly unsinkable liner hit the iceberg in the middle of the Atlantic. After the tragedy had been announced the New York newspaper, *The American*, devoted a leader to it. The leader was devoted entirely to the death of John Jacob Astor, the millionaire; and at the end of it, almost casually, it was mentioned that 1,800 others were also lost. The only one who really mattered, the only one with real news value, was the millionaire. The other 1,800 were of no real importance. Men can be like that, but God can never be like that. Bain, the psychologist, said in a very different connection that the sensualist has what he calls " a voluminous tenderness." In the highest and the best sense there is a voluminous tenderness in God. James Agate said of G. K. Chesterton: " Unlike some thinkers, Chesterton understood his fellow-men; the woes of a jockey were as familiar to him as the worries of a judge. . . . Chesterton, more than any man I have ever known, had the common touch. He would give the whole of his attention to a boot-black. He had about him that bounty of heart which men call kindness, and which makes the whole world kin." That is the reflection of the love of God to which no man is lost in the crowd.

This is something to remember in a day and an age when the individual is tending to get lost. Men tend to become numbers in a system of social security; they tend to become members of an association or union in which they almost lose their right to be individuals at all. W. B. Yeats said of Augustus John, the famous artist and portrait painter: " He was supremely interested in the revolt from all that makes one man like another." To God one man is never like another; each is His individual child, and each has all God's love and all God's power at his disposal. To Jesus this woman was not lost in the crowd; in her hour of need to Him she was all that mattered. Jesus is like that for every one of us.

FAITH'S TEST AND FAITH'S REWARD

Matthew 9: 27-31

> And, as He passed on from there, two blind men followed Him, shouting. " Have pity on us," they said, " you Son of David." When He came into the house, the blind men came to Him. Jesus said to them, " Do you believe that I am able to do this? " " Yes, Lord," they said. Then He touched their eyes. " Be it to you," He said, " according to your faith." And their eyes were opened. And Jesus sternly commanded them, " See, let no one know of this." But they went out and spread abroad the story of Him all over the country.

BLINDNESS was a distressingly common disease in Palestine. It came partly from the glare of the eastern sun on unprotected eyes, and partly because people knew nothing of the importance of cleanliness and hygiene. In particular the swarms and clouds of unclean flies carried the infections which led to loss of sight.

The name by which these two blind men addressed Jesus was *Son of David*. When we study the occurrences of that title within the gospels, we find that it is almost always used by crowds or by people who knew Jesus only, as it were, at a distance (*Matthew* 15: 22; 20: 30, 31; *Mark* 10: 47; 12: 35, 36, 37). The term *Son of David* describes Jesus in the popular conception of the Messiah. For generations and for centuries the Jews had awaited the promised deliverer of David's line, the leader and the commander who would not only restore their freedom, but who would lead them to power and glory and greatness and world conquest. It was in that way that these blind men thought of Jesus; they saw in Him the wonder-worker who would lead the people to victory, to freedom and to conquest. They came to Jesus with a very inadequate idea of who and what He was, and yet He healed them. The way in which Jesus dealt with these men is very illuminating.

(i) Clearly He did not answer their shouts at once. Jesus wished to be quite sure that they were sincere and earnest in their desire for what He could give to them. It might well have been that they had taken up a popular cry just because everyone else was shouting, and that, as soon as Jesus had passed by, they would simply forget. He wanted first of all to be sure that their request was genuine, and that their sense of need was real. After all there were advantages in being a beggar; a man was rid of all the responsibility of working and of making a living; there are advantages in being an invalid. There are people who in actual fact do not wish their chains to be broken. W. B. Yeats tells of Lionel Johnson, the scholar and poet. Johnson was an alcoholic. He had, as he said himself, " a craving that made every atom of his body cry out." But, when it was suggested that he should undergo treatment to overcome this craving, his answer quite frankly was: " I do not want to be cured." There are not a few people who in their heart of hearts do not dislike their weakness; and there are many people, who, if they were honest, would have to say that they do not wish to lose their sins. Jesus had first of all to be sure that these men sincerely and earnestly desired the healing He could give.

(ii) It is interesting to note that Jesus in effect compelled these people to see Him alone. Because He did not answer them in the streets, they had to come to Him in the house. It is the law of the spiritual life that sooner or later a man must confront Jesus alone. It is all very well to take a decision for Jesus on the flood tide of emotion of some great gathering, or in some little group which is charged with spiritual power. But after the crowd a man must go home and be alone; after the fellowship he must go back to the essential isolation of every human soul; and what really matters is not what a man does in the crowd, but what he does when he is alone with Christ. Jesus compelled these men to face Him alone.

(iii) Jesus only asked these men one question: " Do you believe that I am able to do this? " The one essential for a miracle is faith. There is nothing mysterious or theological about this. No doctor can cure a sick person, if the person goes to him in a completely hopeless frame of mind. No medicine will do a man any good, if the man thinks he might as well be drinking water. The way to a miracle is to place one's life in the hands of Jesus Christ, and to say, " I know that you can make me what I ought to be."

THE TWO REACTIONS

Matthew 9: 32-34

As they were going away, look you, they brought to Him a dumb man who was demon-possessed; and, when the demon had been expelled from him, he spoke. And the crowds were amazed. " Nothing like this," they said, " was ever seen in Israel." But the Pharisees said, " He casts out the demons by the power of the prince of the demons."

THERE are few passages which show better than this passage does the impossibility of an attitude of neutrality towards Jesus Christ. Here we have the picture of two reactions to Jesus. The attitude of the crowds was amazed wonder; the attitude of the Pharisees was virulent hatred. It must always remain true that what the eye sees depends upon what the heart feels. The feelings within a man's heart can and do colour everything which he sees.

The crowds looked on Jesus with wonder, because the crowds were composed of simple people with a crying sense of need; and they saw that in Jesus that need could be supplied in the most astonishing way. Jesus will always appear wonderful to the man with a sense of need; and the deeper the sense of need the more wonderful Jesus will appear to be.

The Pharisees looked on Jesus and saw Him as one who was in league with all the powers of evil. They did not deny His wondrous powers; but they attributed them to the fact that Jesus was in league with the prince of the devils. This verdict of the Pharisees was due to certain attitudes of mind.

(i) They were too set in their ways to change. As we have seen, to them not one word could be added or subtracted from the Law. To them all the great things belonged to the past. To them to change a tradition or a convention was a deadly sin. Anything that was new was wrong. And when Jesus came with a new interpretation of what real religion was, they hated Him, as they had hated the prophets long ago.

(ii) They were too proud in their self-satisfaction to submit. If Jesus was right, they were wrong. Jesus can do nothing with a man until a man surrenders his will and his life to Him. The Pharisees were so well satisfied with themselves that they saw no need to change; and they hated anyone who wished to change them. Repentance is the gate whereby all men must enter the Kingdom, and repentance means the recognition of the error of our ways, the realization that in Christ alone there is life, and the surrender to Him and to His will and power, whereby alone we can be changed.

(iii) They were too prejudiced to see. Their eyes were so blinded by their own ideas and their own prejudices that they could not see in Jesus Christ the truth and the power of God.

The man with a sense of need will always see wonders in Jesus Christ. The man who is so set in his ways that he will not change, the man who is so proud in his self-righteousness that he cannot submit, the man who is so blinded by his prejudices that he cannot see, will always resent and hate and seek to eliminate Jesus Christ.

THE THREEFOLD WORK

Matthew 9: 35

> And Jesus made a tour of all the towns and villages, teaching in their synagogues, and heralding forth the good news of the Kingdom, and healing every disease and every illness.

HERE in one sentence we see the threefold activity which was the essence of the life of Jesus.

(i) Jesus was the *herald*. The herald is the man who brings a message from the king: Jesus was the one who brought a message from God. The duty of the herald is the proclamation of certainties. Preaching must always be the proclamation of certainties. No church can ever be composed of people who are certain, as it were, by proxy. It is not only the preacher who must be certain. The people must be certain too. There never was a time when this certainty was more needed than it is to-day. Geoffrey Heawood, who is headmaster of a great English public school, has written that the great tragedy and problem of this age in which we live is that we are standing at the cross-roads, and the signposts have fallen down.

Mr. Beverley Nichols once wrote a book which was composed of interviews with famous people. One of the interviews was with Mr. Hilaire Belloc who was one of the most famous English Roman Catholics. After the interview Mr Nichols wrote: " I was sorry for Mr. Belloc because I felt that he had nailed at least some of his colours to the wrong mast; but I was still sorrier for myself and for my own generation, because I knew that we had no colours of any kind to nail to any mast." We live in an age of uncertainty, an age when people have ceased to be sure of anything. Jesus was the herald of God, who came proclaiming the certainties by which men live; and we too must be able to say, " I know whom I have believed."

(ii) Jesus was *teacher*. It is not enough to proclaim the Christian certainties and to let it go at that; we must also be able to show the significance of these certainties for life and for living, for that is teaching. The importance of this, and the problem of this, lies in the fact that we teach Christianity, not by talking about it, but by living it. It is not the Christian's duty to discuss Christianity with others, so much as it is to show them in life what Christianity is. A writer who lived in India writes like this: " I remember a British battalion, which like most battalions came to parade service because they had to, sang hymns they liked, listened to the preacher if they thought him interesting, and left the Church alone for the rest of the week. But their rescue work at the time of the Quetta earthquake so impressed a Brahmin that he demanded immediate baptism, because only the Christian religion could make men behave like that." The thing which taught that Brahmin what Christianity was like was Christianity in action. To put this at its highest: our duty is not to talk to men about Jesus Christ, but to show men Jesus Christ. A saint has been defined as someone in whom Christ lives again. Every Christian must be a teacher, and he must teach others what Christianity is, not by his words, but by his life.

(iii) Jesus was *healer*. The gospel which Jesus brought did not stop at words; it was translated into deeds. If we read through the gospels, we will see that Jesus spent far more time healing the sick, and feeding the hungry, and comforting the sorrowing than He did merely talking about God. He turned the words of Christian truth into the deeds of Christian love. We are not truly Christian until our Christian belief issues in Christian action. The priest would have said that religion consists of sacrifice; the Scribe would have said that religion consists of Law; but Jesus Christ said that religion consists of love

THE DIVINE COMPASSION

Matthew 9: 36

> When He saw the crowds, He was moved with compassion to the depths of His being, for they were bewildered and dejected, like sheep who have no shepherd.

WHEN Jesus saw the crowd of the ordinary men and women, He was *moved with compassion*. The word which is used for *moved with compassion* (*splagchnistheis*) is the strongest word for compassionate pity in the Greek language. It is formed from the word *splagchna*, which means *the bowels*, and it describes the pity and the compassion which move a man to the very deepest depths of his being. In the gospels, apart only from its use in some of the parables, it is used only of Jesus (*Matthew* 9: 36; 14: 14; 15: 32; 20: 34; *Mark* 1: 41; *Luke* 7: 13). When we study these passages, we are able to see the things which moved Jesus most of all.

(i) He was moved to compassion by the *world's pain*. He was moved with compassion for the sick (*Matthew* 14: 14); for the blind (*Matthew* 20: 34); for those in the grip of the demons (*Mark* 9: 22). In all our afflictions He is afflicted. He could not see a sufferer but He longed to ease the pain.

(ii) He was moved to compassion by the world's *sorrow*. The sight of the widow at Nain, following the body of her son out to burial, moved His heart (*Luke* 7: 13). He was filled with a great desire to wipe the tear from every eye.

(iii) He was moved to compassion by the world's *hunger*. The sight of the tired and hungry crowds was a call upon His power (*Matthew* 15: 32). No Christian can be content to have too much while others have too little.

(iv) He was moved to compassion by the world's *loneliness*. The sight of a leper, banished from the society of his fellow-men, living a life which was a living death of loneliness and universal abandonment, called forth His pity and His power (*Mark* 1: 41).

(v) He was moved to compassion by the world's *bewilderment*. That is what moved Jesus on this occasion. The common people were desperately longing for God; and the Scribes and the Pharisees, the priests and the Sadducees, the pillars of orthodox religion of His day, had nothing to offer them. The orthodox teachers had neither guidance, nor comfort, nor strength to give. Milton, in *Lycidas*, describes almost savagely the religious leaders who have nothing to offer:

> " Blind mouths! that scarce themselves know how to hold
> A sheep-hook, or have learnt aught else the least
> That to the faithful herdman's art belongs!
> . . . Their lean and flashy songs
> Grate on their scrannel pipes of wretched straw,
> The hungry sheep look up and are not fed."

The words that are used to describe the state of the common people are vivid words. The word that we have translated *bewildered* is *eskulmenoi*. It can describe a corpse which is *flayed* and *mangled*; someone who is *plundered* by rapacious men, or *vexed* by those without pity, or treated with *wanton insolence*; some who is utterly *wearied* by a journey which seems to know no end. The word that we have translated *dejected* is *errimenoi*. It means *laid prostrate*. It can describe a man prostrated with drink, or a man laid low with mortal wounds.

The Jewish leaders, who should have been giving men strength to live, were bewildering men with subtle arguments about the Law, which had no help and comfort in them. When they should have been helping men to stand upright, they were bowing them down under the intolerable burden of the Scribal Law. They were offering men a religion which was a burden instead of a support. We must always remember that the Christian religion exists, not to discourage, but to encourage, not to weigh men down with burdens, but to lift them up with wings.

THE WAITING HARVEST

Matthew 9: 37, 38

> Then He said to His disciples, " The harvest is great, but the workers are few. Therefore, pray to the Lord of the harvest to send out workers for His harvest."

HERE is one of the most characteristic things that Jesus ever said. When He and the orthodox religious leaders of His day looked on the crowd of ordinary men and women, they saw them in quite different ways. The Pharisees saw the common people as chaff to be destroyed and burned up; He saw them as a harvest to be reaped and to be saved. The Pharisees in their pride looked for the destruction of sinners; Jesus in His love died for the salvation of sinners.

But here also is one of the great Christian truths and one of the supreme Christian challenges. That harvest will never be reaped unless there are reapers to reap it. It is one of the great blazing basic truths of the Christian faith and life that *Jesus Christ needs men*. When He was upon this earth, His voice could reach so few. He was never outside Palestine, and there was a world which was waiting. He still wants men to hear of the good news of the gospel, but men will never hear unless other men will tell them. Jesus Christ wants a child taught; that child will never be taught unless a teacher emerges to teach him. Jesus Christ wants all men to hear the good news; men will never hear it unless there are those who are prepared to cross the seas and the mountains and bring the good news to them.

Nor is prayer enough. A man might say, " I will pray for the coming of Christ's Kingdom every day in life." But in this, as in so many things, prayer without works is dead. Martin Luther had a friend who felt about the Christian faith as he did. The friend was also a monk. They came to an agreement. Luther would go down into the dust and heat of the battle for the Reformation in the world; the friend would stay in the monastery and uphold Luther's hands in prayer. So they began that way. Then, one night, the friend had a dream. He saw a vast field of corn as big as the world; and one solitary man was seeking to reap it—an impossible and a heart-breaking task. Then he caught a glimpse of the reaper's face; and the reaper was Martin Luther; and Luther's friend saw the truth in a flash. " I must leave my prayers," he said, " and get to the work." And so he left his pious solitude, and went down to the world to labour in the harvest.

It is the dream of Christ that every man should be a missionary and a reaper. There are those who cannot do other than pray, for life has laid them helpless, and their prayers are indeed the strength of the labourers. But that is not the way for most of us, for those of us who have strength of body and health of mind. Not even the giving of our money is enough. If the harvest of men is ever to be reaped, then every one of us must be a reaper, for there is someone whom each one of us could—and must—bring to God.

THE GOSPEL OF MATTHEW

THE MESSENGERS OF THE KING

Matthew 10: 1-4

> And when He had summoned His twelve disciples,
> He gave them power over unclean spirits, so that
> they were able to cast them out, and so that they were
> able to heal every disease and every sickness. These
> are the names of the twelve apostles: first and fore-
> most Simon, who is called Peter, and Andrew, his
> brother; James, the son of Zebedee, and John, his
> brother; Philip and Bartholomew; Thomas and
> Matthew, the tax-collector; James, the son of Alphaeus,
> and Thaddaeus; Simon the Cananaean and Judas
> Iscariot, who was also His betrayer.

METHODICALLY, and yet with a certain drama, Matthew
unfolds his story of Jesus. In the story of the Baptism
Matthew shows us Jesus accepting His task. In the story
of the Temptations Matthew shows us Jesus deciding on
the method which He will use to embark upon His task.
In the Sermon on the Mount we listen to Jesus' words of
wisdom. In *Matthew* 8 we look on Jesus' deeds of power.
In *Matthew* 9 we see the growing opposition gathering
itself against Jesus. And now we see Jesus choosing His
men. If a leader is about to embark upon any great undertaking, the first thing that he must do is to choose his staff.
On them the present effect and the future success of his
work both depend. Here Jesus is choosing His staff, His
right-hand men, His helpers in the days of His flesh, and
those who would carry on His work when He left this
earth and returned to His glory.

There are two facts about these men which are bound
to strike us at once.

(i) They were very ordinary men. They had no wealth;
they had no academic background; they had no social
position. They were chosen from the common people,
men who did the ordinary things, men who had no special
education, men who had no social advantages. It has been
said that Jesus is looking, not so much for extraordinary
men, as for ordinary men who can do ordinary things

extraordinarily well. Jesus sees in every man, not only what that man is, but also what He can make him. Jesus chose these men, not only for what they were, but also for what they were capable of becoming under His influence and in His power. No man need ever think that he has nothing to offer Jesus Christ; Jesus Christ can take what the most ordinary man can offer and use it for greatness.

(ii) They were the most extraordinary mixture. There was, for instance, Matthew, the tax-gatherer. All men would regard Matthew as a quisling, as one who had sold himself into the hands of his country's masters for gain, as the very reverse of a patriot and a lover of his country. And with Matthew there was Simon. The Authorized Version calls him the *Canaanite*; that is a mistranslation; it ought to be the *Cananaean*. Luke (*Luke* 6: 16) calls him Simon *Zelōtēs*, which means Simon the *Zealot*. Josephus (*Antiquities*, 8. I. 6.) describes these Zealots; he calls them the fourth party of the Jews; the other three parties were the Pharisees, the Sadducees, and the Essenes. He says that they had " an inviolable attachment to liberty," and that they said that " God is to be their ruler and Lord." They were prepared to face any kind of death for their country, and did not shrink to see their loved ones die in the struggle for freedom. They refused to give to any earthly man the name and the title of king. They had an immovable resolution which would undergo any pain. They were prepared to go the length of secret murder and stealthy assassination to seek to rid their country of foreign rule. They were the patriots *par excellence* among the Jews, the most nationalist of all the nationalists. The plain fact is that if Simon the Zealot had met Matthew anywhere else than in the company of Jesus, he would have stuck a dagger in him. Here is the tremendous truth that men who hate each other can learn to love each other when they both love Jesus Christ. Too often religion has been a means of dividing men. It was meant to be—and in the presence of the living Jesus it was—a means of bringing together men who without Christ were sundered from each other.

We may ask why Jesus chose *twelve* special apostles. The reason is very likely because there were *twelve tribes*; just as in the old dispensation there had been twelve tribes of Israel, so in the new dispensation there are twelve apostles of the new Israel. The New Testament itself does not tell us very much about these men. As Plummer has it: " In the New Testament it is the work, and not the workers, that is glorified." But, although we do not know much about them, the New Testament is very conscious of their greatness in the Church, for the *Revelation* tells us that the twelve foundation stones of the Holy City are inscribed with their names (*Revelation* 21: 14). These men, simple men with no great background, men from many differing spheres of belief, were the very foundation stones on which the Church was built. It is on the stuff of common men and women that the Church of Christ is founded.

THE MAKING OF THE MESSENGERS

Matthew 10: 1-4 (*continued*)

WHEN we put together the three accounts of the calling of the Twelve (*Matthew* 10: 1-4; *Mark* 3: 13-19; *Luke* 6: 13-16) certain illuminating facts emerge.

(i) He *chose* them. *Luke* 6: 13 says that Jesus called His disciples, and *out of them He chose twelve*. It is as if Jesus' eyes moved over the crowds who followed Him, and the smaller band who stayed with Him when the crowds had departed, and as if all the time He was searching for the men to whom He could commit His work. As it has been said, " God is always looking for hands to use." God is always saying, " Whom shall I send, and who will go for us? " (*Isaiah* 6: 8). There are many tasks in the Kingdom, the task of him who must go out and the task of him who must stay at home, the task of him who must use his hands and the task of him who must use his mind, the task which will fasten the eyes of all upon the doer of it and the task which no one will ever see. But always Jesus' eyes are searching the crowds for those who will do His work.

(ii) He *called* them. Jesus does not compel a man to do His work; He offers him work to do. Jesus does not coerce; He invites. Jesus does not desire conscripts; He desires volunteers. As it has been put, a man is free to be faithful and free to be faithless. But to every man there comes the summons which he can accept or refuse.

(iii) He *appointed* them. The Authorized Version has it that He ordained them (*Mark* 3: 14). The word which is translated *ordain* is the simple Greek word *poiein*, which means *to make* or *to do*; but which is often technically used for *appointing a man to some office*. Jesus was like a king appointing his men to be his ministers; He was like a general allocating their tasks to his commanders. It was not a case of drifting unconsciously into the service of Jesus Christ; it was a case of definitely being appointed to it. A man might well be proud, if he was appointed to some earthly office by some earthly king; how much more shall he be proud when he is appointed by the King of kings?

(iv) These men were appointed from *amongst the disciples*. The word disciple means *a learner*. The men whom Christ needs and desires are the men who are willing to learn. The shut mind cannot serve Jesus Christ. The servant of Christ must be willing to learn more every day in life. Each day he must be a step nearer Jesus and a little nearer God.

(v) The reasons why these men were chosen are equally significant. They were chosen *that they should be with Jesus* (*Mark* 3: 14). If they were to do His work in the world, they must live in His presence, before they went out to the world; they must go from the presence of Jesus Christ

into the presence of men. It is told that on one occasion
Alexander Whyte preached a most powerful and a most
moving sermon. After the service a friend said to him:
" You preached today as if you had come straight from
the presence of Jesus Christ." Whyte answered: " Perhaps
I did." No work from Christ can ever be done except by
him who comes from the presence of Christ. Sometimes
in the complexity of the activities of the modern Church
we are so busy with committees and courts and administration and making the wheels go round that we are in
danger of forgetting that none of these things matter, if
they are carried on by men who have not been with Christ
before they have been with men.

(vi) They were called to be *apostles* (*Mark* 3: 14; *Luke*
6: 13). The word apostle literally means *one who is sent
out*; it is the word for an *envoy* or an *ambassador*. The
Christian is Jesus Christ's ambassador to men. He comes
into the presence of Christ in order that he may go forth
to men from that presence, bearing with him the word
and the beauty of Jesus Christ.

(vii) They were called to be the *heralds* of Christ. In
Matthew 10: 7 they are bidden *to preach*. The word is
kērussein, which comes from the noun *kērux*, which means a
herald. The Christian is the herald of Jesus Christ; he
brings to men the announcement from Jesus Christ. That
is why he must begin in the presence of Christ. The
Christian is not meant to bring to men his own opinions
or his views; he brings a message of divine certainties
from Jesus Christ—and he cannot bring that message
unless first in the presence he has received it.

THE COMMISSION OF THE KING'S
MESSENGER

Matthew 10: 5-8a

Jesus sent out these twelve, and these were the orders
He gave them: " Do not," He said, " go out on the

road to the Gentiles, and do not enter into any city of the Samaritans; but go rather to the sheep of the house of Israel who have perished. As you go make this proclamation: The Kingdom of Heaven is near. Heal the sick, raise the dead, cleanse the leper, cast out demons."

HERE we have the beginning of the King's commission to His messengers. The word which is used in the Greek for Jesus *commanding* His men, or *giving them orders* is interesting and illuminating. It is the word *paraggellein*. This word in Greek has four special usages. (i) It is the regular word of military command: Jesus was like a general sending his commanders out on a campaign, and briefing them before they went. (ii) It is the word used of calling one's friends to one's help. Jesus was like a man with a great ideal summoning his friends to make that ideal come true. (iii) It is the word which is used of a teacher or a philosopher giving rules and precepts to his students or disciples. Jesus was like a teacher sending his students out into the world, equipped with his teaching and his message. (iv) It is the word which is regularly used for an imperial command. Jesus was like a king despatching his ambassadors into the world to carry out his orders and to speak for him.

This passage begins with what everyone must find a very difficult instruction. It begins by forbidding the twelve to go to the Gentiles or to the Samaritans. There are many who find it very difficult to believe that Jesus ever said this at all; this apparent exclusiveness is very unlike Him; and it has been suggested that this saying was put into His mouth by those who in the later days wished to keep the gospel for the Jews, by the very men who were the bitter opponents of Paul, when he wished to take the gospel to the Gentiles. But there are certain things to be remembered. This saying is so unlike the mind of Jesus that no one could have invented it; He must have said it, and there must be some explanation.

We can be quite certain that it was not a *permanent* command. Within the gospel itself we see Jesus talking graciously and intimately and revealing Himself to a woman of Samaria (*John* 4: 4-42); we see Him telling one of His immortal stories of which the hero is a Samaritan (*Luke* 10: 30); we see Him healing the daughter of a Syro-Phoenician woman (*Matthew* 15: 28); and it is Matthew himself who tells us of Jesus' final commission to His men to go out into all the world and to bring all nations into the gospel (*Matthew* 28: 19, 20). What then is the explanation of this?

The twelve are forbidden to go to the Gentiles; that meant that they could not go north into Syria, nor could they even go east into the Decapolis, which was largely a Gentile region. They could not go south into Samaria for that was forbidden. The effect of this order is in actual fact to limit the first journeys of the twelve to Galilee. There are three good reasons for that. (i) The Jews had in God's scheme of things a very special place; in the justice of God they had to be given the first offer of the gospel. It is true that they rejected it, but the whole of history was designed to give them the first opportunity to accept. (ii) Very definitely the twelve were not equipped to preach to the Gentiles. They had neither the background, nor the knowledge nor the technique. Before the gospel could be effectively brought to the Gentiles a man with Paul's life and background had to emerge. A message has little chance of success, if the messenger is ill-equipped to deliver it. If a preacher or teacher is wise, he will realize his own limitations, and will see clearly what he is fitted and what he is not fitted to do. (iii) But the great reason for this command is simply this—any wise commander knows that he must limit his objectives. He must direct his attack at one chosen point. If he diffuses his forces here there and everywhere, he dissipates his strength and invites failure. The smaller his forces the more limited his objective must at the moment be. To attempt to attack on too broad a front is simply to court disaster. Jesus knew that, and His aim was to concentrate his attack on Galilee, for Galilee, as we have seen, was the most open of all parts of Palestine to a new gospel and a new message (cp. on *Matthew* 4: 12-17). This command of Jesus was a *temporary* command. He was the wise commander who refused to diffuse and dissipate His forces; He skilfully concentrated His attack on one limited objective in order to achieve an ultimate and universal victory.

THE WORDS AND WORKS OF THE KING'S
MESSENGER

Matthew 10: 5-8a (*continued*)

THE King's messengers had words to speak and deeds to do.

(i) They had to announce the imminence of the Kingdom. As we have seen (cp. on *Matthew* 6: 10, 11) the Kingdom of God is a society on earth, where God's will is as perfectly done as it is in heaven. Of all persons who ever lived in the world Jesus was, and is, the only person who ever perfectly did, and obeyed, and fulfilled, God's will. Therefore in Him the Kingdom had come. It is as if the messengers of the King were to say, " Look! You have dreamed of the Kingdom, and you have longed for the Kingdom. Here in the life of Jesus *is* the Kingdom. Look at Him, and see what being in the Kingdom means." In Jesus the Kingdom of God came to men.

(ii) But the task of the twelve was not confined to speaking words; it involved doing deeds. They had to heal the sick, to raise the dead, to cleanse the lepers, to cast out demons. All these injunctions are to be taken in a double sense. They are to be taken *physically*, because Jesus Christ came to bring health and healing to the bodies of men. But they are also to be taken *spiritually*. They describe the change wrought by Jesus Christ in the souls of men.

(a) They are to *heal the sick*. The word used for *sick* is very suggestive. It is a part of the Greek verb *asthenein*, the primary meaning of which is *to be weak*; *asthenēs* is the standard Greek adjective for *weak*. When Christ comes to a man, He strengthens the weak will, He buttresses the weak resistance, He nerves the feeble arm for fight, He confirms the weak resolution. Jesus Christ fills our human weakness with His divine power.

(b) They are to *raise the dead*. A man can be dead in sin. His will to resist can be broken; his vision of the good can be darkened until it does not exist; he may be helplessly and hopelessly in the grip of his sins, blind to goodness and deaf to God. When Jesus Christ comes into a man's life, He resurrects him to goodness. Jesus Christ revitalizes the goodness within us which our sinning has killed.

(c) They are to cleanse *the lepers*. As we have seen, the leper was regarded as polluted. *Leviticus* says of the leper, " All the days wherein the plague shall be in him he shall be *defiled*; he is *unclean*; he shall dwell alone; outside the camp shall his habitation be " (*Leviticus* 13: 46). 2 *Kings* 7: 3, 4 shows us the lepers who only in the day of deadly famine dared to enter into the city. 2 *Kings* 15: 5 tells us how Azariah the king was smitten with leprosy, and unto the day of his death he had to live in a lazar house, separated from all men. It is interesting to note that even in Persia this pollution of the leper was believed in. Herodotus (1: 138. 1) tells us that, " if a man in Persia has the leprosy he is not allowed to enter into a city or to have any dealings with any other Persians; he must, they say, have sinned against the sun." So, then, the twelve are to bring cleansing to the polluted. A man can stain his life with sin; he can pollute his mind, his heart, his body with the consequences of his sin. His words, his actions, his influence can become so befouled that they are an unclean influence on all those with whom he comes into contact. Jesus Christ can cleanse the soul that has stained itself with sin; He can bring to men the divine antiseptic against sin. Jesus Christ cleanses human sin with the divine purity.

(iv) They were to *cast out demons*. A demon-possessed man was a man in the grip of an evil power; he was no longer master of himself and of his actions; the evil power within him had him in its mastery. A man can be mastered by evil; he can be dominated by evil habits; evil can have a mesmeric fascination and attraction for him. Jesus comes not only to cancel sin, but to break the power of cancelled sin. Jesus Christ brings to men enslaved by sin the liberating power of God; He emancipates the slave of sin.

THE EQUIPMENT OF THE KING'S
MESSENGER

Matthew 10: 8b-10

> " Freely you have received; freely give. Do not set out to get gold or silver or bronze for your purses; do not take a bag for the journey, nor two tunics, nor shoes, nor a staff. The workman deserves his sustenance."

THIS is a passage in which every sentence and every phrase would ring an answering bell in the mind of the Jews who heard it. In it Jesus was giving to His men the instructions and the orders which the Rabbis at their highest and their best gave to their students and disciples.

" Freely you have received," says Jesus, " freely give." A Rabbi was bound by law to give his teaching freely and for nothing; the Rabbi was absolutely forbidden to take money for teaching the Law which Moses had freely received from God. In only one case could a Rabbi accept payment. He might accept payment for teaching a child, for to teach a child is the parent's task, and no one else should be expected to spend time and labour doing that which it is the parent's own duty to do; but higher teaching had to be given without money and without price. In the *Mishnah* the Law lays it down that, if a man takes payment for acting as a judge, his judgments are invalid; that, if he takes payment for giving evidence as a witness, his witness is void. Rabbi Zadok said, "Make not the Law a crown wherewith to aggrandize thyself, nor a spade wherewith to dig." Hillel said, "He who makes a worldly use of the crown of the Law shall waste away. Hence thou mayest infer that whosoever desires a profit for himself from the words of the Law is helping on his own destruction." It was laid down: "As God taught Moses gratis—so do thou." There is a story of Rabbi Tarphon. At the end of the fig harvest he was walking in a garden; and he ate some of the figs which had been left behind. The watchmen came upon him and beat him. He told them who he was, and because he was a famous Rabbi they let him go. All his life he regretted that he had used his status as a Rabbi to help himself. "Yet all his days did he grieve, for he said, 'Woe is me, for I have used the crown of the Law for my own profit!'" When Jesus told His disciples that they had freely received and must freely give, He was telling them what the teachers of His own people had been telling their students for many a day. If a man possesses a precious secret it is surely his duty, not to hug it to himself until he is paid for it, but willingly to pass it on. It is a privilege to share with others the riches God has given us.

Jesus told the twelve not to set out to acquire gold or silver or bronze for their *purses*; the Greek literally means for their *girdles*. The girdle, which the Jew wore round his waist, was rather broad; and at each end for part of its length it was double; money was carried in the double part of the girdle; so that the girdle was the usual purse of the Jew. Jesus told the twelve not to take a *bag* for the journey. The bag may be one of two things. It may simply be a bag like a haversack in which provisions would ordinarily have been carried. But there is another possibility. The word is *pēra*, which can mean a beggar's *collecting bag*; sometimes the wandering philosophers took a collection in such a bag after addressing the crowd.

In all these instructions Jesus was not laying upon His men a deliberate and calculated discomfort. He was once again speaking words which were very familiar to a Jew. The *Talmud* tells us that: " No one is to go to the Temple Mount with staff, shoes, girdle of money, or dusty feet." The idea was that when a man entered the temple, he must make it quite clear that he had left everything which had to do with trade and business and worldly affairs behind. What Jesus is saying to His men is: " You must treat the whole world as the Temple of God. If you are a man of God, you must never give the impression that you are a man of business, out for what you can get." Jesus' instructions mean that the man of God must show by his attitude to material things that he is a man of God, and that his first interest is God and not material things.

Finally, Jesus says that the workman deserves his sustenance. Once again the Jews would recognize this. It is true that a Rabbi might not accept payment, but it was also true that it was considered at once a privilege and an obligation to support a Rabbi, if he was truly a man of God. Rabbi Eliezer ben Jacob said: " He who receives a Rabbi in his house, or as his guest, and lets him have his enjoyment from his possessions, the scripture ascribes it to him as if he had offered the continual offerings." Rabbi Jochanan laid it down that it was the duty of every Jewish community to support a Rabbi, and the more so because a Rabbi naturally neglects his own affairs to concentrate on the affairs of God.

Here then is the double truth; the man of God must never be over-concerned with material things, but the people of God must never fail in their duty to see that the man of God receives a reasonable support. This is a passage which lays an obligation on teacher and on people alike.

THE GOSPEL OF MATTHEW

THE CONDUCT OF THE KING'S MESSENGER

Matthew 10: 11-15

" When you enter into any city or village, make inquiries as to who in it is worthy, and stay there until you go out of it. When you come into a household, give your greetings to it. If the house is worthy, let your peace come upon it; if it is not worthy, let your peace return to you. If anyone will not receive you, and will not listen to your words, when you leave that house or that city, shake off the dust of it from your feet. This is the truth I tell you—it will be easier for the land of Sodom and Gomorrah on the day of judgment than for that city."

HERE is a passage which is full of the most practical advice for the King's messengers.

When they enter a city or a village, they are to seek a house that is worthy. The point is that if they took up their residence in a house which had an evil reputation for morals or for conduct or for fellowship, it would seriously hinder their usefulness. They were not to identify themselves with anyone who might prove to be a handicap. That is not for a moment to say that they were not to seek to win such people for Christ, but it is to say that the messenger of Christ must have a care whom he makes his intimate friend.

When they entered a house, they were to stay there until they moved on to another place. This was a matter of courtesy. They might well be tempted, after they had won certain supporters and converts in a place, to move on to a house which could provide more luxury, more comfort, and better entertainment. The messenger of Christ must never give the impression that he courts people for the sake of material things, and that his movements are dictated by the demands of his own comfort.

The passage about giving a greeting, and, as it were, taking the greeting back again, is typically eastern. In the east a spoken word was thought to have a kind of active and independent existence. It went out from the mouth as independently as a bullet from a gun. This idea emerges regularly in the Old Testament, especially in connection with words spoken by God. Isaiah hears God say, " I have sworn by myself, the word is gone out of my mouth in righteousness, and shall not return " (*Isaiah* 45: 23). " So shall my word be that goeth out of my mouth; it shall not return unto me void, but it shall accomplish that which I please, and it shall prosper in the thing whereto I sent it " (*Isaiah* 55: 11). Zechariah sees the flying roll, and hears the voice: " This is the curse that goeth forth over the face of the whole earth " (*Zechariah* 5: 3). To this day in the east, if a man speaks his blessing to a passer-by, and then discovers that the passer-by is of another faith, he will come and take his blessing back again. The idea here is that the messengers of the King can send their blessing to rest upon a house, and, if the house is unworthy of it, can, as it were, recall the blessing, and take it back again.

If in any place their message is refused, the messengers of the King are to shake the dust of that place off their feet and to move on. To the Jew the dust of a Gentile place or road was defiling; therefore, when the Jew crossed the border of Palestine, and entered into his own country, after a journey in Gentile lands, he shook the dust of the Gentile roads off his feet, that the last particle of pollution might be cleansed away. So Jesus said, " If a city or a village will not receive you, you must treat it like a Gentile place." Again, we must be clear as to what Jesus is saying. In this passage there is both a temporary and an eternal truth.

(i) The temporary truth is this. Jesus was not saying that certain people had to be abandoned as being outside the message of the gospel and beyond the reach of grace. This is an instruction like the opening instruction not to go to the Gentiles and to the Samaritans. It comes from the situation in which it was given. It was simply due to the time factor; time was short; as many as possible must hear the proclamation of the Kingdom; at that time there was not time to argue with the disputatious and to seek to win the stubborn; that would come later. At the moment the disciples had to tour the country as quickly as possible, and therefore at the moment they had to move on when there was no immediate welcome for the message which they brought.

(ii) The permanent truth is this. It is one of the great basic facts of life that time and time again an opportunity comes to a man—and it does not come back. To those people in Palestine there was coming the opportunity to welcome and to receive the gospel, but if they did not take it, it was an opportunity which might well never return. As the proverb has it: " Three things come not back— the spoken word, the spent arrow, and the lost oppostunity." This happens in every sphere of life. In his autobiography, *Chiaroscuro*, Augustus John, the famous artist, tells of an incident and adds a laconic comment. He was in Barcelona in Spain: " It was time to leave for Marseilles. I had sent forward my baggage and was walking to the station, when I encountered three Gitanas engaged in buying flowers at a booth. I was so struck by their beauty and flashing elegance that I almost missed my train. Even when I reached Marseilles and met my friend, this vision still haunted me, and I positively had to return. But I did not find these gypsies again. *One never does.*" The artist was always looking for glimpses of beauty to transfer to his canvas—but he knew well that if he did not paint the beauty when he found it, all the chances were that he would never catch that glimpse again. The tragedy of life is so often the tragedy of the lost opportunity.

Finally, it is said that it will be easier for Sodom and Gomorrah in the day of judgment than for the town or the village which has refused the message of Christ and the Kingdom. Sodom and Gomorrah are in the New

Testament proverbial for wickedness (*Matthew* II: 23, 24; *Luke* 10: 12, 13; 17: 29; *Romans* 9: 29; 2 *Peter* 2: 6; *Jude* 7). It is interesting and relevant to note that just before their destruction Sodom and Gomorrah had been guilty of a grave and vicious breach of the laws of hospitality (*Genesis* 19: 1-11). They, too, had rejected the messengers of God. But, even at their worst, Sodom and Gomorrah had never had the opportunity to reject the message of Christ and His Kingdom. That is why it would be easier for them at the last than for the towns and villages of Galilee; for it is always true that the greater the privilege has been the greater the responsibility is.

THE CHALLENGE OF THE KING TO HIS MESSENGERS

Matthew 10: 16-22

" Look you, it is I who am sending you out as sheep in the midst of wolves. Show yourself as wise as serpents, and as pure as doves. Beware of men! For they will hand you over to the councils, and they will scourge you in their synagogues. You will be brought before rulers and kings for my sake, that you make your witness to them and to the Gentiles. But when they hand you over, do not worry how you are to speak, or what you are to say. What you are to speak will be given to you in that hour, for it is not you who speak, but the Spirit of your Father who speaks in you. Brother will hand over brother to death, and father will hand over child. Children will rise up against parents, and will murder them; and you will be hated by all for my name's sake. But he who endures to the end will be saved."

BEFORE we begin to deal with this passage in detail, we may note two things about it in general.

When we were studying the Sermon on the Mount (vol. i, pp. 78-82), we saw that one of Matthew's great characteristics was his love of orderly arrangement (vol. i, pp. xx-xxii). We saw that it was Matthew's custom to collect in one place all the material on any given subject, even if it was spoken by Jesus on different occasions. Matthew was the teacher and the systematizer of his material. This passage is one of the instances where Matthew collects his material from different times. Here he collects the things which Jesus said on various occasions about persecution. There is no doubt that even when Jesus sent out His men for the first time, He told them what to expect. But at the very beginning Matthew tells how Jesus told His men not to go at that time to the Gentiles or to the Samaritans; and yet here in this passage Matthew shows us Jesus foretelling persecution and trial before rulers and kings, that is to say, far beyond Palestine. The explanation is that Matthew collects Jesus' references to persecution and he puts together, both what Jesus said when He sent His men out on their first expedition, and what Jesus told them after His Resurrection, when He was sending them out into all the world. Here we have the words of Jesus, not only when for the first time He was sending His men out into Galilee, but also, after He had risen from the dead, and when He was sending them out to all nations and to the ends of the earth. Here are words, not only of Jesus of Galilee, but also of the Risen Christ.

Further, we must note in these words Jesus was making use of ideas and pictures which were part and parcel of Jewish thought. We have seen again and again how it was the custom of the Jews, in their pictures of the future, to divide time into two ages. There was this present age, which is wholly bad; there was the age to come, which would be the golden age of God; and in between there was the Day of the Lord, which would be a terrible time of chaos and destruction and judgment. Now in Jewish thought one of the ever-recurring features of the Day of the Lord was that it would split friends and kindred into two, and that the dearest bonds of earth would be destroyed in bitter enmities. "All friends shall destroy each other"

(2 *Esdras* 5: 9). " At that time shall friends make war one against another like enemies " (2 *Esdras* 6: 24). " And they will strive with one another, the young with the old, and the old with the young, the poor with the rich, and the lowly with the great, and the beggar with the prince " (*Jubilees* 23: 19). " And they will hate one another, and provoke one another to fight; and the mean will rule over the honourable, and those of low degree shall be extolled above the famous " (*Apocalypse of Baruch* 70: 3). " And they shall begin to fight among themselves, and their right hand shall be strong against themselves, and a man shall not know his brother, nor a son his father or his mother, till there be no number of the corpses through their slaughter " (*Enoch* 56: 7). " And in those days the destitute shall go forth and carry off their children, and they shall abandon them, so that their children shall perish through them; yea they shall abandon their children that are still sucklings, and not return to them; and shall have no pity on their loved ones " (*Enoch* 99: 5). " And in those days in one place the fathers together with their sons shall be smitten and brothers one with another shall fall in death till the streams flow with their blood. For a man shall not withhold his hand from slaying his sons and his sons' sons, and the sinner shall not withhold his hand from his honoured brother; from dawn to sunset they shall slay each other " (*Enoch* 100: 1, 2). All these quotations are taken from the books which the Jews wrote and knew and loved, and on which they fed their hearts and their hopes, in the days between the Old and the New Testament. Jesus knew these books; His men knew these books; and when Jesus spoke of the terrors to come, and of the divisions which would tear apart the closest ties of earth, He was in effect saying: " *The Day of the Lord has come.*" And His men would know that He was saying that, and would go out knowing that they were living in the greatest days of history.

THE KING'S HONESTY TO HIS MESSENGERS

Matthew 10: 16-22 *(continued)*

No one can read this passage without being deeply impressed with the honesty of Jesus. He never hesitated to tell men what they might expect, if they followed Him. It is as if He said, " Here is my task for you—at its grimmest and at its worst—do you accept it? " Plummer comments: " This is not the world's way to win adherents." The world will offer a man roses, roses all the way, comfort, ease, advancement, the fulfilment of his worldly ambitions. Jesus offered His men hardship and death. And yet the proof of history is that Jesus was right. In their heart of hearts men love a call to adventure; there is an adventurer somewhere hidden in the heart of every man.

After the siege of Rome, in 1849, Garibaldi issued the following proclamation to his followers: " Soldiers, all our efforts against superior forces have been unavailing. I have nothing to offer you but hunger and thirst, hardship and death; but I call on all who love their country to join with me "—and they came in their hundreds. After Dunkirk, Churchill offered his country " blood, sweat and tears ". Prescott tells how Pizarro, that reckless adventurer, offered his little band the tremendous choice. The choice was between the known safety of Panama, and the as yet unknown splendour of Peru. He took his sword and he traced a line with it on the sand from east to west: " Friends and comrades! " he said, " on that side are toil, hunger, nakedness, the drenching storm, desertion and death; on this side, ease and pleasure. There lies Peru with its riches; here, Panama and its poverty. Choose each man what best becomes a brave Castilian. For my part I go south." and he stepped across the line. And thirteen men, whose names are immortal, chose adventure with him. When Shackleton proposed his march to the South Pole he asked for volunteers for that trek amidst the blizzards across the polar ice. He expected to have difficulty in

THE GOSPEL OF MATTHEW

finding any. He was inundated with letters, from young and old, rich and poor, the highest and the lowest, who all desired to share in that great adventure.

It may be that the Church must learn again that we will never attract men to an easy way; it is the call of the heroic which ultimately speaks to the hearts of men.

Jesus offered His men three kinds of trial.

(i) The *state* would persecute them; they would be brought before councils and kings and governors. Long before this Aristotle had wondered if a good man could ever really be a good citizen, for, he said, it was the duty of the citizen ever to support and to obey the state, and there were times when the good man would find that impossible. When they were brought to court and to judgment, they were not to worry about words; for God would give them words. " I will be with thy mouth and teach thee what to say," God promised Moses (*Exodus* 4: 12). It was not the humiliation which the early Christian dreaded, not even the cruel pain and the agony. But many of them feared that their own unskilfulness in words and defence might injure rather than commend the faith. It is the promise of God that when a man is on trial for his faith, the words will come to him.

(ii) The *Church* would persecute them; they would be scourged in the synagogues. The Church does not like to be disturbed, and has its own ways of dealing with disturbers of the peace. The Christians were, and are, those who turn the world upside down (*Acts* 17: 6). It has often been true that the man with a message from God has had to undergo the hatred and the enmity of a fossilized orthodoxy.

(iii) The *family* would persecute them. Their nearest and dearest would think them mad, and shut the door against them. Sometimes the Christian is confronted with the hardest choice of all—the choice between obedience to Christ and obedience to kindred and to friends.

Jesus warned His men that in the days to come they might well find state and Church and family conjoined against them.

THE REASONS FOR THE PERSECUTION OF THE KING'S MESSENGER

Matthew 10: 16-22 (*continued*)

LOOKING at things from our own point of view, we find it hard to understand why any government should wish to persecute the Christians, whose only aim was to live with purity, with charity and with reverence. But in later days the Roman government had what it considered good reason for persecuting the Christians (see on this subject vol. i, pp. 108-110).

(i) There were certain slanders current about the Christians. They were accused of being cannibals because of the words of the sacrament, which spoke of eating Christ's body and drinking His blood. They were accused of immorality because the title of their weekly feast was the *agapē*, the love feast. They were accused of incendiarism because of the pictures which the Christian preachers drew of the coming of the end of the world. They were accused of being disloyal and disaffected citizens because they would not take the oath to the godhead of the Emperor.

(ii) It is doubtful if even the heathen really believed these slanderous charges. But there were other charges which were more serious. The Christians were accused of "tampering with family relationships." It was the truth that Christianity often split families, as we have seen. And to the heathen Christianity appeared to be something which divided parents and children, and husbands and wives.

(iii) A real difficulty was the position of slaves in the Christian Church. In the Roman Empire there were 60,000,000 slaves. It was always one of the terrors of the

Empire that these slaves might rise and rebel. If the structure of the Empire was to remain intact these slaves must be kept in their place; nothing must be done by anyone to encourage them to revolt, or the consequences would be terrible beyond imagining. Now the Christian Church made no attempt to free the slaves, or to condemn slavery; but it did, within the Church at least, treat the slaves as equals. Clement of Alexandria pleaded that "slaves are like ourselves," and the golden rule applied to them. Lactantius wrote: " Slaves are not slaves to us. We deem them brothers after the Spirit, in religion fellow-servants." It is a notable fact that, although there were thousands of slaves in the Christian Church, the inscription *slave* is never met with in the Roman Christian tombs. Worse than that, it was perfectly possible for a slave to hold high office in the Christian Church. In the early second century two bishops of Rome, Callistus and Pius, had been slaves. And it was not uncommon for elders and deacons to be slaves. And still worse, in A.D. 220 Callistus, who, as we have seen, had been a slave, declared that henceforth the Christian Church would sanction the marriage of a highborn girl to a freed man, a marriage which was in fact illegal under Roman law, and, therefore not a marriage at all. In its treatment of slaves the Christian Church must necessarily have seemed to the Roman authorities a force which was disrupting the very basis of civilization, and threatening the very existence of the Empire by giving slaves a position which they should never have had, as Roman law saw it.

(iv) There is no doubt that Christianity seriously affected certain vested interests connected with heathen religion. When Christianity came to Ephesus, the trade of the silversmiths was dealt a mortal blow, for far fewer desired to buy the images which they fashioned (*Acts* 19: 24-27). Pliny was governor of Bithynia in the reign of Trajan, and in a letter to the Emperor (Pliny, *Letters*, 10: 96) he tells how he had taken steps to check the rapid growth of Christianity so that " the temples which had been deserted now begin to be frequented; the sacred festivals, after a long intermission, are revived; while there is a general demand for sacrificial animals, which for some time past have met with few purchasers." It is clear that the spread of Christianity meant the abolition of certain trades and activities; and those who lost their trade and lost their money not unnaturally resented it.

Christianity preaches a view of man which no totalitarian state can accept. Christianity deliberately aims to obliterate certain trades and professions and ways of making money. It still does—and therefore the Christian is still liable to persecution for his faith.

THE PRUDENCE OF THE KING'S MESSENGER

Matthew 10: 23

" When they persecute you in one city, flee into another. This is the truth I tell you—you will not complete your tour of the cities of Israel, until the Son of Man shall come."

THIS passage counsels a wise and a Christian prudence. In the days of persecution a certain danger always threatened the Christian witness. There always were those who actually courted martyrdom; they were wrought up to such a pitch of hysterical and fanatical enthusiasm that they went out of their way to become martyrs for the faith. Jesus was wise. He told His men that there must be no wanton waste of Christian lives; that they must not pointlessly and needlessly throw their lives away. As some one has put it, the life of every Christian witness and missionary is precious, and these lives must not be recklessly thrown away. " Bravado is not martyrdom." Often the Christians had to die for their faith, but they must not throw away their lives in a way that did not really help the faith. As it was later said, a man must contend *lawfully* for the faith.

When Jesus spoke like this, He was speaking in a way which Jews would recognize and understand. No people were ever more persecuted than the Jews have always been; and no people were ever clearer as to where the duties of the martyr lay. The teaching of the great Rabbis was quite clear. When it was a question of *public sanctification* or *open profanation* of God's name, duty was clear—a man must be prepared to lay down his life. But when that public declaration was not in question, a man might save his life by breaking the law; but for no reason must he commit idolatry, unchastity, or murder. The case the Rabbis cited was this: suppose a Jew is seized by a Roman soldier, and the soldier says mockingly, and with no other intention that to humiliate and to make a fool of the Jew: " Eat this pork." Then the Jew may eat, for " God's laws are given for life and not for death." But suppose the Roman says: " Eat this pork as a sign that you renounce Judaism; eat this pork as a sign that you are ready to worship Jupiter and the Emperor," then the Jew must die rather than eat. In any time of official persecution the Jew must die rather than abandon his faith. As the Rabbis said, " The words of the Law are only firm in that man who would die for their sake." The Jew was forbidden to throw away his life in a needless act of pointless martyrdom; but when it came to a question of true witness, he must be prepared to die.

We do well to remember that, while we are bound to accept martyrdom for our faith, we are forbidden to court martyrdom. If suffering for the faith comes to us in the course of duty, it must be accepted; but it must not be needlessly invited; for to invite it does more harm than good to the faith we bear. The self-constituted martyr is too common in all human affairs.

It has been said that there is sometimes more heroism in daring to fly from danger than in stopping to meet it. There is real wisdom in recognizing when to escape. Andre Maurois in *Why France Fell* tells of a conversation he had with Mr. Winston Churchill, as he then was. There was a time at the beginning of the Second World War when England seemed strangely inactive and unwilling to action. Churchill said to Maurois: " Have you observed the habits of lobsters? " " No," answered Maurois to this somewhat surprising question. Churchill went on: " Well, if you have the opportunity, study them. At certain periods in his life the lobster loses his protective shell. At this moment of moulting even the bravest crustacean retires into a crevice in the rock, and waits patiently until a new carapace has time to grow. As soon as this new armour has grown strong, he sallies out of the crevice, and becomes once more a fighter, lord of the seas. England, through the faults of imprudent ministers, has lost its carapace; we must wait in our crevice until the new one has time to grow strong." There was a time when inaction was wiser than action; and when to escape was wiser than to attack.

If a man is weak in the faith, he will do well to avoid disputations about doubtful things, and not to plunge into them. If a man knows that he is susceptible to a certain temptation, he will do well to avoid the places where that temptation will speak to him, and not to frequent them. If a man knows that there are people who anger and irritate him, and who bring the worst out of him, he will be wise to avoid their society, and not to seek it. Courage is not recklessness; there is no virtue in running needless risks; God's grace is not meant to protect the foolhardy, but the prudent.

THE COMING OF THE KING

Matthew 10: 23 *(continued)*

THIS passage contains one strange saying which we cannot honestly neglect. Matthew depicts Jesus as sending out His men, and, as He does so, saying to them, " You will not complete your tour of the cities of Israel, until the Son of Man shall come." On the face of it that seems to mean that Jesus said that before His men had completed their preaching tour, His day of glory and His return to power would have taken place. The difficulty about that saying is just this—that it did not in fact happen, and, if at that moment Jesus had that expectation, He was mistaken and wrong. If He said this in this way, He foretold something which actually did not take place. There is a perfectly good and sufficient and satisfying explanation of this apparent difficulty.

The people of the early Church believed intensely in the second coming of Jesus, and they believed that it would happen soon, certainly within their own lifetime. There could be nothing more natural than that, because they were living in days of savage persecution, and they were longing for the day of their release and their glory. The result was that they fastened on every possible saying of Jesus which could be interpreted as foretelling His triumphant and glorious return; and sometimes they quite naturally used things which Jesus said, and read into them something more definite than was actually originally there. We can see this process happening within the pages of the New Testament itself. There are in the New Testament three versions of the one saying of Jesus. Let us set them down one after another:

> Verily I say unto you, there be some standing here, which shall not taste of death, till they see the Son of man coming in His Kingdom (*Matthew* 16: 28).

> And He said unto them, Verily I say unto you, That there be some of them that stand here, which shall not taste of death, till they have seen the Kingdom of God come with power (*Mark* 9: 1).

> But I tell you of a truth, there be some standing here, which shall not taste of death, till they see the Kingdom of God (*Luke* 9: 27).

Now it is clear that these are three versions of the same saying. *Mark* is the earliest gospel, and therefore Mark's version is most likely to be strictly accurate. *Mark* says that there were some who were listening to Jesus who would not die until they saw the Kingdom of God coming with power. That was gloriously true, for within thirty years of the Cross the message of the Cross and of Christ had swept across the world and had reached Rome, the capital of the world. Indeed men were being swept into the Kingdom; indeed the Kingdom was coming with power. *Luke* transmits the saying in the same way as *Mark.*

Now look at *Matthew.* His version is slightly different; he says that there are some who will not die until they see the Son of Man coming in power. That, in fact, did not happen. The explanation is that Matthew was writing between A.D. 80 and 90, in days when terrible persecution was raging. Men were clutching at everything which promised release from agony; and he took a saying which foretold the spread of the Kingdom and turned it into a saying which foretold the return of Christ within a lifetime —and who shall blame him?

That is what Matthew has done here. Take this saying in our passage and write it as Mark or Luke would have written it: " You will not complete your tour of the cities of Israel, until the *Kingdom of God* shall come." That was blessedly true, for as the tour went on, men's hearts opened to Jesus Christ, and they took Him as Master and Lord.

In a passage like this we must not think of Jesus as being mistaken; we must think that Matthew read into a promise of the coming of the Kingdom a promise of the second coming of Jesus Christ. And he did so because, in days of terror, men clutched at the hope of Christ; and Christ did come to them in the Spirit, for no man ever suffered for Christ alone.

THE GOSPEL OF MATTHEW

THE KING'S MESSENGER AND THE KING'S
SUFFERINGS

Matthew 10: 24, 25

> " The scholar is not above his teacher, nor is the slave
> above his master. It is enough for the scholar that
> he should be as his teacher, and the servant that he
> should be as his master. If they have called the master
> of the house Beelzeboul, how much more shall they
> so call the members of his household."

It is Jesus' warning to His disciples that they must expect
what happened to Him to happen to them. The Jews well
knew this sentence: " It is enough for the slave to be
as his master." In the later days they were to use it in a
special way. In A.D. 70 Jerusalem was destroyed, and
destroyed so completely that a plough was drawn across
the devastation. The Temple of God and the Holy City
were in ruins. The Jews were dispersed throughout the
world, and many of them mourned and lamented and
complained about the terrible fate which had befallen
them personally. It was then that the Rabbis said to them:
" When God's Temple has been destroyed, how can any
individual Jew complain about his own personal misfortunes? "

In this saying of Jesus there are two things.

(i) There is a *warning*. There is the warning that, as
Christ had to carry a cross, so also the individual Christian
must carry a cross. The word that is used for *members
of his household* is the one Greek word *oikiakoi*; this word
has a technical use; it means *the members of the household
of a government official*: that is to say, the official's *staff*.
It is as if Jesus said, " If I, the leader and commander,
must suffer, you who are the members of my staff cannot
escape." Jesus calls us, not only to share His glory, but
to share His warfare and His agony; and no man deserves
to share the fruits of victory, if he refuses to share the
struggle of which these fruits are the result.

(ii) There is the statement of a *privilege*. To suffer for

394

Christ is to share the work of Christ; to have to sacrifice
for the faith is to share the sacrifice of Christ. When
Christianity is hard, we can say to ourselves, not only,
" Brothers, we are treading where the saints have trod,"
we can also say, " Brothers, we are treading where the
feet of Christ have trod." There is always a thrill in
belonging to a noble company. Eric Linklater in his
autobiography tells of his experience in the disastrous
March retreat in the First World War. He was with the
Black Watch, and they had come out of the battle with
one officer, thirty men, and a piper left of the battalion.
" The next day, marching peacefully in the morning light
of France along a pleasant road, we encountered the
tattered fragments of a battalion of the Foot Guards,
and the piper, putting breath into his bag, and playing
so that he filled the air like the massed bands of the High-
land Division, saluted the tall Coldstreamers, who had
a drum or two and some instruments of brass, that made
also a gallant music. Stiffly we passed each other, swollen
of chest, heads tautly to the right, kilts swinging to the
answer of the swagger of the Guards, and the Red Hackle
in our bonnets, like the monstrance of a bruised but
resilient faith. We were bearded and stained with mud.
The Guards—the fifty men that were left of a battalion—
were button-bright and clean shaved—we were a tatter-
demalion crew from the coal mines of Fife and the back
streets of Dundee, but we trod quick-stepping to the
brawling tune of ' Hielan' Laddie ', and suddenly I was
crying with a fool's delight and the sheer gladness of
being in such company." It is one of life's great thrills
to have the sense of belonging to a goodly company and
a goodly fellowship.

When Christianity costs something we are closer than
ever we were to the fellowship of Jesus Christ; and if
we know the fellowship of His sufferings, we shall also
know the power of His resurrection.

THE KING'S MESSENGER'S FREEDOM FROM FEAR

Matthew 10: 26-31

" Do not fear them; for there is nothing which is
covered which shall not be unveiled, and there is
nothing hidden which shall not be known. What
I tell you in the darkness, speak in the light. What
you hear whispered in your ear, proclaim on the
housetops. Do not fear those who can kill the body,
but who cannot kill the soul. Rather fear Him who
is able to destroy both soul and body in Gehenna.
Are two sparrows not sold for a halfpenny, and not
one of them shall light on the ground without your
Father's knowledge? The hairs of your head are all
numbered. So then do not be afraid; you are of
more value than many sparrows."

THREE times in this short passage Jesus bids His disciples
not to be afraid. In the King's messenger there must be
a certain courageous fearlessness which marks him out
from other men.

(i) The first commandment is in verses 26, 27, and it
speaks of a double fearlessness. (*a*) They are not to be
afraid because there is nothing covered that will not be
unveiled, and nothing hidden which will not be known.
The meaning of that is that *the truth will triumph.* " Great
is the truth," ran the Latin proverb, " and the truth will
prevail." When James the Sixth threatened to hang or
exile Andrew Melville, Melville's answer was: " You
cannot hang or exile the truth." Even when the Christian
is involved in suffering and sacrifice and even martyrdom
for his faith, he must remember that the day will come
when things will be seen as they really are; and then the
power of the persecutor and the heroism of the Christian
witness will be seen at their true value, and each will have
its true reward. (*b*) They are not to be afraid to speak with
boldness the message they have received. What Jesus
has told them, they must tell to men. Here in this one
verse (verse 27) there lies the true function of the preacher.

First, the preacher must *listen*; he must be in the secret place with Christ, that in the dark hours Christ may speak to him, and that in the loneliness Christ may whisper in his ear. No man can speak for Christ unless Christ has spoken to him; no man can proclaim the truth unless he has listened to the truth; for no man can tell that which he does not know. In the great days in which the Reformation was coming to birth, Colet invited Erasmus to come to Oxford to give a series of lectures on Moses or Isaiah; but Erasmus knew he was not ready. He writes back: " But I who have learned to live with myself, and know how scanty my equipment is, can neither claim the learning required for such a task, nor do I think that I possess the strength of mind to sustain the jealousy of so many men, who would be eager to maintain their own ground. The campaign is one that demands, not a tyro, but a practised general. Neither should you call me immodest in declining a position which it would be most immodest for me to accept. You are not acting wisely, Colet, in demanding water from a pumice stone, as Plautus said. With what effrontery shall I teach what I have never learned? How am I to warm the coldness of others, when I am shivering myself? " He who would teach and preach must first in the secret place listen and learn. Second, the preacher must speak what he has heard from Christ, and he must speak even if his speaking is to gain him the hatred of men, and even if, by speaking, he takes his life in his hands. Men do not like the truth, for, as Diogenes said, truth is like the light to sore eyes. Once Latimer was preaching when Henry the king was present. He knew that he was about to say something which the king would not relish. So in the pulpit he soliloquised aloud with himself. " Latimer! Latimer! Latimer! " he said, " be careful what you say. Henry the king is here." Then he paused, and then he said, " Latimer! Latimer! Latimer! be careful what you say. The King of kings is here." The man with a message speaks to men, but he speaks in the presence of God. It was said of John Knox, as they buried him, " Here lies one who feared God so much that he never feared the face of any man."

The Christian witness is the man who knows no fear, because he knows that the judgments of eternity will correct the judgments of time. The Christian preacher and teacher is the man who listens with reverence and who speaks with courage, because he knows that, whether he listens or speaks, he is in the presence of God.

THE KING'S MESSENGER'S FREEDOM FROM FEAR—THE COURAGE OF THE RIGHT

Matthew 10: 26-31 (*continued*)

(ii) The second commandment is in verse 28. To put it very simply, what Jesus is saying is that no punishment that men can ever lay upon a man can compare with the ultimate fate of a man who has been guilty of infidelity and disobedience to God. It is true that men can kill a man's physical body; but God can condemn a man to the death of the soul. There are three things that we must note here.

(a) There is a kind of belief in immortality which is called belief in *conditional immortality*. This belief holds that the reward of goodness is that the soul of the good man climbs up and up until he is one with all the immortality, the bliss and the blessedness of God; and that the punishment of the evil man, who will not mend his ways in spite of all God's appeals to him, is that his soul goes down and down and down until it is finally obliterated, extinguished and annihilated, and ceases to be. We cannot erect a doctrine on a single text, but that is something very like what Jesus is saying here. The Jews knew the awfulness of the punishment of God.

" For Thou has power over life and death,
And Thou leadest down to the gates of Hades, and
    leadest up again.
But though a man can kill by his wickedness,
Yet the spirit that is gone forth he bringeth not back,
Neither giveth release to the soul that Hades has
    received " (*Psalms of Solomon,* 16: 13, 14).

During the killing times of the Maccabean struggle, the
seven martyred brothers encouraged each other by saying,
" Let us not fear him who thinketh he kills; for a great
struggle and pain of the soul awaits in eternal torment
those who transgress the ordinance of God " (4 *Maccabees*
13: 14, 15). We do well to remember that the penalties
which men can exact are as nothing to the penalties which
God can exact and to the rewards which He can give.

(*b*) The second thing which this passage teaches us is
that there is still left in the Christian life a place for what
we might call a holy fear. The Jews well knew this fear of
God. One of the rabbinic stories tells how Rabbi Jochanan
was ill. " His disciples went in to visit him. On beholding
them he began to weep. His disciples said to him, ' O
Lamp of Israel, righthand pillar, mighty hammer! Where-
fore dost thou weep? ' He replied to them, ' If I was
being led into the presence of a human king who today is
here and tomorrow in the grave, who, if he were wrathful
against me, his anger would not be eternal, who, if he
imprisoned me, the imprisonment would not be eternal,
who, if he condemned me to death, the death would not
be for ever, and whom I can appease with words and bribe
with money—even then I would weep. But now, when
I am being led into the presence of the King of kings, the
Holy One, blessed is He, who lives and endures for all
eternity, who, if He be wrathful against me, His anger is
eternal, who, if He imprisoned me, the imprisonment
would be for ever, who if He condemned me to death,
the death would be for ever, and whom I cannot appease
with words or bribe with money—nay more, when before
me lie two ways, one the way of the Garden of Eden and

the other the way of Gehenna, and I know not in which I am to be led—shall I not weep?"

It was not that the Jewish thinkers forgot that there is love, and that love is the greatest of all things. "The reward of him who acts from love," they said, "is double and quadruple. Act from love, for there is no love where there is fear, or fear where there is love, except in relation to God." The Jews were always sure that in relation to God there was both fear and love. "Fear God and love God, the Law says both; act from both love and fear; from love, for, if you would hate, no lover hates; from fear, for, if you would kick, no fearer kicks." But the Jew never forgot—and neither must we—the sheer holiness of God. And for the Christian the matter is even more compelling, for our fear is not that God will punish us, but our fear is that we may grieve His love. The Jew was never in any danger of sentimentalizing the love of God, and neither was Jesus. God is love, but God is also holiness, for God is God; and there must be a place in our hearts and in our thought both for the love which answers God's love, and the reverence, the awe and the fear which answer God's holiness.

(c) Further, this passage tells us that there are things which are worse than death; and disloyalty is worse than death. If a man is guilty of disloyalty, if he buys security at the expense of dishonour, life is no longer tolerable. He cannot face men; he cannot face himself; and ultimately he cannot face God. There are times when comfort, safety, ease, life itself can cost too much.

THE KING'S MESSENGER'S FREEDOM FROM FEAR—GOD CARES!

Matthew 10: 26-31 (*continued*)

(iii) The third commandment not to fear is in verse 31; and it is based on the certainty of the detailed care of God. If God cares for the sparrows, surely He will care for men.

Matthew says that two sparrows are sold for a halfpenny and yet not one of them falls to the ground without the knowledge of God. Luke gives us that saying of Jesus in a slightly different form: "Are not five sparrows sold for two halfpennies, and not one of them is forgotten before God?" (*Luke* 12: 6). The point is this—two sparrows were sold for one halfpenny. (The coin is the *assarion*, which was one-sixteenth of a *denarius*; a *denarius* was approximately ninepence; therefore the *assarion* was about a halfpenny). But if the purchaser was prepared to spend two halfpennies, he got, not four sparrows, but *five*. The extra one was thrown into the bargain as having no value at all. God cares even for the sparrow which is thrown into the bargain, and which on man's counting has no value at all. Even the forgotten sparrow is dear to God. The thing is even more vivid than that. The Authorized Version—and it is a perfectly correct translation of the Greek—has it that not one sparrow *falleth* to the ground without the knowledge of God. In such a context the word *fall* makes us naturally think of *death*; but in all probability the Greek is a translation of an Aramaic word which means to *light* upon the ground. It is not that God marks the sparrow when the sparrow falls dead; it is far more; it is that God marks the sparrow every time it lights and hops upon the ground. So it is Jesus' argument that, if God cares like that for sparrows, much more will He care for men.

Once again the Jews would well understand what Jesus was saying. No nation ever had such a conception of the detailed care of God for His creation. Rabbi Chanina said, "No man hurts his finger here below, unless it is so disposed for him by God." There was a rabbinic saying, "God sits and feeds the world, from the horns of the buffalo to the eggs of the louse." Hillel has a wonderful interpretaton of *Psalm* 136. That psalm begins by telling the story in lyric poetry about the God who is the God of creation, the God who made the heavens and the earth, and the sun and the moon and the stars (verses 1-9); then it goes on to tell the story about the God who is the God of history, the God who rescued Israel from Egypt and who fought her battles for her (verses 11-24); then finally it goes on to speak of God as the God " who giveth food to all flesh " (verse 25). The God who made the world, the God who controls all history, is the God who gives men food. The coming of our daily bread is just as much an act of God as the act of creation, and the saving power of the deliverance from Egypt. God's love for men is seen not only in the omnipotence of creation and in the great events of history; it is also seen in the day-to-day nourishment of the bodies of men.

The courage of the King's messenger is founded on the conviction that, whatever happens, he cannot drift beyond the love and care of God. He knows that his times are for ever in God's hands; that God will not leave him or forsake him; that he is surrounded for ever by the care of God. And if that is so—of whom then shall we be afraid?

THE LOYALTY OF THE KING'S MESSENGER AND ITS REWARD

Matthew 10: 32, 33

> " I too will acknowledge before my Father every one who acknowledges me before men. I too will deny before my Father who is in heaven every one who denies me before men."

HERE there is laid down the double loyalty of the Christian life. If a man is loyal to Jesus Christ in this life, Jesus Christ will be loyal to him in the life to come. If a man is proud to acknowledge that Jesus Christ is his Master, Jesus Christ will be proud to acknowledge that he is His servant. It is the plain fact of history that if there had not been men and women in the early Church who in face of death and suffering and agony refused to deny

Jesus Christ, there would be no Christian Church today. The Church of today is built and founded on the unbreakable loyalty of those who held fast to their loyalty and to their faith. Pliny, the governor of Bithynia, writes to Trajan, the Roman Emperor, about how he treated the Christians within his province. Anonymous informers laid information that certain people were Christian. Pliny tells how he gave these men the opportunity to invoke the gods of Rome, to offer wine and frankincense to the image of the Emperor, and how he demanded that as a final test they should curse the name of Christ. And then he adds: " None of these acts, it is said, those who are really Christians can be compelled to do." Even the Roman governor confesses his helplessness to shake the loyalty of those who were truly Christian.

It is still possible for a man to deny Jesus Christ.

(i) We may deny Him with our *words*. It is told of J. P. Mahaffy, the famous scholar and man of the world from Trinity College, Dublin, that, when he was asked if he was a Christian, his answer was: " Yes, but not offensively so." He meant that he wished to make it quite clear that he did not propose to allow his Christianity to interfere with the society he kept and the pleasures he loved. Sometimes we say to other people, practically in so many words, that we are Church members, but not to worry about it too much; that we have no intention of being different; that we are prepared to take our full share in all the pleasures of the world; and that we do not expect people to take any special trouble to respect any vague principles that we may have. The Christian can never escape the duty of being different from the world. It is not our duty to be conformed to the world; it is our duty to be transformed from it.

(ii) We can deny Him by our *silence*. A French writer tells of bringing a young wife into an old family. The old family had not approved of the marriage, although they were too conventionally polite ever to put their objections into actual words and criticisms. But the young wife afterwards said that her whole life was made a misery by " the menace of things unsaid." There can be a menace of things unsaid in the Christian life. Again and again life brings us the opportunity to speak some word for Christ, to utter some protest against evil, to take some stand, and to show what side we are on. Again and again on such occasions it is easier to keep silence than to speak. But such a silence is in itself a denial of Jesus Christ. It is very probably true that far more people deny Jesus Christ by their cowardly silence than by their deliberate words.

(iii) We can deny Him by our *actions*. We can live in such a way that our life is a continuous denial of the faith which in words we profess. He who has given his allegiance to the gospel of purity may be guilty of all kinds of petty dishonesties, and breaches of strict honour. He who has undertaken to follow the Master who bade him take up a cross can live a life which is dominated by attention to his own ease and comfort. He who has entered the service of Him who Himself forgave and who bade His followers to forgive can live a life of bitterness and resentment and variance with his fellow-men. He whose eyes are meant to be on that Christ who died for love of men can live a life in which the idea of Christian service and Christian charity and Christian generosity are conspicuous by their absence. A special prayer was composed for the Lambeth Conference of 1948:

> " Almighty God, give us grace to be not only hearers, but doers of Thy holy word, not only to admire, but to obey Thy doctrine, not only to profess, but to practise Thy religion, not only to love, but to live Thy gospel. So grant that what we learn of Thy glory we may receive into our hearts, and show forth in our lives: through Jesus Christ our Lord. Amen."

That is a prayer which every one of us would be well to remember and continually to use.

THE WARFARE OF THE KING'S MESSENGER

Matthew 10: 34-39

> " Do not think that I came to send peace on earth:
> I did not come to send peace, but a sword. I came
> to set a man at variance against his father, and a
> daughter against her mother, and a daughter-in-law
> against her mother-in-law; and a man's enemies
> shall be the members of his own household. He that
> loves father or mother more than he loves me is not
> worthy of me; and he who does not take up his cross
> and follow after me is not worthy of me. He who
> finds his life will lose it; and he who loses his life
> for my sake shall find it."

NOWHERE is the sheer honesty of Jesus more vividly
displayed than it is here. Here He sets the Christian demand
at its most demanding and at its most uncompromising.
He tells His men exactly what they may expect, if they
accept the commission to be the messengers of the King.
Here in this passage Jesus offers four things.

(i) He offers a *warfare*; and in that warfare it will
often be true that a man's foes will be those of his own
household. It so happens that Jesus was using language
which was perfectly familiar to the Jew. The Jews believed
that one of the features of the Day of the Lord, the day
when God would break into history, would be the division
of families. The Rabbis said: " In the period when the
Son of David shall come, a daughter will rise up against
her mother, a daughter-in-law against her mother-in-law."
" The son despises his father, the daughter rebels against
the mother, the daughter-in-law against her mother-in-law,
and a man's enemies are they of his own household."
It is as if Jesus said, " The end you have always been
waiting for has come; and the intervention of God in
history is splitting homes and groups and families into
two." When some great cause emerges, it is bound to
divide people; there are bound to be those who answer,
and those who refuse the challenge. To be confronted
with Jesus is necessarily to be confronted with the choice

whether to accept Him or to reject Him; and the world
is always divided into those who have accepted Christ
and those who have not.

The bitterest thing about this warfare was that a man's
foes would be those of his own household. It can happen
that a man loves his wife and his family so much that he
may refuse some great adventure, some avenue of service,
some call to sacrifice, either because he does not wish to
leave them, or because to accept it would involve them in
danger and in risk. T. R. Glover quotes a letter from
Oliver Cromwell to Lord Wharton. The date is 1st January,
1649, and Cromwell had in the back of his mind that
Wharton might be so attached to his home and to his
wife that he might refuse to hear the call to adventure
and to battle, and might choose to stay at home: "My
service to the dear little lady; I wish you make her not
a greater temptation than she is. Take heed of all relations.
Mercies should not be temptations; yet we too often
make them so." It has happened that a man has refused
God's call to some adventurous bit of service, because
he allowed personal attachments to immobolize him.
Lovelace, the cavalier poet, writes to his Lucasta, *Going
to the Wars*:

> " Tell me not (Sweet) I am unkind,
>   That from the nunnery
> Of thy chaste breast, and quiet mind,
>   To war and arms I fly.
>
> True; a new mistress now I chase,
>   The first foe in the field;
> And with a stronger faith embrace
>   A sword, a horse, a shield.
>
> Yet this inconstancy is such,
>   As you too shall adore.
> I could not love thee (Dear) so much,
>   Loved I not honour more."

It is very seldom that any man is confronted with this
choice; a man may well go through life and never be
confronted with it; but the fact remains that it is possible

for a man's loved ones to become in effect his enemies, if the thought of them keeps him from doing what he knows God wishes and wants him to do.

(ii) He offers a *choice*; and in that choice a man has to choose sometimes between the closest ties of earth and loyalty to Jesus Christ. Bunyan knew all about that choice. The thing which troubled him most about his imprisonment was the effect which it would have upon his wife and children. What was to happen to them, bereft of his support? " The parting with my wife and poor children hath often been to me in this place, as the pulling the flesh from my bones; and that not only because I am somewhat too fond of these great mercies, but also because I should have often brought to my mind the many hardships, miseries, and wants that my poor family was like to meet with, should I be taken from them, *especially my poor blind child*, who lay nearer my heart than all I had besides. O the thought of the hardship I thought my blind one might go under, would break up my heart to pieces. . . . But yet, recalling myself, thought I, I must venture you all with God, though it goeth to the quick to leave you; O I saw in this condition, I was a man who was pulling down his house upon the head of his wife and children; yet thought I, I must do it, I must do it."

Once again, this terrible choice will come very seldom; in God's mercy to many of us it may never come; but the fact remains that all loyalties must give place to loyalty to God.

THE COST OF BEING A MESSENGER OF THE KING

Matthew 10: 34-39 (*continued*)

(iii) Jesus offered them a *cross*. People in Galilee well knew what a cross was. When the Roman general, Varus, had broken the revolt of Judas of Galilee, he crucified two thousand Jews, and placed the crosses by the wayside along the roads of Galilee. In the ancient days the criminal did actually carry the cross-beam of his cross to the place of crucifixion, and the men to whom Jesus spoke had seen people staggering under the weight of their crosses and dying in agony upon them.

The great men, whose names are on the honour roll of faith, well knew what they were doing. After his trial in Scarborough Castle, George Fox wrote, " And the officers would often be threatening me, that I should be hanged over the wall . . . they talked much then of hanging me. But I told them, ' If that was it they desired, and it was permitted them, I was *ready*.' " When Bunyan was brought before the magistrate, he said, " Sir, the law (the law of Christ) hath provided two ways of obeying: The one to do that which I in my conscience do believe that I am bound to do, actively; and where I cannot obey it actively, there I am willing to lie down and to suffer what they shall do unto me."

The Christian may have to sacrifice his personal ambitions, the ease and the comfort that he might have enjoyed, the career that he might have achieved; he may have to lay aside his dreams, to realize that shining things of which he caught a glimpse are not for him. He will certainly have to sacrifice his will, for no Christian can ever again do what he likes; he must do what Christ likes. In Christianity there is always some cross, for Christianity is the religion of the Cross.

(iv) He offered them an *adventure*. He told them that the man who found his life would lose it; and the man who lost his life would find it. Again and again that has been proved true in the most literal way. It has always been true that many a man might easily have saved his life; but, if he had saved it, he would have lost it, for no one would ever have heard of him, and the thing he did in history would never have been done, and the place he holds in history would have been lost to him. Epictetus says of Socrates: " Dying, he was saved, because he did not flee." Socrates could easily have saved his life, but if he had done so the real Socrates would have died, and no man would ever have heard of him. When Bunyan was charged with refusing to come to public worship and with running forbidden meetings of his own, he thought seriously whether it was his duty to flee to safety, or to stand by what he believed to be true. As all the world knows, he chose to take his stand. T. R. Glover closes his essay on Bunyan thus: " And supposing he had been talked round and had agreed no longer ' devilishly and perniciously to abstain from coming to Church to hear divine service,' and to be no longer ' an upholder of several unlawful meetings and conventicles to the great disturbance and distraction of the good subjects of the kingdom contrary to the laws of our sovereign lord the king '? Bedford might have kept a tinker the more—and possibly none of the best at that, for there is nothing to show that renegades make good tinkers—and what would England have lost? "

There is no place for a policy of safety first in the Christian life. The man who seeks first ease and comfort and security and the fulfilment of personal ambition may well get all these things—but he will not be a happy men; for he was sent into this world to serve God and to serve his fellow-men. A man can hoard life, if he wishes to do so. But that way he will lose all that makes life valuable to others and worth living for himself. The way to serve others, the way to fulfil God's purpose for us, the way to true happiness is to spend life, for only thus will we find life, here and hereafter.

THE REWARD OF THOSE WHO WELCOME THE KING'S MESSENGER

Matthew 10: 40-42

He who receives you, receives me; and he who receives me, receives Him that sent me. He who receives a prophet because he is a prophet will receive a prophet's reward; and he who receives a righteous man because he is a righteous man will receive a righteous man's reward. And whoever gives one of these little ones a drink of cold water because he is a disciple—this is the truth I tell you—he will not lose his reward.

WHEN Jesus said this, He was using a way of speaking which the Jews regularly used. The Jew always felt that to receive a person's envoy or messenger was the same as to receive the person himself. To pay respect to an ambassador was the same as to pay respect to the king who had sent him. To welcome with love the messenger of a friend was the same as to welcome the friend himself. The Jew always felt that to honour a person's representative was the same as to honour the person whose representative he was. This was particularly so in regard to wise men and to those who taught and brought God's truth. The Rabbis said: " He who shows hospitality to the wise is as if he brought the first-fruits of his produce unto God." " He who greets the learned is as if he greeted God." If a man is a true man of God, to receive him is to receive the God who sent him.

In this passage we can see set out the links in the chain of salvation. In that chain there are four links. (i) There is God out of whose love the whole process of salvation began. (ii) There is Jesus who brought that message to men. (iii) There is the human messenger, the prophet who speaks, the good man who is an example, the disciple who learns, who in turn all pass on to others the good news which they themselves have received. (iv) There is the believer who welcomes God's men and God's message and who thus finds life to his soul.

In this passage there is something very lovely for every simple and for every humble soul.

(i) We cannot all be prophets, and preach and proclaim the word of God, but he who gives God's messenger the simple gift of hospitality will receive no less a reward than the prophet himself. There is many and many a man who has been a great public figure; there is many and many a man whose voice has kindled the hearts of thousands of people; there is many and many a man who has carried an almost intolerable burden of public service and public responsibility, all of whom would have gladly borne witness that they could never have survived the effort and the demands of their task, were it not for the love and the care and the sympathy and the service of someone at home, who was never in the public eye at all. When true greatness is measured up in the sight of God, it will be seen again and again that the man who greatly moved the world was entirely dependent on someone who, as far as the world is concerned, remained unknown. Even the prophet must get his breakfast, and have his clothes attended to; even the prophet must have his home. Let those who have the often thankless task of making a home, cooking meals, washing clothes, shopping for household necessities, caring for children, never think of it as a dreary and a weary round; it is God's greatest task; and they will be far more likely to receive the prophet's reward than those whose days were filled with committees and whose homes were comfortless.

(ii) We cannot all be shining examples of goodness; we cannot all stand out in the world's eye as righteous; but he who helps a good man to be good receives a good man's reward. H. L. Gee has a lovely story. There was a lad in a country village who, after a great struggle, reached the ministry. His helper in his days of study had been the village cobbler. The cobbler, like so many of his trade, was a man of wide reading and far thinking, and he had done much for the lad. In due time the lad was licenced to preach. And on that day the cobbler said to him, " It was always my desire to be a minister of the gospel, but the circumstances of my life made it impossible. But you are achieving what was closed to me. And I want you to promise me one thing—I want you to let me make and cobble your shoes—for nothing—and I want you to wear them in the pulpit when you preach, and then I'll feel you are preaching the gospel that I always wanted to preach standing in my shoes." And beyond a doubt the cobbler was serving God as the preacher was, and his reward would one day be the same.

(iii) We cannot all teach the child; but there is a real sense in which we can all serve the child. We may not have either the knowledge or the technique to teach, but there are simple duties to be done, without which the child cannot live. It may be that in this passage it is not so much *children in age* of whom Jesus is thinking as it is *children in the faith*. It seems very likely that the Rabbis called their disciples *the little ones*. Again it may be that in the technical, academic sense we cannot teach, but there is a teaching by life and example which even the simplest person can give to another.

The great beauty of this passage is its stress on simple things. The Church and Christ will always need its great orators, its great shining examples of sainthood, its great teachers, those whose names are household words; but the Church and Christ will also always need those in whose homes there is hospitality, on whose hands there is all the service which makes a home, and in whose hearts there is the caring which is Christian love; and, as Mrs. Browning said, " All service ranks the same with God."